Regulation and the Courts

R. SHEP MELNICK

Regulation and the Courts:
The Case of the Clean Air Act

THE BROOKINGS INSTITUTION
Washington, D.C.

Library of Congress Cataloging in Publication data:

Melnick, R. Shep, 1951–
  Regulation and the courts.

  Includes index.
  1. Air—Pollution—Law and legislation—United States.
2. Judicial review of administrative acts—United States.
3. Administrative procedure—United States. 4. Administrative law—United States. I. Title.
KF3812.M44 1983 344.73'046342 83-7694
ISBN 0-8157-5662-3 347.30446342
ISBN 0-8157-5661-5 (pbk.)

9 8 7 6 5 4 3 2 1

THE BROOKINGS INSTITUTION is an independent organization devoted to nonpartisan research, education, and publication in economics, government, foreign policy, and the social sciences generally. Its principal purposes are to aid in the development of sound public policies and to promote public understanding of issues of national importance.

The Institution was founded on December 8, 1927, to merge the activities of the Institute for Government Research, founded in 1916, the Institute of Economics, founded in 1922, and the Robert Brookings Graduate School of Economics and Government, founded in 1924.

The Board of Trustees is responsible for the general administration of the Institution, while the immediate direction of the policies, program, and staff is vested in the President, assisted by an advisory committee of the officers and staff. The by-laws of the Institution state: "It is the function of the Trustees to make possible the conduct of scientific research, and publication, under the most favorable conditions, and to safeguard the independence of the research staff in the pursuit of their studies and in the publication of the results of such studies. It is not a part of their function to determine, control, or influence the conduct of particular investigations or the conclusions reached."

The President bears final responsibility for the decision to publish a manuscript as a Brookings book. In reaching his judgment on the competence, accuracy, and objectivity of each study, the President is advised by the director of the appropriate research program and weighs the views of a panel of expert outside readers who report to him in confidence on the quality of the work. Publication of a work signifies that it is deemed a competent treatment worthy of public consideration but does not imply endorsement of conclusions or recommendations.

The Institution maintains its position of neutrality on issues of public policy in order to safeguard the intellectual freedom of the staff. Hence interpretations or conclusions in Brookings publications should be understood to be solely those of the authors and should not be attributed to the Institution, to its trustees, officers, or other staff members, or to the organizations that support its research.

Foreword

OVER THE PAST two decades federal judges—who for years had quietly deferred to the expertise of administrators—have become increasingly aggressive in their oversight of administrative action. This judicial activism has drawn praise from critics of bureaucracy spanning the political spectrum, but surprisingly little attention has been paid to its consequences for national policy and national institutions. Have the courts in fact improved policymaking? Or have they, as Felix Frankfurter might have predicted, exceeded their institutional capacity?

In this book R. Shep Melnick, assistant professor of government at Harvard University and former research fellow and research associate in the Brookings Governmental Studies program, examines how the federal courts have influenced policymaking in one highly significant and controversial area, the regulation of air pollution. He probes the long-term effects of a variety of court decisions that have helped to shape environmental policy during the 1970s. His analysis of the bureaucratic and congressional politics of air pollution control provides insight into the process of environmental regulation as well as the effects of judicial activism.

Melnick shows not only that court decisions had consequences unforeseen by judges and legal commentators, but also that the net effect of a large number of trial and appellate court decisions was to widen the gap between the promise and performance of the programs administered by the Environmental Protection Agency. He explains how these difficulties resulted from the peculiar institutional characteristics of the judicial branch.

In his research Melnick benefited greatly from the cooperation of Environmental Protection Agency officials in Washington, Durham, and many regional offices. Without their cooperation both in granting interviews and making files available this work could not have been completed.

A number of scholars, especially at Brookings and Harvard, offered invaluable guidance to the author. Arthur Maass and Martha Derthick provided both direction and encouragement throughout nearly five years of research and writing. Robert A. Katzmann, Andrew S. McFarland, Bernard J. Steigerwald, Richard B. Stewart, and Paul J. Quirk wrote extensive comments. Nancy D. Davidson edited the manuscript. Diane Hodges provided administrative assistance in addition to massive amounts of typing. Joan P. Milan assisted with the typing, and Diana Regenthal prepared the index. The Ford Foundation and an anonymous donor provided generous financial support.

Finally, the author thanks his wife, Katherine M. Hanna, for the many hours she devoted to discussing with him the relation between politics and the law.

The views expressed in this book are the author's alone, and should not be ascribed to the persons whose assistance is acknowledged above, to the Ford Foundation, or to the trustees, officers, or other staff members of the Brookings Institution.

BRUCE K. MACLAURY
President

March 1983
Washington, D.C.

Contents

To the memory of my father, Charles H. Melnick

Abbreviations and Acronyms

ACP   area classification plan
API   American Petroleum Institute
BACT   best available control technology
CASAC   Clean Air Scientific Advisory Committee
COWPS   Council on Wage and Price Stability
ECAO   Environmental Criteria and Assessment Office
EDF   Environmental Defense Fund
EDP   emission density plan
EPA   Environmental Protection Agency
FEA   Federal Energy Administration
ICS   intermittent control systems
ISR   indirect source review
NAAQS   national ambient air quality standards
NAS   National Academy of Sciences
NRDC   Natural Resources Defense Council
NSPS   new source performance standards
OAQPS   Office of Air Quality Planning and Standards
OGC   Office of General Counsel
OMB   Office of Management and Budget
OPE   Office of Planning and Evaluation
ORD   Office of Research and Development
PSD   prevention of significant deterioration
SAB   Science Advisory Board
SIP   state implementation plan
TCP   transportation control plan

CHAPTER ONE

Law and Regulation: The Dual Transformation

We stand on the threshold of a new era in the history of the long and fruitful collaboration of administrative agencies and reviewing courts.
—Chief Judge David Bazelon in
Environmental Defense Fund v. *Ruckelshaus,* 1971

Recent history would indicate that the prime mover behind implementation of the Clean Air Act has not been Congress or EPA, but the courts—specifically this court. —Judge Malcolm Wilkey in *Ethyl Corp.* v. *EPA,* 1976

LITTLE MORE than a decade ago a book on the influence of federal court decisions on national air pollution control policy would have been a short one indeed. Before 1970 the norm of judicial deference to agency expertise guided the courts in their review of the relatively minor regulatory decisions made by federal administrators. State courts handled the few public nuisance suits brought by private citizens against individual polluters. Yet by 1980 the federal courts had not only heard hundreds of cases dealing with air pollution, but had issued scores of rulings profoundly affecting national environmental policies.

The federal courts have done far more than adjudicate disputes between private parties or prevent administrators from exceeding their statutory authority. They have announced sweeping rulings on policy issues left unresolved by existing legislation, often expanding the scope of government programs in the process. Consider, for example, the following decisions issued under the Clean Air Act of 1970.[1]

—In *Sierra Club* v. *Ruckelshaus,* the district court for the District of Columbia instructed the Environmental Protection Agency (EPA) to design a program that would prevent the "significant deterioration" of air quality in areas already meeting statutory air quality standards.[2] The court based its decision on the act's preface, which announced Congress's

1. 84 Stat. 1676. For an extensive review of the Clean Air Act decisions, see William H. Rodgers, Jr., *Handbook on Environmental Law* (West, 1977).

2. *Sierra Club* v. *Ruckelshaus,* 344 F. Supp. 253 (D.D.C. 1972), upheld by an equally divided Supreme Court, *sub nom. Fri* v. *Sierra Club,* 412 U.S. 541 (1973).

intention "to protect and enhance the quality of the Nation's air resources." The court of appeals for the D.C. Circuit and the Supreme Court upheld this decision. The resulting program has become one of the largest and most complex administered by the EPA, affecting nearly every new industrial facility in the country.

—In *Natural Resources Defense Council* v. *Environmental Protection Agency* the D.C. Circuit ordered the EPA to produce within a few months elaborate "transportation control plans" for cities with high levels of carbon monoxide and ozone (smog).[3] The court also told the agency to find ways to maintain air quality standards once achieved. Shortly thereafter, a reluctant EPA announced a long series of draconian and highly unpopular measures to curtail driving and parking in major metropolitan areas.

—While the Clean Air Act requires polluters to comply with all pollution control requirements necessary to meet health-based air quality standards, the courts have refused to impose sanctions on polluters unless convinced that the requisite control technology is economically and technologically feasible. The courts have used their "equity" power to fashion compliance schedules extending well past the act's deadline for meeting air quality standards.[4]

—To facilitate judicial review of agency action and to encourage public participation, the courts have required the EPA to adopt rule-making procedures more elaborate than those specified by the Administrative Procedures Act.[5] These judicially designed procedures affect nearly every action taken by the EPA.

—In a number of cases brought by environmental groups, the federal courts have required the EPA to formulate pollution control programs for airborne lead, vinyl chloride, asbestos, beryllium, and mercury.[6]

As remarkable as this flurry of activity seems when compared with the preceding period of quiescence, these decisions are not aberrations. On the contrary, they represent the convergence of two major political

3. *Natural Resources Defense Council* v. *Environmental Protection Agency*, 475 F.2d 968 (D.C. Cir. 1973).

4. *Union Electric Co.* v. *Environmental Protection Agency*, 427 U.S. 246 (1976), and, for example, *U.S.* v. *West Penn Power Co.*, 460 F. Supp. 1305 (W.D. Penn. 1978).

5. *Kennecott Copper Corp.* v. *Environmental Protection Agency*, 462 F.2d 846 (D.C. Cir. 1972) and *Portland Cement Assoc.* v. *Ruckelshaus*, 486 F.2d 375 (D.C. Cir. 1973).

6. *Natural Resources Defense Council* v. *Train*, 545 F.2d 320 (2d Cir. 1976) and *Environmental Defense Fund* v. *Ruckelshaus*, 3 *Environmental Law Reporter* 20173 (D.D.C. 1973).

developments of the late 1960s and the 1970s: the rapid expansion of federal health and safety regulation and the increased activism of the federal judiciary. The courts have helped to shape a wide array of federal regulatory programs, including those for environmental protection, occupational safety and health, natural resources development, consumer protection, transportation, and telecommunications. While judicial opinions written in Clean Air Act cases ushered in what Judge David Bazelon termed the "new era" in administrative law, the patterns of judicial behavior established in this litigation extend far beyond the realm of pollution control.

Since these two developments, growth of federal regulation and heightened judicial scrutiny of administrative action, began at about the same time, one might suppose that the latter was an inevitable consequence of the former. The courts, it would seem, expanded their supervision of regulatory agencies to prevent bureaucrats from abusing their newly gained powers. According to this explanation, federal judges simply adapted old principles to fit a new reality. Their traditional activities became more significant and more visible as the reach of the federal government increased. If this is the case, then the apparent activism of the federal courts, far from representing a grasp for imperial power, reveals nothing more than the judiciary's continuing effort to safeguard limited constitutional government.

As convincing as it may at first seem, this explanation for judicial activism in regulatory matters suffers from two critical flaws. First, the seeds of the new era of administrative law were sown and began to take root in the mid-1960s, shortly before the explosion of regulatory legislation. The agencies reprimanded in these early decisions were not young agencies eager to expand their power, but rather entrenched bureaucracies administering well-established programs—the Federal Power Commission, the Federal Highway Administration, the Army Corps of Engineers, the Federal Communications Commission, and the Department of Agriculture. In each case the court voiced concern not about the novelty of the program, but about the agency's failure to consider novel approaches to old problems. Second, far from constraining the growth of governmental power, court decisions led to further increases in the size of government programs. Indeed, judges commonly criticized administrators for being too timid in their wielding of public authority rather than for arbitrarily encroaching upon private property. Thus, the "growth of government" argument not only distorts the history of judicial review of agency action, but fails to recognize the qualitative changes that took place in judicial review during the 1960s and 1970s.[7]

The new era in administrative law was not an attempt by the courts to lean against prevailing political winds favoring a larger federal government nor one to round off the sharp edges of new government programs. To use a more appropriate metaphor, the courts were among the first to ride a rising political wave. Their efforts to increase the government's role in protecting the health and safety of its citizens and to decrease the influence of industry in regulatory policymaking preceded those of Congress and the White House. The courts did not follow, they led. And even when they followed, they did so with surprising eagerness and aggressiveness.

The legal literature is filled with articles, books, even entire journals that describe this flood of decisions and trace the evolution of environmental and administrative law. Such analysis focuses almost entirely on the development of legal *doctrines,* not on the *consequences* of judicial activity. If the courts were attempting primarily to follow instructions from legislators or to define and vindicate constitutional rights, then this approach might be adequate for understanding and evaluating court action. But, as will be shown, this is not the case. The federal courts have sought to reform both the regulatory policies of the national government and the agencies that help to develop them. For this reason, evaluating the courts' performance in administrative and environmental law requires detailed analysis of the long-term consequences of court action.

This book examines how a large number of court decisions have influenced policymaking under the Clean Air Act. Congress passed the

7. By far the best review of these developments is Richard B. Stewart, "The Reformation of American Administrative Law," 88 *Harvard Law Review* 1667 (1975). Also see Kenneth Culp Davis, *Administrative Law of the Seventies* (Lawyers Co-operative Publishing, 1976). Early cases include *Scenic Hudson Preservation Conference* v. *Federal Power Commission,* 354 F.2d 608 (2d Cir. 1965); *Citizens to Preserve Overton Park* v. *Volpe,* 401 U.S. 402 (1971) (Federal Highway Administration); *Office of Communication of the United Church of Christ* v. *Federal Communications Commission,* 359 F.2d 994 (D.C. Cir. 1966); and *Environmental Defense Fund* v. *Hardin,* 428 F.2d 1093 (D.C. Cir. 1970) (Department of Agriculture).

Cases decided under the National Environmental Policy Act of 1969, which requires environmental impact statements for all major federal actions, provide examples of how the courts have used legislation passed by Congress to justify doctrines they had themselves announced previously. See Frederick Anderson, "The National Environmental Policy Act," in Erica Dolgin and Thomas Guilbert, eds., *Federal Environmental Law* (West, 1974), p. 412.

Clean Air Act in late 1970, only a few weeks after President Richard M. Nixon created the Environmental Protection Agency by executive order. As one of the earliest and most far-reaching examples of the health and safety regulation that flowered in the 1970s, the act spawned litigation that in turn produced a series of landmark decisions. Several of these decisions remain cornerstones of the new administrative law. These decisions and their consequences deserve detailed analysis not because they are unusual, but because they are part of a larger pattern of political and institutional behavior.

The New Regulation

Between 1968 and 1978 Congress passed more regulatory statutes than it had in the nation's previous 179 years. These laws include the Occupational Safety and Health Act, the Consumer Product Safety Act, the Traffic Safety Act, the Child Protection and Toy Safety Act, the Coal Mine Health and Safety Act, the Surface Mining Control and Reclamation Act, the Truth in Lending Act, the Age Discrimination Act, the Equal Employment Opportunity Act, the Clean Water Act, the Toxic Substances Control Act, and, of course, the Clean Air Act—to name but a few. New agencies appeared to administer these laws: the EPA, the Occupational Safety and Health Administration, the Equal Employment Opportunity Commission, the National Highway Traffic Safety Administration, the Consumer Product Safety Commission, the Mining Enforcement and Safety Administration, the Office of Surface Mining, and the Federal Energy Regulatory Commission. By 1980 the new regulatory agencies employed more than 60,000 people and spent over $5 billion per year. The total annual cost of these programs, while hard to estimate, must be counted in the tens of billions of dollars.[8]

The new social regulation of the 1960s and 1970s differs from the economic regulation that originated in the Progressive and New Deal eras in more ways than just costliness and rapidity of enactment. While the precise nature of these differences is subject to dispute, and while

8. David Vogel, "The 'New' Social Regulation in Historical and Comparative Perspective," in Thomas K. McGraw, ed., *Regulation in Perspective: Historical Essays* (Harvard University Press, 1981), pp. 155–64. Murray Weidenbaum, former chairman of the Council of Economic Advisers, has estimated the total yearly costs of federal regulation to be over $100 billion. "On Estimating Regulatory Costs," *Regulation*, vol. 2 (May–June 1978), p. 14. Many economists have questioned this figure.

some programs (such as those administered by the Food and Drug Administration and the Federal Trade Commission) seem to fall between the two categories, most students of regulation agree that the health and safety regulation of the recent period differs from most previous regulation in its purpose, scope, and structure.[9]

Purpose

While traditional economic regulation focuses above all on the problem of monopoly and its effect on prices, the new regulation focuses primarily on the quality of the products of the industrial system, namely consumer goods and externalities. The purpose of most traditional regulation is to prevent firms from using their monopoly position to charge excessive prices or to curtail service. To do this, regulators can break up existing monopolies ("trust-busting"), prevent new ones from forming (stopping mergers and outlawing unfair trade practices), or set maximum rates and minimum service levels. The purpose of most recent regulation, in contrast, is to reduce the health and safety risk created by consumer goods (such as automobiles, drugs, and toys) and by externalities (such as air pollution, water pollution, and hazards in the workplace).

The goal of protecting the well-being of citizens brings with it more political controversy than does the goal of ensuring fair and efficient pricing. It is relatively easy to delegate the task of achieving the latter to economists and other experts. But experts cannot so readily claim to know whether a consumer product is sufficiently safe and effective or whether the environment is sufficiently healthy, enjoyable, or even aesthetically pleasing. It is, moreover, somewhat easier to become angry about cancer-causing pollution than about windfall profits.

Scope

This change in the purpose of the regulation in turn expands its scope. Traditional regulation selected a few natural monopolies, near monop-

9. There is a large and growing literature on this subject, including the following: Walter Lilley III and James C. Miller III, "The New 'Social Regulation,'" *The Public Interest*, no. 47 (Spring 1977), p. 49; Paul H. Weaver, "Regulation, Social Policy, and Class Conflict," *The Public Interest*, no. 50 (Winter 1978), p. 45; Mark Green and Ralph Nader, "Economic Regulation vs. Competition: Uncle Sam the Monopoly Man," 82 *Yale Law Journal* 871 (1973); Ralph K. Winter, Jr., "Economic Regulation vs. Competition: Ralph Nader and Creeping Capitalism," 82 *Yale Law Journal* 890 (1973); and James Q. Wilson, ed., *The Politics of Regulation* (Basic Books, 1980).

olies, or supposed monopolies for special treatment. The Interstate Commerce Commission first regulated only railroads and later added trucking and inland water transport. The Civil Aeronautics Board regulates interstate airlines; the Federal Communications Commission, broadcasters and interstate telephone service; state public utilities commissions, intrastate electric power and telephone service. The new regulatory agencies exercise control over hundreds of industries and thousands of companies. The EPA's actions directly affect every facility that produces air pollution, water pollution, noise, solid waste, radiation, or pesticides—which means virtually every firm and government unit in the country. Similarly the Occupational Safety and Health Administration regulates working conditions in nearly every factory, store, and construction site in the nation. The Consumer Product Safety Commission has authority to set standards for almost any consumer good sold by American industry.

Not only does the new regulation directly touch more lives than does the old, but officials administering these new laws are less likely to see their job as promoting the effective management of one sector of the economy. This helps explain the continuing hostility between these agencies and the business community.[10]

Structure

The authors of the regulatory statutes passed in the late 1960s and 1970s attempted to meet criticisms aimed at traditional regulation and to instill in regulators an enduring sense of mission. Lectured incessantly about its failure to provide regulators with specific standards, Congress wrote lengthy statutes that did far more than tell administrators to grant licenses "in the public interest" or to guarantee "fair and reasonable rates." Many of the laws passed during this period included relatively specific standards, deadlines, and procedures. For example, the Clean Air Act, which by 1977 had expanded to cover almost 200 pages, specifies which industries must comply with emission limitations by 1977, which by 1979, and which by 1981; that the levels of sulfur dioxide in the air over national parks can increase by only two micrograms

10. Vogel, "The 'New' Social Regulation," pp. 164–79. This is not the only reason for the continuing hostility between businessmen and regulators. See Paul J. Quirk, *Industry Influence in Federal Regulatory Agencies* (Princeton University Press, 1981), especially his discussion of the National Highway Traffic Safety Administration and the Food and Drug Administration.

per cubic meter over 1977 levels; and that cars produced in 1981 can emit no more than one gram of nitrogen oxides per mile.

While these statutes still leave administrators with considerable discretion, Congress played a far more active and continuing role in the formulation of policy than it had in the past. To increase the efficiency with which administrators carry out these statutory mandates, Congress and the president usually created single-headed agencies located squarely within the executive branch rather than multimember independent commissions.

Another key instrument used by the authors of these new regulatory statutes to promote effective, aggressive regulation was greater opportunity for judicial review. Previous statutes had required citizens wishing to sue administrators to show that they had suffered direct, concrete harm at the hands of an agency. Almost all the regulatory laws passed in the 1970s, though, authorized "any citizen" to file suit against administrators either for taking unauthorized action or for failing to perform "nondiscretionary" duties. Some statutes even reimburse litigants in such suits for their trouble. When combined with detailed statutes, these opportunities for judicial review provided fledgling environmental and consumer groups with powerful resources within the regulatory process.

This liberalization of judicial review provisions resulted in part from the Democratic Congress's distrust of the administrations of Richard Nixon and Gerald Ford. A surprising amount of the regulatory legislation passed during this period was written primarily by Congress, with little assistance from the White House. After seeing how the Republican administrations used administrative means to prune Great Society programs, the Democrats in Congress attempted to protect their initiatives from executive branch sabotage. One way to force administrators to execute laws faithfully is to allow public interest groups to sue them when they do not. Thus, when the Nixon administration tried to remove the "citizen suit" provision from the Clean Air Act, it met defeat after a bitter partisan debate.[11]

---

11. *A Legislative History of the Clean Air Amendments of 1970*, prepared for the Senate Committee on Public Works, 93 Cong. 2 sess. (Government Printing Office, 1974), pp. 138–44, 214–15. For an overview of President Nixon's efforts to use administrative means to change national policies, see Richard Nathan, *The Plot That Failed: Nixon and the Administrative Presidency* (Wiley, 1975). For Congress's response, see James L. Sundquist, *The Decline and Resurgence of Congress* (Brookings Institution, 1981).

Judicial review provisions were more than pawns in a temporary partisan battle, however. They were part of a broad-gauged effort backed by Congress, the press, academic observers, and the legal community to open up the policymaking process to groups other than regulated industries. For years critics of regulation as varied as Ralph Nader and conservative Chicago school economists had argued that the dominant influence of regulated industries had perverted government regulation of business, leading it to serve the private interest of the regulated rather than the broader public interest.[12] Rules on standing and timeliness that limited access to the courts reinforced this bias. Efforts to open the courts to new public interest groups, so it was thought, would help to reduce or eliminate it. Although liberalization of judicial review provisions received little public attention in the early 1970s, this reform captures the essence of almost all the others enacted by Congress.

The New Era in Administrative Law

The regulatory statutes of the 1960s and the 1970s offered the courts an invitation to engage in searching oversight of newly created programs and agencies. This was an offer the courts could easily have refused. For years judges had claimed that standing requirements, which limited access to the courtroom, were based on constitutional principle, not just statutory provision. Article III of the Constitution authorizes federal courts to decide "cases and controversies." According to long-standing judicial doctrine, unless plaintiffs have a concrete, personal stake in the matter at hand, judges will be forced to rule on speculative questions, not lively "cases and controversies." The traditional restrictive reading

12. The literature on this theme is enormous. Paul Quirk provides a useful summary in the first chapter of *Industry Influence in Federal Regulatory Agencies*. Among the leading works on "capture" theory are the following: Marver Bernstein, *Regulating Business by Independent Commission* (Princeton University Press, 1955); George J. Stigler, "The Theory of Economic Regulation," 2 *Bell Journal of Economics and Management Science* 3 (1971); Theodore J. Lowi, *The End of Liberalism: Ideology, Politics, and the Crisis of Public Authority* (Norton, 1969); Roger G. Noll, ed., *Reforming Regulation: An Evaluation of the Ash Council Proposals* (Brookings Institution, 1971); Gabriel Kolko, *Railroads and Regulation: 1877–1916* (Princeton University Press, 1965); and James M. Landis, *Report on Regulatory Agencies to the President-Elect* (GPO, 1960). On the acceptance of this critique by influential judges, see J. Skelly Wright, "Beyond Discretionary Justice," 81 *Yale Law Journal* 575 (1972); and Stewart, "Reformation of American Administrative Law," especially pp. 1681–88 and 1713–60.

of Article III contained a large element of modesty: judges considered themselves unfit to decide abstract policy issues. It also contained an element of self-defense: judges feared being pulled into what Felix Frankfurter called "the political thicket."[13]

Changes in judicial doctrines on standing, which in turn allowed more rigorous scrutiny of agency action, were part and parcel of the reassertion of judicial power that began in the Supreme Court under Chief Justice Earl Warren. The most widely publicized, savagely attacked, and tenaciously defended examples of this activism were constitutional law rulings on racial integration, reapportionment, school prayer, pornography, criminal procedure, women's rights, and abortion. The new administrative law exhibits several of the central characteristics of the constitutional doctrines announced in these cases: egalitarianism, eagerness to use the power of the federal government to redistribute economic and political power, and willingness to become entangled in the day-to-day operation of government programs.[14] Because administrative law decisions immediately affect federal bureaucrats, not private citizens, and because they bring judges directly into conflict with appointed rather than elected officials, they have not incited as much passion or received as much scholarly attention as have constitutional rulings. But their effect has been profound nonetheless.

The lowering of standing requirements is only the most obvious of the changes that occurred during what Richard Stewart has termed "the reformation of American administrative law."[15] The groups benefiting from these new standing rules would have had little reason to use their newly acquired access to the courts if they always lost their cases on the merits. On what other matters, then, did these new litigants prevail?

First, the courts increasingly have read the Administrative Procedures Act and other federal statutes to guarantee a wide variety of groups the right to participate directly in agency deliberations as well as to bring their complaints to court. Several key courts, especially the D.C. Circuit

13. *Colgrove* v. *Green*, 328 U.S. 549 at 556 (1946).

14. The literature on the Warren court and constitutional law is even larger and more imposing than that on regulation. For a conventional, generally sympathetic view, see Archibald Cox, *The Role of the Supreme Court in American Government* (Oxford University Press, 1976). For thoughtful criticism, see Alexander Bickel, *The Supreme Court and the Idea of Progress* (Harper and Row, 1970). Laurence H. Tribe's treatise *American Constitutional Law* (Foundation Press, 1978) provides an extensive review and analysis of these doctrines and decisions.

15. Stewart, "Reformation of American Administrative Law."

(which hears more administrative law cases than any other court), have interpreted the act to require agencies to expand the number and scope of their public hearings as well as to respond to the comments of intervenors. The courts have also used the environmental impact statement requirements of the National Environmental Policy Act of 1969 to force agencies to listen to those opposed to their proposed projects. When in doubt, the courts have read the law to encourage, not limit, participation by nontraditional interest groups.

Second, in reviewing the reasonableness of agency action under the Administrative Procedures Act, the courts have increased the burden on the agencies to explain the rationale for their decisions and to demonstrate that they have considered other policy options. To use the jargon of the new administrative law, judges now take a "hard look" at agency decisions to make sure they have given "adequate consideration" to competing objectives. The purpose of this "searching and careful review" is clear: requiring agencies to uncover more information produces better policy; requiring them to offer clear explanations encourages full public debate; and requiring them to hear a variety of viewpoints discourages administrators from bowing to the nearest interest group. The "adequate consideration" requirement has often merged with the command to expand public participation. A court can be sure that an agency has considered many viewpoints only if it has heard from many groups. Consequently, these doctrines too have increased participation by those previously excluded from agency deliberations.

Third, the courts have become increasingly willing to second-guess agencies on their reading of statutes and their interpretation of evidence—especially when they fear the agency lacks aggressiveness in pursuing its statutory mission. While claiming not to substitute their opinions for those of the administrator, judges frequently disagree with agencies on the meaning of statutory terms and insist upon an expansive reading of "nondiscretionary duties." For example, while the EPA found that the Clean Air Act's statement of purpose by itself conferred no regulatory authority, the courts read the "protect and enhance" clause to embody a prohibition on the "significant deterioration" of air quality. In another set of cases several circuit courts interpreted the words "emission limitations" in the Clean Air Act to mean "emission standards requiring the use of constantly operating technological controls," even though the EPA had taken a less restrictive view. When the EPA tried to classify "variances" as "revisions," several courts ruled they must be handled under the more elaborate procedures designed for "postponements."[16] One can find hundreds of similar decisions under other statutes.

What all these changes show is that judges who had long deferred to the decisions of administrators no longer trusted administrators to develop well-balanced policies. This does not mean that courts increased their efforts to circumscribe the reach of administrative power. On the contrary, the courts frequently pushed agencies to be more aggressive in protecting citizens' "fundamental personal interests in life, health, and liberty," which, according to Judge Bazelon, "have always had a special claim to judicial protection, in comparison with the economic interests at stake in a ratemaking or licensing proceeding."[17] The suspicion arose not that regulators do too much, but that they listen either to too few people or to the wrong people.

In his pathbreaking article on the new administrative law, Richard Stewart summarizes these developments in the following way:

> Faced with the seemingly intractable problem of agency discretion, courts have changed the focus of judicial review (in the process expanding and transforming traditional procedural devices) so that its dominant purpose is no longer the prevention of unauthorized intrusions on private autonomy, but the assurance of fair representation for all affected interests in the exercise of the legislative power delegated to agencies.[18]

These "affected interests" include not just traditional, economic-based interest groups—who already wield substantial, perhaps excessive, influence in the administrative process—but a wide array of new forms of political organizations that would receive little attention without judicial assistance.

In sum, the heart of the new administrative law is an assessment of the nature of and possible cures for what is often called the "bureaucracy problem."[19] The judges who developed these doctrines joined academic critics of bureaucracy and regulation in claiming that administrators often lose sight of their original goals, become bogged down in red tape, fail to announce or defend coherent policies, suffer from the parochialism

16. These cases are *Sierra Club* v. *Ruckelshaus; Natural Resources Defense Council* v. *Environmental Protection Agency*, 489 F.2d 390 (5th Cir. 1974); and *Natural Resources Defense Council* v. *Environmental Protection Agency*, 478 F.2d 875 (1st Cir. 1973).

17. *Environmental Defense Fund* v. *Ruckelshaus*, 439 F.2d 584 at 598 (D.C. Cir. 1971).

18. Stewart, "Reformation of American Administrative Law," p. 1712.

19. James Q. Wilson reviews the many criticisms aimed at bureaucracy in "The Bureaucracy Problem," *The Public Interest*, no. 6 (Winter 1967), p. 3.

that comes from specialization, and, most seriously, develop such close relations with those they regulate that they come to serve the very groups originally believed to threaten the public interest. The legislators who sponsored the new regulation adopted this theme in the early 1970s. It was a theme that influential judges not only had already embraced, but had helped to define and disseminate.

Evaluating the Courts: Judges and Bureaucrats

This discussion of the goals of the new administrative law raises two questions about its consequences. First, have the courts correctly identified the nature of the bureaucracy problem? And second, have they proved capable of designing reforms adequate for solving or at least alleviating the problem? For years judges, lawyers, politicians, scholars, and citizens have argued about whether and when judges should intervene in policy disputes. But obviously what happens when they do intervene is an important factor for deciding whether they should.

While lacking in attention to policy outcomes, the continuing debate over the role of the courts has produced a useful description of the institutional characteristics of the courts and their relevance to the policymaking process. Investigating these institutional characteristics is particularly important in the study of administrative law: here judges challenge the policymaking expertise of agencies specially created by lawmakers to carry out particular programs. To justify their intervention courts must claim either special competence in some aspects of policy-making or special attentiveness to the public interest. It is useful to review the chief institutional characteristics of the courts, comparing their strengths and weaknesses with those of administrative agencies.[20]

First, federal judges are generalists with lifetime tenure. Administrators are specialists whose tenure (especially for political executives) is shorter

20. The following works provide a good summary of this debate: Abram Chayes, "The Role of the Judge in Public Law Litigation," 89 *Harvard Law Review* 1281 (1976); Owen M. Fiss, "Foreword: The Forms of Justice," 93 *Harvard Law Review* 1 (1979); Donald L. Horowitz, *The Courts and Social Policy* (Brookings Institution, 1977); Nathan Glazer, "Should Judges Administer Social Services?" *The Public Interest*, no. 50 (Winter 1978), p. 64; Stuart A. Sheingold, *The Politics of Rights: Lawyers, Public Policy, and Political Change* (Yale University Press, 1974); J. Woodford Howard, Jr., "Adjudication Considered as a Process of Conflict Resolution: A Variation on Separation of Powers," 18 *Journal of Public Law* 339 (1969); and Ralph Cavanaugh and Austin Sarat, "Thinking

and less secure. As generalists who must hear cases on everything from tax fraud, medical malpractice, and contract disputes to antitrust and desegregation cases, judges are unencumbered with the parochialism bred by specialization. The scope of their responsibilities encourages judges to ask whether the programs of an agency are consistent with broad national policies. Moreover, insulated from the pressures of electoral politics and from the demands of narrow but vocal interests, judges can take action painful in the short run but beneficial and popular in the long run. By intervening at critical junctures in the administrative process, skillful judges may be able to help agencies broaden their perspective, clarify their goals, and develop the courage and foresight to innovate.

The virtues of the politically independent generalist, though, entail corresponding vices. Far removed from the daily operation of administrative agencies, judges may fail to appreciate the complexity of the issues before them and consequently hand down sweeping but inappropriate orders. In addition, independence can breed arrogance. Judges may simply impose their policy preferences on administrators who, unlike judges, are subject to considerable control by elected officials. Political executives can be fired; civil servants can be reassigned or reprimanded by budget cuts. Congress and the president have no such control over judges. The role of the politically insulated generalist is a precarious one in a political community facing complex policy choices and dedicated to popular government.

Second, courts must act when—and only when—litigants bring cases before them. Individuals and groups dissatisfied with administrative decisions can raise their claims in court and have their arguments evaluated by those without previous commitments on the policy issues at stake. While the resources needed to mount a court suit may be

about Courts: Toward and Beyond a Jurisprudence of Judicial Competence," 14 *Law and Society Review* 371 (1980). The discussion that follows relies heavily on the Chayes article and the Horowitz book.

The "judicial impact" literature, while small in comparison with traditional legal writing, is growing in size and quality. For bibliographies see Theodore Becker and Malcolm Feeley, eds., *The Impact of Supreme Court Decisions* (Oxford University Press, 1973); and Lawrence Baum, "Implementation of Judicial Decisions," *American Politics Quarterly*, vol. 4 (January 1976), p. 86. Few of these studies concentrate on administrative law. Two exceptions are Martin M. Shapiro, *The Supreme Court and Administrative Agencies* (Free Press, 1968); and Daniel J. Fiorino, "Judicial-Administrative Interaction in Regulatory Policy Making: The Case of the Federal Power Commission," 28 *Administrative Law Review* 41 (1976).

considerable, often they are less than required to lobby administrators or legislators. Thus the courts provide an alternative point of access to those who believe they have been excluded from the political process, unfairly harmed by government action, or deprived of promised government aid.

The courts' dependence on litigants over whom they have no control, however, prevents them from planning or setting their own priorities and often presents them with highly atypical cases. The accident of who gets to court first can affect the outcome of important cases. Moreover, the judge usually must accept at face value a party's claim to represent a certain constituency. It is important to remember that increasing access, if it is anything more than a formality, means increasing the power of those given access. When these participants gain power, others lose. Those who win in the administrative process stand pat; those who lose appeal to the courts. There is no obvious reason to suppose that the latter are more deserving on the whole than the former. Increasing the opportunities for those who lose at the agency level to renew their battle at the judicial level is desirable only if their claims have previously been unfairly dismissed.

Third, litigants present their arguments and evidence to judges in a highly structured, adversarial process. Since judges have little staff of their own, they must rely on litigants to explain their positions, recite supporting data, and attack the arguments of their opponents. Each side has the incentive to discover information that will aid its case and the opportunity to present it. The judge must then consider all evidence collected before coming to a decision. This open, intellectually coherent process in which each side probes the reasoning of the other contrasts with the "muddling through" that many observers claim characterizes administrative decisionmaking.[21]

Of course, the adjudicatory process gains its intellectual coherence by focusing narrowly on the case before the court. The larger policy implications of the case—the long-term effect on parties not before the court—are often ignored altogether. Adjudication focuses on what has happened in the past, not on what may happen in the future, and far more on legal wrongs and rights than on suitable remedies. In addition, since adjudication is so time consuming, it is susceptible to manipulation by those who seek delay. In recent years most agencies have abandoned

21. Charles E. Lindblom, "The Science of 'Muddling Through,' " *Public Administration Review*, vol. 19 (Spring 1959), p. 79.

formal adjudication in favor of more informal rulemaking procedures because adjudication is cumbersome and diverts attention from overriding policy issues. For better or worse, the courts remain wedded to this form of decisionmaking.

Finally, the federal courts are organized in a loosely coordinated hierarchy. At the bottom of this hierarchy 516 district court judges initially hear the evidence in most cases. Parties dissatisfied with their decisions can appeal first to one of the twelve circuit courts of appeal and then to the Supreme Court. While district court judges can immerse themselves in the details of particular cases, they must follow the principles announced by higher courts and show due respect for precedent. Decentralization allows lower courts to undertake extensive fact finding, to consider extenuating circumstances, and to ensure that justice is done in the individual case. Judges can thus temper the foolish or harsh uniformity imposed on private citizens by statutes and bureaucratic regulations. Conversely, since courts are linked together by publicly announced rules, they can escape from the morass of particularism and keep in mind broad principles and overarching goals.

Reconciling principledness and responsiveness, uniformity and flexibility is easier to applaud than to achieve. Expected to be consistent and principled on the one hand and responsive to the peculiar exigencies of individual cases on the other, the courts, like other institutions, can end up rejecting one for the other or oscillating between the two extremes rather than finding a happy medium. Unbending commitment to the rule of law can lead judges to impose rigid requirements on agencies and private parties, purposely ignoring the costs of the resulting regulation and the obstacles to compliance. Conversely, judges who see their role as ensuring that justice be done in the individual case can undermine national policies and weaken centralized leadership.[22] Decentralization allows disagreements among courts to persist for years, leading to confusion and unequal treatment of citizens living in different judicial districts.

This description of the judicial process by itself does not allow one to predict how judicial intervention will affect policymaking or to evaluate the institutional capacity of the courts. One reason is that judges are not automatons who act in a predetermined manner once they put

22. Robert A. Kagan provides a perceptive analysis of the conflict between "stringency" and "accommodation" in *Regulatory Justice: Implementing a Wage-Price Freeze* (Russell Sage Foundation, 1978), especially chaps. 1, 5, and 10.

on black robes. Judges, like all public figures, need intelligence and prudence to make good policy. There are competent and incompetent judges just as there are wise and foolish, corrupt and honest, foresighted and narrow-minded congressmen, bureaucrats, and presidents. Only by looking at specific cases can one know how well these men and women have performed within their institutions.

Second, just as policy issues differ substantially one from another, so do federal agencies and their political environments. Some issues are easily understood by those without specialized training; others are not. Some issues are "bipolar," that is, they affect only two well-defined sets of interests. Others are, to use Lon Fuller's term, "polycentric."[23] Here many parties are involved in such a way that whatever happens to one has an effect on all the others. Moreover, some government policies are susceptible to the formulation of clear general rules; others inevitably require the application of discretion by lower-level officials. Some government agencies are closely supervised by both Congress and the White House. Others are more autonomous. One would expect some of these policy arenas to be more in need of—and more amenable to—judicial intervention than others.

To complicate matters further, describing the consequences of court decisions is a necessary but not sufficient condition for evaluating the policymaking capacity of the judiciary. The term *capacity* implies a comparison: More capable than whom? Other government institutions as they exist? Government institutions as we would create them? A perfectly rational benevolent despot? A bevy of economists? The study of administrative law provides a useful comparison: Did the court working through the agency do a better job than the agency would have done by itself? But this raises an even more difficult question: How can one rank policy outcomes? The issues that come to court are controversial ones, or they would not be in court at all. Observers will disagree on the goodness of outcomes even when these outcomes are evident.

To appreciate the problem this creates for evaluating the capacity of the courts, consider the differences between national policymaking and the National Pastime. One of the greatest aspects of baseball is the batting average. This statistic not only provides interesting reading material, but helps settle disputes. Everyone knows that George Brett is a better hitter than Mark Belanger because Brett's average is higher. No

23. Lon L. Fuller, "The Forms and Limits of Adjudication," 92 *Harvard Law Review* 353 (1978).

matter that in 1980 Brett failed to get a hit in more than 60 percent of his trips to the plate. He was still without doubt a "capable" hitter—in fact, that year he was the best. In the world of politics, though, batting averages are harder to compile. The problem is that there is no clear definition of hits, strikeouts, and errors, nor are there impartial umpires to help settle rhubarbs between contentious players.

Evaluating the performance and assessing the capacity of political institutions requires a standard of good and bad policy. Many of those who comment upon the institutional capacity of the courts seek to provide such a standard by reducing policymaking to problem solving. Problems have solutions, which capable institutions find. Those who favor judicial intervention often attempt to identify what they call "political failures" and to explain why the courts will not similarly fail. A political failure occurs when nonjudicial institutions arrive at an incorrect solution to a societal problem or deny a problem exists. Identifying political failures, however, is hardly a nonpartisan, scientific undertaking. One person's political failure may be another person's conscious—and proper—political choice.

Conversely, the anticourt faction calls attention to the mistakes the courts frequently make in trying to solve the problems they lay out for themselves. Yet deciding whether the unfortunate unintended consequences of a court action outweigh its expected or even unexpected benefits requires coming to some agreement on the importance of the goal the court chose in the first place. Often these critics of the courts question the merits of the courts' ends as well as the adequacy of their means. Thus, all attempts to evaluate the courts' institutional capacity inevitably raise the issue of whether one can reasonably view political controversies requiring choice as problems requiring solutions.

The Clean Air Act as Case Study

The purpose of this work is first to describe the influence of federal court decisions on policymaking in an area characterized by extensive judicial intervention and then to evaluate the courts' ability to understand these complex issues and to control the activity of a large bureaucracy. It seeks to enlighten the reader not just on the subject of environmental regulation (as important as this is), but above all on the question of the institutional capacity of the courts.

Three aspects of judicial oversight of air pollution regulation make it a particularly useful and interesting object of study. The preceding discussion has already alluded to two of these. First, not only has the Clean Air Act had a major effect on the economy and environment, but it presents a leading example of the new regulation. One finds here the key issues of how to define acceptable social risk, how to enforce costly control requirements, and how to reconcile protection of public health with economic growth and energy development.

Second, the judicial decisions issued under the act have themselves become models provoking emulation. Many doctrines developed in Clean Air Act cases rank as the guiding principles of the new administrative law. Since these decisions have received praise from the academic legal community, Congress, and even the EPA, they provide a test case, not a straw man or a sideshow.[24]

Third, the number of court decisions issued under the act allows one to examine several different types of cases without leaving the field of pollution control. The decisions examined in this book involve everything from standard setting to the writing of guidelines for state agencies to enforcing emission limitations. Some issues are technically complex, others far simpler. District courts, circuit courts, and the Supreme Court have all issued important rulings. Environmental groups won some cases, industry others, the EPA still others. These differences allow a number of useful comparisons.

Chapters 2 and 3 provide an overview of air pollution regulation and the Clean Air Act decisions issued between 1970 and 1980. One purpose of these chapters is to help the reader understand the legal and policy issues arising in the chapters that follow. Another is to encourage comparative study of the consequences of judicial decisions by explaining the basic characteristics of the EPA's implementation of the act and the courts' reaction to it.

The heart of this work consists of the six case studies in chapters 4 through 9. Each of these chapters focuses on a major program or policy issue. Table 1-1 provides a brief summary of the major court decisions

---

24. For a sampling of this favorable response, see the following: National Academy of Sciences, *Decisionmaking in the Environmental Protection Agency* (NAS, 1977), pp. 90–95; *Clean Air Act Amendments of 1977*, H. Rept. 95-294, 95 Cong. 1 sess. (GPO, 1977), pp. 318–25; William H. Rodgers, Jr., "A Hard Look at *Vermont Yankee:* Environmental Law under Close Scrutiny," 67 *Georgetown Law Journal* 699 (1979); William F. Pedersen, Jr., "Formal Records and Informal Rulemaking," 85 *Yale Law Journal* 38 (1975); and Richard B. Stewart, "The Development of Administrative and Quasi-Constitutional Law in Judicial Review of Environmental Decisionmaking: Lessons from the Clean Air Act," 62 *Iowa Law Review* 713 (1977).

Table 1-1. *Major Court Decisions Interpreting the Clean Air Act*

Subject	Case	Ruling
Prevention of significant deterioration (PSD)	*Sierra Club* v. *Ruckelshaus*, 344 F. Supp. 253 (D.D.C. 1972)	Ordered EPA to disapprove state implementation plans (SIPs) not preventing significant deterioration of air quality
	Citizens to Save Spencer County v. *EPA*, 600 F.2d 844 (D.C. Cir. 1979)	Upheld EPA rule on effective date of 1978 regulation
	Alabama Power Co. v. *Costle*, 636 F.2d 323 (D.C. Cir. 1979)	Overturned EPA rules implementing PSD section of 1977 Clean Air Act Amendments
Dispersion	*NRDC* v. *EPA*, 489 F.2d 390 (5th Cir. 1974)	Instructed EPA to permit substitution of dispersion enhancement for constant controls only if they are "unavailable"
	Big Rivers Electric Corp. v. *EPA*, 523 F.2d 16 (6th Cir. 1975)	Upheld EPA rules limiting use of intermittent control systems
	NRDC v. *EPA*, 529 F.2d 755 (5th Cir. 1976)	Upheld rules limiting stack height credit; dismissed contempt motion against EPA
Variances	*NRDC* v. *EPA*, 478 F.2d 875 (1st Cir. 1973) (and similar decisions in 2d, 5th, and 8th Circuits)	Prohibited EPA from approving variances granted by the states extending beyond 1975
	Train v. *NRDC*, 421 U.S. 60 (1975)	Overruled circuits; reinstated previous EPA policy permitting variances not causing violation of national standards
Enforcement	*Buckeye Power Co.* v. *EPA*, 481 F.2d 162 (6th Cir. 1973) (and similar decisions of other courts)	Prohibited EPA from enforcing SIP regulations without demonstrating that necessary control equipment is technically and economically feasible
	Union Electric Co. v. *EPA*, 427 U.S. 246 (1976)	Ruled that EPA can approve and enforce SIP regulations without proving their feasibility; suggested that courts and EPA can consider feasibility in fashioning relief
	Hancock v. *Train*, 426 U.S. 167 (1976)	Prohibited states from requiring federal facilities to comply with permits issued under SIPs
	Adamo Wrecking Co. v. *U.S.*, 434 U.S. 275 (1978)	Prohibited EPA from enforcing "work practice rule" for hazardous pollutants
	Cleveland Electric Illuminating Co. v. *EPA*, 572 F.2d 1150 (6th Cir. 1978)	Upheld EPA's SIP for most of Ohio

Table 1-1 *(continued)*

Subject	Case	Ruling
	Cincinnati Gas and Electric Co. v. EPA, 578 F.2d 660 (6th Cir. 1978)	Invalidated EPA's SIP for two Ohio counties
	U.S. v. West Penn Power Co., 460 F. Supp. 1305 (W.D. Penn. 1978)	After examining feasibility of controls, court ordered utility to install scrubbers
Standards	*Kennecott Copper Corp. v. EPA*, 462 F.2d 846 (D.C. Cir. 1972)	Invalidated secondary standard for sulfur dioxide
	EDF v. Ruckelshaus, 3 *Environmental Law Reporter* 20173 (D.D.C. 1973)	Ordered EPA to promulgate regulations for asbestos, beryllium, and mercury
	Portland Cement Assoc. v. Ruckelshaus, 486 F.2d 375 (D.C. Cir. 1973)	Invalidated new source performance standard; established more elaborate rulemaking procedure
	NRDC v. Train, 545 F.2d 320 (2d Cir. 1976)	Ordered EPA to set air quality standards for airborne lead
	Ethyl Corp. v. EPA, 541 F.2d 1 (D.C. Cir. 1976)	Upheld EPA regulation limiting lead in gasoline; ruled that EPA can rely on "hypotheses" and can "err on the side of overprotection"
	Lead Industries Assoc. v. EPA, 647 F.2d 1130 (D.C. Cir. 1980)	Upheld air quality standard for airborne lead; prohibited EPA from considering cost in standard setting
	American Petroleum Institute v. Costle, 665 F.2d 1176 (D.C. Cir. 1981)	Upheld revision of ozone standard
Transportation controls	*City of Riverside v. Ruckelshaus*, 4 *Environment Reporter Cases* 1728 (C.D. Cal. 1972)	Ordered EPA to write transportation control plans (TCPs) for California
	NRDC v. EPA, 475 F.2d 968 (D.C. Cir. 1973)	Overturned EPA decision to give states more time to produce TCPs; ordered EPA to devise program to maintain air quality standards
	South Terminal Corp. v. EPA, 504 F.2d 646 (1st Cir. 1974)	Invalidated parts of EPA's TCP for Boston
	Texas v. EPA, 499 F.2d 289 (5th Cir. 1974)	Invalidated parts of EPA's TCP for Texas
	Brown v. EPA, 521 F.2d 827 (9th Cir. 1975) (and several other similar cases)	Ruled that EPA does not have authority to force states to enforce federal TCPs

discussed in these chapters. These case studies are long—perhaps too long for many readers. The length of each story, though, indicates how long it can take for the full impact of court decisions to appear. If a controversy does not end when a judge issues his opinion, neither does it stop when an agency revises its regulations. A court decision often precipitates a long series of negotiations involving the original litigants, a variety of agency officials, other members of the executive branch, state officials, congressmen, lobbyists, and even the president. Uncovering the links between court decisions and policy revision requires careful attention to each stage in the development of administrative and legislative policy and often calls for creative reconstruction of what would have happened had the court acted differently.

While each of these six chapters concentrates on the consequences of a relatively small number of decisions, the work as a whole attempts to transcend this programmatic perspective. Two other types of judicial influence on policymaking will receive intermittent attention in these chapters and considerably more in the conclusion. First, I will examine how well these many court decisions—with all their expected and unintended consequences—fit together. Just as air pollutants can be synergistic or antagonistic in their effects, so too can court decisions. It is important to know whether court intervention fragments or brings unity to the policymaking process.

Second, the influence of a court decision can extend far beyond the policy issues before the court. A victory even in an insignificant case can increase the bargaining power of the winner on other matters. Anticipation of future court actions can affect the way members of Congress write laws, the extent to which the president tries to control administrative behavior, the relative influence of various parts of the bureaucracy, and the manner in which the members of the public respond to agency orders. Since policymaking in administrative agencies is a political process, investigators must pay attention to the shifting political power of the participants.

The final chapter of this book summarizes the findings of each case study and examines the larger patterns that emerge when they are considered as a whole. It comes back to the question "Can one evaluate the policymaking capacity of the courts?" and presents a standard for such an evaluation. Chapter 10 argues that while one can indeed identify a political and bureaucratic failure in air pollution control, it is not the one identified by the courts.

Most of this introductory chapter has been devoted to discussion of the courts. But the book is at least as much about regulation as about the courts. Most of the book's action takes place within the Environmental Protection Agency. Much of the evidence supporting the analysis comes from EPA documents and files and from interviews with EPA officials. Viewed in one way, this book is about how a regulatory bureaucracy reacts to stimuli from an outside force. Viewed in another, it is a description of how various institutions and private interests—the agency, Congress, the White House, the courts, industry, and environmentalists— seek to resolve troublesome regulatory issues. It is my hope that even those with no interest in the courts can learn something about bureaucratic decisionmaking and the nature of regulatory issues from this study. For if judges sometimes make mistakes in their efforts to reform the regulatory process, part of the blame must go to those political scientists, economists, and journalists who helped to create the stereotypes upon which these judges rely. This study attempts to present a fuller picture both of the activities of the courts and of the paradoxes of government's regulation of its citizens.

CHAPTER TWO

Air Pollution Regulation, 1970–80

The air program is probably the most intellectually thin program we've got and it is the most overbuilt in terms of the law and the structure and the size. . . . That's a program that really has a church history problem. Every single congressional battle and staff battle is relevant to understanding why you're at the point you are now. —EPA Administrator Douglas Costle

WHEN President Ronald Reagan took office in 1981, many environmentalists feared his administration would convince Congress to weaken the Clean Air Act, the flagship of the environmental protection fleet. Reducing the burden of federal regulation was a major plank in Reagan's platform, and much of his criticism was aimed at environmental regulation. To make matters worse, the act's authorization ran out in 1981, necessitating some form of congressional action. The Senate, which in the past had strongly supported the act, was now in Republican hands. Especially after Reagan's surprising legislative victories on the budget and taxes, major revision of the act seemed near.

In December 1982, though, proposed amendments to the act died quietly in committee. The House committee remained internally divided. Legislation supported by the Senate committee was unacceptable to the White House. Some observers doubt that a major revision of the Clean Air Act will become law before the 1984 presidential election.

What is most striking about this sequence of events is not the failure of the Reagan administration to produce quick, major changes in the act, but the similarities between 1981–82 and two prior periods, 1973–74 and 1976–77. In 1973, after the Arab oil embargo, President Richard M. Nixon proposed emergency energy legislation that would relax key provisions of the Clean Air Act. Despite calls for action to meet the energy crisis, Congress did not pass a bill Nixon would sign until mid-1974. That legislation, the Energy Supply and Environmental Coordination Act,[1] contained few revisions of the Clean Air Act. The sponsors

1. 88 Stat. 258.

24

of the 1970 act had successfully resisted retrenchment. In 1976 another Republican president, Gerald R. Ford, supported amendments to relax air pollution regulation, and Congress geared up for action. With inflation and unemployment running high and energy shortages on everyone's mind, environmentalists were once again on the defensive. Yet Congress did not produce amendments to the act until 1977, and these amendments strengthened the act in many ways.

This brief history of clean air legislation emphasizes the continuities of environmental politics. While presidents—especially Republican ones— have favored relaxing regulatory demands, Congress has strengthened the act more than it has weakened it. Air pollution regulation is so complex and controversial that Congress usually takes action a year or two after everyone announces that it "must" act "immediately." In the meantime other institutions—especially the Environmental Protection Agency, the states, and the courts—have tried to cope with the problems created by the act.

1970: The Policy Breakthrough

Air pollution presents a classic example of a market externality or spillover. And the evolution of air pollution control in the United States provides an equally classic example of how the American political system typically handles such regulatory issues.[2] In the absence of government action, air pollution imposes costs on society in the form of adverse health effects, harm to vegetation and materials, and reduced visibility. Polluters, though, are seldom forced to compensate those who suffer this harm. As a result, those who use the air as a dumping ground fail to put a price on the consumption of a scarce natural resource—clean, breathable air. While it is generally conceded that government has a legitimate role to play in controlling such pollution, the federal government took almost no part in the process until the 1960s. Pollution control remained the domain of state and municipal public health agencies, which, with varying degrees of success, attempted to reduce the amount of visible pollution in the air of industrialized cities.

2. For a useful summary of the problem of externalities, see Stephen Breyer, *Regulation and Its Reform* (Harvard University Press, 1982). Two works that summarize the early history of pollution control are Richard B. Stewart and James E. Krier, *Environmental Law and Policy*, 2d ed. (Bobbs-Merrill, 1978); and James E. Krier and Edmund Ursin, *Pollution and Policy: A Case Essay on California and Federal Experience with Motor Vehicle Air Pollution, 1940–1975* (University of California Press, 1977).

Industrial growth after World War II produced increasing concern over air pollution. Utilities met growing demand for electricity by building coal-burning power plants that emitted large amounts of sulfur dioxide and particulate matter. In the late 1940s and early 1950s pollution from power plants and steel mills contributed to several "killer fogs" in Britain and the United States, causing thousands of premature deaths. Meanwhile, use of the automobile—which emits carbon monoxide, nitrogen oxides, and hydrocarbons—rose dramatically. Scientists investigating the origin of Los Angeles's famous smog discovered that the latter two pollutants interact to produce the brownish cloud that frequently caused eye irritation and various respiratory difficulties in residents of that city.

States such as California, Pennsylvania, and New York took the lead in addressing these problems, and Congress took halting steps to help them (see table 2-1). Federal involvement started in 1955 with small

Table 2-1. *Major Provisions of Federal Legislation on Air Pollution Control*

	Legislation		
Major provision	Air Quality Act of 1967[a]	Clean Air Amendments of 1970[b]	Clean Air Act Amendments of 1977[c]
Air quality standards	Set by states on basis of studies by federal government	Uniform primary (health) and secondary (welfare) ambient air quality standards set by EPA	"Precautionary" nature of standards emphasized
Attainment deadlines	None	Primary standards: 1975 or 1977 if extension granted. Secondary: within reasonable time	Primary: 1979 for stationary source pollutants; 1982 for mobile source pollutants or 1987 if extension granted. Secondary: no change
Implementation plans	States responsible for devising plans to meet air quality standards	State implementation plans (SIPs) due in 1972; must include enforceable emission limitations and schedules; EPA must either approve or set alternative emission limits	Systematic reassessment of SIPs for nonattainment areas required by 1979; prevention of significant deterioration (PSD) and offset programs expanded; limits placed on use of dispersion enhancement; special provisions for problem sources

Table 2-1 (*continued*)

Major provision	Air Quality Act of 1967[a]	Clean Air Amendments of 1970[b]	Clean Air Act Amendments of 1977[c]
		Legislation	
Enforcement	Left to states, except for cumbersome conference procedure	Emission limitations enforceable by both state and federal government; criminal penalties and injunctions authorized; provision for citizen suits	Civil penalties and noncompliance penalties added; construction ban and other sanctions for failing to attain air quality standards
New sources	No provisions	Uniform new source performance standards (NSPS) set by EPA	Attainment areas: best available control technology plus review of PSD increment consumption. Nonattainment: lowest achievable emission rate plus offset review. Coalburning power plants: percentage reduction of sulfur in fuel
Motor vehicle emissions	Federal government sets "feasible" emission standards for new vehicles	New vehicles must reduce emissions to 90 percent of 1970 level no later than 1975–76	Deadline for hydrocarbon and carbon monoxide standards extended; nitrogen oxides standard relaxed
Transportation controls	No provisions	State plans must include "land-use and transportation controls" necessary to attain air quality standards	Deadline for transportation controls extended; indirect source review made discretionary for states
Judicial review	Administrative Procedure Act governs	Challenges of regulations in "appropriate circuit"; citizen suits in federal district court	D.C. Circuit identified as "appropriate circuit" for regulations of national applicability

a. 81 Stat. 485; preceded by Air Pollution Control Act of 1955, 69 Stat. 322; Clean Air Act of 1963, 77 Stat. 392; and Motor Vehicle Air Pollution Control Act of 1965, 79 Stat. 992.
b. 84 Stat. 1676.
c. 91 Stat. 685.

research projects and grants to the states. During the 1960s the federal government glided slowly, almost imperceptibly, into recommending safe pollution levels for various pollutants. The Air Quality Act of 1967 (the immediate predecessor of the legislation passed in the 1970s) charged the National Air Pollution Control Administration, a small unit within the Department of Health, Education and Welfare, with setting technologically feasible emission standards for new automobiles and helping the states devise pollution control programs. Yet progress in reducing pollution levels remained painfully slow. By 1969 most observers had labeled the federal program a nearly complete failure.[3]

The year 1970 was a political watershed for pollution control. The Earth Day activities of that spring called attention to the nation's many environmental problems. Politicians and the media claimed that air and water pollution were creating an environmental crisis. New organizations formed to promote environmental protection. President Nixon introduced a bill to strengthen air pollution legislation and later issued a reorganization plan creating the Environmental Protection Agency.[4] Senator Edmund S. Muskie, Democrat of Maine, the author of previous air pollution legislation and chairman of the Senate Subcommittee on Environmental Pollution, moved quickly to ensure that Nixon would neither receive political credit for jumping on the environmental protection bandwagon nor produce a new act with more bark than bite. Not only had Muskie long advocated stronger pollution control measures, but he also expected to be running for president against Nixon in 1972. A 1970 report by Ralph Nader's Center for Study of Responsive Law charging Muskie with being soft on polluters strengthened the senator's resolve to push a tough bill through Congress.[5] After months of one-upmanship, Muskie succeeded in creating a very ambitious law.[6]

The section of the 1970 act that received most attention in Congress and the press was the requirement that by 1975 auto manufacturers

3. Richard J. Tobin, *The Social Gamble: Determining Acceptable Levels of Air Quality* (Lexington Books, 1979); J. Clarence Davies III and Barbara Davies, *The Politics of Pollution,* 2d ed. (Bobbs-Merrill, 1975).

4. 35 Fed. Reg. 15623 (1970).

5. John C. Esposito, *Vanishing Air* (Grossman, 1970).

6. Useful accounts of the passage of the 1970 act include Charles O. Jones, *Clean Air: The Policies and Politics of Pollution Control* (University of Pittsburgh Press, 1975); Alfred Marcus, "Environmental Protection Agency," in James Q. Wilson, ed., *The Politics of Regulation* (Basic Books, 1980); and Helen Ingram, "The Political Rationality of Innovation: The Clean Air Act Amendments of 1970," in Ann F. Friedlaender, ed., *Approaches to Controlling Air Pollution* (MIT Press, 1978).

reduce the emissions of new cars by 90 percent. Detroit and the Nixon administration claimed this was technologically infeasible. Senator Muskie responded that the 90 percent figure was based on estimates of the pollution reduction necessary to protect human health and that setting such federal standards would force the development of new technology. Thus was born the concept of "technology forcing," which has since become a major theme of the act.[7]

The sections of the act involving stationary sources received much less attention in the press and on the House and Senate floor, but were no less sweeping. The act required the EPA to set new source performance standards (NSPS) for all major categories of polluting facilities. Each standard was required to "reflect the degree of emission limitation achievable through the application of the best system of emission reduction which . . . has been adequately demonstrated" (section 111). The administrator was also instructed to set emission limitations for "hazardous pollutants," to regulate fuel and fuel additives, and to establish emission standards for aircraft.

As important as these provisions were, the centerpiece of the 1970 act was the national ambient air quality standard (NAAQS). The act created a three-step process to define and achieve adequate air quality:

1. The EPA must set "primary" and "secondary" standards for all pollutants that "endanger the public health or welfare." Primary standards must be adequate to "protect the public health" by incorporating "an adequate margin of safety." Secondary standards must be adequate to "protect the public welfare from any known or anticipated adverse effects" (sections 108 and 109).

2. States must submit by 1972 state implementation plans (SIPs) adequate to meet primary standards by 1975 and secondary standards within "a reasonable time." These SIPs must include "emission limitations, schedules, and timetables for compliance with such limitations, and such other measures as may be necessary to insure attainment and maintenance of such primary or secondary standard, including, but not limited to, land-use and transportation controls" (section 110). If the EPA determines that all or part of a SIP is inadequate, it must promptly promulgate an adequate plan of its own.

7. John E. Bonine, "The Evolution of 'Technology-Forcing' in the Clean Air Act," *Environment Reporter*, Monograph 21 (Bureau of National Affairs, 1975); and Jones, *Clean Air*, chap. 7.

3. The requirements of each SIP are enforceable in both federal and state courts. The EPA can ask federal courts to impose criminal penalties for "knowing violators" of SIP rules or to issue injunctions stopping further violation (section 113).

The 1970 act was far more detailed than most previous regulatory statutes. Most sections included deadlines for administrative action. Not only did the act specify precise emission limitations for new cars, but the Senate report suggested exact numerical standards for several key pollutants. Yet much was left to administrative discretion. As mentioned in the previous chapter, the need for discretion, coupled with congressional distrust of the Nixon administration, led the authors of the act to include liberal judicial review provisions.

Political scientists have noted that when the direct costs of regulation fall on a small, well-defined group (such as polluters) and benefits accrue to a large, dispersed collection of individuals (such as those who breathe the air), the former often come to dominate the administrative process once the initial enthusiasm for regulation dissipates.[8] Those who benefit from controls find it hard to organize lobbying efforts to counterbalance the ability of those being regulated to maintain a daily presence in the administrative process. As a result, victories achieved in a legislative breakthrough slowly evaporate as administrators develop a specific program to carry out statutory commands.

Although the Environmental Protection Agency was not as brash or aggressive by 1980 as it was in the early 1970s, it maintained a strong sense of mission and an adversarial relation with industry throughout the decade. None but the most unrelenting environmentalist would claim (at least until the Reagan administration made its appointments in 1981) that polluters had "captured" the EPA.

This is particularly surprising in light of the changing economic and political context of regulation. The 1960s and early 1970s were years of constant economic growth. Just as politicians looked for ways to spend the fiscal surplus, they expected business to be able to finance pollution control from its substantial profits. In the mid- and late 1970s, however, inflation, unemployment, and energy dominated political dis-

8. Marver Bernstein, *Regulating Business by Independent Commission* (Princeton University Press, 1955), chap. 3; James Q. Wilson, "The Politics of Regulation," in James W. McKie, ed., *Social Responsibility and the Business Predicament* (Brookings Institution, 1974); and Mancur Olson, Jr., *The Logic of Collective Action* (Harvard University Press, 1965).

course. Many costly EPA regulations came into effect just as the nation was sliding into the recession of 1974–75. The EPA often received blame for fueling inflation and adding to the unemployment rolls. In addition, air pollution regulations that increased energy consumption (such as restrictions on the use of leaded gasoline) or that limited the use of domestic fuels (such as sulfur dioxide standards limiting the burning of coal) led to constant battles between the EPA and those whose primary concern was reducing American dependence on foreign oil. To see why large-scale administrative and legislative retreat did not occur in the 1970s one must look in greater detail first at the political coalition supporting regulation and then at the agency administering it.

Political Actors and Coalitions

By imposing burdens on a wide variety of polluters and consumers and by promising benefits to an equally wide variety of groups and citizens, the Clean Air Act has drawn a multitude of participants into the debate over regulation of air pollution. On occasion these groups have formed strange coalitions. For example, in 1977 environmentalists united with eastern high-sulfur coal interests to impose further restrictions on low-sulfur western coal.[9] Yet coalitions on clean air issues have remained nearly constant since 1970. Environmentalist groups have received strong support from congressional committees, especially in the Senate. Industry has sought help from the White House, other federal agencies, and the states. Caught between its two masters, Congress and the president, the EPA has sided more often with the former than the latter.

Congress and the Executive

From the time he sponsored the Clean Air Acts of 1965, 1967, and 1970 until he left Congress to become secretary of state, Senator Edmund S. Muskie was the political figure with the greatest influence on air pollution policy. With years of experience in the field, the respect of the vast majority of the Senate, the ability to command media attention, and an enviable capacity for outmaneuvering his opponents, Muskie

9. Bruce A. Ackerman and William T. Hassler, *Clean Coal/Dirty Air* (Yale University Press, 1981).

controlled the tempo as well as the substance of congressional action. Time and again Muskie staved off attempts to amend the act until the political environment was favorable to his cause. As chairman of the Subcommittee on Environmental Pollution of the Senate Committee on Public Works (later renamed the Committee on Environment and Public Works), Muskie held detailed annual oversight hearings on the implementation of the act. He expected the EPA to consult with him or his staff on major policy decisions. Muskie made clear what he thought Congress had intended in 1970—especially when he believed the administration was pressuring the EPA to act differently.[10]

Senator Muskie had two sets of allies within the Senate. The first was a dedicated, aggressive, knowledgeable staff. Muskie aides, particularly Leon Billings, developed a reputation for both influence and arrogance. Without their assistance the Subcommittee on Environmental Pollution— which became known as "the Muskie committee"—would not have been able to write such detailed legislation and reports, conduct its many hearings, and keep abreast of daily activities at the EPA.

The second set of allies was the Republicans on the subcommittee. Senator Muskie developed close working relations with those minority members who participated actively in policymaking for pollution control, including Howard Baker, Robert Stafford, Pete Domenici, John Chafee, and even the more conservative James Buckley. These senators, like their Democratic colleagues, chose to devote their attention to environmental issues because they believed that the federal government should take strong action to prevent environmental degradation. At times Republicans on the committee have offered stronger support for environmental programs than have Democrats. One of the ironies of the 1980 election, which brought the Senate under control of the Republicans, is that the two men who became chairmen of the full committee and the subcommittee—Robert Stafford and John Chafee—have resisted relaxation of the act more vigorously than have their ranking Democratic counterparts.

The House of Representatives did not play a major role in the writing of the 1970 act, but has since steadily gained influence over regulatory policy. The Clean Air Act falls within the jurisdiction of the Subcommittee on Health and the Environment of the House Energy and Commerce

10. Bernard Asbell chronicles many of Muskie's activities in *The Senate Nobody Knows* (Johns Hopkins University Press, 1978). This journalistic account provides an interesting view of Muskie's influence on the 1977 amendments.

Committee. Until 1978 this subcommittee (which was one of the two busiest in the House) was chaired by Representative Paul G. Rogers, Democrat of Florida. While Senator Muskie was known as "Mr. Environment," Representative Rogers gained his reputation as "Mr. Health." His subcommittee treated the act as a preventive health measure and sought to strengthen its health-related features.

Rogers, like Muskie, assembled a young, competent, hard-driving staff, but he had trouble keeping committee members and the rest of the House in line. Rogers faced frequent challenges from Republicans in the subcommittee, Democrats in the full committee, and even other subcommittees—most notably the House Appropriations Committee's Subcommittee on Agriculture, Environmental and Consumer Protection, chaired until 1975 by the fiercely anti-EPA Jamie Whitten. In 1977 the Rogers subcommittee lost two key votes on the floor, the first on auto standards and the second on prevention of significant deterioration. When Rogers retired in 1978, a lively battle for the subcommittee chairmanship ensued. Henry Waxman of California, the most liberal of the candidates, eventually won. But his control over policymaking has been constantly challenged, especially by John Dingell of Michigan, the new chairman of the full committee. The difference between House and Senate reflects not just the personalities of legislative leaders, but also the greater skepticism about environmental programs expressed by the membership of the lower house.

Both the House and Senate subcommittees have frequently complained about presidential hostility to air pollution programs. This was particularly true during the Nixon administration. Despite the fact that Nixon created the EPA and signed some of the most ambitious environmental protection legislation in the country's history, he never received the trust of environmentalists in Congress or the loyalty of the EPA. Generally suspicious of the federal bureaucracy and concerned about the costs the Clean Air Act placed on industry, the president and his White House staff carefully reviewed activity in the EPA, sought to block many agency regulations, and introduced legislation to reduce the EPA's goals and authority. By 1974, antagonism between the Nixon administration and the EPA had become so great that Administrator Russell Train (recently appointed by Nixon) refused to support legislative revisions proposed by the White House and other federal agencies. The weakening of the presidency in the wake of Watergate strengthened the position of the

EPA and congressional committees. As one insider put it, Train survived only "because Richard Nixon did not."[11]

Hostility between Congress and the president and cool relations between the EPA and the White House continued under Gerald Ford. More surprising was the reemergence of this pattern under President Jimmy Carter. Carter received the support of environmental groups in the 1976 election, appointed several leaders of these organizations to top positions in the EPA, and endorsed much of the legislation developed by the Muskie and Rogers committees. Yet he, too, was eventually attacked by environmentalists for trying to water down EPA rules and was criticized in special hearings of the Muskie committee for "interfering" with air pollution regulation.[12] However, President Reagan's appointment of many political executives with close ties to industry and his major cuts in the EPA's budget have made many environmentalists and congressmen look upon his predecessor more positively.

What accounts for the constant sparring between the president on one side and the EPA and the Congress on the other? Partisanship is an important part of the explanation, but not the only part. Another is institutional. All recent presidents have established mechanisms for subjecting major decisions of the EPA and other regulatory bodies to interagency review. Under Nixon and Ford the Office of Management and Budget (OMB) coordinated what it called the "quality of life review," which gave those agencies opposed to EPA actions a chance to attack them. First the Department of Commerce and later the Federal Energy Administration objected to many EPA rules, often delaying their promulgation. President Carter created the Regulatory Analysis Review Group, an interagency committee staffed by personnel from the Council on Wage and Price Stability, to perform similar oversight. President Reagan has reinstituted and strengthened OMB review. While observers disagree on the effect these mechanisms have had on substantive policy, there is little doubt that they have contributed to the hard feelings

11. Robert Sansom, *The New American Dream Machine: Toward a Simpler Lifestyle in an Environmental Age* (Doubleday, 1976), p. 25. Sansom was assistant administrator for air programs. Deputy Administrator John Quarles tells a similar story in *Cleaning Up America: An Insider's View of the Environmental Protection Agency* (Houghton Mifflin, 1976).

12. *Executive Branch Review of Environmental Regulation*, Hearings before the Subcommittee on Environmental Pollution of the Senate Committee on Environment and Public Works, 96 Cong. 1 sess. (Government Printing Office, 1979), pp. 1–2, 231–60, 329–63.

between the EPA's supporters and those who have established and conducted the review.[13]

Behind these institutional arrangements lies a difference in perspective that often puts presidents at odds with the EPA and its congressional patrons. Presidents are expected not just to protect the environment, but also to promote economic growth, employment, and energy self-suffi-ciency. They are charged with coordinating the activities of many agencies whose missions bring them into conflict with one another—the EPA, the Department of Energy, the Department of Commerce, the Council of Economic Advisers, and OMB, to name but a few. Thus, presidents, even those who start with strong positions on environmental protection, come more and more to seek what they call "balance," and what their opponents decry as "leniency."

Interest Groups, the States, and Public Opinion

For many years industry kept effective pollution control off the agenda of the federal government. The National Coal Association and the leading automakers spearheaded this opposition. No major environmental group emerged to push for stronger regulation. All this changed in 1970. Industry groups suffered a major setback; they were effectively excluded from decisionmaking on the 1970 act. New environmental organizations appeared to monitor EPA activities. While industry has slowly recuperated from its defeat, environmental groups have remained remarkably active and strong.

It is difficult to generalize about the role business firms have played in the development of air pollution regulation. The Clean Air Act affects many industries and in different ways. Those especially hard hit by regulation—the auto, steel, nonferrous smelting, and electric power industries—have managed to win delays both from the EPA and from Congress. (The key to Detroit's success was gaining the support of the United Auto Workers.)[14] At first most firms sought above all to avoid

13. "Special Report: Office of Management and Budget Plays Critical Part in Envi-ronmental Policymaking, Faces Little External Review," 7 *Environment Reporter—Current Developments* 693; Stanley Bach, "Governmental Constraints on Environmental Regula-tion," in National Academy of Sciences, *Decisionmaking in the Environmental Protection Agency,* vol. 2b (NAS, 1977), p. 163; and Christopher C. DeMuth, "Constraining Regulatory Costs," *Regulation,* vol. 4 (January–February 1980), p. 13 and (March–April 1980), p. 29.

14. Norman J. Ornstein and Shirley Elder, *Interest Groups, Lobbying and Policymaking* (Congressional Quarterly Press, 1978), chap. 6.

making pollution control expenditures at their own facilities. More recently, as this has become harder to achieve, trade associations and broader industry coalitions have grown in number and influence. They have met with mixed success. The newly formed American Industrial Health Council successfully opposed the carcinogen policy proposed by the EPA in 1979. The American Petroleum Institute waged a campaign for a major relaxation of the national standard for ozone (smog), but succeeded only in making the standard slightly more lenient. The Lead Industries Association lost its battle against a stringent standard for airborne lead; the Utilities Air Regulatory Group failed to defeat a restrictive standard for coal-burning power plants in 1979. The Business Roundtable and a new coalition called the National Economic Development Association have focused on convincing Congress to prune the act. They have yet to achieve a significant legislative victory.[15]

Industry has had greatest success resisting pollution controls when it has enlisted the aid of state governments. The Clean Air Act states that the states, not the federal government, bear "primary responsibility" for controlling pollution. It gives them authority to write and enforce state implementation plans. Since state agencies provide much of the personnel, money, and expertise in this exercise in "cooperative federalism," federal regulators cannot ignore their opinions. State governors and legislators frequently offer instructions to these state agencies.

Although several states have developed highly competent regulatory agencies and stringent pollution controls, most are sensitive to the threat of losing jobs as a result of industry closing or relocating. Nevada and Arizona have refused to impose strict requirements on nonferrous smelters, which face serious foreign competition and constitute the largest—or the only—employer in some western towns. Ohio, an economically depressed state highly dependent on electric power generated from the burning of coal, has for years opposed the EPA's efforts to reduce sulfur dioxide emissions. Strangely enough, the states' desire to protect employment does not always put them at odds with environmentalists. For example, many eastern states struggling to retain existing industry have supported programs that impose greater restrictions on pollution in the West and the Sun Belt.

---

15. Most of these examples are discussed at length in subsequent chapters. For a discussion of why industry lobbying is sometimes less effective than one might expect, see Raymond A. Bauer, Ithiel de Sola Pool, and Lewis Anthony Dexter, *American Business and Public Policy: The Politics of Foreign Trade,* 2d ed. (Aldine, 1972).

In contrast to industry and the states, environmental groups are relatively few in number and united in purpose. They have worked hard to establish close links with EPA officials, congressional committee members and staff, and the national media. They have also made extensive use of the federal courts.

Environmental groups active in air pollution control include both old-line conservation organizations and younger public interest groups. The most important of the former is the Sierra Club, which led the fight to limit pollution in the Rocky Mountains. Others include the National Audubon Society and the National Wildlife Federation. The environmental groups that have most closely monitored regulation under the Clean Air Act are the Natural Resources Defense Council (NRDC) and the Environmental Defense Fund (EDF), two organizations formed in the late 1960s largely through grants from the Ford Foundation. Both have combined litigation with lobbying Congress and the EPA. While the EDF has emphasized regulation of hazardous pollutants, especially carcinogens, the NRDC has specialized in matters relating to national air quality standards and state implementation plans. A variety of other groups, including the American Lung Association, the League of Women Voters, and a few labor unions, have united with these core groups to form the National Clean Air Coalition, which tries to present a united front to Congress and the media. Their ability to agree on a common course of action has been a key to their success.

Environmentalists have had to deal with two problems in achieving this unanimity. The first is the different priorities of various groups. While some groups (the "smoggies") emphasize the goal of reducing urban pollution, others (the "greenies") seek above all to protect wilderness areas. Policies aimed at reducing urban pollution by encouraging industrial relocation threaten to divide these two groups. Second, maintaining organizations based on what James Q. Wilson has called "purposive incentives" requires emphasizing the threat of immediate and serious danger to the environment.[16] Rhetoric used and positions taken to build support for the organization can make negotiation with agency officials, industry spokesmen, and congressmen difficult. Environmental groups have coped with these problems by stating ambitious environ-

16. James Q. Wilson, *Political Organizations* (Basic Books, 1973), chaps. 3 and 9. Also see Jeffrey Berry, *Lobbying for the People: The Political Behavior of Public Interest Groups* (Princeton University Press, 1977); and David Vogel, "The Politics of the Public Interest Movement," Hudson Institute Paper HI-2950-P (December 1978).

mental protection goals—aimed not just at reducing air pollution but at reducing automobile use and encouraging land use planning—while accepting long delays in their achievement. They have managed both to paint environmental issues in symbolic terms (pitting the moral goods of health and respect for nature against the evils of pollution and the quest for corporate profits) and reach pragmatic agreements with those whose support they need.

Another reason environmental groups have remained politically influential is that public opinion has continued to support aggressive pollution control. A 1979 poll found that 54 percent of its sample agreed with the statement that "protecting the environment is so *important* that requirements and standards cannot be too high, and continued improvements must be made *regardless* of cost." Of the respondents, 53 percent thought the government was moving too slowly to clean up the air, and only 5 percent thought it was moving too fast. A 1981 Harris poll found that 80 percent of the public oppose any relaxation of the Clean Air Act; 65 percent oppose any cost-based constraint on health standards.[17]

Public opinion on pollution control in part rests on perceptions of who is paying for it. The national media have usually focused on the harm caused by pollution and implied that control costs will be taken out of profits, not passed along to consumers. When the EPA has imposed controls that fall directly on private citizens (such as restrictions on driving or threats to close down a factory), it has met stiff popular opposition. The agency has learned to avoid such measures. In recent years industry has tried to change public perceptions on environmental issues, charging that the real battle lines are between the vast majority of consumers and workers on the one hand and a small minority of environmental purists and individuals with arcane respiratory ailments on the other. How an issue is framed—as an environmental issue, a consumer issue, an employment issue, an energy issue, or a local control issue—often determines who wins and who loses. So far, environmental groups have been far more effective in framing issues than have their opponents.

The EPA: The Administrative Core

Despite the specificity of the Clean Air Act and the extensive oversight performed by Congress and the executive branch, it is the EPA that must

17. *Public Opinion*, vol. 2 (August–September 1979), pp. 22–23; 12 *Environment Reporter—Current Developments* 789.

apply the words of the statute and find solutions to environmental and administrative problems not recognized by legislators. The EPA is the largest federal regulatory agency, as well as one of the newest and most controversial. In 1970 President Nixon created the EPA by pulling together administrative units from the Departments of Agriculture, Interior, and Health, Education and Welfare. By 1980 it employed over 10,000 people and spent more than $3 billion annually. While air pollution control is the EPA's single largest program, the agency is also responsible for regulating water pollution, noise, pesticides, solid waste, toxic substances, radiation, and hazardous waste.[18]

Within the EPA air pollution policy is made jointly by a number of administrative components. The most visible decisionmakers are the agency's political executives: the administrator, the deputy administrator, and the several assistant administrators responsible for specific program areas. All are appointed by the president and are formally accountable to him. The four EPA administrators—William Ruckelshaus (1971–73 and 1983–), Russell Train (1974–77), Douglas Costle (1977–81), and Anne Gorsuch Burford (1981–83)—have all been lawyers, though with varying degrees of familiarity with pollution control. William Ruckelshaus's lack of experience in the area originally made environmentalists skeptical. By taking aggressive positions on a number of issues in his first year, however, he both established the EPA's reputation as a defender of the environment and developed pride and a sense of mission within the EPA. Russell Train, previously chairman of the Council on Environmental Quality and subsequently president of the Conservation Foundation, expanded the EPA's regulatory programs and kept the agency at arm's length from the White House. Douglas Costle, who had headed Connecticut's Department of Environmental Protection, became known as a manager and mediator. The appointment of Anne Gorsuch Burford reversed the trend toward increasing experience in environmental protection and interrupted the pattern of administrators opposing major relaxation of environmental regulation.

The units that offer advice to the administrator on air pollution questions have frequently been shifted around on organizational charts (receiving a new name each time), but their number and characteristics have remained relatively stable. An assistant administrator heads the agency's air program office. Most have been lawyers and strong environmental advocates. During the Carter administration, for example,

18. Alfred Marcus, *Promise and Performance: Choosing and Implementing an Environmental Policy* (Greenwood Press, 1980), pp. 31–49.

David Hawkins, a chief litigator for the NRDC, served in this position. The most important bureau under this assistant administrator's control is the Office of Air Quality Planning and Standards (OAQPS), located in Durham, North Carolina.

More than distance separates the OAQPS from Washington. It is an organization composed of technical personnel: mechanical and chemical engineers, meteorologists, and other specialists. While the EPA's Washington office tends to view the OAQPS as too cautious, the OAQPS tends to distrust the adversarial techniques of lawyers and to suspect that Washington fails to understand technical issues. The tenure of most agency lawyers and political executives is between two and four years, but OAQPS personnel stay much longer. Many current OAQPS officials came to the EPA from the National Air Pollution Control Administration. The OAQPS expects results in years, not months. Moreover, it generally seeks engineering solutions and hesitates to attempt to spur innovation by writing technologically infeasible regulations. Seeing themselves as air pollution control professionals, OAQPS officials have resisted efforts to use the Clean Air Act to achieve ends other than pollution reduction—such as reducing reliance on the automobile or stimulating land use planning. These attributes have caused friction between the OAQPS and the assistant administrator and have led to the creation of special-purpose units directly under the control of the assistant administrator.[19]

Separated from the air office are those lawyers and engineers whose job it is to enforce EPA regulations. The Office of Enforcement has a small staff in Washington and many more people scattered throughout the ten regional offices. The Office of Enforcement has an institutional preference for tough, even infeasible, regulations: such rules can improve the agency's bargaining position in negotiations with polluters. Enforcers deal with the hard cases—the "bad apples"—and consequently tend to view polluters as the enemy and negotiations over SIP requirements as the battlefield. The Office of Enforcement has generally opposed attempts to revise SIP provisions, both because such revisions create temporary uncertainty and because this office has a larger role in informal revisions of SIPs (through the negotiating of consent decrees) than in the formal revision process, which is dominated by dispersion modelers in the OAQPS. Enforcement lawyers who expect quick environmental victories

19. In 1974, for example, Assistant Administrator Roger Strelow created the Office of Transportation and Land Use Planning, removing these responsibilities from the OAQPS (see chap. 9).

usually leave the agency after a year or two of fighting what seem to be never-ending battles against sophisticated polluters. Those who remain—especially in the regional offices—gradually develop the long-range perspective and more accommodating views of the OAQPS's professionals.

While lawyers in the Office of Enforcement prepare the agency's suits against polluters, the Office of General Counsel (OGC) defends the agency from legal challenges.[20] The OGC carries more prestige than the Office of Enforcement. Its lawyers are young, ambitious, and eager to set environmental policy. The OGC forms the bridge between the courts and the rest of the agency. It explains the agency's position to reviewing courts and explains to the agency what the courts require it to do. Because the courts have played such an active role under the Clean Air Act, the OGC has a hand in almost every major decision the agency makes. At times OGC lawyers have been more interested in pleasing reviewing courts than in devising workable control programs. This is not surprising in light of their lack of technical background and the fact that they will be blamed if the EPA loses a suit or is found in contempt of court. In the early 1970s OGC lawyers developed a reputation as aggressive "Young Turks." How they earned this label and the effect they had on the air program will be a major theme of this book.

In recent years a new force has arisen to challenge the preeminence of lawyers within the EPA: the economists. The Office of Planning and Management, staffed by economists and systems analysts, was originally established by Administrator Ruckelshaus to respond to the criticism EPA regulation received in interagency review. As the economic and energy consequences of EPA rules have grown and as opposition to environmental regulation has stiffened, the Office of Planning and Management has gained institutional stature. This office carries on a running dialogue with the Department of Energy, OMB, the president's Council of Economic Advisers, industry lobbyists, and the EPA's academic critics. The Office of Planning and Management has pushed the EPA to develop quantitative analysis for evaluating the benefits and costs of regulation. In recent years the administrator has relied more heavily on the assistant administrator for planning and management for advice that is in tune with the political mood of the country.

20. The Office of General Counsel has from time to time been put under the same assistant administrator as the Office of Enforcement. These reorganizations, though, have not altered the tasks or perceptions of the two offices.

Much of the important work of administering the Clean Air Act takes place in the EPA's regional offices. Regulation is decentralized both because pollution problems vary greatly from area to area and because substantial responsibility under the act rests with the states. The regional offices constitute a bridge between the states and the EPA's Washington office. Regional officials must become familiar with state programs and politics, explain the EPA's regulations to the states, and express state and local concerns to those who set agency policy. Not surprisingly, regional officials are often torn between their dedication to consistent rule application on the one hand and their desire to recognize distinctive local problems and to cut through red tape on the other. Many of the tensions within the Clean Air Act are felt most keenly at this organizational level.

With all these offices involved in making decisions on air pollution control, coordination becomes a problem. The EPA has developed interoffice working groups and a steering committee of senior officials to facilitate discussion and review. One consequence of these various levels of review, though, is delay. Controversial regulations often sit on the back burner for months while participants either look for compromises or try to avoid difficult issues altogether. At times it takes a dramatic event—such as a court order—to force the agency to make a decision.

As important as it is to understand the different perspectives EPA officials bring to policymaking, one should not forget that the EPA is a single organization with a distinctive sense of purpose. Throughout the 1970s almost all agency personnel shared a strong commitment to environmental protection. While recognizing the shortcomings of the Clean Air Act, the agency defended its air program vociferously. Few within the EPA recommended sweeping changes. To some observers this represents bureaucratic inertia and entrenchment: no one wants to change an elaborate program he has spent years building up. But it also reflects a recognition that industry and the states have made major investments with the expectation that existing regulations will remain in place. Rapid change can be unfair, economically wasteful, and administratively disastrous.

Contributing to the EPA's defense of the Clean Air Act was a surprisingly strong and pervasive siege mentality. Despite the support the EPA received from Congress and the steady expansion of its programs,

EPA officials saw enemies everywhere. Former Assistant Administrator Robert Sansom expressed vividly the prevalent attitude:

> Most in Congress lacked the vision to see the problem, much less the solution. The few who did understand EPA's plight were fearful of opening any environmental legislation for amendment. They were afraid because the anti-environmental energy forces in the Congress might have been able to turn an effort to devise national growth, land-use, and transportation policies consistent with a clean environment into an effort to overturn the finest set of laws in the world for abating industrial pollution.[21]

The overriding desire to save the Clean Air Act led the EPA not to disregard political opposition, but, when possible, to avoid it. This occasionally put the agency at odds with pro-environmental congressmen and their staffs. While agency officials may have agreed with the objectives of this group, they realized that the EPA and the Clean Air Act, not individual congressmen or staff members, would receive the blame for overly stringent requirements or mistakes. For this reason, the EPA resisted being pushed too hard by environmental enthusiasts and avoided going to the mat with politically powerful opponents.

The Regulatory Scheme

The act that the EPA fought so hard to preserve provided the framework within which most policy disputes were resolved during the 1970s. It also created innumerable headaches for agency officials. The authors of the 1970 act made two key choices that have guided the nation's pollution policy ever since. First, they chose to impose direct controls on polluters. Rather than offer subsidies for pollution control, impose taxes on pollution, or establish a system of marketable emission rights, Congress and the executive branch opted—almost without thought—for what has become known as "command and control" regulation. Second, the act established an ambient air quality, or air quality management, approach to regulation. Congress did debate the merits of this scheme and its alternative, one that sets performance standards based on "available technology." The 1970 act applied the latter approach to new sources but not to existing sources. To understand the ensuing conflicts over implementation of the act it is essential to understand the implications of the ambient air quality scheme.

21. Sansom, *New American Dream Machine,* p. 20.

While an emission-based approach to regulating air pollution starts with a definition of "available technology," an ambient approach starts with standards for local air quality (for example, a maximum hourly average concentration of 0.12 part per million of ozone) and sets emission limitations for each pollution source on that basis. Focusing directly on air quality has several advantages. It ensures that polluters who locate in relatively unpopulated and clean areas will not be burdened with the expensive control requirements appropriate for heavily industrialized areas where pollution levels threaten the health of millions of citizens. Conversely, it prevents new polluters from further degrading air quality in those areas where the air is already unhealthy. Politically, stressing air quality makes it easier to present pollution control as a health measure—and few issues are more attractive than protection of the public health. At the same time, setting national air quality standards rather than national emission standards gives the states the opportunity to choose any pollution control mix adequate to meet these standards.

Despite these advantages, the EPA has slowly moved away from the ambient approach under the Clean Air Act. Congress also rejected the ambient approach when it passed legislation on water pollution control in 1972. The reason for this is that regulation based on ambient standards is technically and administratively complex and is based on several assumptions that do not hold up under careful scrutiny. This becomes apparent when one looks at the three stages of regulation under this approach: setting air quality standards, writing individual emission limitations, and bringing sources into compliance.

Standard Setting: The Threshold Problem

The Clean Air Act requires the EPA to set primary (health-based) and secondary (welfare-based) national ambient air quality standards for all those pollutants emitted by "numerous sources" that "endanger the public health and welfare." By 1980 the EPA had established standards for seven criteria pollutants, so named because the EPA must set them after reviewing criteria documents on their effects. These standards are uniform throughout the entire country; the same standard that applies to Littleton, New Hampshire, also applies to New York City and Los Angeles. The 1970 act allowed heavily polluted areas to apply for two-year extensions of the 1975 deadline for meeting health-based standards, but by 1977 every air pollution control region was expected to attain the primary standards.

Since existing pollution levels vary greatly from area to area, so too does the cost of meeting the standards. Many areas complied with the act simply by requiring utilities to burn lower-sulfur coal. But Los Angeles could have attained the ozone and carbon monoxide standards only by reducing auto traffic by about 90 percent—a reduction that would have wreaked havoc with that city's entire economic and social structure. Generally the marginal cost of pollution control—the cost of removing the final pound of a pollutant—rises rapidly as the extent of control increases.

The authors of the 1970 act justified imposing very heavy costs on some areas by claiming that primary standards represent the minimum air quality necessary to protect public health. Primary standards are not based on cost-benefit analysis, but on a medical determination of safe pollution levels. Even if it were possible to find such safe levels, it would not necessarily make sense to spend huge amounts of money achieving these levels instead of using these resources for, say, hospitals or dental clinics.[22] Basing pollution control programs on uniform national standards becomes even more questionable when one realizes that it is usually impossible to set a "safe" pollution level.

Most scientists now agree that for most pollutants there is no health effects threshold, that is, a concentration below which there are no serious health effects and above which there are. In the words of a study conducted by the National Academy of Sciences, "health damage varies with the upward and downward variations in the concentration of the pollutant, with no sharp lower limit."[23] The House Commerce Committee's 1977 report concluded that "the 'safe threshold' concept is, at best, a necessary myth to permit the setting of some standards."[24] The arbitrariness of any nonzero air quality standard makes it difficult for the EPA to justify its demands that polluters spend large amounts of money to attain it. It also calls into question the wisdom of allowing pollution levels to rise to the national standards in areas currently below

22. James E. Krier, "The Irrational National Air Quality Standards: Macro- and Micro-Mistakes," 22 *UCLA Law Review* 323 (1974).

23. National Academy of Sciences–National Academy of Engineering, *Air Quality and Automobile Emission Control* (GPO, 1974), vol. 1, p. 17.

24. *Clean Air Act Amendments of 1977*, H. Rept. 95-294, 95 Cong. 1 sess. (GPO, 1977), p. 111. For an extended discussion of this issue, see chap. 8.

them. Thus, the national standards, the foundation of the air quality scheme, may be too lenient for some areas and too stringent for others.

Emission Limitations: Dispersion and Transport Problems

An effective pollution control program requires clear, specific emission limitations for each pollution source. It is nearly impossible to prove that a particular polluter has contributed to a violation of an ambient air quality standard on any given day. Usually the combined emissions of a number of sources cause such violations. The relative size of their contributions depends on a number of variables, including daily operation levels and weather patterns. Moreover, enforcement action taken against those causing ambient air violations always comes too late; the harm has already occurred. Consequently the Clean Air Act requires state implementation plans to contain specific "emission limitations, schedules, and timetables for compliance with such limitations," which are enforceable even without a showing that a source caused a particular ambient violation.

The act gives the states the job of writing emission limitations sufficient to attain national standards, but requires the EPA to make sure these plans are adequate. The first problem that the states and the EPA face is that techniques for plotting the dispersion of pollutants through the atmosphere are highly inexact. In 1971 most states used crude "rollback" models to estimate required emission reductions. If the pollution concentration in the most heavily polluted part of the state exceeded the standard by x percent, then all polluters in the state (or at least in that control region) would be required to reduce their emissions by x percent. While such calculations are simple, the worst-case assumptions built into rollback analysis frequently led to more control than necessary to meet the standards.

As polluters and state agencies searched for ways to reduce control requirements, they relied more heavily on dispersion models. Dispersion models are computer simulations that predict how the plumes emanating from smokestacks will be dispersed through the atmosphere. Modeling is technically complex, expensive, and inexact. Even the best models supplied with extensive monitoring data may underpredict actual concentrations by 50 percent or overpredict by as much as 100 percent. Models vary widely in their assumptions and predictive ability. For every model the EPA produces that shows a violation of a national standard, industry can usually find one that predicts that no violation will occur. Such modeling battles can go on for years.

Predicting air quality levels is even more difficult for secondary pollutants, that is, pollutants formed by the interaction of two or more precursors. Ozone (smog) is produced in a complex chemical reaction involving several components, including hydrocarbons and nitrogen oxides. The amount of ozone produced by given quantities of these two components depends on temperature, humidity, and the presence of various catalysts. Similarly, sulfur dioxide, particulate matter, and other pollutants combine to produce various forms of sulfates. Most health experts consider the complex sulfate molecule far more dangerous to health than sulfur dioxide. Moreover, the acid precipitation caused by the joining of sulfur dioxide derivatives with moisture in the air decreases the pH of lakes and streams, killing fish and plant life.

Secondary pollutants not only make it difficult to predict how much pollution will be created, but also make it nearly impossible to determine with precision where this pollution will settle. Pollutants emitted in New York City may not create ozone until they reach Hartford, Connecticut. Recent evidence has shown that ozone can travel hundreds, even thousands, of miles in the upper atmosphere. Sulfur dioxide and particulate matter, too, travel hundreds of miles in the upper atmosphere, becoming more dangerous the longer they remain in the air. This phenomenon has become known as long distance transport. Increases in the amount of pollution so transported have become known as atmospheric loading.

These difficulties not only strain the technical capacity of state and federal regulations, but call into question the local basis of air pollution control under the Clean Air Act. By regulating local air quality levels the act assumes that what goes up in one state comes down in that state. It offers no effective recourse to states such as those in New England that receive the acid rain and high sulfate levels produced by coal burning in states such as Ohio and Illinois. The exporting of pollution has added to the demands for uniform emission limitations on all sources regardless of their location.

Enforcement: Administrative Overload

Thousands of stationary sources and millions of mobile sources pour pollutants into the atmosphere. Although meeting the act's air quality standards requires that a large number of sources install costly pollution controls, many polluters have delayed spending money on these controls until forced to do so by the government. With so many sources initially in violation of SIP requirements, noncompliance has carried little stigma. This meant that in many areas of the country the states and the EPA had to undertake a massive administrative effort, first to inform polluters of their responsibilities and then to threaten sanctions against those who balked. Success in such an undertaking requires that applicable regulations be known, clear, achievable, and testable; that enforcement resources be commensurate with the task; and that sanctions for noncompliance be credible. Unfortunately, this has not been the case.

The act gave the states little more than a year to write their SIPs. Most state plans included broad requirements that state agencies expected to tailor to particular sources as the occasion arose. Many such occasions arose when the Arab oil embargo caused the price of low-sulfur fuel to skyrocket, when sources such as steel mills realized that they could not possibly meet their SIP limitations no matter how much they spent, when smelters and paper mills claimed they would go out of business unless the states relaxed control requirements, and when state and federal enforcement officials learned that most state plans did not include definitions of test methods that would allow them to prove that a violation had indeed occurred. The states granted (and the EPA often approved) revision after revision, changing not just cleanup schedules but final control requirements as well. At times it became impossible just to locate the applicable regulation—to say nothing of understanding or enforcing it. When the EPA disapproved a revision, the source could challenge its dispersion modeling. Industry had a strong incentive to cause as much uncertainty as possible, since serious enforcement efforts could not begin until the regulations were clearly established.

The EPA did not have a large enough enforcement staff to inspect or insist upon compliance by more than a small percentage of polluters. It had to rely on the states for most enforcement. To make matters worse, it did not have authority to ask for civil penalties until 1977. This meant the EPA depended on both federal district court judges and the states to get tough with polluters. Generally they did not. The EPA itself often backed away from aggressive enforcement, realizing that trying to shut down many factories would invite congressional backlash. Thus all the shortcomings of the statutory pollution control scheme—technical, economic, and political—became evident in enforcement. Serious enforcement did not start until about 1975, the year the standards were to be achieved. Given the problems created by the act, it is a tribute to the EPA and state agencies that it took place at all.

The Evolution of Regulation

Regulation of air pollution went through three phases in the 1970s, each corresponding roughly to the term of office of the incumbent administrator and president, and each punctuated by the enactment of new legislation. The period of organization and experimentation lasted from 1970 to 1973, while the EPA was under the direction of William Ruckelshaus. A period of consolidation and growth began with the appointment of Russell Train and the passage of the Energy Supply and Environmental Coordination Act in 1974. In early 1977 a new phase began with President Carter's appointment of Douglas Costle and, later, the passage of the 1977 amendments. During this period the EPA directed its energies to implementing the amendments. Enforcement actions became more numerous and regulation became more complex. This era came to a close in 1981 as Anne Gorsuch Burford became administrator and Congress considered further amendments to the act.

1970–73: Organization and Experimentation

The first years of the EPA and the Clean Air Act were ones of confusion, experimentation, and high expectations. The EPA rushed to meet the many deadlines of the act, promulgating six sets of NAAQS in April 1971, publishing its first NSPS in December 1971, and approving most SIPs on schedule in May 1972. To meet this succession of deadlines the agency based its decisions on any information readily available and tried to put off as many problems as possible. The one air quality standard challenged in court was eventually dropped by the EPA for lack of any scientific justification.[25] The courts also found the EPA's documentation supporting several NSPSs deficient.[26] The SIPs approved in 1972 lacked compliance schedules for individual sources. Facing the dual challenge of enforcing its rules and defending them from attacks, the agency chose to avoid new, controversial tasks, such as writing

25. *Kennecott Copper Corp.* v. *Environmental Protection Agency*, 462 F.2d 846 (D.C. Cir. 1972).

26. *Portland Cement Assoc.* v. *Ruckelshaus*, 486 F.2d 375 (D.C. Cir. 1973) and *Essex Chemical Corp.* v. *Ruckelshaus*, 486 F.2d 427 (D.C. Cir. 1973).

transportation control plans for major cities. It concentrated its energies on inducing major pollution sources to install technological controls necessary to meet the primary standards as quickly as possible.

Meanwhile events outside the EPA's control had dropped three new issues into its lap. First, the federal courts ordered the EPA to devise a program to prevent the significant deterioration of air quality in areas already meeting primary and secondary standards. The prevention of significant deterioration (PSD) program the agency began to develop in 1973 grew rapidly and quickly became politically controversial. Second, the courts also ordered the EPA to limit automobile traffic in those major cities that could not otherwise meet national standards for carbon monoxide and ozone. These transportation control plans proved to be a disaster that severely wounded the EPA's public reputation. Third, even before the oil embargo of October 1973, the EPA realized that the aggregate SIP-induced demand for clean low-sulfur fuel would exceed near-term supplies. Aware that flue gas scrubbers, even if reliable, take years to design and install, the EPA issued a clean fuels policy that encouraged states with sulfur dioxide regulations more stringent than required by the act to relax their SIPs in order to make low-sulfur fuel available in areas with higher pollution levels. While the states did little to respond at first, they flooded the EPA with requests for emergency variances once the embargo occurred. By the time Congress began to consider emergency energy legislation in late 1973, the golden years of environmentalism were over.

1974–76: Consolidation and Growth

In the middle years the EPA began to enforce its regulations, to establish extensive new programs, and to implement the provisions of the Energy Supply and Environmental Coordination Act. It beefed up its enforcement staff in the regions and pursued a strategy of seeking informal agreements committing polluters to installation of "reasonably available technology." The EPA conceded that not all areas would be able to meet primary standards by 1975 or even 1977. It asked Congress to extend the deadline and announced its "offset" policy, which allowed some new sources to locate in areas not meeting national standards.[27]

27. This policy required new facilities to "offset" their emissions by buying emission rights from existing polluters. 41 Fed. Reg. 55558 (1976).

Congress waited until 1977 to revise the statutory deadlines and accepted most of the EPA's offset policy.

This period also saw the fall of transportation control plans and the rise of PSD. The transportation plans and related programs ran into so much resistance in 1974–75 that the EPA finally abandoned all pretensions of enforcing them. In 1976 it announced a strategy for controlling mobile source pollutants that deemphasized controls on automobile use. In contrast, agency support for the program to limit pollution increases in relatively clean areas blossomed. The EPA published final PSD regulations in late 1974 and began to issue permits to new sources under this increasingly elaborate scheme. The EPA was slowly moving toward a policy of requiring the use of best available control technology everywhere rather than focusing primarily on those areas exceeding the national standards.

1977–81: Increasing Enforcement and Complexity

While most EPA officials and congressmen expected mid-course corrections to the Clean Air Act to pass in 1976, a filibuster by senators opposed to PSD delayed congressional action until 1977. In large part that legislation ratified changes made informally by the EPA. It replaced the original 1975 and 1977 deadlines with more realistic ones geared to the seriousness of particular pollution problems. It also gave the agency new enforcement powers, including civil penalties. With these powers, the backing of Congress, and the support of the Carter administration, the EPA made major strides toward putting some of the nation's worst polluters on compliance schedules. By 1980 almost all air pollution control regions had met primary standards for stationary source pollutants (sulfur dioxide and particulate matter), though not for mobile source pollutants (ozone and carbon monoxide).

The 1977 amendments also added new and administratively burdensome requirements for PSD, visibility protection, plan revisions for nonattainment areas, transportation control measures, nonferrous smelter orders, and mandatory assessment of noncompliance penalties. As a result the EPA's air program has grown enormously in size and complexity. By 1981 state air officials and the EPA itself joined industry in requesting further legislative action to simplify regulation. As explained earlier, such revisions had not appeared by the time the Ninety-seventh Congress adjourned in December 1982.

A decade of federal regulation of air pollution has produced substantial achievements. The number of violations of primary standards has been significantly reduced in urban areas. The President's Council on Environmental Quality reported that between 1974 and 1978 the number of "unhealthy days" in major cities (using a composite index combining levels for five criteria pollutants) decreased by 18 percent, the number of "very unhealthful" days dropped 35 percent, and the number of "hazardous" days declined by 55 percent. Average annual pollution levels and total emissions also dropped, though not as dramatically.[28]

Serious problems remain nonetheless. Many polluters continue to exceed their legal emission limitations. Many areas continue to violate national standards, especially for ozone. Sulfate levels have failed to decline in the Northeast; acid rain might be getting worse. In short, not only has the act failed to achieve the ambitious goals established in 1970, but new and serious environmental problems have come to light in intervening years.

28. Council on Environmental Quality, *Environmental Quality: Eleventh Annual Report of the Council on Environmental Quality* (GPO, 1980), p. 147; and Lester B. Lave and Gilbert S. Omenn, *Clearing the Air: Reforming the Clean Air Act* (Brookings Institution, 1981).

CHAPTER THREE

The Dilemmas of Judicial Review

Although this inquiry into the facts is to be searching and careful, the ultimate standard of review is a narrow one. The court is not empowered to substitute its judgment for that of the agency.
 —Justice Marshall in *Citizens to Preserve Overton Park* v. *Volpe*, 1971

NEARLY EVERY Clean Air Act case that comes to court presents the judges who must decide it with a dilemma. On the one hand, judges hear plaintiffs claim that they have suffered irreparable harm as a result of the bureaucracy's overzealousness, callousness, inattention, timidity, ignorance, or ineptitude. Judges see that the administrators who carry out the Clean Air Act have the power to destroy firms, put thousands of people out of work, and increase American dependence on foreign oil, as well as to protect the health of millions of Americans and the beauty of pristine wilderness areas. The harm caused by agency action or inaction is often both serious and permanent.

On the other hand, most judges recognize their limited expertise in this regulatory area. The Environmental Protection Agency's decisions frequently rest on judgments made after long deliberation by scientists, engineers, economists, and experienced enforcement officials and on political agreements painstakingly negotiated among officials from several agencies, Congress, the White House, and the states. It can take days for judges just to figure out what the key issues are. It is not surprising therefore, that judges usually uphold agency decisions. As the administrative apparatus of the federal government extends its reach, judges hear more complaints about the bureaucracy running out of control, but find it difficult to provide adequate supervision.

In offering guidance to the lower courts, the Supreme Court and Congress have restated rather than resolved this dilemma. In its landmark *Overton Park* opinion—cited in nearly every subsequent administrative and environmental law case—the Supreme Court explained that the decisions of administrators are "entitled to a presumption of regularity." Yet the courts must conduct "a thorough, probing, in-depth review."[1] In 1977 the report of the House Commerce Committee paraphrased the *Overton Park* opinion to explain the role it envisioned for judicial review under the Clean Air Act:

> The purpose of the committee's provision in this regard is to endorse the court's practice of engaging in searching review without substituting their judgment for that of the Administrator and to assure that no retreat to a less searching approach take place.[2]

Here is advice worthy of Polonius.

One fact about judicial review of agency action is clear: of the thousands of regulations, orders, and other rulings announced by federal agencies, only a very small percentage are invalidated or modified by court decisions. This does not mean that court decisions are unimportant. By intervening at critical junctures courts can direct the flow of agency decisionmaking. The paucity of decisions overturning agency actions can at times indicate administrative compliance with prior judicial orders. However, this raises the question: What accounts for the particular instances of judicial intervention? Why do judges who usually defer to administrative expertise sometimes decide that administrators have acted "arbitrarily," "unreasonably," or "unfairly" or have failed to perform "nondiscretionary duties"?

The simple answer is that in these instances judges have found violations of the law. But this begs the question: What is "the law" and how do judges know what it says? Usually "the law" means the authorizing statute, in this case the lengthy Clean Air Act. While the act is relatively specific compared to many other federal statutes, litigation usually involves conflicting interpretation of ambiguous words. Is a "variance" a "revision" or a "postponement"? Is a highway that attracts automobile traffic an "emission source"? What constitutes an "adequate margin of safety"? The problem of interpretation is even greater under the Administrative Procedures Act, the generic statute governing agency procedures and the norms of judicial review. This act tells judges to reverse agency action that is "arbitrary and capricious," "contrary to constitutional right," "in excess of statutory jurisdiction," or "without

---

1. *Citizens to Preserve Overton Park* v. *Volpe,* 401 U.S. 402 at 415 (1971).

2. *Clean Air Act Amendments of 1977,* H. Rept. 95-294, 95 Cong. 1 sess. (Government Printing Office, 1977), p. 323. The committee was explaining its recommendations that courts employ the "substantial evidence" test in reviewing EPA decisions.

observation of procedures required by law."[3] These phrases pose questions rather than resolve disputes.

"The law" also means past judicial decisions and accepted canons of interpretation. An enormous case law has grown up on the Administrative Procedures Act, and court decisions have gradually clarified the duties and authority of the EPA under the Clean Air Act. But this, too, begs the question: How did these judicial doctrines develop? What reasoning stands behind the precedent judges now follow?

This chapter focuses on the reasons judges have given for circumscribing administrative discretion under the Clean Air Act. But before exploring this theme it is useful first to review the types of cases that reach the federal courts and the form they take. This requires a brief summary of the judicial review provisions of the Clean Air Act.

The Forms of Judicial Review

The 1970 Clean Air Act authorized three different types of suits: challenges to EPA rules and regulations; citizen suits seeking the performance of nondiscretionary duties by the EPA; and enforcement suits against polluters. The act offers guidance on which court must hear each type of suit, when they must be filed, and who can bring them. In 1977 Congress added greater specificity to these judicial review provisions, incorporating into the act major court rulings issued between 1971 and 1976.

Challenges to Agency Rules

The Clean Air Act provides for expedited review of most EPA actions in the federal courts of appeal. According to section 307, challenges to agency regulations that are either "nationally applicable" or "based on a determination of nationwide scope or effect" must be brought to the Court of Appeals for the District of Columbia Circuit (the D.C. Circuit). This includes all air quality standards, new source performance standards, emission limitations for hazardous pollutants, and most rules on prevention of significant deterioration (PSD). Challenges to regulations that are "locally or regionally applicable" must be filed in the U.S. Court of Appeals for the "appropriate circuit." This includes EPA decisions to

3. 5 U.S.C. 706 (2).

approve or disapprove portions of state implementation plans (SIPs) and agency promulgation of substitute plans. Section 307 requires that petitions for review be filed within sixty days of the date the EPA took the challenged action. It does not specify who can bring such suits.

Congress has allowed plaintiffs to proceed directly to circuit courts without stopping first at federal district courts, both to prevent delay and to promote uniformity. The former concern is reflected in the strict deadlines for filing suit; the latter in the expansive jurisdiction of the D.C. Circuit. The authors of these judicial review provisions assumed that section 307 cases would involve primarily abstract questions of "law" rather than questions of "fact." Circuit courts, unlike district courts, cannot conduct trials. They cannot listen to testimony from witnesses or allow attorneys to engage in discovery proceedings. The circuit courts, which have become the central focus of Clean Air Act litigation, have, as a result, experimented with new mechanisms for investigating policy issues.

Two jurisdictional disputes have arisen under section 307. The first involves the division of power between the D.C. Circuit and other circuits. It is often hard to say whether a rule that directly affects a particular state or facility is part of a broader regulation of national applicability or is based on "a determination of nationwide scope." Business firms and state governments usually prefer to sue in local circuits. The EPA and environmental groups prefer the D.C. Circuit. Throughout the 1970s court decisions and congressional action have tended to favor centralization of review in the District of Columbia.

The second dispute concerns the line between challenging regulations and contesting enforcement orders. Section 307 precludes private parties from raising in enforcement proceedings issues they could have raised in suits challenging regulations. The purpose of this provision is to prevent polluters from waiting until the last moment before calling agency rules into question. Often, however, the implications of a regulation are not clear until the EPA tries to enforce it. Most district courts allow those subject to air pollution regulations to dispute the EPA's interpretation of general rules either in preenforcement review or, more frequently, in defending themselves in enforcement cases brought by the EPA. This has allowed polluters to keep their challenges alive long after the sixty-day period runs out.[4]

4. This difficulty is discussed in David P. Currie, "Judicial Review under Federal Pollution Laws," 62 *Iowa Law Review* 1221 (1977), and in chap. 7 below.

Citizen Suits

As noted in chapter 1, the 1970 act authorized any citizen to bring suit against either (a) polluters for failing to comply with valid emission limitations or (b) the administrator of the EPA for failing "to perform any act or duty under this act which is not discretionary." This citizen suit provision (section 304) does not require challengers to be "adversely affected by agency action," as does the Administrative Procedures Act. It thus seems to confer standing on all potential litigants. Citizen suits brought against polluters go to the federal district court in the area where the alleged violation has occurred. Suits against the administrator can be brought in any district court.

Section 304 was originally viewed as a method for speeding up enforcement of the act. In 1970 Senator Muskie's committee presented even the "nondiscretionary duty" half of the provision as a way for citizens to push the EPA to bring more enforcement suits.[5] As disputes mounted between Congress and the Nixon administration and between the EPA and environmental groups, however, section 304 developed into a mechanism not for facilitating enforcement, but for forcing the EPA to institute new programs. Environmental groups have brought very few section 304 suits against polluters. They have, however, frequently sued the EPA under the "nondiscretionary duty" clause. These cases have resulted in major victories for environmentalists on PSD, transportation controls, regulation of airborne lead, visibility protection, and several other important issues.

Enforcement Suits

While sections 304 and 307 authorize private citizens to sue the EPA, section 113 gives the EPA authority to bring actions against those who violate the act. Enforcement cases go to the federal district court for the area in which the alleged violation occurred. Judges who hear these cases must first decide whether the defendant has violated the law, and, if so, what constitutes "appropriate relief." The act allows courts to impose criminal penalties of up to $25,000 per day and one year in jail for knowingly violating pollution laws. Since criminal intent is hard to

5. A Legislative History of the Clean Air Amendments of 1970, prepared for the Senate Committee on Public Works, 93 Cong. 2 sess. (GPO, 1974), pp. 436–39.

prove, the EPA usually brings civil actions against polluters. In these cases courts can impose temporary or permanent injunctions and (after passage of the 1977 amendments) "assess and recover a civil penalty of not more than $25,000 per day of violation."

Elaborate, well-established judicial rules govern the presentation of evidence in enforcement cases and establish where the burden of proof lies. The same cannot be said about the determination of "appropriate relief." Under the 1970 act, section 113 allowed the EPA to issue to polluters administrative orders specifying "a time for compliance which the administrator determines is reasonable, taking into account the seriousness of the violation and any good faith efforts to comply." Most district courts hearing section 113 cases have claimed that the act and the inherent equity power of federal courts allow them virtually unlimited discretion in defining "appropriate relief." This flexible approach to remedies seems to fly in the face of the statement of the 1970 Senate committee that "existing sources of pollutants either should meet the standard of the law or be closed down."[6] But Congress has done little to circumscribe judicial discretion. The "balancing of equities" by district court judges in enforcement proceedings has become a well-known and generally accepted safety valve or loophole (depending on one's perspective).

Rationales for Judicial Restraint

One frequently hears the assertion that judges cannot avoid deciding the cases that come before them. In a sense this is true: judges must somehow dispose of each of the many complaints they hear. Judges cannot simply ignore plaintiffs. This does not mean, however, that judges must always make an independent judgment on the merits of the case before them. They have many ways of avoiding such judgment. They can deny plaintiffs standing, declare the case moot or premature, rule that the parties have not exhausted their administrative remedies, or even leave the case sitting on the bottom of the court docket. More important, when they finally get to the merits of the case they can simply defer to the agency's expertise and judgment. Indeed, it is a cardinal rule of administrative law that agency determinations are "entitled to a

6. Ibid., p. 403.

presumption of regularity." When courts avoid decision or defer to administrators, they resolve cases without exercising an independent influence on policymaking.

Judges have dismissed many Clean Air Act cases before reaching the merits. They have rejected suits not filed in a timely fashion, ruled that others were brought to the wrong court, and found that still others were not yet ripe for decision.[7] While most courts have not questioned the standing of public interest law firms (which by traditional standards frequently do not have a concrete interest in the cases they bring), a few have. The Tenth Circuit, for example, stated, "It seems to us unreasonable to interpret [section 304] as expressing a congressional intent to permit a New York subway rider to challenge in the Court of Appeals for the Tenth Circuit actions of the Administrator affecting the Four Corners area of New Mexico, Utah, and Colorado."[8] One district court judge dismissed an enforcement suit brought by the EPA because he claimed the EPA had not aggressively pursued the case. Other judges have pushed the EPA to negotiate settlements with polluters to avoid protracted trials.[9]

Judges tend to go to greater lengths to avoid the merits in enforcement cases than in challenges to EPA regulations. There is a simple reason for this: in enforcement cases, once the court finds that a violation has occurred, it inevitably becomes entangled in fashioning appropriate relief; in judicial review of agency action, in contrast, it is usually easy for the court to find a reason for deferring to the agency, thus avoiding further involvement. This serves to emphasize the importance of the deference option in cases which judges consider somehow unfit for judicial resolution. Judges have pointed out many characteristics of Clean Air Act cases that make them difficult for courts to handle. These considerations not only help explain instances of judicial deference and

7. *Getty Oil Co.* v. *Ruckelshaus,* 467 F.2d 349 (3d Cir. 1972) and *Lloyd A. Fry Roofing Co.* v. *Environmental Protection Agency,* 554 F.2d 885 (8th Cir. 1977) (filing deadline); *Natural Resources Defense Council* v. *Environmental Protection Agency,* 465 F.2d 492 (1st Cir. 1972) and *Friends of the Earth* v. *Environmental Protection Agency,* 499 F.2d 1118 (2d Cir. 1974) (wrong court); *West Penn Power Co.* v. *Train,* 522 F.2d 203 (3d Cir. 1975) and *Utah International* v. *Environmental Protection Agency,* 478 F.2d 126 (10th Cir. 1973) (ripeness).

8. *Natural Resources Defense Council* v. *Environmental Protection Agency,* 481 F.2d 116 at 120 (10th Cir. 1973).

9. For reasons explained in chap. 7, these rulings are seldom published. But see, for example, *U.S.* v. *Associated Electric Cooperative,* 15 *Environment Reporter Cases* 1533 (D.E. Mo. 1980).

avoidance but also constitute obstacles that judges must overcome when they do intervene.

Technical Complexity

The scientific and engineering issues that arise in many clean air cases are enough to humble even the most self-confident judge. Chief Judge David Bazelon stated in one such case:

> Socrates said that wisdom is the recognition of how much one does not know. I may be wise if that is wisdom, because I recognize that I do not know enough about dynamometer extrapolations, deterioration factor adjustments, and the like to decide whether or not the government's approach to these matters was statistically valid.[10]

It is often impossible to separate legal issues from disputes over the reliability of the EPA's air quality monitoring data, the adequacy of meteorological assumptions used in dispersion models, the extent to which studies of the effects of pollution on rats are applicable to humans, or whether mild impairment of hemoglobin production in children constitutes an "adverse health effect."[11] Most judges hate to immerse themselves in these controversies and recognize the danger of resolving them on the basis of what Judge Bazelon has called "homespun scientific aphorisms."[12]

Polycentric Issues

Most air pollution issues involve not two well-defined parties, but a variety of dispersed groups whose interests are difficult to assess. Business firms, environmentalists, state officials, officials in a variety of federal agencies, consumers, drivers, and breathers all are affected by air pollution regulations. Most judges recognize this. Federal courts have lowered standing requirements so that individuals who separately have only a small interest in a controversy but together have a substantial interest

10. *International Harvester Co.* v. *Ruckelshaus,* 478 F.2d 615 at 650–51 (D.C. Cir. 1973).

11. *South Terminal Corp.* v. *Environmental Protection Agency,* 504 F.2d 646 (1st Cir. 1974); *Cleveland Electric Illuminating Co.* v. *Environmental Protection Agency,* 572 F.2d 1150 (6th Cir. 1978); *American Petroleum Institute* v. *Costle,* 665 F.2d 1176 (D.C. Cir. 1981); and *Lead Industries Assoc.* v. *Environmental Protection Agency,* 647 F.2d 1130 (D.C. Cir. 1980).

12. *Ethyl Corp.* v. *Environmental Protection Agency,* 541 F.2d 1 at 67, note 7 (D.C. Cir. 1976). Bazelon added, "On more subtle, and less visible, matters of scientific judgement we judges are well beyond our institutional competency."

can be heard in court. This by itself ensures that most Clean Air Act cases will involve at least three parties (the EPA, the beneficiaries of regulation, and those who must bear its cost). In recent years the number of parties joining such cases has increased to such an extent that judges have had to experiment with new methods for organizing the presentation of arguments. These cases do not fit the "bipolar" model of traditional adjudication, but rather conform to the "polycentric" model that legal scholars for years claimed was not appropriate for judicial resolution.[13]

Neither Sword nor Purse

Some judicial orders are virtually self-executing. If a court invalidates an agency regulation, for example, the agency cannot enforce the rule until it is declared legally valid. However, when a court orders an agency to perform a "nondiscretionary duty" or to make its regulations more stringent, or when it orders a polluter to reduce its emissions, achieving compliance is not nearly so simple. The court must force the agency or the polluter to take positive steps to come into compliance. Not only do courts lack regular staff capable of monitoring compliance, but they must frequently rely on other institutions to supply the resources agencies need to follow court orders.

In several Clean Air Act cases the courts have instructed the EPA to expand its program or to speed up the regulatory process. The EPA has missed most of the deadlines set by the courts, claiming that Congress has not provided it with enough money or trained personnel. The court cannot appropriate more funds. Unless agency officials have acted in bad faith, courts hesitate to find them in contempt. Judges have found themselves in similar difficulty after ordering state officials to implement programs opposed by state legislators. Judicial threats to fine state officials and even to jail legislators have stiffened resistance to federal "encroachment." In the words of one district court judge who (against his better judgment) became involved in such a confrontation with the state and city of New York, "courts should not, in the exercise of sound discretion, grant relief which requires 'continuous judicial supervision.' "[14]

13. Lon L. Fuller, "The Forms and Limits of Adjudication," 92 *Harvard Law Review* 353 (1978). For an example, see the discussion of *Alabama Power* v. *Costle* in chap. 4.
14. *Friends of the Earth* v. *Wilson*, 389 F. Supp. 1394 at 1396 (S.D.N.Y. 1974), quoting *Unicon Management Corp.* v. *Koppers Co.*, 366 F.2d 199 (2d Cir. 1966). This *Friends of the Earth* decision and its consequences are discussed in chap. 9.

In some policy areas it is possible to justify judicial intervention on the grounds that the other branches of government have failed to oversee the agency in question.[15] No such claim can be made about air pollution control. Congress, the president, and the states have all competed to influence air pollution policy. That is why judicial intervention frequently brings the courts into conflict with those institutions that directly wield the sword and control the purse strings.

Rationales for Intervention

Given these difficulties, why have federal judges overturned the EPA on so many important issues? One possible answer is that the reviewing courts simply disagreed with the policy choices made by the EPA. While one must be attentive to the possibility that judges have policy preferences that they express in their opinions, one should not exaggerate the idiosyncratic nature of judicial decisionmaking. Judges must explain their decisions in written opinions that can be reviewed by higher courts. This both inhibits them from simply voting their policy preferences and produces legal doctrines that help to reveal the patterns of judicial action. The reasons judges give for their decisions have an important influence on agencies' responses since they provide guidance on what the court will accept in the future.[16] Administrative agencies and reviewing courts engage in a dialogue over policymaking; and in dialogues, words count. The remainder of this chapter reviews the objectives announced by judges who have sought to influence the EPA's air pollution policy.

The Law as Limit

Fundamental to the protection of individual liberty in the United States is the idea that the executive branch cannot take actions against private citizens without being authorized to do so by the law. A corollary of "no taxation without representation" is "no regulation without legislation." One cannot always expect an agency pursuing its particular

15. See, for example, Martin Shapiro, *The Supreme Court and Administrative Agencies* (Free Press, 1968), chap. 3.

16. On this point, see Daniel J. Fiorino, "Judicial-Administrative Interaction in Regulatory Policy Making: The Case of the Federal Power Commission," 28 *Administrative Law Review* 41 (1976).

mission to respect the limits placed upon its power by authorizing legislation. The agency, after all, is an interested party. The courts, in contrast, have responsibility for preventing government officials from disturbing the lives of private citizens in ways not explicitly condoned by statute.

Authorizing statutes often give broad powers to administrative agencies. The judiciary, nonetheless, seeks to discern the limits of the power delegated to agencies by Congress, considering both the "plain meaning" of the statute and the legislative history of the act. For example, the Clean Air Act allows the EPA to regulate "fuel additives" that contribute to auto emissions. The EPA used this provision to justify its regulation of motor oil, claiming that oil can leak into a car's combustion chamber and affect emissions. When oil companies questioned the EPA's authority to do this, the reviewing court found that the "commonsense meaning" of the term "fuel additive" does not include substances not added directly to fuel, and that Congress nowhere evidenced an intent to allow the EPA to regulate every factor that could influence auto emissions. It invalidated the EPA's motor oil regulation.[17] Congress later expanded the EPA's statutory authority, and the agency reinstated its rule. The courts have similarly prevented the EPA from taking an expansive interpretation of the terms "potential to emit" and "adequately demonstrated technology."[18]

The right that courts have traditionally sought to protect from unauthorized administrative intrusion is that of private property. While the federal courts are not as solicitous of the property rights of business firms as they once were, judges—especially those in district courts—are well aware of the devastating impact regulatory agencies can have on individual firms and the economy of entire states. They have often taken steps to keep the EPA within the outer bounds set by the Clean Air Act.

The courts have sought to prevent the EPA from encroaching on other rights as well. In one of the rare instances when the EPA threatened individuals with criminal penalties—and thus the deprivation of liberty—the Supreme Court adopted an extremely restrictive reading of the EPA's statutory authority.[19] Several circuit courts have prohibited the EPA

17. *Lubrizol Corp.* v. *Environmental Protection Agency,* 562 F.2d 807 (D.C. Cir. 1977).

18. *Alabama Power* v. *Costle,* 636 F.2d 323 (D.C. Cir. 1979) and *Portland Cement Assoc.* v. *Ruckelshaus,* 486 F.2d 375 (D.C. Cir. 1973).

19. *Adamo Wrecking Co.* v. *United States,* 434 U.S. 275 (1978).

from taking actions that invade the right of state and municipal governments to manage local transportation systems.[20]

In all these cases the courts have sought to moderate the zeal of agencies single-mindedly pursuing limited objectives and to bring greater balance to public policies. In the words of Judge Harold Leventhal, principal author of what has become known as the "hard look" doctrine of judicial review of agency action, "The rule of administrative law, as applied to the congressional mandate for a clean environment, ensures that mission-oriented agencies . . . will take due cognizance of environmental matters. It ensures at the same time that environmental protection agencies will take into account the congressional mandate that environmental concern be reconciled with other social and economic objectives of our society."[21]

The Law as Mandate

The regulatory statutes that place limits on agency authority also mandate administrative action. There are two ways of looking at these mandates. First, one can view them as commands issued to administrators by Congress. Regulators' sense of mission and desire for continued funding will lead them to carry out these mandates to the best of their ability. If Congress wants more aggressive action, it can appropriate more money, embarrass administrators in hearings, or issue more explicit statutory commands. This, at least, was the traditional view. More recently the courts have accepted a different approach, ruling that statutory commands create legally enforceable entitlements. According to this understanding, the Clean Air Act gives every citizen of the United States the right not just to breathe air as clean as that required by the act, but the right to see the EPA carry out each requirement of the statute. Judicial vindication of these rights both protects the health of private individuals against harm done by polluters and gives Congress an additional mechanism for ensuring that its laws are faithfully executed.

Federal courts have issued many "action-forcing" decisions under the act. The best example is the D.C. Circuit's ruling that the EPA must

20. *Brown* v. *Environmental Protection Agency*, 521 F.2d 827 (9th Cir. 1975); *Brown* v. *Environmental Protection Agency*, 566 F.2d 665 (9th Cir. 1977); *State of Maryland* v. *Environmental Protection Agency*, 530 F.2d 215 (4th Cir. 1975); and *District of Columbia* v. *Train*, 521 F.2d 971 (D.C. Cir. 1975).

21. "Environmental Decisionmaking and the Role of the Courts," 122 *University of Pennsylvania Law Review* 509 at 555 (1974).

promulgate transportation control plans adequate to assure the attainment and maintenance of air quality standards by 1975. Several action-forcing decisions have gone beyond the letter of the law, insisting that the EPA act in accordance with what the courts see as the spirit of the act. For example, in ordering the EPA to set an air quality standard for lead, the Second Circuit conceded that "the literal language of section 108(a)(1)(C) is somewhat ambiguous," but found that the EPA's interpretation of that section "would vitiate the public policy underlying the enactment of the 1970 Amendments as set forth in the Act and in its legislative history."[22] When in doubt, some courts have acted to strengthen the EPA's regulation of air pollution.

The courts have done more than prevent the EPA from using loopholes to avoid taking controversial actions; they have added to the law to solve problems that they believe Congress would have or should have addressed but did not at the time recognize. For example, the Fifth Circuit relied on ambiguous statutory phrases and pieces of legislative history to prevent polluters from building "tall stacks" that could exacerbate the acid rain and sulfate problems. The courts have been remarkably assertive in claiming to understand the act's basic aims and to anticipate the concerns of its authors. Underlying their assertiveness is the assumption that regulatory agencies are inclined to engage in bureaucratic foot-dragging and to ignore new problems.

Procedures and Their Purposes

The most common reason courts give for striking down agency actions is failure to comply with procedure specified by law or required by judicial precedent. Judges can easily spot an agency's failure to abide by procedural requirements. This does not explain, though, why judges add their own procedural demands as well as enforce statutory requirements. In a few cases, no doubt, judges simply invent new procedures to prevent agencies from instituting policies they oppose on substantive grounds. More important, the courts use procedural requirements to increase the accuracy of agency decisionmaking and to ensure that all interested parties receive an opportunity to present their views.

According to traditional legal principles, due process requires that a person adversely affected by a proposed agency action have an oppor-

22. *Natural Resources Defense Council* v. *Train*, 545 F.2d 320 at 327 and 324 (2d Cir. 1976).

tunity to explain why the proposal should be dropped, amended, or not applied to him. The type of procedure required by due process depends on the nature of the information relevant to rulemaking. If the agency must make a determination about the facts of a particular case, then the parties directly involved have a right to hear and dispute the findings of the agency, often with the right to cross-examine agency witnesses and to have the cases decided by agency personnel not responsible for initiating the investigation.[23] Such detailed knowledge about how a rule will affect individual commenters is seldom relevant to the making of broad, essentially legislative choices. Consequently, when an agency writes a rule of general applicability, it must invite comments from the general public but need not allow oral testimony or cross-examination. The Administrative Procedures Act recognizes this difference by distinguishing "formal adjudication" from "notice and comment rulemaking."

In Clean Air Act cases the courts have avoided imposing cumbersome adjudicatory hearings on the EPA, but have insisted that the EPA do more than simply follow the minimal "notice and comment" procedures of the Administrative Procedures Act.[24] When the EPA sets new source performance standards or national ambient air quality standards, for example, the courts require it to disclose the assumptions and technical justification for its proposal, to solicit comments on this technical analysis, and to respond to all significant criticism.[25] The courts have justified these additional procedural requirements by claiming that greater debate within the scientific community will prevent the EPA from making technical mistakes, and that more widespread citizen participation in rulemaking will prevent the EPA from listening to only a narrow segment of the political spectrum. The adequacy of these assumptions is probed in chapter 8.

23. Walter Gellhorn and Clark Byse, *Administrative Law*, 6th ed. (Foundation Press, 1974), pp. 575–89.

24. *Kennecott Copper Corp.* v. *Environmental Protection Agency*, 462 F.2d 846 (D.C. Cir. 1972). "Notice and comment" or "informal" rulemaking refers to the issuing of regulations under sec. 553 of the Administrative Procedures Act. This section requires agencies (a) to publish a "general notice of proposed rule making" in the Federal Register; (b) to "give interested persons an opportunity to participate in the rule making through submission of written data, views, or arguments with or without opportunity for oral presentation"; and (c) to promulgate—"after consideration of the relevant matter presented"—final rules, which must be accompanied by a "general statement of their basis and support."

25. *Portland Cement Assoc.* v. *Ruckelshaus; Lead Industries Assoc.* v. *EPA;* also see William F. Pedersen, Jr., "Formal Records and Informal Rulemaking," 85 *Yale Law Journal* 38 (1975).

Reviewing the Facts

No matter how many procedural hoops the courts make an agency jump through, there is always a danger that an incompetent, biased, or negligent agency will make a decision that cannot withstand careful review even by the layman. If the courts do not prevent agencies from acting on the basis of faulty findings, then agencies will in effect be able to act in a manner unauthorized by law. Judges generally avoid declaring administrative actions "arbitrary and capricious," preferring instead to send questionable decisions back to the agency for a better explanation. Whatever form rejection of agency action takes, it is clear that courts must at times decide whether such a mistake has been made.

The courts have invalidated several EPA decisions on these grounds. The First Circuit found that the EPA's transportation control plan for Boston was based on unduly pessimistic monitoring data. Upon remand the EPA discovered that its data did indeed exaggerate the extent of control necessary to meet the standards.[26] Similarly, after the D.C. Circuit remanded the EPA's secondary standard for sulfur dioxide, the agency discovered that it had originally misread important technical evidence.[27] Such cases have convinced judges that they can at times spot errors that would otherwise have gone unnoticed.

How clear and serious must a technical or factual mistake be before a judge will overturn an agency action based upon it? The courts generally address this question by deciding who carries the burden of proof. In enforcement cases the agency carries the burden of proving that a violation of the law has occurred. In a challenge to an agency rule the private party must show that a "reasonable person" could not support the decision made by the agency. In a few unusual cases the courts have consciously shifted the burden of proof according to their perception of the relative costs and benefits of mistaken agency actions.[28]

Granting Relief

Once a judge finds that the EPA has proved "upon a preponderance of the evidence" that a polluting facility has exceeded its legal emission limitations, he will usually insist that the agency recommend appropriate

26. *South Terminal Corp.* v. *EPA* (see chap. 9).
27. *Kennecott Copper Corp.* v. *EPA* (see chap. 8).
28. *International Harvester Co.* v. *Ruckelshaus.*

relief, including necessary control technology, compliance schedules, and possibly fines. But judges seldom accept these recommendations in full. They jealously guard their prerogative to impose penalties on private parties.

One reason for this is the suspicion that an agency might act unnecessarily harshly or in a discriminatory manner against an individual who has violated its regulations. Conversely, when agencies themselves impose penalties there is a danger of corruption. In enforcement, where the force of the law confronts the isolated individual, impartiality—and the appearance of impartiality—are prized commodities.

A second reason why the courts play an active role in fashioning relief is that they view this phase of the regulatory process as a final opportunity to add balance to an inflexible regulatory scheme. The Clean Air Act makes no provision for the EPA to consider the cost of the air quality standards upon which state implementation plans are based. Balancing the equities in enforcement proceedings provides a safety value, a check policies. Since the EPA is an *environmental protection* agency, it cannot always be relied upon to strike a reasonable balance. While cynics might claim that this balancing of equities makes a mockery of the Clean Air Act's deadlines and standards, most judges, congressmen, and even agency officials view it as an acceptable way of moderating an extremely demanding statute and ensuring that justice is done in the individual case.[29]

The Constitution and Beyond

Courts in the United States follow the Constitution as well as individual statutes. They overturn laws that they deem contrary to their reading of that basic document and interpret statutes so as to make them compatible with the Constitution. In fact one can view all administrative law as an effort by the courts to ensure that agencies do not deprive citizens of life, liberty, or property without due process of law in violation of the Fifth Amendment. The courts have relied upon the Fifth Amendment as well as the Fourth and Tenth Amendments to restrict the EPA's authority to request criminal penalties, to conduct inspections, and to issue commands to state officials.[30]

In a few instances the courts have relied on constitutional arguments to require an expansion of EPA programs, rather than to limit the

29. This theme and cases supporting it are discussed in chap. 7.

30. *Adamo Wrecking Co.* v. *U.S.; Stauffer Chemical Co.* v. *Environmental Protection Agency*, 647 F.2d 1075 (10th Cir. 1981); *Brown* v. *EPA* (1977).

authority of the federal government. No federal court has yet followed the lead of those environmental advocates who find a right to a "healthy environment" implicit in the First and Fourteenth Amendments.[31] Several influential jurists have, nonetheless, alluded to constitutional considerations in requiring more aggressive agency action. In *Environmental Defense Fund* v. *Ruckelshaus*, for example, Judge Bazelon stated:

> Courts are increasingly asked to review administrative action that touches on fundamental personal interests in life, health, and liberty. These interests have always had a special claim to judicial protection, in comparison with the economic interests at stake in a ratemaking or licensing proceeding.[32]

The D.C. Circuit has used this argument to push for stringent air quality standards under the Clean Air Act.

Some writers have suggested another Constitution-based rationale for judicial activism, that courts should correct "political failure." According to this argument the judiciary has an obligation to counterbalance the political biases of Congress and the executive branch. One such potential bias is the short time horizon of officeholders who are elected for two-, four-, or six-year terms. Saving the ecosystem from disaster, they maintain, requires the judiciary, with its longer-range perspective, to push administrators to take actions that appear politically risky in the short run.[33]

No court has yet given official recognition to this "political failure" rationale for judicial intervention. But some court actions are difficult to explain on any other grounds. Moreover, the new administrative law as a whole is based on a variation of this analysis: the political branches of government have failed to gain control of regulatory bureaucracies and often contribute to agency capture by giving special treatment to well-organized interests. The role of the court is to enfranchise those groups disenfranchised by other institutions. While proponents of judicial modesty consider this argument a convenient veil for the imposition of

31. For example, William D. Kirchick, "The Continuing Search for a Constitutionally Protected Environment," 4 *Environmental Affairs* 515 (1975); Ronald E. Klipsch, "Aspects of a Constitutional Right to a Habitable Environment: Toward an Environmental Due Process," 49 *Indiana Law Journal* 203 (1974); Christopher D. Stone, "Should Trees Have Standing?—Toward Legal Rights for Natural Objects," 45 *Southern California Law Review* 450 (1972); and Laurence H. Tribe, "Ways Not to Think about Plastic Trees: New Foundations for Environmental Law," 83 *Yale Law Journal* 1315 (1974).

32. *Environmental Defense Fund* v. *Ruckelshaus*, 439 F.2d 584 at 598 (D.C. Cir. 1971).

33. See, for example, Joseph L. Sax, *Defending the Environment: A Strategy for Citizen Action* (Knopf, 1971); and David Sive, "Some Thoughts of an Environmental Lawyer in the Wilderness of Administrative Law," 70 *Columbia Law Review* 612 (1970).

judges' and law professors' upper-middle-class conservation ethic, others see such judicial activism as a necessary step toward the development of a new environmental ethos.[34]

Judicial Discretion and Judicial Conflict

Judicial review under the Clean Air Act and all other statutes calls for the exercise of judicial discretion. As a result, judges often disagree on the controversies they face. One judge may decide that the EPA has acted in an overzealous fashion. Another judge may view the same agency action as insufficient to meet the congressional mandate to protect the environment. While one court may give a polluter years to comply with SIP requirements, others may consider meeting the deadlines of the Clean Air Act critical to the protection of citizens' health.

Several times conflicts among circuit courts have led the Supreme Court to hear Clean Air Act cases. Intercircuit disputes can last for years. Sometimes disagreements between courts are more subtle and more resistant to resolutions by higher courts. For example, while a district court hearing a section 304 "mandatory duty" case may set strict deadlines for the EPA, circuit court rulings adding procedural requirements to the act may make it impossible for the agency to comply. Judges not only differ in their political viewpoints, but see different parts of the administrative process.

Another consequence of the exercise of judicial discretion is "forum shopping." Courts develop reputations on various issues. Some, such as the First, Second, and D.C. Circuits, are seen as particularly hospitable to environmental groups. Industry is more likely to receive a sympathetic hearing in the Fourth, Ninth, or Tenth Circuits, or in its favorite district court, the Eastern District of Louisiana. Forum shopping has become so intense under environmental statutes that the EPA has written elaborate rules specifying the exact minute when the "race to the courthouse" begins.[35] It is, in short, misleading to speak of "the courts" as a unified entity. Different judges react in different ways to the dilemmas of judicial review.

34. Compare, for example, William Ophuls, *Ecology and the Politics of Scarcity: Prologue to a Political Theory of the Steady State* (W. H. Freeman, 1977), and Aaron Wildavsky, "Aesthetic Power or Triumph of the Sensitive Minority over the Vulgar Mass: A Political Analysis of the New Economics," *Daedalus*, vol. 96 (Fall 1967).
35. 45 Fed. Reg. 26048 (1980).

CHAPTER FOUR

Significant Deterioration: A Tiger by the Tail

MR. ZARB: *The significant deterioration question is one of complete vagueness. I don't know what it means and Administrator Train doesn't know what it means.*
REP. HASTINGS: *I might add the Congress to that list, we don't know what it means, either . . . and let us add the court to that. The Supreme Court didn't seem to come down too strong on deciding it.*
        —FEA Administrator Frank Zarb and Rep. James Hastings, 1975

IN THE early 1970s environmental groups won two court battles that fundamentally altered the goals of the Environmental Protection Agency's air pollution control program. In the first case, *Sierra Club* v. *Ruckelshaus,* the District Court for the District of Columbia, later upheld by the D.C. Circuit and the Supreme Court, ruled that state implementation plans (SIPs) must include provisions not just to assure the attainment and maintenance of national air quality standards, but also to prevent the "degradation" of air currently cleaner than required by the standards.[1] This decision in effect replaced the Clean Air Act's uniform national ambient air quality standards with a multiplicity of standards based on previous air quality levels, not on health or welfare effects.

In the second case, *Natural Resources Defense Council* v. *Environmental Protection Agency,* the Fifth Circuit prohibited polluters from achieving air quality standards through "dispersion enhancement" (spreading pollutants over a wider area) rather than through emission reduction.[2] The EPA eventually accepted this reading of the act, forgoing an appeal to the Supreme Court. Limiting the use of "dispersion enhancement" in effect adds the goal of reducing total emissions to the goal of meeting ambient air quality standards.

The statutory basis for both sets of judicial decisions was slim at best.

1. *Sierra Club* v. *Ruckelshaus,* 344 F. Supp. 253 (D.D.C. 1972), upheld by an equally divided Supreme Court, *sub nom. Fri* v. *Sierra Club,* 412 U.S. 541 (1973).
2. *Natural Resources Defense Council* v. *Environmental Protection Agency,* 489 F.2d 390 (5th Cir. 1974).

This does not mean that the judges who wrote these opinions did not have good reasons for acting as they did. As discussed in chapter 2, the Clean Air Act does not address two key air pollution problems: the loading of the atmosphere with dangerous pollutants that can travel hundreds of miles downwind, and subtle health and welfare effects below the national standards. By cracking down on polluters in urban areas, the EPA's original program gave polluters incentives to disperse their pollution over a larger area and to expand or relocate in less developed areas. This meant that some areas would become more polluted as others became cleaner. While this policy reduced pollution levels in metropolitan areas and satisfied the requirements of the act, it ignored serious environmental problems not directly addressed by the act. Relying more on the spirit than on the letter of the law, the courts instructed the EPA to take a broader view of its environmental protection responsibilities.

Both the EPA and Congress later decided that the courts were right. The agency's original ambivalence and mild opposition to these rulings turned into support as it developed programs to carry out the courts' demands. The 1977 amendments ratified the core of the judicially developed policy on dispersion and added provisions on prevention of significant deterioration (PSD) that were even more demanding than those published by the EPA. It is not surprising, therefore, that those who support an active role for the courts in environmental policymaking use these cases as illustrations of the foresight of the judiciary.[3]

Two complications plague this positive assessment of the courts' performance in the *Sierra Club* and *NRDC* cases. First, a major reason the courts won political vindication was that they shifted the balance of power between Congress and the president. On both PSD and dispersion the president and his top advisers disagreed with the courts, while the key congressional committees supported the courts' policies. The court decisions allowed the EPA to ignore the White House. They also allowed the House and Senate committees to achieve their preferred policies merely by blocking White House proposals to reverse the court decisions.

3. See, for example, Richard B. Stewart, "The Development of Administrative and Quasi-Constitutional Law in Judicial Review of Environmental Decisionmaking: Lessons from the Clean Air Act," 62 *Iowa Law Review* 713 (1977); N. William Hines, "A Decade of Nondegradation Policy in Congress and the Courts: The Erratic Pursuit of Clean Air and Clean Water," 62 *Iowa Law Review* 643 (1977); and Grant P. Thompson, "The Role of the Courts," in Erica Dolgin and Thomas Guilbert, eds., *Federal Environmental Law* (West, 1974).

Second, both decisions have created major administrative problems for the EPA and have produced widespread confusion over the objectives of the agency's control strategies. The courts altered the basic goals of the federal government's air pollution program without considering administrative feasibility and without examining in detail the nature and importance of these goals. As will be shown in both this chapter (on PSD) and the next (on dispersion), these court decisions intensified controversy without clarifying public debate.

The Evolution of PSD

PSD was born in the courtroom and has resided there almost constantly for the past decade. Nothing captures its evolution better than a comparison of the first and most recent court cases on the subject. In late May 1972, two days before the deadline for approving implementation plans for all fifty-four states and territories, the Sierra Club asked the federal District Court for the District of Columbia to issue an emergency order restraining the EPA from approving any state plan that permitted the "significant deterioration" of air quality anywhere in the state. Judge John H. Pratt gave the EPA only five days to prepare its case. The Department of Justice attorney who argued the case for the EPA knew little about the structure of the new Clean Air Act and even less about the details of air pollution control. Industry did not intervene. Several state attorneys general supported the Sierra Club, but few of them consulted with state air agencies before doing so.

The District Court issued a brief, handwritten order enjoining the EPA from approving state plans that

permit the significant deterioration of existing air quality in any portion of any state where the existing air quality is better than one or more of the secondary standards promulgated by the Administrator.[4]

Judge Pratt's order did not say what "significant deterioration" means. In fact, he several times identified the term with the more absolute term "nondegradation." The judge seemed to assume that the EPA knew what "significant deterioration" meant. His chief legal argument was that by including in the 1970 act the statement that one purpose of the legislation

4. Preliminary injunction issued by Judge John H. Pratt, May 30, 1972, reprinted in *The Nondegradation Policy of the Clean Air Act*, Hearings before the Subcommittee on Air and Water Pollution of the Senate Committee on Public Works, 93 Cong. 1 sess. (Government Printing Office, 1973), p. 5.

was "to protect and enhance the quality of the Nation's air resources," Congress had indicated its approval of a nondegradation objective previously announced by Department of Health, Education, and Welfare officials under the Air Quality Act of 1967.

The EPA received no more guidance from the appellate courts. The D.C. Circuit upheld the decision without writing an opinion—a highly unusual occurrence. The Supreme Court reviewed the case, but split 4–4, leaving the lower court's decision intact. Again there was no explanation. The District Court opinion, written in a hurry after an extremely brief discussion of the issues, became the law of the land.

The *Sierra Club* decision touched off a long series of administrative, congressional, and judicial disputes. After conducting an unusually elaborate rulemaking process involving two sets of proposals and two opportunities for public comment, the EPA finally published PSD regulations in December 1974.[5] Both environmental groups and industry challenged these regulations in court. The D.C. Circuit upheld the EPA in the summer of 1976.[6] By this time Congress was in the midst of considering legislation that would modify the EPA's program. A filibuster on PSD killed this legislation in 1976, but Congress passed an extremely detailed provision in 1977.[7] The EPA proposed regulations implementing the 1977 amendments in November. But intense controversy over the regulations led the agency to wait until June 1978 before publishing final rules.[8] Three national environmental groups and scores of industry plaintiffs challenged these regulations. In its first decision on the regulations, *Citizens to Save Spencer County* v. *Environmental Protection Agency*, the D.C. Circuit upheld the EPA.[9] But in the second, more important one, *Alabama Power* v. *Costle*, the Circuit Court overturned an array of EPA actions, siding at times with industry and at times with environmentalists.[10] The EPA proposed and then published further regulations in response to the court order.[11]

5. The initial litigation is described in Cynthia J. Bolbach, "The Courts and the Clean Air Act," *Environment Reporter,* Monograph 19 (Bureau of National Affairs, 1974). The key steps in the first rulemaking process are recorded in: 38 Fed. Reg. 18986 (1973) (first proposal); 39 Fed. Reg. 31000 (1974) (second proposal); 39 Fed. Reg. 42510 (1974) (promulgation).

6. *Sierra Club* v. *Environmental Protection Agency,* 540 F.2d 1114 (D.C. Cir. 1976).

7. 91 Stat. 685, Clean Air Act Amendments of 1977, pt. C, secs. 160–69A.

8. 42 Fed. Reg. 57459 (1977); 43 Fed. Reg. 26380 (1978).

9. 600 F.2d 844 (D.C. Cir. 1979).

10. 606 F.2d 1068 (D.C. Cir. 1979) and 636 F.2d 323 (D.C. Cir. 1979).

11. 44 Fed. Reg. 51924 (1979); 45 Fed. Reg. 52676 (1980).

Alabama Power is one of the most complex environmental cases ever decided by an appellate court. So many litigants brought so many issues before the court that the D.C. Circuit experimented with new procedures to structure the presentation of legal arguments. The court's staff divided the issues presented by the more than eighty parties into seventeen categories. Oral argument lasted a day and a half—far more than the hour or two most cases receive before appellate courts. The court then took the unprecedented step of issuing a preliminary opinion, waiting for the agency to propose new regulations and for the challengers to comment on them, and assigning each member of the three-judge panel a section of the final court opinion. The final opinion was extraordinarily detailed, not just explaining to the EPA why some of its regulations were invalid, but also giving examples of the types of replacement rules that would survive court review. The court's handling of the *Alabama Power* case was as organized, detailed, and time consuming as the ruling in the *Sierra Club* case was hurried, cavalier, and ambiguous.

Like many governmental programs, PSD grew from a good idea, a gleam in the eye of policy entrepreneurs, to a complex set of regulations that attempt to address a large number of problems and local circumstances. As the program took effect, those adversely affected by it complained about some rules and discovered ways to evade others. A variety of questions of interpretation arose. Administrators became more sophisticated in writing precise rules, and the number of regulations grew. Parties unhappy with the agency's decisions appealed to the courts, to Congress, and to other sectors of the executive branch in their efforts to overturn agency decisions. In the *Sierra Club* case one sees the humble origins of PSD. In *Alabama Power* one sees the later stages of the policy process, characterized both by more focused controversy and by better understanding of the significance of the issues by all those involved, including the judges.

PSD, though, is a program that became more than ordinarily complex. One expects the opponents of regulatory programs to criticize their complexity. Thus it is hardly unusual that David Stockman, while a member of the House of Representatives, described PSD as "the codification of a bureaucratic nightmare that is lacking in scientific, economic, or practical justification."[12] Considerably more surprising is the dissatisfaction with PSD expressed by past and present EPA officials and other

12. Additional Views of Representative David Stockman, *Clean Air Act Amendments of 1977*, H. Rept. 95-294, 95 Cong. 1 sess. (GPO, 1977), p. 534.

observers generally supportive of environmental programs. Former Deputy EPA Administrator John Quarles warned a congressional committee that PSD is "teetering on the edge of administrative impossibility."[13] State air pollution officials have called for the repeal of the PSD sections of the 1977 amendments. A report by the Ford Foundation predicted that PSD had become so convoluted that it could not long survive.[14] The National Commission on Air Quality, established by the 1977 amendments and chaired by Senator Gary Hart, recommended that a large portion of the PSD program be abolished.[15] Even EPA officials who have worked on the program for years now despair at understanding the regulations they have helped to write. One experienced and knowledgeable EPA official concluded that "most state and federal air pollution professionals agree that if PSD isn't simplified soon, it will come crashing down under its own weight."[16] The issue debated within the EPA is not whether PSD needs revision, but only when change should come and how fundamental it should be.

PSD has few friends and more than its share of enemies because it is incredibly cumbersome, causes unnecessary delays in the construction of industrial facilities, and diverts regulators' resources from more effective programs. These defects in the program—defects few would deny—resulted from the way in which PSD originated. The issues before the court in *Alabama Power* were especially difficult and confusing because the court that initiated the PSD program in the *Sierra Club* case issued a sweeping order without examining either the objectives or the costs of PSD. The following history of the program will show that PSD has never outgrown the deficiencies of the method of its conception.

The Sierra Club Litigation

The district court's decision in *Sierra Club* v. *Ruckelshaus* presents a startling anomaly: it directed the EPA to prevent the "significant

13. Quoted in 11 *Environment Reporter—Current Developments* 268.

14. Study Group Sponsored by the Ford Foundation and Administered by Resources for the Future, *Energy: The Next Twenty Years* (Ballinger, 1979), pp. 398–402.

15. National Commission on Air Quality, *To Breathe Clean Air* (GPO, 1981), pp. 2.2-12 to 2.2-15.

16. Personal interview with Bernard Steigerwald (OAQPS), October 2, 1980. In 1981 the National Clean Air Coalition, a coalition of national environmental groups, recommended various changes in PSD "to simplify the program and to ease the permitting

deterioration" of air quality, but neglected to inform the agency what this critical term meant. There is no indication that Judge Pratt intended to prohibit all new pollution in areas with clean air. Even the Sierra Club conceded that its victory "does not prevent all increases in pollution."[17] Yet the judge gave the EPA no legal or policy basis for deciding what pollution increases between zero and the secondary standards must be considered "significant."

The absence of such guidance was not simply a result of oversight or undue haste. Judge Pratt justified his decision by claiming that Congress and previous administrators had already established a policy preventing "significant deterioration." Noting the "protect and enhance" language of the act's preface, he remarked:

> On its face, this language would appear to declare Congress's intent to improve the quality of the nation's air and to prevent deterioration of that air quality, no matter how presently pure that quality in some sections of the country happens to be.[18]

Pratt buttressed this extrapolation by referring to five fragments of legislative history, only three of which actually preceded passage of the 1970 act: (1) a 1969 National Air Pollution Control Administration guideline announcing that state air quality standards that "result in significant deterioration of air quality" conflict with the "protect and enhance" goal of the 1967 Air Quality Act;[19] (2) a statement of HEW officials claiming that under amendments to the 1967 act proposed by the Nixon administration in 1970 this policy would remain intact;[20] (3) a sentence in the 1970 Senate report stating that the EPA should disapprove SIP provisions for clean air areas that do not "provide, to the maximum extent practicable, for the continued maintenance of such

process." *Clean Air Act,* Hearings before the Subcommittee on Health and the Environment of the House Committee on Energy and Commerce, 97 Cong. 1 sess. (GPO, 1981), p. 307. EPA Assistant Administrator Kathleen Bennett claimed that PSD "regulations are so complex that they virtually assure uncertainty and delay with little air quality benefit" (p. 369).

17. Statement of Laurence I. Moss of the Sierra Club, originally made in hearings before the Muskie committee in 1973, quoted in 38 Fed. Reg. 18987 (1973).

18. *Sierra Club* v. *Ruckelshaus* at 255.

19. National Air Pollution Control Administration, "Guidelines for the Development of Air Quality Standards and Implementation Plans," pt. 1, sec. 1.51, p. 7 (NAPCA, 1969).

20. Statements of the Secretary of HEW Robert Finch and Under Secretary John Veneman, reprinted in *A Legislative History of the Clean Air Amendments of 1970,* prepared for the Senate Committee on Public Works, 93 Cong. 2 sess. (GPO, 1974), p. 1365.

ambient air quality";[21] (4) a guideline, proposed by the EPA in 1971 but later withdrawn, explaining that promulgation of national air quality standards "shall not be considered in any manner to allow significant deterioration of existing air quality in any portion of any state";[22] and (5) statements made by members of the House and Senate committees in 1972 oversight hearings linking the "protect and enhance" language of the 1970 act with "prevention of significant deterioration."[23] Judge Pratt implied that "significant deterioration" was either a term of art or the subject of a long policy debate, that the EPA had dropped PSD only after industry and the White House objected, and that all the EPA had to do was reinstate its previous policy.

Unfortunately, the "nondegradation policy" previously announced by federal air and water pollution control officials remained, in the words of one PSD historian and advocate, "nothing more than an undeveloped program objective."[24] Not only had the federal government never taken action against a state or a polluter for violating this "policy," but it had never even defined what would constitute a violation. Moreover, under the 1967 act, the federal government had no authority to define acceptable air quality levels or to set emission limits for new sources. The National Air Pollution Control Administration saw its 1969 statement on "significant deterioration" as a way to encourage the states to prevent unnecessary pollution increases.

The 1970 act changed all this. In 1972 Administrator Ruckelshaus and his top advisers eliminated references to "significant deterioration" not because they were under political pressure to do so, but because the 1970 act provided the EPA with clear, specific methods for deciding what constituted "acceptable" air pollution increases. Unlike the 1967 act, the 1970 act required the EPA to set not just primary or health-based standards, but secondary air quality standards "requisite to protect the public welfare from any known or anticipated adverse effects associated with the presence of such air pollutant in the ambient air."

21. 1970 Senate report, reprinted in ibid., p. 411.

22. 36 Fed. Reg. 8186 (1971).

23. *Clean Air Act Oversight,* Hearings before the Subcommittee on Public Health and the Environment of the House Committee on Interstate and Foreign Commerce, 92 Cong. 1 and 2 sess. (GPO, 1972), pp. 529–31; and *Implementation of the Clean Air Act Amendments of 1970,* Hearings before the Subcommittee on Air and Water Pollution of the Senate Committee on Public Works, 92 Cong. 2 sess. (GPO, 1972), pp. 12–13, 18–21, 271–276.

24. Hines, "A Decade of Nondegradation Policy," p. 660.

Section 116 of the act confers upon the states, not the EPA, authority to insist upon standards more stringent than these. The 1970 act also provided another key tool missing from the 1967 act, the new source performance standard (NSPS). By statutory definition these emission standards constitute the "maximum practicable" controls to which the Senate report referred. The EPA's lawyers advised Administrator Ruckelshaus that secondary air quality standards and NSPSs define permissible "deterioration," and that the EPA had no legal authority to establish additional restrictions.[25]

The EPA had policy as well as legal objections to further restrictions in clean air areas. By discouraging relocation of polluting facilities to clean air areas, such rules could delay the attainment of health-based standards in urban areas. "Dispersion or relocation of existing sources," the agency told the appellate court, "must remain an environmental tool."[26] The EPA's primary task, Administrator Ruckelshaus kept telling his staff, was to protect "people, not prairie dogs."

In its argument before the D.C. Circuit and the Supreme Court, the EPA explained that with the 1970 act's secondary air quality standards and new source performance standards, "it is difficult to imagine what criteria [for defining significant deterioration] might be established that would have any meaningful basis." The agency contended that the District Court's decision in effect represented a rejection of the regulatory scheme of the 1970 act. But the appellate courts neither overturned the decision nor gave the EPA additional guidance on how to supplement the secondary and new source standards. The only indication either appellate court gave of a rationale for upholding Judge Pratt came in a statement Judge Carl McGowan made during oral argument: "If there is any serious doubt about what Congress meant, the least damage is done by following the course taken by the lower court."[27]

It will probably never be known whether Judge Pratt and the appellate courts accepted the legal arguments of the Sierra Club or they simply thought that PSD was good policy. Even those legal commentators who applaud the *Sierra Club* decision admit that its legal underpinnings are so weak as to require justification on policy grounds. Yet the decisions

25. Memorandum of law, Robert Baum (OGC) to Ed Tuerk and John Quarles, "Nondegradation," March 11, 1971.

26. Government reply brief in *Sierra Club* v. *Ruckelshaus*, No. 72-1528 (D.C. Cir. 1972), p. 27.

27. Quoted in Bolbach, "The Courts and the Clean Air Act," p. 22.

did not even come close to announcing a new policy. "Significant deterioration" had no meaning until the EPA gave it meaning.

Policy Issues and Options

The Sierra Club would not have brought suit against the EPA if it had not found the Clean Air Act as interpreted by the EPA deficient in some way. While the courts did not mention the policy arguments of the Sierra Club and the other groups joining the litigation, it is likely that they were swayed by these arguments. Examining the concerns that led the Sierra Club to initiate litigation and the policy arguments for PSD voiced by other groups can help make clear both why the courts acted as they did and what policy options faced the agency after the decision.

The problem of greatest concern to environmentalists was the construction of coal-burning power plants in the Rocky Mountains. The Four Corners power plant in northwestern New Mexico had already reduced visibility over a large section of the Southwest. Other huge facilities, including one for the Kaiparowits Plateau, were in the planning stages. With electricity often cheaper to transport than coal, utilities intended to build large mine-mouth plants adjacent to sources of low-sulfur coal and send electricity to metropolitan areas in southern California. Environmental groups and states such as New Mexico and Colorado were furious that the EPA was doing nothing to inhibit this "exporting of pollution."

Even worse, the EPA's air pollution policies encouraged the building of these plants in two ways. First, the national ambient air quality standards made it more difficult for utilities to build power plants in urban areas, which already had high pollution levels. This was particularly true of southern California. Second, by using the low-sulfur fuel of western mines, utilities could avoid putting flue gas desulfurization scrubbers on new plants. Section 111 of the Clean Air Act requires the EPA to set uniform national new source performance standards that take into account the cost of pollution controls. A standard stringent enough to require western utilities to scrub western coal would be prohibitively expensive for eastern plants burning much higher-sulfur coal. So the EPA set a standard that eastern plants could meet by scrubbing high-sulfur coal and western plants could meet by burning low-sulfur coal without additional controls. Thus the Clean Air Act actually encouraged greater pollution in clean areas of the West.

Goals for PSD

While environmentalists and officials from several states agreed that the EPA's policy was misguided, they did not agree on exactly what was wrong with it or how it should be amended. Supporters of PSD put forth six major reasons for requiring additional controls for sources locating in areas that have met national air quality standards. As the EPA reviewed specific control strategies, it became clear that not all of the goals of PSD supporters were compatible.[28]

The first and most frequently mentioned goal of PSD is to protect visibility in those pristine, low-humidity areas where small increases in pollution levels can detract from the natural beauty of the landscape. The secondary standards, designed to apply to the entire country, do not adequately address the problem of visibility in unique areas such as national parks and designated wilderness areas. Visibility protection was the primary concern of the Sierra Club, which warned that before long visitors would be unable to see across the Grand Canyon.

Second, as chapter 2 explained, the 1970 act focuses on improving local ambient air quality and fails to address directly the problem of atmospheric loading and long distance transport of pollutants such as sulfates and ozone. Throughout the 1970s evidence mounted suggesting that pollutants formed in the atmosphere far from their point of emission are at least as dangerous as emissions breathed by individuals close to the original source. The dispersion of pollutants achieved by locating sources in rural areas does not provide a solution to this problem. To reduce the health threat posed by atmospheric sulfates and to combat acid rain, the EPA must reduce *total* emissions of sulfur dioxide and nitrogen oxides.

Third, medical evidence produced in the 1970s also indicated that the health-based national standards do not fully protect all citizens even from the adverse effects of locally produced pollution. For most pollutants there simply are no safe concentrations above zero. Lowering the national standard to reflect this new information would lead to incredibly expensive control requirements, social disruption, and political backlash.

28. The many rationales for PSD (but not the strategies appropriate for each) are summarized in *Clean Air Act Amendments of 1977,* H. Rept. 95-294, pp. 103–41.

PSD, though, could protect citizens in attainment areas from additional health risks without imposing huge costs on society.

Fourth, environmentalists feared that without additional limits on pollution increases in clean air areas, regulation under the Clean Air Act would not force the development of new control technology. Environmentalists claimed that the requirement of uniform emission standards for new sources discourages innovation: if more effective but more expensive controls become available, all new plants must install them; this leads industry to locate in clean areas and install state-of-the-art technology rather than to devise better technology. PSD would force industry to develop better controls rather than move to clean air areas.

Fifth, environmentalists and residents of rural areas objected not just to the air pollution produced by facilities that locate in rural areas, but also to the changes in land use patterns they bring. Power plants produce boom towns and attract highways, commercial development, and satellite industries. Strip mines produce huge environmental problems, which the federal government had not yet addressed. Many advocates of PSD viewed the program as a way to promote land use planning and to prevent changes in the character of rural areas. This became a major focus of the EPA's 1974 program.

Finally, the twenty states that joined the Sierra Club in its original suit argued that states wishing to retain air cleaner than the secondary standard would be unable to do so without PSD. According to the New Mexico attorney general, PSD "prevents these [rural] areas from attempting to attract industry by enacting lenient emissions control requirements."[29] The House Commerce Committee explicitly adopted this rationale, stating that a primary purpose of PSD was "to prevent competition for industry to be waged among States on the basis of air quality."[30]

There are actually two parts to this "economic blackmail" argument. The first and more limited argument is that a uniform NSPS for coal-burning power plants makes it difficult for western states to insist on any controls other than the use of low-sulfur coal. The second argument is that regardless of how strict standards for new sources are, attainment areas gain an economic windfall from regulation. Nonattainment areas cannot compete with attainment areas for industry either because they cannot allow new growth or because they must impose SIP regulations

29. Brief of New Mexico and other states in *Fri v. Sierra Club*, pp. 2–3.
30. *Clean Air Act Amendments of 1977*, H. Rept. 95-294, p. 141.

more stringent than NSPS limitations. As the PSD debate progressed, support for the program came less from those rural states that compete for new industry than from urban states that feared losing existing industry. PSD became in the eyes of some a way to "shield the developed and polluted States from the natural advantages which otherwise may be enjoyed by less developed and cleaner States," and to prevent "flight of industry—and jobs—from areas where pollution levels are approaching or exceed the minimum Federal standards."[31]

Control Strategies

Not surprisingly, the specific programs proposed by PSD supporters varied according to the priorities they placed on achieving these several goals. The Sierra Club, for example, devised a complex "volumetric emission density plan" that would have effectively prevented the construction of large power plants. Those who desired to protect pristine areas without barring all major facilities from locating in attainment areas proposed plans to create extremely restrictive tertiary ambient air quality standards for a few parts of the country. These standards would have protected the visibility of a few "cherished places" by preventing large facilities from locating near them.[32]

However, tertiary air quality standards and siting restrictions designed to protect pristine areas do not directly address the atmospheric loading problem. Atmospheric loading is a problem under the Clean Air Act precisely because the act focuses exclusively on ambient air quality and not on total emissions. Coping with this problem requires placing tighter restrictions on new facilities wherever they are located—whether in the Grand Canyon, the Wyoming desert, or the Tennessee Valley. Unfortunately, regulations that increase restrictions on new plants can also discourage replacement of old, dirty plants, thus exacerbating the problem of atmospheric loading. This is a problem that constantly vexed those writing PSD regulations.

Achieving the goal of protecting citizens against low-level health effects involves a similar regulatory dilemma. While it makes sense to

31. The first quotation comes from the Separate View of Representative David E. Satterfield III in ibid., p. 504. The second comes from the body of the report, ibid., p. 133.

32. The EPA described the plans proposed by the Sierra Club and other environmental groups and explained their shortcomings in 39 Fed. Reg. 31006 (1974).

provide additional protection to rural citizens because the cost of this
protection is lower for them than for urban citizens, there is no easy
answer to the question of how much additional protection is desirable.
Quantitative analysis of this issue is impossible for the very reason that
the national standards are insufficient to protect health completely: very
little is known about the effects of low-level concentrations of criteria
pollutants. As the EPA noted in 1973:

> Pending the development of adequate scientific data on the kind and extent
> of adverse effects of air pollutant levels below the secondary standards,
> significant deterioration must necessarily be defined without a direct quanti-
> tative relationship to specific adverse effects on public health and welfare.[33]

What is known is that health risks increase as pollution levels rise, and
that levels are currently highest in areas of high population density. If,
as the EPA originally feared, PSD provides speculative health benefits to
a few people by preventing industrial relocation that would reduce the
more certain health risks many people now face, then PSD would hardly
serve a public health purpose. For this reason both HEW and the
Department of Housing and Urban Development vigorously opposed
PSD.[34]

While arguments over the contours of a PSD program threatened at
times to divide environmentalists concerned with protecting pristine
areas from those concerned with reducing urban pollution levels, almost
any PSD program would provide further impetus for technology forcing,
a goal both sets of environmental protection advocates could support.
Case-by-case determination of the best available control technology
would increase use of scrubbers and speed the dispersion of new
technology. Increasing the scarcity of emission rights would similarly
stimulate research and development. By stressing the technology-forcing
aspect of PSD, environmental groups could unite in common cause
against industry.

Similarly, almost any type of PSD restriction would alter the competitive position of the various states. While environmental groups united
in their support for any PSD program that aided technology forcing, the
states disagreed vigorously on what steps would eliminate alleged
economic blackmail. The reasons for this are readily apparent. States
differ not just in the purity of their air, but in the relative value they put

33. 38 Fed. Reg. 18987 (1973).
34. HUD and HEW comments on July 16, 1973, proposal, contained in EPA public
docket on PSD proposal.

on environmental protection and economic development. New Mexico, for example, supported a stronger NSPS for coal-burning power plants because it wanted to insist on more stringent control requirements without losing industry. In contrast, neighboring Arizona opposed PSD restrictions because it welcomed the economic advantage it gained from having clean air and willingly traded that resource for growth. Urban states trying to retain their industry wanted a PSD program that would reduce the competitive advantage of all clean air states by substantially reducing their margin for growth. One state's economic blackmail is another state's golden opportunity. It is not surprising, therefore, that once the implications of PSD became apparent the states as a whole played no important role in the development of a specific PSD program other than complaining about federal intrusion on state autonomy.

Finally, a PSD program that attempts to encourage land use planning must focus on the local effect of pollution. In its 1974 PSD proposal the EPA stated that "the development of proper land use planning to ensure protection of the environment is one of the most important tasks yet to be undertaken." Yet it warned that

> comprehensive land use planning is a complex process including many variables, only one of which is air quality. Development of land use plans in which air quality represents a single overriding criterion is not, in the Administrator's judgment, a desirable course of action for most areas.[35]

Thus a PSD program designed with this goal in mind must allow planners to consider a number of factors other than air quality in deciding what level of deterioration is significant. Of course, the more discretion given to local decisionmakers, the less able the federal government would be to protect pristine areas, limit atmospheric loading, force technological development, protect citizens from low-level health effects, and reduce economic blackmail.

It is highly doubtful that Judge Pratt had any idea of the plurality of goals encompassed under the rubric "prevention of significant deterioration." Several of these goals are compatible and even complementary. One can imagine a land use planning scheme that would give special, federally mandated protection to a few pristine areas. A tertiary sulfur dioxide standard could both protect rural populations from low-level health risks and help to reduce atmospheric loading. Case-by-case new source review could reduce loading and economic blackmail. But, as has

35. 39 Fed. Reg. 31001 (1974).

been shown, there are potential conflicts among these goals. Keeping clean air clean helps keep dirty air dirty. Federal restrictions on local and total emissions reduce the choices available to the states as they develop land use plans. Ironically, the plan the EPA developed to achieve one of these objectives was converted by the 1977 amendments into a vehicle for achieving a wide variety of partially conflicting goals.

The EPA Develops a Program

Between 1973 and 1975 the EPA's position on PSD changed from mild opposition to strong support. The agency that appealed the *Sierra Club* case all the way to the Supreme Court in 1973 publicly refused to support the Nixon administration's legislative proposal to overturn the decision in 1974. In part this was due to a change in administrators: Russell Train was more sympathetic to PSD than was William Ruckelshaus.[36] But the views of the bureaucracy as a whole changed as well. Many of the agency officials who helped write the original PSD regulations became convinced (much to their surprise) that they had devised a plan that protected wilderness areas while allowing economic growth, encouraged land use planning without depriving the states of needed flexibility, and responded to the court order without imposing impossible demands upon the agency. The PSD regulations issued in late 1974 were not just the product of long hours of careful thought and tedious negotiation. They were, many within the EPA believed, moderate, reasonable, and environmentally beneficial.

Despite this the EPA never made a serious effort to implement this first set of PSD regulations. Because the EPA expected Congress to amend the Clean Air Act momentarily and suspected that the courts might overturn the regulations in the second round of litigation, the agency devoted few resources to this task. The 1974 regulations are important primarily because they formed the link between the 1972 court decision and the 1977 amendments. In 1977 Congress accepted the EPA's basic regulatory scheme. In fact, throughout the long congressional debate over PSD, alternative frameworks hardly received mention. Besides providing Congress with a program on which it could build, the EPA's

36. Senator Muskie may have been instrumental in shaping Train's opinion on PSD. *Nomination of Russell E. Train,* Hearings before the Senate Committee on Public Works, 93 Cong. 1 sess. (GPO, 1973), pp. 13, 55–56.

regulations created a "default" position greatly disliked by some participants, especially state governments. These were the rules that industry and the states would face if Congress failed to reach agreement on modifications. Given the pivotal role played by the 1974 regulations in the legislative process, it is important to see how court action—and the EPA's guesses about what the courts might do in the future—helped to shape the agency's original PSD program.

Shortly after the Supreme Court upheld Judge Pratt in 1973, the EPA took the unusual step of describing and soliciting public comments on a number of possible approaches to PSD. Given the importance of the issue, the EPA stated, "the question of how such a policy should be defined and implemented cannot properly be addressed, much less decided on narrow legal grounds. Rather, it is a question that must be discussed, debated, and decided as a public policy issue, with full consideration of its economic and social implications."[37] The EPA took this position not just because of the potential consequences of PSD, but also because its attorneys could find few hints on what approach would pass legal muster.[38]

Anticipation of judicial review nonetheless influenced the EPA's regulations at two critical junctures. First, it led the agency to choose a program that defined significant deterioration in terms of incremental changes in ambient air quality, rather than in terms of allowable emission increases. While agency engineers warned that this approach created immense technical difficulties, the Office of General Counsel (OGC) insisted that it was more in tune with Judge Pratt's order than was the emission-based scheme favored by the engineers. Second, the OGC argued that the EPA plan would have a better chance of surviving judicial review if the EPA limited the states' authority to allow increased pollution within their territory. Many states resented these federally imposed limitations. Their demands for revision of the PSD program drew Congress into the fray.

Choosing the Ambient Increment Scheme

During 1973 the EPA considered a variety of approaches to defining and controlling significant deterioration. It relied on both legal and

37. 38 Fed. Reg. 18986 (1973).
38. Memorandum, Richard Denney (OGC) to Joseph Padgett (OAQPS), "Significant Deterioration—Legal Strategy Paper," January 18, 1974.

policy arguments to whittle down its options to the two alternatives it examined in detail. The EPA rejected the proposals of the Sierra Club, Natural Resources Defense Council, and Environmental Defense Fund as both too complicated to administer and too limited in their environmental benefits to justify the restrictions on economic growth which they would entail.[39] It dropped the permissive "local definition plan" proposed in its 1973 Federal Register notice when the OGC and Department of Justice attorneys argued that a plan that gave the states complete discretion to define "significant deterioration" would surely be struck down in court.[40] Similarly, the EPA contended that an emission tax, a proposal favored by many economists as well as by the Nixon administration, would not respond to the court order:

> If significant deterioration of air quality is to be prevented by the emission charge, some relationship between the charge rate and the resultant air quality must be found. Such a relationship is not presently available. . . . Consequently, the emission charge, while possessing some desirable attributes, does not appear to be a practical means of preventing significant deterioration of air quality.[41]

This statement illustrates the presumption that the more directly a plan focused on ambient air quality the more likely it would be to receive judicial approval.

The EPA's 1973 announcement described two plans that defined significant deterioration in terms of incremental increases in ambient pollution levels. The first established a single increment that defined significant deterioration for all clean areas of the country. The emission ceiling for any area would equal the area's existing ("baseline") pollution concentration level plus the increment. While this seemed to be what the courts had in mind, a single-increment plan has serious shortcomings:

> It may not be wise to restrict the development of waste land to the same degree that a scenic national park is restricted, particularly if that restriction forces additional air quality deterioration on the heavily populated regions of the nation.[42]

Consequently EPA proposed a variation on this approach, the area classification plan (ACP).

The area classification plan would allow states to choose from among

39. 38 Fed. Reg. 18993–94 (1973) and 39 Fed. Reg. 31006 (1974).
40. Memorandum, Richard Denney (OGC) to Bernard Steigerwald (OAQPS), November 27, 1974.
41. 38 Fed. Reg. 18994 (1973).
42. Ibid., 18991.

three increments to define significant deterioration for each locality. The small Class I increments would protect an area from almost any measurable pollution increase. The Class II increment would allow moderate economic growth. Class III areas could sustain pollution levels up to the secondary standard. As early as 1973 the EPA noted that the ACP, which required the states to zone their land for various purposes, "appears to be superior in many, if not all, respects."[43]

Paradoxically, while the increments in the ACP limit the deterioration of local air quality, the EPA had no air quality justification for the size of the increments. The EPA chose the air quality increments on the basis of the types of sources that would be allowed to locate in each area. The Class I increment was small enough to "prohibit the introduction of even one small fossil fuel fired power plant, municipal incinerator, medium apartment complex (assuming oil heat), or any other medium scale residential or commercial development." Class II increments were designed to allow medium-size coal plants (up to 1,000 megawatts) but to prohibit larger ones. Class III areas could accommodate heavy growth. Thus the ACP's increments were based on land use, not air quality considerations. The EPA noted that a key virtue of the plan was its ability to stimulate "longer range strategic planning" by the states.[44]

The chief competitor of the ACP was the emission density plan (EDP). Under the EDP each section of a state would be allowed to increase its total emissions by a specified amount each year. The EPA suggested that ten tons per year per square mile might be a reasonable figure for sulfur dioxide and three tons per year per square mile for particulate matter. The Office of Air Quality Planning and Standards (OAQPS) favored the EDP for two reasons. First, while it did not focus on local air quality, it had a stronger air quality justification than the ACP. The ACP remained tied to the troublesome ambient air approach. The EDP, in contrast, put a cap on total emission increases. The EPA noted that "emission density (regional emissions/regional area) is an excellent indicator of atmospheric loading."[45] The OAQPS viewed the EDP as a way to cure one of the key deficiencies of the act without departing from its basic purpose of improving air quality and without getting into the messy land use planning business.

The second advantage of the EDP was its relative administrative and

43. Ibid., 18993.
44. Ibid.
45. Ibid., 18991.

technical simplicity. The ACP required establishing what EPA called a baseline concentration for clean air areas. Extensive air quality monitoring data, however, seldom exist for rural areas. Where baseline data are available, they usually show random or yearly variations larger than the increments proposed by the EPA. To make matters worse, the error range of most monitors is larger than the ACP's increments. This means monitoring is useless for deciding whether a new source has "consumed" the increment. Regulatory agencies can check increment consumption only by using dispersion models to determine whether pollution increases caused by a source violate the allowable increment. The OAQPS warned that "even in the best case the possible errors in the modelling process due to, for example, uncertainties in meteorological parameters, may overwhelm the air quality increment under consideration."[46]

In short, the small air quality increment of the ACP exacerbated all the difficulties inherent in a regulatory scheme that focused on local air quality rather than on emissions. The EDP, in contrast, would have been easy to administer: control agencies would simply calculate the total emissions produced by new sources, subtract the emission reductions achieved by old sources, and compare this with the allowable emission increment.

In late 1973 the EPA established a task force to choose a regulatory framework. While OAQPS representatives continued to favor an emission-based plan, most representatives of other offices favored the ACP. The latter group emphasized that under the EDP, sources could concentrate their emissions in one corner of a control region, increasing pollution levels to the secondary standards and defeating all efforts to limit growth or stimulate land use planning. Agency lawyers insisted that a plan based on ambient air quality considerations would stand a much better chance of surviving judicial review than would the EDP. Judges love analogies, they pointed out, and the analogy between the act's ambient air quality standards and the ACP's ambient air quality increments is a strong one. Thus the OAQPS faced a strong coalition of lawyers and land use planning advocates.

The event that finally led the task force to favor the ACP was an economic impact analysis commissioned by the agency. Using the admittedly arbitrary increments suggested in the original proposal, the consultants' report found that the EDP would constrain the construction

46. EPA, OAQPS, "Technical Support Document—EPA Regulations for Preventing Significant Deterioration of Air Quality" (EPA, January 1975), p. 78.

of new coal-burning power plants, while the ACP would not—unless, of course, the states designated large areas as Class I.[47] The task force did not ask the consultants to consider the impact of the two plans using different increment sizes. While the report did not show that the ACP was inherently superior to the EDP, it put the engineers on the defensive and convinced the economists on the task force that the ACP would not have perverse effects on economic growth. The lawyers' presumption in favor of a local air quality approach carried the day.

Adding the Details

The EPA spent 1974 developing the area classification plan. It held lengthy discussions with state officials, environmental groups, industry, and other federal agencies before issuing its second formal proposal in August 1974. It then evaluated public comments, went through an interagency review, and published final rules in December.[48] Throughout this period the states pushed the EPA to grant them maximum flexibility. Environmental groups argued that the EPA should set increments for mobile source pollutants (carbon monoxide, hydrocarbons, and nitrogen oxides), not just for sulfur dioxide and particulate matter. They also sought smaller increments and case-by-case review of best available control technology (BACT). Conversely, the Federal Energy Administration (FEA) fought for larger increments and opposed case-by-case BACT. Industry and its friends at the Department of Commerce devoted their efforts to delaying the EPA's regulations and supporting the administration's proposals to overturn the *Sierra Club* decision. Within the EPA, the OAQPS sought changes in the plan that would make it easier to administer. The OGC looked for ways to strengthen the agency's legal defenses.

While the EPA made a few concessions to PSD opponents, it refused to make changes that would compromise the scheme's basic purpose. For example, the EPA agreed to the FEA's requests to drop case-by-case review of BACT for coal plants and to exclude from PSD review the coal conversions required by energy legislation passed in 1974. But it refused to increase the size of the Class II ambient increment to allow the building of large-scale power plants in these areas. This decision was

47. Harbridge House, "The Impact of Proposed Non-Degradation Regulations on Economic Growth" (November 1973).
48. 39 Fed. Reg. 31000 (1974); 39 Fed. Reg. 42510 (1974).

especially important since under the EPA's plan all areas are originally designated Class II. This meant that all large power plants would need a variance in the form of a redesignation to Class III before construction could begin. The EPA argued that to allow large power plants to locate in rural areas without such specific approval would both defeat the purpose of the ACP and lead the courts to invalidate the entire scheme.[49]

The states played a far different role in the development of EPA regulations than they had in the original *Sierra Club* litigation. When the EPA consulted with representatives of state governors and air agencies, it found that

> most states indicated a preference for no further federal involvement in regard to this issue. It was also mentioned that those states which raised this issue during the *Sierra Club* suit were not necessarily reflecting a state policy concerning economic blackmail.[50]

In fact, the professional association representing state air agency officials called for legislation leaving PSD completely up to the states.[51]

Two provisions provoked strong opposition from several states, those relating to control of federal lands and EPA review of state reclassification. Attorneys in the OGC and the Departments of Justice, Agriculture, and Interior insisted that federal or Indian land could not be subjected to any form of state control. Only the federal government and Indian tribes, they maintained, could redesignate these areas from Class II to Class I or III. Western states—including even the pro-PSD New Mexico—were extremely worried about federally established barriers to growth within their territories. The EPA compounded these fears by noting that a Class I increment could be violated by a source as far as 100 miles from the Class I area. The size of these buffer zones surrounding Class I areas varies according to terrain and weather conditions. Only source-specific dispersion modeling can determine their exact size. Buffer zones are largest in areas of steep terrain. Mountain states with large federal land

49. Memorandums, Richard Denney (OGC) to Assistant Administrator Roger Strelow, "No Significant Deterioration Regulations," July 17, 1974; Strelow to OGC, July 1974.

50. Memorandum, Joseph Padgett (OAQPS) to OGC, January 25, 1974. An April 2, 1974, draft action memo stated, "It was noted [at a meeting with state air pollution control officials] that many States had filed *amicus curiae* briefs on behalf of the Sierra Club, but in most cases the air pollution control agencies were not in agreement with those briefs, most of which were filed by the State Attorney General" (p. 5).

51. *Clean Air Act Amendments, 1975,* Hearings before the Subcommittee on Health and the Environment of the House Committee on Interstate and Foreign Commerce, 94 Cong. 1 sess. (GPO, 1975), p. 627. Only one state, California, urged stricter PSD regulations. California's comments were written by the state attorney general's office.

holdings—such as Utah, Colorado, and Idaho—feared that these buffer zones would put huge sections of their territory under de facto federal control.

The EPA's final regulations gave the states authority to classify federal lands, but allowed federal land managers (the secretaries of the departments with jurisdiction over the land) to reclassify their lands to a more restrictive classification. The OGC claimed that the courts would look much more favorably on regulations that gave such special protection to national parks and official wilderness areas.[52] This section of the EPA's regulations later provided a major bargaining chip to congressional supporters of PSD who wished to gain the states' support for PSD legislation. As it turned out, some states were willing to agree to almost any change in PSD in return for amendments reducing the extent of federal control over the buffer zones surrounding federal lands.

The second major federalism issue involved EPA review of area reclassification proposed by the states. The Sierra Club threatened to challenge the EPA's regulation if it allowed the states to redesignate their entire territory as Class III. The OGC warned that the Sierra Club had a strong legal argument: if a state classified each of its control regions as Class III, pollution levels could reach the secondary standards everywhere in the state—precisely the situation Judge Pratt told the EPA to prevent. To convince the reviewing court that this would not occur, the EPA required the states to submit records similar to environmental impact statements to support reclassifications and promised to invalidate "arbitrary" redesignations. The EPA officials did not expect to use this authority extensively. Indeed the agency's general counsel told the assistant administrator he hoped the EPA could "get away with a fairly cursory review."[53] But the agency obviously could not publicly reassure the states that the purpose of the provision was simply to strengthen its position in court.

While the EPA was fighting these battles with the states, industry, environmentalists, and the FEA, the OAQPS was waging a rear guard action to reduce the administrative and technical burden imposed by

52. Memorandum, Richard Denney (OGC) to Kent Berry (OAQPS), October 31, 1974; April 2, 1974, draft action memo, p. 18.

53. Memorandum, Robert Zener (general counsel) to Roger Strelow, June 1975. This paragraph also relies on the following memos: Richard Denney (OGC) to Roger Strelow, October 2, 1974; Denney to Strelow, June 20, 1975; Denney to Zener, June 25, 1975; draft action memo, April 2, 1974.

PSD. Much to the displeasure of environmental groups, the EPA continued to insist that mobile source pollutants could not be covered by PSD. More important, the OAQPS convinced the EPA's political executives that it was technically impossible to treat the baseline-plus-increment ceiling as a tertiary air quality standard. Since this issue gained prominence after passage of the 1977 amendments, it demands special attention.

Agency deliberation over the status of air quality increments focused on monitoring rules, which experienced what one EPA memo described as a "turbulent history."[54] The OAQPS opposed monitoring-based checks on increment consumption, claiming that using monitoring data for this purpose presupposes "the existence of information and/or techniques which do not always exist." It recommended that increment consumption be tallied on the basis of dispersion modeling estimates alone. Everyone recognized that models are often highly inaccurate predictors of actual air quality. But models have the virtue of simplicity and consistency. "Mathematical simulation," the EPA explained in its technical support document on PSD, "provides a consistent, reproducible way to estimate 'hypothetical' air quality increments" for sulfur dioxide and particulate matter.[55]

Proposing an elaborate regulatory scheme that included no real-world checks on administrative discretion made many EPA officials nervous. Some recognized that PSD review would become entangled in arcane modeling disputes and that actual air quality could deteriorate much more than the EPA's paper calculation indicated. But the OAQPS convinced the rest of the agency that using monitoring as a postconstruction check on modeling would have even more perverse results. If EPA models underpredicted concentrations, the source would be forced to close down or add costly new controls shortly after it began operation. The source would then challenge the EPA's monitoring, pointing out that the recorded violations could well have resulted from measurement error, random yearly variations in the baseline, or emissions produced by minor sources or other types of sources exempted from PSD review. Conversely, sources denied permits could point to monitoring data that the EPA considered unreliable to argue for a more lenient permit. To make matters worse, the monitoring data required to establish a baseline could take a year or more to collect and interpret. This would both

54. Memorandum, Richard Rhoads (OAQPS) to Roger Strelow, "Deletion of Ambient Monitoring Requirements from the Significant Deterioration Regulation," July 26, 1974.
55. OAQPS, "Technical Support Document," pp. 71, 78.

delay granting of permits and add substantial regulatory costs. For these reasons the EPA maintained that a monitoring-based program was "virtually unworkable."[56]

Fortunately the rationale for the regulatory scheme did not demand real-world checks on increment consumption, for the increments had no intrinsic significance. Rather, they were chosen on the basis of the types of sources that would normally cause dispersion models to predict increment violations. If the EPA's conservative dispersion models predicted that a major source would violate an increment, then the state would have to decide whether to reclassify the area to allow construction. The EPA readily admitted:

> The basic purpose of this classification procedure would be to require a conscious decision, made publicly with public input, that the intention of the State and the desire of the local population is to provide for the general type of air quality implied by the classification.[57]

In other words, given the land use planning focus of this PSD program, actual air quality was of little importance.

The EPA's 1974 PSD program was at the same time far more and far less than it appeared to be. On the one hand, as environmental groups noted, it was extremely limited in scope and purpose. It regulated only sulfur dioxide and particulate matter. It did not prevent air quality levels from reaching the secondary standards. It did not even measure the actual deterioration of air quality. Most important, it established land use planning and air quality management *procedures* without setting substantive goals. Missing from the program were the goals of reducing atmospheric loading, forcing technology, reducing exposure to low-level concentrations of criteria pollutants, and eliminating economic blackmail. The EPA's regulations did not even specify which pristine wilderness areas deserved special protection. This task was left to federal land managers.

On the other hand, many groups foresaw substantial problems even with this limited program. Many western states feared that federal bureaucrats, especially those in the Department of Interior, would classify large sections of federal land as Class I, thus preventing growth in substantial portions of state-controlled land. They also worried about the EPA's review of their efforts to reclassify state land and about the regulatory burden placed upon state air agencies. Energy watchers voiced

56. Ibid., p. 9.
57. 39 Fed. Reg. 31004 (1974).

concern that decisions made by both state and federal officials under PSD could seriously inhibit coal use and exploitation of new energy resources.

When the EPA published its final regulations in December 1974, environmentalists and industry challengers presented all these criticisms to the D.C. Circuit. The EPA expected the environmentalists to win on some issues, but the court surprised everyone by upholding the program in its entirety. That decision—*Sierra Club* v. *Environmental Protection Agency*—came in mid-1976, just as the amendments to the Clean Air Act were reaching the floor of the Senate. This court action, like the original *Sierra Club* decision, significantly affected the congressional debate.

Congress Expands the Program

Next to the relaxation of auto emission standards, PSD was the most controversial section of the 1977 amendments. Western senators opposed to PSD filibustered the amendments to death in 1976. The debate continued in 1977. The House report of that year announced that PSD "is one of the most carefully and completely studied issues to come before Congress in many years."[58] The amendments that finally became law in 1977 not only endorsed PSD, but added to the act a long and unusually detailed section that tightened and extended the EPA's program. PSD did not merely survive congressional review, it flourished.

How was it that a Congress that did not even mention the words "significant deterioration" in an act passed at the height of the environmental enthusiasm of the early 1970s took such a strongly pro-PSD position in 1977, when energy shortages and recession were on everyone's mind? One possible explanation is education. Several years' experience with air pollution control had shown Congress that uniform air quality standards would not provide adequate protection for all parts of the country; that the 1970 act ignored the long distance transport problem; and that new source performance standards had not ended economic blackmail. The EPA's PSD program not only forced Congress to confront these problems, but provided it with a vehicle for reform. Thus one can argue that the *Sierra Club* decision induced Congress to conduct a thorough review of its air pollution program.

58. *Clean Air Act Amendments of 1977,* H. Rept. 95-294, p. 172.

Congress's education, though, did not extend to the mechanisms and consequences of the EPA's ambient increment scheme. The PSD section of the 1977 amendments contains several glaring and embarrassing mistakes. It contains two incompatible effective dates. More important, it treats the baseline-plus-increment figure as a measurable tertiary standard—despite the EPA's insistence that this makes no sense at all. The amendments require a year of preconstruction monitoring, which the EPA still maintains is completely useless. While the EPA's original plan gave the states a great deal of flexibility to redesignate regions from Class II to Class I or III, Congress made reclassification extremely difficult. In effect, the arbitrary increments, originally chosen to facilitate land use planning, became binding air quality ceilings.

The Political Context: Congress and Its Committees

To understand congressional action on PSD—particularly the paradox of such a flawed and poorly understood program passing after long and heated debate—it is necessary to consider the relations between Congress as a whole and its committees. Members of Congress generally defer to committee recommendations unless they have strong reasons for doing otherwise. This is particularly true when technical issues are involved, as was the case with PSD. Overturning a committee recommendation usually requires a clear issue and either presidential leadership or loud complaints from constituents. None of these prerequisites applied to PSD. The Senate and House subcommittees led by Senator Muskie and Representative Rogers convinced Congress that something must be done about atmospheric loading, low-level health effects, visibility protection, and economic blackmail. Members of Congress not on these committees left what they considered mere details to the committees. After defeating efforts by congressmen and senators from western states to delete PSD altogether, the committees were essentially on their own.

Most members of the Muskie and Rogers committees—even the Republicans—were strong environmental protection advocates who had long supported some version of PSD. The EPA's PSD program gave them a concrete proposal to support and amend. It also gave them powerful bargaining chips to use against PSD opponents. They used this opportunity to fashion a very stringent PSD program—in fact, even more stringent than they, their staff, or the EPA realized at the time. To some extent their success reflects the general popularity of air pollution control programs in Congress and the respect members had for Senator Muskie and Representative Rogers. But the peculiar circumstances of 1976–77— especially the existence of a court-mandated PSD program—gave added strength to these committees and made it particularly difficult for opponents to defeat this proposal. Seven factors help explain the clout of these committees and thus the stringency of the PSD section of the 1977 amendments.[59]

First, the auto industry and the Republican administration desperately wanted to relax the auto emission standards scheduled to go into effect for the 1977 model year. While Senator Muskie admitted that these standards were probably infeasible, he announced that he would not support any amendments to the act that did not include ratification of PSD. When he introduced his committee's bill in 1976 Muskie stated:

> What apparently has not been understood, however, is that I think the Clean Air Act as it was enacted in 1970 is basically sound law. . . . Amendments may be desirable, not essential. In my opinion, with one exception, the judicial and administrative processes are available to overcome any hurdles which may be presented by the act in its present form. . . . I think the courts and the Administrator can resolve the nondegradation issue.[60]

Muskie in effect held revision of the auto standards and other deadlines hostage to passage of a PSD program at least as strong as the EPA's.

Second, the states were eager to remove those details of the EPA's program to which they strongly objected, particularly restrictions on areas surrounding federal land. Muskie and Rogers skillfully traded concessions on these high-salience issues for changes that strengthened and enlarged the regulatory scheme proposed by the EPA. The D.C. Circuit helped their cause by rejecting the states' challenge to the EPA's plan in the 1976 *Sierra Club* case.

Third, many state officials and businessmen simply wanted Congress to act in some way to end the uncertainty over the legal validity of the EPA's program. The EPA shared this interest in a congressional resolution of the issue. EPA political executives repeated that any legislation was

59. The congressional debate on PSD was extensive, both in 1976 and 1977. Relevant excerpts from the *Congressional Record* are compiled in *A Legislative History of the Clean Air Act Amendments of 1977*, prepared for the Senate Committee on Environment and Public Works, 95 Cong. 2 sess. (GPO, 1978), pp. 705–1185, 3031–3233, 4411–4501, 4938–5466, 6225–6546.

60. *Congressional Record* (May 19, 1976), p. 14562. The "one exception" mentioned by Muskie was the nitrogen oxides standard for new cars, which Muskie believed was infeasible.

)

better than no legislation. For this reason the agency preferred to accept without complaint some provisions in the committee bills it considered unwise rather than to endanger passage of amendments by objecting.

Fourth, the opponents of PSD seriously hurt their own cause by taking a hard-line position and by circulating information of questionable validity. Instead of proposing a less ambitious alternative to the proposals of the EPA and the congressional committees, the Ford administration and the Chamber of Commerce (which led industry's lobbying effort) pushed for total elimination of PSD. This would have left the visibility of areas such as the Grand Canyon and the Tetons completely unprotected. It also allowed Muskie to claim that "Ford supports dirty air." The administration rejected the pleas of the Republican members of the Senate committee to put forth a proposal to limit PSD to a few wilderness areas. Most of these Republicans eventually sided with Muskie. To make matters worse, the Chamber of Commerce made exaggerated claims it could not substantiate about the economic effects of PSD. The opponents of PSD simply lost their credibility.

Fifth, cities and states that had not met the 1975 deadline for achieving national air quality standards began to realize that PSD could provide economic protection for developed areas as well as environmental protection for the undeveloped. The 1977 House report noted that the National League of Cities endorsed PSD as a way to address "the need to protect against massive industrial migration to clean air regions."[61] The National Association of Counties and the state of Ohio (the state with the most severe stationary source pollution problem in the country) supported PSD for similar reasons. The managers of the 1977 amendments did not allow these political advantages to go to waste.

Sixth, because PSD placed restrictions not on existing facilities, but on new sources that might locate in a member's district, members tended to hear few complaints from their districts. Except in a handful of western states, the costs of the program seemed speculative; they did not fall directly on constituents. Only businessmen who planned to expand or to move foresaw the possible consequences of the program and complained. This left business virtually alone, facing an alliance of environmentalists and labor unions who feared losing jobs in developed areas. It was thus easy for PSD supporters to paint the issue as "business versus the public interest."

61. *Clean Air Act Amendments of 1977*, H. Rept. 95-294, p. 134.

Finally, EPA's ambient increment scheme added a crucial ingredient to this mix of political forces. Because this scheme is complex and at times counterintuitive, committee staff members and the few congressmen who studied the details of the program played an especially important role. Most members were primarily concerned about the types of sources that could locate in each area. The only way to make such predictions was to insert various assumptions into dispersion models. The debate over PSD thus turned into a "war of models" with each side using its own assumptions about weather conditions, wind speeds, stack heights, plume rise, and other such parameters. As industry spokesmen lost their credibility, most members of Congress relied on the analyses provided by the EPA and committee staff without understanding their limited predictive value. When the EPA later changed some of its modeling assumptions, the economic impact of the whole program changed concomitantly.[62]

The regulatory scheme proposed by the EPA also made it easy for those familiar with the plan to present major changes as "merely technical." The best example of this was the House committee's addition of monitoring requirements. While this drastically altered the nature of the regulatory scheme, it received no attention on the floor or even in committee reports. The House committee similarly added requirements that the EPA expand PSD to cover mobile source pollutants and develop a scheme to protect visibility. The staffs of both committees were particularly eager to squeeze as much environmental control out of PSD as they could. They adeptly used their knowledge of the operation of the EPA's scheme and the details of the legislation to include additional restrictions on polluters.

The New Program Emerges

Senator Muskie, Representative Rogers, and their staffs skillfully pressed their tactical advantage. The bill that came out of the Senate committee responded to the complaints of the states by removing EPA review of state classifications, greatly reducing the amount of federal

---

62. Judge Robinson discussed this problem in *Alabama Power* v. *Costle,* 636 F.2d 323 at 387. He ruled that the EPA was not legally required to use the modeling assumptions of studies cited by sponsors of the amendment.

land subject to classification by federal land managers, and claiming to eliminate the buffer zone surrounding Class I areas.[63] But at the same time the bill added provisions to (1) eliminate the states' option of reclassifying areas as Class III; (2) establish *mandatory* Class I areas that included almost all national parks and national wilderness areas as well as other selected federal lands; and (3) require case-by-case review of best available control technology for *all* major sources, not just the few categories of large sources covered by the EPA's regulations.

Moreover, while Senator Muskie kept repeating that the bill eliminated buffer zones, the bill recognized the obvious fact that emissions outside an area can cause violations of that area's increment. The bill provided that when a dispersion model predicts a violation of a Class I increment by a source outside the Class I area, the federal land manager can authorize the state to grant a permit to the source, provided the manager finds its emissions will have "no adverse impact on the air quality-related values of such land." This in effect leaves the size of the buffer zone up to the federal land manager. Since the bill charges each manager with an "affirmative responsibility to protect the air quality-related values," and the Senate report instructs them to "err on the side of protecting air quality-related values for future generations," environmentalists could probably delay the permitting process by challenging such waivers in court. In addition, the bill authorizes federal land managers to ask a state to *deny* a permit that would allow emissions producing an "adverse impact on the air quality-related values of such land" even though models predict no increment violation.[64] Thus the Senate committee's bill not only strengthened PSD, but did not reduce federal control substantially in those areas most likely to be designated as Class I under the EPA's original scheme.

The Muskie committee consistently commanded the votes of nearly two-thirds of the entire Senate. The hostile one-third, led by western senators, was able to delay passage of the bill but not to defeat it or even to force Muskie to make major concessions. The situation was somewhat different in the House. In 1976 the Rogers committee just barely won a vote to postpone the effective date of the committee bill pending additional study of the impact of PSD. The next year the

63. *Clean Air Amendments of 1977*, S. Rept. 95-127, 95 Cong. 1 sess. (GPO, 1977), pp. 27–37.

64. Ibid., pp. 36, 152.

committee lost a floor vote on a provision to loosen controls in Class I areas.[65]

Realizing that the House would not go as far as the Senate on PSD, the Rogers committee offered a proposal, billed as a compromise, that stood halfway between the Senate bill and the EPA's program on some issues but expanded PSD still further on other matters. The House bill reinstated Class III, which the EPA insisted was necessary to allow expected economic growth through the 1980s. But it substantially reduced the size of the Class III increment and made it very hard for states to reclassify areas as Class III. The House bill included fewer mandatory Class I areas but added discretionary Class I areas. The states could redesignate these areas as Class II, but could not move them to Class III. At the same time the bill tightened the three-hour Class II increment for sulfur dioxide, the increment most likely to cause polluters problems. The bill also added provisions to extend PSD to mobile source pollutants, to define and protect visibility-related air quality values, to force emission rollbacks in areas that exceed their PSD increments, and to require a year's monitoring before granting permits.

After each house had approved the committees' recommendations, the conference committee met hurriedly to put together a final bill before the auto companies began production runs on their new cars. In general the conferees split the difference between the PSD provisions of the two houses. For example, they accepted the Senate's list of mandatory Class I areas, the House's plan to retain Class III, the Senate's increments for Class I and language on buffer zones, and the House's increments for Class II. It also included the new provisions proposed by each committee: the Senate's expansion of the number of sources subject to review and its complex provisions on protection of air quality in Class I areas, and the House's provisions on visibility, mobile source pollutants, monitoring, and enforcement. Dominated by members of the two environmental protection committees, the conferees made little attempt to restrict the

65. In 1976 the closest vote in the Senate was on the Moss amendment to postpone action on PSD for one year. It lost 31–63. (*Congressional Record* [August 3, 1976], p. 25192.) In 1977 an amendment to relax PSD requirements failed by a vote of 33–61. (*Congressional Record,* daily edition [June 9, 1977], p. S9278.) A challenge to the House committee's 1976 PSD proposal was defeated 156–199. (*Congressional Record* [September 8, 1976], p. 29255.) But in 1977 the "Breaux amendment"—opposed by both the committee and the administration—passed by a vote of 237–172. (*Congressional Record,* daily edition [May 25, 1977], p. H5051.)

size of the PSD program—even when EPA staff warned that the scheme would be nearly impossible to administer as written.

The 1977 amendments transformed the EPA's original effort to stimulate land use planning by the states into the largest air pollution control program administered by the EPA. The existence of the EPA's court-ordered plan did more than educate Congress to the possible virtues of PSD. Its very existence gave PSD supporters—including those seeking economic as well as environmental protection—key strategic advantages in the legislative battle. Moreover, the ambient increment approach of the plan made it all too easy for a handful of congressmen and staff members to expand—and confuse—the program by making a few seemingly technical adjustments. Congress voted overwhelmingly to support the 1977 amendments. But it is doubtful that the average congressman had any idea how the much-debated PSD provisions of that legislation would be translated into an administrative program. Even those EPA officials who had worked on PSD for years were surprised when they realized what the amendments required the agency to do.

The Cycle of Cumulative Litigation

One of the principal objectives of the PSD portion of the 1977 amendments was to establish a clear congressional PSD policy. Senator Muskie claimed that specific legislation on this issue would eliminate uncertainty and delay, reduce the role of the courts in policymaking, and "avoid having legislation by regulation."[66] Judged by these standards, the amendments were a complete failure. The EPA took almost a year to publish final regulations implementing the PSD section of the law. The court reviewing these regulations noted that the EPA had "proceeded with vigor and industry to carry out the Herculean task Congress has assigned to it," but invalidated many parts of the regulation nonetheless.[67] The PSD programs of the EPA and the states remained in limbo until the EPA revised its regulations in late 1980. Everyone expected Congress to make further revisions quickly, but no action had been taken by the end of 1982.

---

66. Quoted in 8 *Environment Reporter—Current Developments* 964.
67. *Alabama Power* v. *Castle*, 606 F.2d 1068 at 1093.

It would take an entire book to explain the development of PSD regulations since 1977. The following discussion attempts merely to provide examples of the problems arising under the act, the ways in which the EPA has tried to cope with them, and how the courts have further complicated the EPA's tasks. This analysis will focus on three issues that came before the D.C. Circuit in the *Spencer County* and *Alabama Power* cases: the effective date of the new PSD provisions, the number of sources subject to PSD review, and the use of monitoring data.

What Effective Date?

The dispute over the effective date of new PSD requirements shows the trouble Congress can get into when it tries to write extremely specific legislation. Either through oversight or inability to reach agreement, the 1977 conferees included two different effective dates in the act. Section 165 subjects all facilities beginning construction after August 7, 1977, to the permit requirement of the new act. But section 168 provides that regulations in effect before passage of the amendments would stay in effect until the states revised their SIPs to conform to the amendments. These revisions were due in December 1978. The EPA first tried to escape this awkward choice by following section 165 and requesting technical amendments confirming its decision. While Senator Muskie claimed this to be the "clear intent" of the conferees, industry and the Department of Energy strenuously objected. They argued that Congress had not intended to impose a twelve- to eighteen-month moratorium on new construction, which they claimed would result from adherence to section 165. They successfully blocked Muskie's attempt to resolve the dispute by technical amendment. Shortly thereafter the EPA announced a compromise deadline midway between the effective dates of the two sections.[68]

Both industry and environmentalists immediately sued the EPA. The D.C. District Court prohibited the EPA from issuing final permits until the D.C. Circuit had resolved the issue. After reviewing the "baroque complexity" of this "imperfect statute," the court upheld the EPA's

---

68. These events are recounted in *Citizens to Save Spencer County* at 851–60. Muskie presented and explained his amendments in *Congressional Record*, daily edition (November 1, 1977), p. S18371.

regulation. The court stated, "It is indisputable that the one section allows what the other prohibits." It traced this conflict to unresolved policy differences between the two houses. Surprisingly, the court indicated that it would have been unfair for the EPA to accept *either* of these two effective dates. The agency properly exercised its responsibility "to pursue a middle course that vitiates neither provision but implements to the fullest possible extent the directives of each."[69]

This controversy not only put the courts in the awkward position of admitting that the law makes no sense, but created confusion within the agency and hardships for firms wanting to know their obligations under the law. While the case remained on the court docket the EPA issued provisional permits to sources that complied with its original regulation. But it informed permit holders that in the event of an adverse court decision, their permits could be revoked even if construction had already begun. The resulting uncertainty impeded corporate planning and increased cynicism among that portion of the public that deals with the EPA.

How Many Sources?

A second problem created by the 1977 amendments was the administrative and technical burdens they placed on control agencies and permit applicants. Under the EPA's previous regulations, state and federal regulators reviewed about 165 permit applications per year. Since the 1974 plan did not include case-by-case determination of BACT, review consisted solely of consideration of modeling evidence for sulfur dioxide and particulate matter, as well a check on compliance with NSPS. The 1977 amendments increased both the number of sources requiring review and the difficulty of each review. The EPA estimated that the number of sources subject to PSD jumped from 165 to 4,000 per year as a result of the amendments. This figure does not even include review of the thousands of small modifications required by a strict reading of the act. The EPA also estimated that requiring the smallest 60 percent of new sources to follow PSD requirements would reduce emissions by only 1 percent. The states claimed they could not possibly take over such an enormous task, whatever the environmental benefits.[70]

69. *Citizens to Save Spencer County* at 859, 864, 862, and 871.
70. 43 Fed. Reg. 26391–92 (1978).

Hesitating to devote its resources to reviewing a large number of small sources, the EPA attempted to reduce its PSD workload. It refused to initiate rulemaking on visibility protection until ordered to do so by the courts. It has done very little to meet the act's deadlines for applying PSD to mobile source pollutants. Most important, the EPA's 1978 regulations attempted to reduce the number and scope of permit applications. The agency established a "two-tier" review process that subjected only the largest facilities to careful scrutiny. At the same time it ruled that modifications do not require PSD permits unless they cross the threshold of 100 tons per year in potential emissions that the act uses to define a "major source." The agency also announced that it would conduct a BACT review only for those pollutants for which the source is "major" under the act—not for all pollutants emitted by a major source. While the EPA could point to little statutory support for these actions, it justified them by claiming that the direct and administrative cost of added control greatly exceeded the resulting environmental benefits.[71]

When environmentalists challenged these shortcuts in the *Alabama Power* case, Judge Harold Leventhal ruled that the "EPA does not have broad authority in this statute to create exemptions on the basis of an analysis of cost-effectiveness."[72] The court ordered the EPA to eliminate its two-tier system, to conduct case-by-case BACT for all those pollutants regulated by the act, and to require permits for all modifications producing a net pollution increase—regardless of the size of this increase.

The *Alabama Power* court did take a major step toward reducing the EPA's administrative burden: it ruled that the EPA's definition of a major source was broader than Congress had intended when it wrote the 1977 amendments. While the court's reading of the legislative history is questionable at best, most EPA officials responsible for implementing PSD consider the court's new definition of a major source a wise policy choice. In fact, the OAQPS and the regional offices originally supported a more restrictive definition, but were overruled by OGC attorneys who argued that such a definition could not survive judicial review. Yet even with the new definition, the *Alabama Power* decision produced a large

---

71. Ibid., 26381.
72. *Alabama Power* v. *Costle*, 606 F.2d 1068 at 1076.

increase in the PSD workload. The EPA must now spend even more time working on permits for smaller sources than it did in 1978.[73]

Monitoring or Modeling?

The third problem posed by the 1977 amendments and the courts' interpretation of them is the most serious. For reasons explained above, the EPA envisioned its original PSD program as an elaborate accounting system based on dispersion modeling and designed to force the states to make conscious decisions about the amount of growth they desired. The EPA did not intend to establish a real-world baseline to which increments would be added to form an area-specific tertiary standard. Nor did it intend to bring enforcement actions against existing sources that complied with permit requirements but contributed to violations of the increment. The 1974 regulations merely required the EPA to prohibit the construction of large sources that, according to EPA predictions, would result in pollution increases greater than the allowable increments.

Congress either rejected or misunderstood this approach. At several key junctures the amendments assume that both the baseline and the increment can be measured by air quality monitors as well as calculated by modeling. Section 165(e)(2) requires PSD permits to include one year's worth of monitoring data "gathered for the purpose of determining whether emission from such facilities will exceed the maximum allowable increases." Section 169(4) defines the "baseline concentration" as

> the ambient concentration levels which exist at the time of the first application for a permit in an area subject to this part, based on air quality data available in the Environmental Protection Agency or a State air pollution control agency and on such monitoring data as the permit applicant is required to submit.

Thus Congress clearly indicated that the EPA must establish a real-world baseline concentration to which it can add the PSD increment to produce an area-specific tertiary standard. Consistent with this understanding of the baseline-plus-increment ceiling, the conference report instructed the EPA and the states to use SIP regulations to rectify any increment violations, regardless of their cause.[74]

---

73. EPA, OAQPS, "Regulatory Impact Assessment for the September 5, 1979 Proposed Regulations for Prevention of Significant Deterioration" (EPA, June 1980), pp. iv–xii.

74. *Clean Air Amendments of 1977*, Conf. Rept. 95-564, 95 Cong. 1 sess. (GPO, 1977), p. 153.

At the same time that Congress was instructing the EPA to set measurable PSD air quality standards, it was requiring it to add and subtract various types of emissions from the air quality levels it discovered through monitoring. Emission increases resulting from some coal conversions would not count toward increment consumption. Emissions from sources receiving PSD permits under the EPA's 1974 regulations would consume increments—even though the baseline concentrations established by the monitoring data collected by the first permit applicant would probably include these emissions. For reasons explained in greater detail in the next chapter, the act also prohibits the EPA from giving a source dispersion modeling credit for stack heights in excess of "good engineering practice." If a source uses such a tall stack, the EPA must charge it with consuming more increment than it does in real life. Thus the EPA cannot simply check its monitors to determine whether a PSD violation has occurred—not just because such monitoring data is highly unreliable, but also because the act itself requires the EPA to combine modeling and monitoring calculations in complicated ways.

The EPA flatly refused to go along with these congressional instructions. In 1978 it announced its intention to revert to its original approach:

> It is apparent that Congress included the monitoring requirements as a means of checking the accuracy of the modeling results. However, in many cases, monitoring data may not provide an adequate "real world" check on the accuracy of modeling as it applies to increment consumption.
>
> As proposed, EPA has decided generally not to require preconstruction or postconstruction ambient monitoring to determine how much of the increment has been used up. . . . In actual practice, assessment of the available increment will normally be accomplished through an accounting procedure whereby atmospheric modeling of individual sources will be used to keep track of changes in actual and allowable emissions as appropriate.[75]

The EPA explained that while it would use monitoring data to calibrate dispersion models, preconstruction monitoring data was practically useless for this endeavor. It therefore relieved permit applicants of this burden, which is not only expensive, but can delay permit approval for well over a year. The EPA similarly ignored the statute's command to establish area-specific baseline dates instead of the uniform baseline date it preferred.[76] In effect the EPA told Congress that its statute made no sense.

The D.C. Circuit did not let the EPA get away with this "remarkable

75. 43 Fed. Reg. 26399 (1978).
76. Ibid., 26400.

assertion of administrative power to revise what Congress has wrought." It ordered the EPA to reinstate the preconstruction monitoring requirement and the variable-date baseline. While conceding that courts should not force agencies to perform clearly irrational actions, the court found a rationale for these sections of the act in their "technology-forcing objective":

> Congress intended that monitoring would impose a certain discipline on the use of modeling techniques, which would be the principal device relied upon for the projection of the impact on air quality of emissions from a regulated source.[77]

While the *Alabama Power* decision led the EPA to monitoring data, it did not succeed in making the agency drink: the EPA still maintains that this information is nearly useless and makes little effort to use it for checking increment consumption.[78] This means that permit applicants must conduct a year's worth of monitoring and the EPA must employ an administratively bewildering variable-date baseline to comply with a section of a law and court order that produces virtually no environmental, economic, or administrative benefits.

If unnecessary cost and delay are currently the biggest problems with the post–*Alabama Power* PSD program, more serious difficulties loom on the horizon. Use of a variable-date baseline means that the emissions of a given source can count toward baseline in some affected areas but consume increment in other areas where the baseline has already been triggered by a permit application. To calculate increment consumption, control agencies must have exact figures on when sources increased their emissions and by what amounts. Firms seldom have exact records on this, and the figures they do have can easily be interpreted in many different ways.

More important, if the courts take monitoring data seriously—as the D.C. Circuit says they must—then both industry and environmental groups can use this highly unreliable information to challenge the EPA's permit decisions, which the EPA still maintains must be made on the basis of modeling calculations alone. Environmentalists can bring enforcement suits under section 304 to shut down sources with PSD permits in areas where monitors show increment violations—even if, as will

77. *Alabama Power* v. *Costle*, 636 F.2d 323 at 372.
78. This becomes clear when one compares the EPA's post–*Alabama Power* statements on modeling, 44 Fed. Reg. 51943–44 (1979) and 45 Fed. Reg. 52723–24 (1980), with the previous statement on the subject, 43 Fed. Reg. 26399–400 (1978).

often happen, such apparent violations result from the natural variability of background pollution concentrations, from measurement error, or from the many categories of emissions not subject to PSD review. Likewise, a source can bring suit against the EPA if monitoring results indicate that the EPA's models are too conservative—even if the models' overprediction results from an unusually low annual background level, from measurement error, or from the use of tall stacks by other sources in the area.

It is still too early to tell how district and local circuit courts of appeal will react to these suits. They could simply dismiss all challenges based on monitoring data. But it is more than likely that many courts—especially those concerned about the burdens federal regulations place on the private sector—will follow the doctrines announced in *Alabama Power* and will use monitoring data to restrict the EPA's discretion in using modeling calculations to set permit requirements. As increments slowly run out, business firms will spend large amounts of money trying to find flaws not just in the EPA's models, but in its application of a modeling-based accounting system to their proposed facilities.

Even before the D.C. Circuit gave renewed legitimacy to a PSD accounting system composed of two sets of books (one based on modeling and one on monitoring), former EPA Deputy Administrator John Quarles warned that "the bookkeeping problems as an increasing number of plants are built may become overwhelming, and it is not hard to visualize extended litigation over the disputes that might arise."[79] With *Alabama Power* the likelihood of "extended litigation" increased significantly. Perhaps it is only fitting that the federal judiciary, which initiated EPA's PSD program in the *Sierra Club* case, will be asked to untangle the resulting regulatory snarl in individual disputes over PSD permits.

Correcting Institutional Failures through Court Action

Even PSD's most enthusiastic supporters admit that the legal reasoning used to justify the 1972 *Sierra Club* decision was weak at best. The District Court relied on a few ambiguous fragments of legislative history to mandate a regulatory program of huge proportion. Some who praise the ruling argue that subsequent congressional action vindicates the courts. This, though, is circular. Congress approved and strengthened PSD in large part because the existence of the EPA's PSD program gave

79. John Quarles, "Federal Regulation of New Industrial Plants" (n.p., 1979), p. 57.

a substantial tactical advantage to its advocates. Other writers, noting this, have advanced a more subtle argument in support of the *Sierra Club* decision. The courts, they claim, intervened to correct an "institutional failure" that prevented Congress from recognizing the importance of wilderness preservation.

There are several variations on this "institutional failure" theme. According to one, without the help of the courts Congress would not have been able to protect unique wilderness areas from despoliation because the politics of congressional coalition building prevent it from demanding that some states—in this case, those in the Rocky Mountains—"forego economic development so that the rest of the country can continue to enjoy the benefits, both actual and psychic, of natural areas preserved in a pristine condition."[80] Others argue that the chief beneficiaries of wilderness preservation are future generations, who are not represented in legislatures. Richard Stewart adds that special solicitude for wilderness preservation can be found "in principles of diversity that underlie the first amendment and the federal structure of our political system."[81] The *Sierra Club* decision, in effect, gave priority to wilderness preservation by shifting the usual burden of political proof, requiring developers to build a majority coalition to defeat PSD rather than forcing environmentalists to construct a coalition to enact it.

If this is what Judge Pratt had in mind (and there is no indication that he did), then his decision produced far more than he expected. The PSD program currently in effect does not apply just to wilderness areas, but to every attainment area in the country. Only one city in the nation (Los Angeles) is a nonattainment area for all pollutants. This means that virtually every major new source in the country must undergo PSD review. PSD has become a scheme for forcing technology, stimulating land use planning, protecting developed areas from economic competition, and reducing atmospheric loading. PSD, in short, is an environmental "Christmas tree" on which supporters of new environmental protection efforts have hung their many experiments.

The *Sierra Club* litigation produced these far-reaching consequences by culminating in a sweeping, categorical judicial order. The courts told the EPA to prevent the "significant deterioration" of *all* clean air—not

---

80. Hines, "A Decade of Nondegradation Policy," p. 654.

81. Stewart, "The Development of Administrative and Quasi-Constitutional Law," p. 750. But see Marc J. Roberts and Richard B. Stewart, "Energy and the Environment," in Henry Owen and Charles L. Schultze, eds., *Setting National Priorities: The Next Ten Years* (Brookings Institution, 1976), pp. 444–45.

just clean air in wilderness areas, and not just to the extent economically reasonable or administratively feasible or environmentally desirable. The EPA tried to moderate the comprehensive nature of the order by introducing a three-class scheme, by limiting review to a few large sources, by allowing states to reclassify areas, and by basing permits on modeling data alone. To increase its plan's chances of surviving subsequent judicial review, though, the EPA presented it as something more than it was: the ambient increment approach seemed to set real, monitorable ceilings on pollution levels, but in actuality did not; the increments chosen by the EPA did not even have any air quality justifications, but were based on land use criteria; the EPA promised to review each reclassification, but did not expect to. These subtleties escaped not just the states and the reviewing court, but most congressmen as well.

The *Sierra Club* decision enhanced the power of already powerful committee members and their staffs. The court ruling provided congressional advocates of PSD with a concrete proposal (which the Republican administration would not otherwise have allowed the EPA to produce), a number of bargaining chips to trade for further environmental restrictions, and a counterintuitive regulatory scheme susceptible to manipulation by those familiar with the confusing details of the program. The PSD section of the 1977 amendments has provoked considerable criticism of Congress—by the courts, the EPA, state officials, and economists as well as the business community. Even the most dedicated environmentalists have conceded that the present law should be amended and simplified. But Congress alone is not to blame for the 1977 amendments. The courts contributed directly to their shortcomings by putting congressional supporters of PSD in a position to ignore cries for restraint.

Even if one accepts the "institutional failure" argument used to justify the *Sierra Club* decision, it is difficult to ignore the corresponding "institutional failures" of the courts. The courts never explained what "significant deterioration" is or why it is worth preventing. Their decisions discouraged the EPA from taking into account the economic effect or administrative feasibility of various regulatory schemes. Court decisions destroyed the veto power of those who opposed PSD by greatly increasing the power of those who sought an expansion of federal regulation. The cumbersome PSD program, which emerged from a surprisingly successful environmental blitzkrieg, now threatens to become the environmental movement's waterloo.

CHAPTER FIVE

Dispersion: Collusion or Contempt?

Dilution is not the solution to pollution.—An old EPA proverb

IN LATE 1973 and early 1974 the Environmental Protection Agency found itself locked in battle with the White House, the Federal Energy Administration (FEA), and the electric utility industry. The EPA insisted that coal-burning power plants comply with the requirements of the Clean Air Act either by switching to low-sulfur fuel or by installing flue gas desulfurization scrubbers, which the EPA considered available technology. The opponents of this policy claimed that scrubbers were unreliable, that the EPA's policy would lead to very high compliance costs, and that it would discourage substitution of American coal for Middle Eastern oil. They recommended that power plants be allowed to meet national air quality standards by dispersing pollutants more widely, rather than by reducing total emissions. Dispersion can be increased either by building taller smokestacks or by varying emissions according to meteorological conditions. The EPA had two objections to substituting these "dispersion enhancement" techniques for controls that reduce total emissions: they are hard to enforce, and they do nothing to reduce the loading of the atmosphere with sulfur compounds that are harmful to human health and contribute to acid rain.

The Muskie and Rogers committees were even more strongly opposed to use of dispersion enhancement techniques than was the EPA, but the 1973 Arab oil embargo put the EPA and these committees on the defensive on energy-versus-environment issues. In late 1973 the House approved an amendment to pending emergency energy legislation (which eventually became the Energy Supply and Environmental Coordination

Act) specifically authorizing use of dispersion enhancement.[1] The Senate refused to agree to this. Before Congress had resolved the issue, the Fifth Circuit Court of Appeals ruled that the EPA could allow polluters to substitute dispersion for emission reductions only when technological controls were "unavailable."[2] The court accepted the argument of the Natural Resources Defense Council (NRDC) that the EPA could not legally approve Georgia's state implementation plan, which authorized polluters to raise their smokestacks to whatever height necessary to prevent violations of national air quality standards.

Although the EPA lost this case, it was far from displeased with the outcome. The agency appealed other sections of the Fifth Circuit's *NRDC* decision to the Supreme Court, but declined to appeal the court's ruling on dispersion. When the administration introduced legislation to overturn the Fifth Circuit's decision, Administrator Russell Train refused to endorse the proposal. He explained that the EPA had gone through "trauma" trying to resolve the dispersion issue, that the agency accepted the Fifth Circuit's resolution of the question, and that it would not support any amendment to its policy of allowing dispersion enhancement only where no adequate technological controls exist.[3]

Officials in the White House, the Department of Commerce, the Federal Energy Administration, and the utility industry suspected that the EPA had colluded with the NRDC in the Fifth Circuit case to gain support for its policy position. Their suspicions grew as the EPA increasingly relied on the decision to justify its refusal to change its policy. But there was little these groups could do to change either the EPA's position or the law. Senator Muskie successfully blocked the administration's legislation on dispersion—as he had done on prevention of significant deterioration (PSD). Eventually the EPA and FEA worked out a compromise that came far closer to the EPA's position than the FEA's. Congress accepted the outlines of this resolution in the 1977 amendments. Thus at a crucial juncture the Fifth Circuit Court tipped the balance of power in the EPA's direction.

The controversy over dispersion, however, did not end there. Despite the fact that several other courts later agreed with the Fifth Circuit, the EPA never fully complied with that court's order. In 1975 the NRDC

1. 88 Stat. 246.

2. *Natural Resources Defense Council* v. *Environmental Protection Agency*, 489 F.2d 390 (5th Cir. 1974).

3. 4 *Environment Reporter—Current Developments* 1927, 2133.

brought a contempt motion against the agency, which scrambled madly to put together stack height regulations and to explain the delay to the court. Clearly concerned about its tenuous legal position, the agency conceded to several of the NRDC's demands.[4] The court grudgingly accepted the complex stack height regulations the agency finally announced.[5] The 1977 amendments required the EPA to make substantial changes in these regulations within the year. The EPA did not announce new rules until 1982—eight years after the *NRDC* decision.[6]

To understand why the EPA had such trouble carrying out a policy it long advocated, it is necessary to appreciate the complexity of the dispersion issue. While the courts treated dispersion as a simple yes-or-no issue—dispersion enhancement versus emission reduction—closer analysis reveals that this is not the case. The term "dispersion enhancement techniques" includes two different approaches to diluting emissions: varying emissions over time and building smokestacks. It is one thing for the EPA to demand that sources install control equipment adequate for meeting national air quality standards under all weather conditions. It is quite another to require them to meet air quality standards without using smokestacks. All stacks disperse pollutants. The key question is *how much* stack height to allow. There is no clear technical way to distinguish a normal stack from a "tall stack." The EPA has struggled for years to maintain its general antidispersion policy while striking a reasonable balance between economic and environmental considerations in its stack height regulations. The courts' failure to comprehend this aspect of the dispersion issue made it difficult for the EPA to confront the stack height problem in a straightforward manner or to design an adequate solution to the problem of atmospheric loading.

The Policy Issues

The authors of the 1970 Clean Air Act rejected a regulatory scheme based on national emissions standards in favor of one based on national

4. 41 Fed. Reg. 7450 (1976).

5. *Natural Resources Defense Council* v. *Environmental Protection Agency,* 529 F.2d 755 (5th Cir. 1976).

6. Section 123 of the new act contains requirements for stack height credit. The EPA proposed regulations under section 123 in 44 Fed. Reg. 2608 (1979) and finally promulgated them in 47 Fed. Reg. 5864 (1982).

air quality standards. The act allowed the states to decide how to meet these standards. But those who wrote the act also realized that control agencies cannot prevent violations of air quality standards merely by taking post hoc enforcement actions against polluters who have contributed to violations of air quality standards. Not only does such enforcement action come too late, but it is nearly impossible to decide which of the many sources located in a nonattainment area contributed to particular violations. Thus the act required the states to establish specific requirements for each source and gave the EPA authority to bring enforcement action against polluters who fail to comply with these rules—whether or not the EPA can show that an air quality violation has occurred.

The legal debate over dispersion centers on section 110(a)(2)(B) of the act, which specified that state implementation plans (SIPs) must include enforceable "emission limitations, schedules, and timetables for compliance with such limitations, and such other measures as may be necessary to insure attainment and maintenance of such primary or secondary standards." The 1970 act failed to define either "emission limitations" or "other measures." Environmental groups as well as Senator Muskie and Representative Rogers read "limitations" to mean "performance standards requiring constant emission reductions." Their opponents argued that the use of the word "limitations" rather than "emission standards" emphasized Congress's desire to give the states maximum flexibility in designing control programs to meet air quality standards. The various participants in the dispersion controversy did not arrive at their conflicting positions by consulting different dictionaries. Behind the semantic debates lay a variety of policy considerations.

The Techniques of Dispersion

As mentioned above, there are two types of dispersion enhancement techniques: stack height increases (called "tall stacks" by their detractors); and what has become known as intermittent control systems (ICS). While ICS usually requires building taller stacks, stack height increases can enhance dispersion without use of ICS.

Sources using ICS vary their pollution emissions according to the assimilative capacity of the ambient air. ICS reduces emissions during periods of atmospheric inversion or unfavorable wind conditions by temporary shutdown, by reducing production at certain plants while increasing production at others (load shifting), or by using cleaner inputs (fuel switching). ICS rests on conditional emission limitations, that is, no more than x amount of pollution can be released under y conditions. While ICS can reduce total emissions, this is not always the case. Sources can increase production during good weather to make up for losses during bad weather. Most sources using ICS curtail operation on only a few days each year. For them it is cheaper to sacrifice a small amount of productive capacity than to install control equipment to prevent ambient violations on the few days of the year with unfavorable weather conditions.[7]

Long before the existence of air pollution control agencies most sources used smokestacks to protect workers and neighbors from the ill effects of high ground-level pollutant concentrations. In general, the taller the stack, the greater the area over which pollution is dispersed and the lower the ambient concentrations surrounding the plant. Since almost no source can meet the national standards without stacks, control agencies ordinarily take into account the height of a source's stack when performing dispersion modeling and writing emission limitations. Every emission limitation designed to ensure attainment of ambient air quality standards includes an assumption about stack height.

Environmentalists did not object to the practice of building smoke-stacks or even to the practice of giving dispersion-modeling credit for existing stack height. Rather they opposed allowing polluters to increase their stack height in order to receive so much dispersion-modeling credit that no further controls would be necessary. They expected the EPA to approve credit for normal stacks, but not for "tall stacks." But how does one draw a line between the two? One way is to deny modeling credit for any stack height increase begun after passage of the act. Unfortunately, this proposal would not only make pollution control requirements dependent on the accident of previous stack height, but would also provide no guidance on allowable stack height for new sources.

For years British air pollution control officials have advocated use of ICS and huge smokestacks. American public health officials, though, have generally argued that a control strategy appropriate for a small

7. The discussion of ICS in this chapter relies heavily on National Academy of Sciences, *Air Quality and Stationary Source Emission Control* (Government Printing Office, 1973); EPA, "Staff Paper, Intermittent Control Systems," prepared by Monitoring and Data Analysis Division, OAQPS, April 1973; the many comments submitted on the EPA's ICS regulations; and EPA, "Position Paper on Regulation of Atmospheric Sulfates" (Office of Air and Waste Management, September 1975).

island would have deleterious consequences in the United States. Britain can ignore Scandinavia's claims that it is exporting pollution more easily than federal regulation can ignore New Hampshire's claim that Ohio's emissions are destroying Granite State lakes. While EPA officials and their predecessors in the National Air Pollution Control Administration opposed wholesale reliance on dispersion, they viewed dispersion techniques as useful tools for meeting environmental goals not easily achieved in other ways. As they learned more about the air pollution problem of various states, they began to appreciate the advantages and disadvantages of dispersion techniques.

The Advantages of Dispersion Enhancement

The most obvious advantage of allowing sources to use dispersion enhancement to meet national ambient air quality standards is lower cost. The Tennessee Valley Authority, for example, estimated that using ICS would cost less than one-tenth as much as installing scrubbers.[8] This made dispersion enhancement popular not just with industry but with public utility commissions who did not want to pass large cost increases along to electricity consumers. While the EPA believed that most major utilities could afford scrubbers at their largest plants, it did not insist that small plants, especially those in rural areas or those scheduled for retirement, install this expensive, controversial technology. Moreover the EPA conceded that nonferrous smelters could not afford to install all necessary technological controls. Dispersion gave the EPA a method for meeting national standards without forcing industrial closures, thus maintaining the "health at any cost" theme of the Clean Air Act without inviting political backlash.

Dispersion also gave control agencies flexibility to deal with the shortage of low-sulfur fuel. Scrubbers take years to design and install. Some older plants simply cannot accommodate scrubbers. Consequently, meeting national standards in the short run requires burning low-sulfur fossil fuels. Even before the oil embargo the EPA recognized that aggregate demand for such fuel would exceed short-run supply. In its 1973 "clean fuels policy" the EPA tried to convince some states to relax their sulfur-in-fuel requirements in order to provide more low-sulfur fuel for use in

8. Testimony of Aubrey Wagner, chairman, Board of Directors, TVA, in *Clean Air Act Oversight*, Hearing before the Subcommittee on Environmental Pollution of the Senate Committee on Public Works, 93 Cong. 2 Sess. (GPO, 1974), pp. 7–8.

areas exceeding primary standards.[9] After the oil embargo the EPA searched frantically for ways to meet national standards with even less low-sulfur fuel. By encouraging states to allow greater use of dispersion in rural areas the EPA could release clean fuels for urban areas; by allowing taller stacks in urban areas it would decrease health risks in the population centers. This allowed the EPA to counter claims that the energy crisis required relaxation of the requirements of the Clean Air Act.

Third, strict limits on the use of dispersion can create serious inequities and produce irrational siting decisions. Many sources constructed before passage of the 1970 act either located on sites with poor natural dispersion characteristics or failed to build their smokestacks tall enough to escape the wind currents caused by the building. The plumes of sources located in river valleys or near high terrain often hit nearby hills, producing highly localized air quality standard violations. Similarly, the plumes of sources constructed with especially short stacks are drawn back toward the source, again causing localized air quality violations. An absolute prohibition on modeling credit for stack height increases would impose very stringent control requirements on sources with poor locations or short stacks. Arguing that the purpose of a smokestack is to prevent high pollutant concentrations in the immediate vicinity of a plant, the EPA's engineers advocated stack height increases sufficient to counteract the vagaries of local terrain and wind currents.

Imposing strict stack height limits can have unfortunate consequences for new sources as well. In the absence of environmental controls, sources often choose to locate in river valleys, near transportation lines. When forced to meet ambient standards such sources would prefer to build stacks tall enough to get their plumes out of the valley. If control agencies were to impose strict stack height limits, a source might reduce its total emissions. But it might satisfy the letter of the law by either (a) moving to the top of a nearby hill, thus increasing its transportation-related costs and emissions, or (b) building two or more geographically dispersed plants rather than one larger one—again increasing both total cost and total pollution. Thus, while in some circumstances stack height restrictions give new sources incentives to reduce their emissions, in other circumstances they can have just the opposite effect.

9. For a description of the EPA's clean fuels policy and the states' response to it, see *Coal Policy Issues*, Hearings before the Senate Committee on Interior and Insular Affairs, 93 Cong. 1 sess. (GPO, 1973), pp. 206–09, 232–45. Chap. 6 provides further discussion of the clean fuels policy.

The Disadvantages of Dispersion Enhancement

Dispersion, Senator Muskie often proclaimed, is the "rhythm method of pollution control."[10] ICS creates serious enforcement problems, only some of which have been cured in recent years. To prevent violation of air quality standards on days with bad weather, sources must both accurately predict when violations will occur and quickly adjust emissions. Weather prediction is a highly inexact science. It is difficult for control agencies to decide whether the prediction system designed by the source is adequate to prevent violations rather than just to reduce emissions after violations occur. While smelters and utilities have improved systems for predicting violations and automatically cutting back production, making sure that these systems are operating properly puts a heavy burden on enforcement officials.

The enforcement question, it is important to note, relates only to ICS, not stack height increases. An emission limitation for a source with a tall stack may be less stringent than one for a source with a shorter stack, but it is no less enforceable.

Use of dispersion enhancement techniques also creates equity problems. Tall stacks can send pollution to other states, increasing their pollution levels and decreasing their room for growth. Even if the pollution in question stays in the same state it can reduce the pollution rights available to new sources. This can be a special problem when sources consume the tiny increments allowed Class I areas under PSD regulation.

The most important disadvantage is that reliance on dispersion rather than emission reduction adds to the problem of atmospheric loading. While ICS and taller stacks reduce local pollutant concentrations, they allow sources to avoid measures aimed at reducing sulfate concentration or combating acid rain. Sulfur dioxide by itself may not pose a major threat to human health, but it becomes particularly dangerous when combined with other pollutants. The longer sulfur dioxide resides in the atmosphere, the more it combines with other pollutants and the more dangerous it becomes. Thus, in the words of the House Commerce Committee:

10. A Legislative History of the Energy Supply and Environmental Coordination Act of 1974, prepared for the Senate Committee on Public Works, 94 Cong. 2 sess. (GPO, 1976), p. 616 (hereafter referred to as Legislative History of ESECA).

In conjunction with tall stacks, ICS may thus increase the health risks associated with SO_2 and NO_x emissions. . . . If SO_2 and NO_x emissions are merely dispersed by tall stacks and intermittent controls and are not reduced, these emissions will be converted to acid rain in significant amounts.[11]

However, if polluters are required to install pollution reduction devices adequate to meet national standards even on those days when the weather is especially bad, both local ambient concentrations and the amount of sulfur dioxide transported to other areas would be reduced. Environmentalists have sought to minimize use of dispersion in order to maximize total emission reduction.

The Policy Trade-offs

To follow the controversy over the dispersion issue, it is important to keep in mind several points. The first has already been mentioned but bears repeating: since all sources use stacks, all use dispersion. While it is possible to ban the use of ICS, it is for all practical purposes impossible to deny dispersion-modeling credit for all stack height. Defining allowable stack height requires deciding how much dispersion to allow.

Second, in making this decision, control agencies must consider not one environmental goal, but two. The EPA noted this in a 1974 statement of its strategy for control of sulfur oxides:

The sulfur oxides control strategy is oriented toward two basic objectives: (1) to *attain the current primary ambient air quality standards* for sulfur dioxide as rapidly as possible and (2) where additional control measures are required on existing sources, to ensure that as rapidly as possible those measures *reduce overall levels of sulfur oxide emissions.*[12]

These two goals are incommensurable. While scientists can say that derivatives of sulfur dioxide are dangerous, they cannot offer a quantitative comparison with the health risks associated with high levels of sulfur dioxide itself. For this reason, the EPA has set its goal as *attaining* national standards but only "minimizing increases in SO_2 and other sulfate precursors."[13]

Third, in practice these two environmental goals can conflict. Reducing total emissions, of course, reduces both loading and local ambient

11. *Clean Air Act Amendments of 1977,* H. Rept. 95-294, 95 Cong. 1 sess. (GPO, 1977), pp. 83, 85.
12. EPA, "National Strategy for Control of Sulfur Oxides from Electric Power Plants" (July 10, 1974), p. 15 (emphasis added).
13. EPA, "Position Paper on Atmospheric Sulfates," p. 74.

concentrations. But when control agencies can force no more emission reductions, they can often achieve national standards by giving sources incentives to make greater use of dispersion. This means giving them dispersion credit that will concomitantly allow them to increase their total emissions. Those who want to protect the citizens of Chicago or Cleveland from dangerously high local pollution concentrations will favor immediate stack height increases. Those whose primary concern is saving lakes from acidification, or protecting downwind communities, or increasing the long-run impetus for technology forcing may be more willing to allow the citizens of Chicago and Cleveland to live with existing pollution levels. Thus dispersion of pollution from given sources raises many of the same dilemmas as do efforts to disperse the polluting sources themselves (see chapter 4).

Fourth, limiting use of dispersion is an indirect and sometimes ineffective method for limiting total emissions. Control agencies must draw artificial lines between acceptable and unacceptable uses of dispersion. In drawing these lines they seldom have adequate information on the aggregate impact of their rulings. Moreover, these regulations invite circumvention. Sources may locate at the top of hills to make use of natural increases in stack height. Or they may disperse pollution more widely by building a greater number of smaller, less efficient, more heavily polluting sources. Stringent stack height limits on new sources may discourage firms from retiring older, dirtier plants, which are often immune from serious enforcement. In short, reducing atmospheric loading by manipulating rules on the use of dispersion is an extremely tricky business.

It is doubtful that the Fifth Circuit or the other courts ruling on the legality of dispersion enhancement ever considered these policy complexities. If they did, they refused to indicate it in their opinions. But the EPA was well aware of them. In fact, the EPA often seemed paralyzed by its recognition of this complexity. It did not formulate a policy on either ICS or stack height until the NRDC and the courts forced its hand.

The Administrative and Political Context

When the EPA issued guidance to the states on preparing SIPs in late 1971 and early 1972, it neither condoned nor rejected the use of ICS or stack height increases for meeting national standards. In 1972 oversight hearings both the Rogers and Muskie subcommittees informed Administrator William Ruckelshaus that they had never intended the EPA to allow polluters to use dispersion enhancement techniques. When Ruckelshaus testified that he would approve ICS if he found it enforceable, Senator Muskie threatened to introduce legislation making clear Congress's intent on the matter.[14] Yet he never did so. From early 1972 until the oil embargo of October 1973, the dispute over dispersion remained within the administrative arena.

The Evolution of the EPA's Policy

Several congressmen and most environmental groups attributed the EPA's original position on dispersion to White House pressure. Such conspiracy theories, however, exaggerate the extent to which the EPA even formulated a policy on the issue. Most EPA officials greeted with skepticism proposals for dispersion enhancement offered by industry and the states. One agency lawyer claimed that the arguments for opposing "tall stacks" are "so compelling that this should be the Agency's position regardless of consequences." Similarly, the head of the EPA's air pollution enforcement unit opposed ICS as "unenforceable because it is too complex and unmanageable."[15] Yet neither Administrator Ruckelshaus nor the Office of Air Quality Planning and Standards (OAQPS) wanted to rule out these options altogether.

The EPA's dispersion "policy" was little more than a series of ad hoc responses to individual requests for advice. Nothing makes this clearer than the agency's actions of May 1972. In approving and disapproving the SIPs submitted by the states, the EPA took two potentially inconsistent positions, both of which were later challenged in court. First, the agency rejected Nevada's plan for using ICS at a Kennecott Copper Company

14. *Implementation of the Clean Air Act Amendments of 1970,* Hearings before the Subcommittee on Air and Water Pollution of the Senate Committee on Public Works, 92 Cong. 2 sess. (GPO, 1972), pp. 245, 269–71, 305–11; *Clean Air Act Oversight,* Hearings before the Subcommittee on Public Health and the Environment of the House Committee on Interstate and Foreign Commerce, 92 Cong. 1 and 2 sess. (GPO, 1972), pp. 529–31; and 4 *Environment Reporter—Current Developments* 1797.

15. Memorandum, Robert Baum (OGC) to John Quarles, April 18, 1972; Memorandum, William Megonnell (Office of Enforcement) to Don Goodwin (OAQPS), "Enforceability of Intermittent Control Systems," April 21, 1972, reprinted in *Legislative History of ESECA,* p. 164.

smelter, explaining that curtailment of operations "is not considered an acceptable substitute for permanent control systems."[16] Second, it approved a Georgia regulation that made sulfur dioxide and particulate emission limitations dependent on stack height—without putting any limits on the height of stack extensions. Georgia announced its intention to allow polluters to install taller stacks rather than experiment with "uncertain SO_2 removal equipment."[17]

One need not look far to discover an explanation for these divergent decisions. ICS was a hot political potato, opposed by EPA enforcement officials as well as key congressmen. The ICS sections of the state plans received adverse publicity and were disapproved to give the EPA more time to devise a consensus position. Stack height, however, was not yet a controversial issue. When the junior engineers who reviewed the state submissions looked at the plans that allowed stack height extensions, they saw that they were adequate for meeting the national ambient air quality standards. In their rush to meet the deadlines of the act, these reviewers tried to avoid raising complex policy questions. The best way to avoid controversy was to treat stack height extensions as just another control technique and to approve the plans. No one paid much attention to stack height regulations—except the NRDC, which in June 1972 filed suit against the EPA for allowing Georgia to give unlimited stack height credit.

The EPA's dispersion policy crystallized slowly in subsequent months. Few EPA officials doubted that smelters could not afford requisite control equipment. The growing gap between aggregate demand and supply of low-sulfur fuels added urgency to the search for an alternative to shutting down noncomplying facilities. Administrator Ruckelshaus ordered the OAQPS to undertake a new analysis of ICS. In April 1973 that office issued a lengthy report that announced:

> The EPA position on ICS is being reevaluated because (a) reliable systems are now being demonstrated and (b) constant control technology may not be available for meeting air quality standards, or may be much more costly than ICS, especially for short-term standards.[18]

The OAQPS recommended allowing ICS for isolated sources with high control costs. This reflected the OAQPS's general approach of insisting only that sources install "reasonably available control technology."

16. 37 Fed. Reg. 10845 (1972); and 37 Fed. Reg. 15095 (1972).
17. Georgia state implementation plan, p. 151, quoted in the NRDC's brief to the Fifth Circuit, p. 28.
18. EPA, "Staff Paper, Intermittent Control Systems," p. 2.

Administrator Ruckelshaus provisionally approved the OAQPS strategy and requested it to draft more specific regulations. This proved to be a difficult task, requiring the OAQPS to specify what types of controls are "available" and which sources are "isolated." Its job was complicated by the continuing hostility of the enforcement office, which objected to the additional burdens ICS could put on it and feared that the OAQPS would accept industry's definition of "available technology." This difference of opinion persisted for years.

While the OAQPS was writing ICS guidelines, the EPA began to take a closer look at the stack height issue. Much of the pressure for this reevaluation came from the NRDC's suit on the Georgia SIP. On May 7, two days before the hearing before the Fifth Circuit, the EPA's Region IV administrator wrote to Governor Jimmy Carter stating:

> Further analysis by the Environmental Protection Agency has shown that the control strategy for attainment and maintenance of standards allows the application of regulations ... which permit unrestricted increases in stack height through[out] the State as a means of compliance. It is the determination of the Environmental Protection Agency that these regulations are not valid control techniques under Section 110(a)(2)(B) of the Clean Air Act.[19]

As the NRDC later pointed out, this letter did not define a stack height policy, but simply prevented Georgia from making use of unrestricted stack height.

While the NRDC accused the EPA of sending this letter simply to moot the Fifth Circuit case, the letter reflected the agency's indecision on the dispersion issue. The EPA generally opposed substituting dispersion enhancement for emission reduction, but could not decide exactly how much pollution reduction was politically, economically, or technically feasible. To make matters worse, the EPA could not announce a stack height policy until it came to a decision on the related ICS regulations.

In September 1973 the EPA finally proposed ICS and stack height regulations. The regulations allowed use of intermittent controls only when "the sole alternatives are either permanent production curtailment or delay of an attainment date for the national standards," and where ICS "will exhibit a high degree of reliability and can be made legally enforceable."[20] While the regulations limited ICS to sulfur dioxide and prohibited its use by power plants burning oil, they left determination of what constitutes "available technology" and "a source sufficiently isolated from others" to be made on a case-by-case basis. The agency

19. Quoted in *NRDC v. EPA*, 489 F.2d 390 at 404.
20. 38 Fed. Reg. 25698 (1973).

estimated that most nonferrous smelters and about fifty coal-fired power plants would qualify. But the NRDC warned that the EPA "has placed itself on the slippery slope, with no clear way of drawing a line between a source where [ICS] is acceptable and where it is not."[21]

Almost as an afterthought, the EPA's proposal announced that the agency would not just allow, but would actively encourage, polluters to increase their stacks to "good engineering practice" height. A sentence that later became highly controversial defined good engineering practice as stack height "sufficiently tall that emissions from the stack are not significantly affected by the atmospheric downwash, eddies, or wakes created by the facility or nearby structures and terrain." For level terrain good engineering practice would be approximately two and one-half times the height of the facility itself and "nearby obstructions." However, "for more complex situations, this rule-of-thumb is too simplistic, and detailed engineering and meteorological investigations of the proposed site should be conducted to determine the appropriate stack height."[22] The EPA would give credit for extension of stack height above good engineering practice only as part of an approved ICS plan.

The stack height section of the regulations was entirely the work of the OAQPS. It had transformed a rough engineering understanding of the *minimum* stack height necessary to prevent localized standard violations into a *maximum* limit on stack height credit. While the Fifth Circuit rejected this approach to limiting stack height, the OAQPS clung to it for years. The slippery concept was the central element of controversy in the NRDC's contempt suit against the EPA.

The Political Standoff

In 1972 the dispersion controversy focused primarily on questions of enforcement and cost. By late 1973 it had become an energy issue. Rapidly rising oil prices eliminated the quick and inexpensive expedient of lowering pollution levels by converting utilities from coal to oil. Government officials seeking to reduce American dependence on foreign oil and utilities seeking a cheaper, more reliable source of fuels urged that sources currently burning oil be allowed (or forced) to convert back to coal. The EPA opposed granting any concessions that might tempt

21. NRDC, "Comments on Proposed Rules Regarding Use of Supplementary Control Systems" (February 14, 1974), pp. 19–20.
22. 38 Fed. Reg. 25700 (1973).

utilities to believe that scrubbing was not inevitable. At the same time the Nixon administration and the FEA saw the oil embargo both as a crisis requiring a forceful response and as an opportunity to revise environmental legislation they viewed as harmful to the economic health of the country.

The political struggle over dispersion climaxed in late 1973 and early 1974 as Congress considered President Nixon's emergency energy bill, which eventually became the Energy Supply and Environmental Coordination Act. Congress's consideration of the bill was fiercely partisan; and the Democratic Congress made so many changes in the original bill that Nixon vetoed it. The next spring, with the sense of crisis waning, a compromise bill that failed to address many key issues finally received the support of the president and both houses of Congress. The lack of political agreement on the dispersion issue was painfully obvious in those sections of the act that amended the Clean Air Act.

Under the leadership of William Simon, the FEA pushed hard for full acceptance of intermittent control systems by Congress and the EPA. When Congress considered the first administration bill, the FEA backed an attempt to allow sources to use *any* means to meet national standards. The House Commerce Committee took a cautious position, allowing coal-burning sources to use ICS for up to six years and asking the EPA to prepare a report on the effectiveness of ICS. The committee recognized "the possibility that the Act's objectives can be achieved through measures other than fuel regulation and constant emission limitations," but thought that the consequences of their use "must be thoroughly explored before they are relied upon as ultimate compliance strategies."[23]

A floor amendment introduced by Representative John Murphy of New York at the urging of the FEA knocked the House off the fence built by the committee. The amendment specified that coal-burning power plants need not comply with applicable "stationary source fuel or emission limitations," but only with "national primary ambient air quality standards." After the House accepted the amendment by voice vote, Murphy claimed these words "say we will permit intermittent or alternative types of mechanisms on our powerplants." This led ICS opponents to offer a further amendment to make the Murphy amendment effective for only six years. The House rejected this, again by voice vote. Thus the House seemed to indicate its support for ICS.[24]

23. *Legislative History of ESECA*, p. 1544.
24. Ibid., pp. 1803, 2088.

The bill passed by the Senate, in contrast, allowed short-term use of ICS, but required sources converting to coal to commit themselves to eventual use of constant controls. The bill also stated that in approving plan revisions relating to fossil fuel the administrator must insist upon the use of "continuous emission reduction measures."[25]

The first conference committee tried to sidestep the controversy. Noting the difference between the two houses, the conference report stated:

> The conference agreement does not include either of the foregoing broad provisions. Instead, the conferees decided to limit the application of this provision to those sources which convert to combustion of coal as a result of the energy emergency.

The committee asked the EPA to prepare a report on sulfur dioxide controls, explaining:

> The Congress intends to review the long term energy problems and environmental needs during the next two years and will consider such relief as may be justified to alleviate the problems presented to facilities, including power plants, which are scheduled to be phased out.[26]

Thus Congress did all it could to avoid making a decision on ICS. The second conference report reflected a similar reluctance to state a permanent policy. As the NRDC's chief litigator later commented, the Energy Supply and Environmental Coordination Act "reflected, rather than resolved, the tense confrontation on the dispersion issue."[27]

While the House and Senate were agreeing to disagree, the EPA was resisting White House and FEA pressure to support legislation explicitly authorizing use of ICS. The confrontation between the EPA and the administration reached its peak in February and March of 1974. EPA Administrator Train refused to accede to President Nixon's request to support the FEA's proposed amendments. Train transmitted to Congress the FEA's proposals to allow use of ICS and to eliminate PSD, but

25. Ibid., pp. 1220, 2660–62.
26. Ibid., pp. 1225, 1227.
27. Richard E. Ayres, "Enforcement of Air Pollution Controls on Stationary Sources under the Clean Air Amendments of 1970," 4 *Ecology Law Quarterly* 441 at 459 (1975). He notes that the conference report was "artfully opaque" (p. 451), but attributes this to the committee's desire "to mollify Congressman Murphy and his supporters" rather than to its desire to sidestep the issue. This constitutes rather tenuous support for the NRDC's claim that Congress "continued" to oppose permanent use of ICS. The only difference between the final conference report and the earlier report was that it emphasized that the EPA must find ICS enforceable before authorizing its use. *Legislative History of ESECA*, pp. 125–35, 158–95.

labeled them "legislative language which would implement the views of other federal agencies." He pointedly refused to endorse them. Train later told the press that he had scored a "great and glorious victory" in resisting White House pressure.[28] Many of the participants in the controversy agree that President Nixon was greatly displeased with the EPA's failure to cooperate with the FEA, but could not afford to fire a man of Train's stature so soon after the preceding fall's "Saturday night massacre." The decision not to accept these amendments represented a turning point for the EPA's political executives. They chose to throw in their lot with Senator Muskie rather than with the administration.[29] The decision announced by the Fifth Circuit in February 1974 both strengthened the EPA's resolve to resist pressure from the White House and eventually played a crucial role in the resolution of the political stalemate.

The Litigation

The dispersion cases provide graphic support for the proposition that how and when a case comes to court can profoundly affect the substantive disposition of the issue before the court. The EPA realized as early as 1972 that either environmentalists or industry would eventually challenge the agency's policy on dispersion. As the EPA moved toward allowing ICS in a few narrowly defined circumstances, the Office of General Counsel (OGC) warned that the agency was treading on soft legal ground and that its chance of success in court might well depend on which court heard the first case.

The OGC's biggest worry was that industry would convince a court that ICS and state regulations based on stack height extensions constitute legal "emission limitations." By admitting that ICS can be enforceable in some circumstances, the EPA forfeited a major argument against its widespread use. The OGC expected that the most important argument against ICS—that it would increase atmospheric loading—would carry little weight in court since the Clean Air Act assumes that the national standards are sufficient to protect the public health and welfare.

The EPA knew that environmentalists would argue that the consid-

28. 4 *Environment Reporter—Current Developments* 1927.

29. Robert Sansom gives an insider's view of this struggle in *The New American Dream Machine: Toward a Simpler Lifestyle in an Environmental Age* (Doubleday, 1976), pp. 42–49.

eration of costs implicit in the EPA policy on ICS ran counter to the spirit of the 1970 act. The OGC warned that the D.C. Circuit, which had recently upheld the *Sierra Club* decision on PSD, might limit use of ICS to those cases where constant controls are technologically infeasible, not just extremely expensive. Consequently, the OGC hoped to get a test case where shutdown was the only alternative to use of ICS, "as opposed, for example, to a suit in the D.C. Court of Appeals solely on the legal questions without a specific factual situation to assess."[30] Most judges would hesitate to shut down a plant on the basis of an ambiguous provision of the act, and focused litigation would inhibit them from insisting on a rigid definition of the word "necessary" in section 110.

The first dispersion case to reach court was a mixed bag for the EPA—but a gold mine for the NRDC. In June 1972, long before the EPA had a coherent policy on dispersion, the NRDC brought suit against the EPA for approving the Georgia SIP. It chose to focus on the stack height provisions of that SIP in part because the Fifth Circuit had in the past looked favorably on environmentalists' suits, but primarily because the plan was so extreme and so explicit. Georgia encouraged sources to build taller stacks to avoid *any* emission reduction.

If the NRDC had brought a more typical case, one in which the SIP combined emission reduction with dispersion enhancement, it would have been harder for environmentalists to present dispersion as a yes-or-no question susceptible to judicial resolution. A court forced to decide how much stack height or how much use of ICS to allow would most likely show more deference to the agency than one asked to decide whether unlimited use of dispersion is acceptable under the act. Moreover, the fact that the EPA had approved the Georgia plan called into question its commitment to environmental protection. Thus, while the first challenge to the EPA came not in the forum it most feared, the D.C. Circuit, and did not involve the most controversial form of dispersion enhancement, ICS, it did pose a serious problem for the agency.

The NRDC Decision

In its 1974 opinion the Fifth Circuit seemed impressed by the NRDC's argument that the EPA was failing to address a significant environmental problem. Yet while the NRDC's brief stressed the policy arguments

---

30. Memorandum, Robert Baum (OGC) to Robert Sansom, April 13, 1973.

against unlimited use of dispersion, the court rested its decision on an analysis of the intrinsic meaning of the word "limitation," on the legislative history of the 1970 act, and on the recent *Sierra Club* decision.

This does not mean that policy considerations did not loom large in the judges' minds. In its subsequent response to the NRDC's contempt motion, the court quoted approvingly the following section of a law review article written by the NRDC's attorney:

> With respect to human health, the scientific community increasingly agrees that damage is related more clearly to the levels of acid sulfates than to concentrations of sulfur dioxide. . . . Thus any system that does not reduce total sulfur dioxide emissions (as well as emission of particulates) will be unavailing to protect the public health.[31]

Nonetheless, in failing to explain explicitly why dispersion is bad, the court's first opinion failed to give the agency useful guidance on how to distinguish acceptable from impermissible dispersion or tall from normal stacks.

The court's first legal argument was that Congress meant "emission limitations" to mean "emission standards," and that neither ICS nor stack height increases are standards. To substantiate this, the court argued that the establishment of national emission standards for new sources and for sources of hazardous emissions reveals "a general preference on the part of Congress for emission standards."[32] This turns on its head the obvious implication of the use of the terms "limitation" in section 110 and "standards" in sections 111 and 112. The purpose of section 110 is to assure that national *ambient* standards are met. The statute gave states maximum flexibility in this area, rejecting a regulatory system based on national emission standards. Sections 111 and 112 carve out exceptions to this broad grant of authority to the states. Several sections of the act—even ones cited by the court—pointedly refer to enforcement of "an emission standard or limitation," further indicating that the two are not identical.[33]

The court's second major argument was that "use of dispersion techniques is at odds with the non-degradation policy" established in

31. *NRDC v. EPA*, 529 F.2d 755 at 756, note 4 (quoting Ayres, "Enforcement of Air Pollution Controls").

32. *NRDC v. EPA*, 489 F.2d 390 at 406.

33. For a clear explanation of Congress's rejection of the uniform standard approach, see the statement of Senator Howard H. Baker, Jr. (the ranking member of the Muskie subcommittee), *Implementation of the Clean Air Act Amendments of 1970*, Hearings, pp. 270–75. This issue is discussed at length in chap. 2.

the *Sierra Club* decision. The court not only accepted without question the highly dubious legal argument of that decision, but asserted without explanation that dispersion enhancement is incompatible with nondegradation. As in the *Sierra Club* decision, the deciding court failed either to present a convincing legal argument or to spell out the advantages of requiring costly controls not necessary simply for meeting national air quality standards.

The court's instructions to the EPA were as perfunctory as its explanation for its rejection of the agency's dispersion policy. The court prohibited the EPA from permitting sources to use dispersion enhancement except when technological controls are "unavailable or infeasible." The court further explained:

> Where a state plan includes both emission limitations and dispersion enhancement controls, a reviewing court must scrutinize the emission limitations included in the plan to determine the relative degrees of reliance the state plan places upon emission limitation and dispersion enhancement.... The objective should be to determine whether the reliance placed upon emission limitation is as great as possible.[34]

Thus the court insisted on a strict reading of both "limitation" and "necessary" in its interpretation of section 110.

Applying this interpretation to the Georgia SIP, the court ruled that the EPA could condone stack height increases

> only (1) if it is demonstrated that emission limitation regulations included in the plan are sufficient *standing alone*, without the dispersion strategy, to attain the standards; or (2) if it is demonstrated that emission limitation sufficient to meet the standard is unachievable or infeasible, and that the state has adopted regulations which will attain the maximum degree of emission limitation achievable.[35]

The court remanded the case to the EPA with instructions to file promptly with the court a report on whether the Georgia plan complied with either of these two conditions. If the administrator were to find the SIP inadequate, the court would "consider issuing further guidelines in accordance with this opinion to govern the process of preparing and publishing substitute regulation" for Georgia.

At first glance the court ruling seems consistent with the EPA's preexisting dispersion policy. The only apparent divergence was the strict reading of "necessary." While the EPA wanted to allow ICS in cases

34. *NRDC v. EPA*, 489 F.2d 390 at 410, note 50.
35. Ibid. at 410.

where technological controls are available but very expensive, the court seemed to limit use of dispersion enhancement to instances of technological infeasibility.

Yet in deciding whether the case before it was moot, the court clearly indicated its dissatisfaction with the EPA's September 1973 rules on stack height:

> The regulations permit the use of stack height increases up to the point consistent with good engineering practice as a control strategy. And they permit the use of unrestricted stack height increases in prescribed circumstances for large, isolated sources. They do not reject the idea of a tall stack control strategy; and they certainly do not reject the more general idea of a dispersion enhancement strategy. Implicit in the Agency's statement that the regulations are faulty because they "permi[t] unrestricted stack height increases through[out] the state" is the message that the Agency would approve a more limited use of a tall stack strategy; and the proposed regulations make it clearer that this was and is the Agency's position. Thus, the EPA's position is still considerably at odds with the position taken by the petitioners.[36]

By ruling that the controversy was still a live one, the court implied that the general policy expressed in these regulations was inconsistent with its decision.

What precisely did the court find objectionable about these regulations? That they allowed increases up to "good engineering practice"? That they allowed stacks taller than good engineering practice where the court found constant controls "available"? Or that the court did not want to allow *any* stack height credit for sources not applying all feasible constant controls? When the NRDC first filed its brief, it gave no explanation of what it expected the EPA or the court to do besides disapprove Georgia's unlimited stack height policy. By 1975 the NRDC had developed a more specific position: existing sources should receive credit for stack height increases only if they apply all technologically feasible controls and if all other sources in the area have also applied such controls; new sources should be allowed credit up to the median stack height for existing sources in that industry in 1970.[37] Not only did the court never mention this proposal in its first decision, but it is doubtful that the NRDC had even formulated it at the time. The court thus failed to explain how the EPA could cure its regulations.

36. Ibid. at 405 (brackets in the original).
37. NRDC, "Language for a Regulation Concerning the Use of Dispersion Enhancement Measures Pursuant to the Clean Air Act," submitted to the Fifth Circuit during the second round of litigation.

The court's weak argument for limiting the use of dispersion and its vague instructions to the EPA indicated that it had not thought out the implication of its general position. As a result, the NRDC and EPA spent years arguing about what the decision really meant. The EPA wanted to avoid an absurd "no stacks" interpretation as well as the interpretation suggested by the NRDC. It kept coming back to the "good engineering practice" approach, which the court had apparently rejected. This led the NRDC to charge that the agency had violated the court's original command.

The Industry Suits

The EPA had a number of reasons for declining to appeal the awkward *NRDC* decision. The most significant reasons were political and are discussed in detail below. But the EPA also saw the Fifth Circuit's decision as a precedent it could employ to fend off pending industry challenges to its ICS policy. The EPA faced suits by the utility and nonferrous smelting industries calling for a relaxation of its restrictions on ICS. The facts of these two cases, *Big Rivers Electric Corp.* v. *Environmental Protection Agency* and *Kennecott Copper Corp.* v. *Train*,[38] were more typical than those in the *NRDC* case. The ICS plans at issue in these cases were designed to reduce total emissions as well as to meet national standards. Moreover, in the *Kennecott* case the challengers claimed that the EPA's policy would cause widespread unemployment. In defending its policy in these cases, the EPA needed all the help it could get.

In its arguments before the Sixth and Ninth Circuits the EPA not only called attention to the *NRDC* decision, but incorporated in its presentation large sections of the brief the NRDC had prepared for the Fifth Circuit. The EPA claimed that "the Fifth Circuit's opinion was correct as to its definition of emission limitations as not including dispersion techniques such as [ICS] and tall stacks." The EPA also tried to convince the courts that Congress had spoken out against ICS when it passed the Energy Supply and Environmental Coordination Act.[39]

The EPA won both cases. Noting the Fifth Circuit precedent and deferring to agency expertise, the Sixth and Ninth Circuits upheld the

38. *Big Rivers Electric Corp.* v. *Environmental Protection Agency,* 523 F.2d 16 (6th Cir. 1975); *Kennecott Copper Corp.* v. *Train,* 526 F.2d 1149 (9th Cir. 1975).

39. Government brief in *Big Rivers Electric Corp.* v. *EPA.*

EPA's disapproval of both ICS plans. The only departure from the opinion of the Fifth Circuit was an indication in the Ninth Circuit's opinion that the EPA would be legally required to allow ICS where it finds constant controls *economically* infeasible, not just where it finds such controls technologically infeasible.[40]

This is what the EPA had wanted from the beginning. The sequence of the dispersion cases—the *NRDC* case first, followed by industry challenges—allowed the EPA to start with a strong environmental protection position and then to make concessions that the plaintiffs in these later cases would hardly want to challenge. Thus the agency used the Fifth Circuit's ruling on stack height to defend its own position on ICS—a policy about which, ironically, the Fifth Circuit had expressed serious reservations. This litigational strategy worked well as long as ICS remained the focus of the legal debate. But when the NRDC began to press its advantage on the stack height issue, the EPA had to pay the piper.

The Aftermath of the Litigation

The decision not to appeal the Fifth Circuit's ruling on dispersion to the Supreme Court was made in a highly politicized environment. The choice was not made by agency lawyers looking for ways to strengthen their legal defense of the agency's position, but by the administrator and his top aides. The political advantages of accepting the decision were significant. The agency had just gone through what Russell Train described as the "trauma" of deciding not to allow permanent use of ICS for most sources. The EPA expected that if it interpreted the Fifth Circuit decision judiciously it could justify the use of ICS for smelters and old rural power plants. However, if it appealed the decision and won, the agency would have to address the ICS issue for a second time, reopening internal wounds and giving the FEA another opportunity to pressure the EPA to extend its use of ICS. Accepting the *NRDC* decision ended internal debate; put the FEA, the White House, and Congress on notice that the EPA opposed use of ICS in all but a few cases; and gave the EPA a legal cloak to cover its policy choice.

While the EPA's decision made good political sense, it is more difficult to understand why the Department of Justice consented to the EPA's

40. *Kennecott Copper Corp.* v. *Train* at 1151.

request to appeal other sections of the Fifth Circuit's NRDC decision (see chapter 6), but not the section on dispersion. To be sure, it would have been highly unusual for Justice to appeal an adverse decision that the agency in question had decided to accept.[41] But surely the FEA or the White House must have expressed to the Department of Justice some opinion on the desirability of Supreme Court review. Perhaps by this point President Nixon was having such legal problems himself that Justice would not tolerate even the remotest appearance of bowing to the command of the administration or its allies. Whatever its motivation, Justice accepted the EPA's request.

The decision to abide by the NRDC ruling paid rich dividends to the EPA on ICS. But it also forced the agency to deal with the court's strange understanding of the stack height question.

The ICS "Compromise"

The EPA's disagreement with the FEA did not end when Congress passed the equivocal dispersion sections of the Energy Supply and Environmental Coordination Act in May 1974. As soon as the act passed, John Sawhill, the new FEA administrator, called upon Congress to amend the Clean Air Act once again to allow greater use of ICS. At the same time the FEA pressed the EPA to employ its enforcement discretion to allow plants currently burning coal to use ICS for the foreseeable future. The EPA had openly conceded that many major sources could not possibly install all necessary control equipment by the 1975 deadline. The EPA's use of post-1975 enforcement orders made it susceptible to lobbying by the FEA and utilities about individual coal-burning plants.[42]

On the legislative front the EPA held the advantage. Agency researchers produced studies alleging that failure to limit total sulfur dioxide emissions would cause "thousands of excess deaths." The FEA commissioned a review of the EPA's findings that concluded that no hard evidence existed to support these claims. In light of this unresolved health evidence dispute, though, Congress was unlikely to take decisive action in one way or another. Given the Muskie and Rogers committees'

41. See Donald Horowitz, *The Jurocracy: Government Lawyers, Agency Programs, and Judicial Decisions* (Lexington Books, 1977).

42. 5 *Environment Reporter—Current Developments* 407–08. See chap. 6 for a discussion of the EPA's use of extended compliance orders.

ability to block new legislation, the FEA's chances of prevailing in Congress were slim.[43]

Recognizing this, the FEA accepted an agreement first put forth by the EPA. The FEA consented to drop its legislative proposal on ICS in return for an EPA pledge to issue enforcement orders allowing some coal-burning sources to use ICS through 1985. The compromise was forged in the Ford administration's interagency Energy Resources Council. Administrator Train called the agreement "a very real breakthrough," and later bragged to the Senate Committee, "Though I hate to tell this to [FEA Administrator Frank] Zarb, I think we came out a little on top in that agreement."[44]

The reasons for the EPA's enthusiasm are not hard to find. The agency could not hope to get most coal plants on scrubbers before 1980. What it most wanted was a sign of commitment by the federal government that would convince utilities that they had no choice but to install constant controls. The "compromise" effectively eliminated the utilities' hope of legislative relief while doing little to delay the EPA's schedule for the installation of scrubbers. The compromise also prevented the EPA's commitment to scrubbing from being abandoned by lower-level bureaucrats or by future political appointees. In short, the FEA-EPA agreement essentially represented the EPA's position. While Senator Muskie at first balked at this extension of time for some utilities, the agreement eventually became part of the 1977 amendments.[45] Thus the NRDC decision played a major role in the EPA's defeat of its adversaries within the executive branch.

---

43. Testimony of FEA Administrator Frank Zarb and EPA Administrator Russell Train, *Implementation of the Clean Air Act—1975,* Hearings before the Subcommittee on Environmental Pollution of the Senate Committee on Public Works, 94 Cong. 1 sess. (GPO, 1975), pp. 282–319. Also see John C. Whitaker, *Striking a Balance: Environment and Natural Resources Policy in the Nixon-Ford Years* (American Enterprise Institute for Public Policy Research, 1976), p. 108; and 5 *Environment Reporter—Current Developments* 14–15.

44. *Implementation of the Clean Air Act—1975,* Hearings, p. 298; and 5 *Environment Reporter—Current Developments* 1232. The administration and the EPA continued, however, to present different proposals on PSD. Letter, Administrator Train to the Senate Public Works Committee, February 3, 1975, reprinted in 5 *Environment Reporter—Current Developments* 1570.

45. *Clean Air Act Amendments of 1976,* H. Rept. 94-1175, 94 Cong. 2 sess. (GPO, 1976), pp. 72–74; *Clean Air Amendments of 1976,* S. Rept. 94-717, 94 Cong. 2 sess. (GPO, 1976), p. 78; *Clean Air Amendments of 1977,* Conf. Rept. 95-564, 95 Cong. 1 sess. (GPO, 1977), pp. 133–35.

The Battle over Stack Height, 1974–76

By the time the EPA had clinched this deal on ICS, the controversy over stack height had just gotten under way. For months the EPA ignored the *NRDC* decision, failing not just to renounce its September 1973 regulations but even to submit a report to the court on the Georgia SIP. The NRDC pushed the EPA to take a harder line on stack height and threatened to embarrass the agency in court if it refused to accept the NRDC proposals. The OAQPS remained committed to its original good engineering practice approach. The OGC hesitated to send the court the report prepared by the agency's technical staff since this report made the OAQPS's intentions clear. After the NRDC took the EPA back to court, the agency finally published an odd array of nationally applicable regulations that emerged from long negotiation between the EPA and the NRDC. A review of these negotiations not only reveals why the EPA acted as it did, but also provides a fascinating example of how courts change the bargaining position of interest groups.

The negotiation over stack height regulation focused on two key questions. First, how much stack height credit could the EPA or the states give existing sources that failed to install what the agency later termed "best available control technology" (BACT)? One alternative— the one that seemed to follow from the logic of the court's argument— was none. Dispersion models could not take into account *any* stack height until the source installed BACT. But even the NRDC saw this as too extreme; it advocated giving credit only for existing stack height unless the sources added BACT. The OAQPS continued to advocate a third position: all sources, regardless of whether they applied BACT, should be allowed—indeed encouraged—to increase stack height to good engineering practice. While the EPA had a variety of environmental, economic, political, and equity arguments for this position, the court had expressed its uneasiness with the good engineering practice approach.

Second, how much credit could control agencies grant to new sources, which presumably would apply BACT when they complied with section 111? The most obvious answer would be unlimited stack height credit. Another would be to give most new sources unlimited credit on the basis of new source performance standards (NSPS), but require case-by-case determination of BACT before giving unlimited credit to coal-burning power plants. (The peculiarities of coal-burning power plants were explained in the previous chapter.) A third alternative would be to apply good engineering practice to new as well as old sources. A fourth would be to accept the NRDC's proposal to give new sources credit up to the median historical stack height for the industry in question. While the latter two options seemed to conflict with the court's statements on stack height for sources employing all feasible controls, they appeared consistent with the court's general position that unlimited stack credit should be granted only where "necessary." Tall stacks are not necessary for sources that can locate in areas with better natural dispersion or lower pollution levels. The more one considers the new source problem, the more one sees the inadequacies of the court's original instructions.

Once the EPA resolved these basic questions, it faced many others. Does BACT review include consideration of cost? Does it differ for new and old sources? Does BACT differ from NSPS? Should coal plants be treated differently from other source categories? If the EPA used the concept of good engineering practice, it added further questions. How should it compute good engineering practice? Is the formula suggested by the EPA a rule of thumb or a hard-and-fast rule? Even after the 1977 amendments gave the EPA additional instructions on how to define best available control technology and good engineering practice, many of these questions remained unresolved.

Throughout the negotiations on stack height the OAQPS supported use of a formula for good engineering practice that allowed its technical staff to determine appropriate stack height on the basis of the peculiar circumstances of each source. The NRDC objected to this policy not only because it would allow stack heights to rise, but also because it deprived national environmental groups, EPA political executives, and the courts of a handle for controlling the discretion of lower-level technocrats. The EPA's Office of Enforcement clearly agreed with the NRDC. This internal disagreement, coupled with the NRDC's legal threats, put the OGC in the position of mediator. The OGC eventually wrote most of the stack height guidelines, consenting to the use of good engineering practice, but substantially reducing the discretion of the OAQPS. While the EPA's technical personnel constantly lost ground to its lawyers, even they saw advantages in the court-induced negotiations: the OAQPS's representatives in the interagency review used the threat of additional court action to resist pressure from the FEA, Tennessee Valley Authority, and Department of Commerce to relax its stack height rules. Thus the court rulings were a resource used by many different groups.

THE INITIAL EPA RESPONSE. The first indication that the EPA might try to ignore the court's decision on stack height came in 1974 when a top OAQPS official stated:

> I am aware of the Fifth Circuit Court decision and the Agency's position that constant emission controls are the preferred method of abatement, but I also understand that stack heights up to engineering good practice are to be allowed without restraint as part of an overall program for attainment and maintenance of ambient air quality standards.[46]

Shortly thereafter, the EPA proposed approval of a revision of the Puerto Rico SIP that allowed all sources to raise their stacks to good engineering practice height.[47] Even more surprisingly, the technical personnel writing the court-ordered review of the Georgia SIP included in their calculations stack height credit up to good engineering practice for several sources.

Not only did EPA engineers continue to rely on good engineering practice, but their definitions of it became increasingly open ended.[48] The OAQPS first suggested removing the "two and one-half times" rule of thumb, finding that "good engineering practice requires a case-by-case judgment based on detailed engineering and meteorological investigation of the specific site." It then added a third reason for increasing stack height to supplement the rationales presented in the September 1973 proposal. According to this new criteria, good engineering practice would dictate stacks tall enough to "minimize the threat of air quality standards being violated during neutral stability, high wind conditions." In other words, the OAQPS wanted to encourage sources to increase their stack height to prevent high pollution concentration caused by unusually unfavorable weather conditions.

The NRDC monitored these developments carefully and protested that the guidelines being circulated within the agency were "too vague and discretionary to assure faithful execution of the Court's injunction against the use of dispersion techniques."[49] The NRDC met often with agency officials to express its misgivings. In the process the environmental group formed an alliance with the Office of Enforcement, which grew increasingly concerned about the OAQPS's policies. When the OAQPS

46. Memorandum, Jean Schueneman (OAQPS) to Tom Helms (Region IV), June 18, 1974.

47. 39 Fed. Reg. 15051 (1974).

48. The following discussion relies heavily on copies of proposed regulations circulated within the EPA and presented to the court by the NRDC and the EPA in the contempt proceedings before the Fifth Circuit.

49. Letter, Richard Ayres (NRDC) to Michael James (OGC), June 28, 1974.

added the "neutral stability, high wind" condition to the good engineering practice formula, Office of Enforcement officials warned:

> If we agree, as the proposal proposes, that stacks may be raised to a height that minimizes the threat to air quality standards during neutral stability, high wind conditions, and that these stacks still not be considered "tall stacks" ... then we will *never see an animal called a "tall stack." However, we will see some 1000-foot stacks that are considered GEP.*[50]

The Office of Enforcement succeeded in having the condition removed from later statements of agency policy. Both the NRDC and the Office of Enforcement continued to push for tougher and more explicit rules on stack height.

Facing this internal and external opposition to its policy, the OAQPS put the stack height issue on the back burner. Fearing that this would encourage sources to increase their stack height and to present control agencies with faits accomplis, the NRDC threatened to bring contempt action against the EPA. At this point the OGC and the assistant administrator for air programs took a more active role in setting agency stack height policy. They circulated a policy that not only tightened up on the definition of good engineering practice, but denied any credit for stack height increases begun after 1972—even if the increase was below good engineering practice. Thus the NRDC was slowly pushing the EPA in the direction suggested by the court.

Despite its successes the NRDC was far from pleased with the agency's progress. One problem was delay. By the first anniversary of the *NRDC* decision the stack height regulations had not even reached interagency review. Just as important, the EPA showed increasing leniency toward new sources. The OAQPS followed its typical policy of demanding only state-of-the-art engineering controls and avoiding requirements that imposed siting restrictions. In addition, the EPA and the FEA agreed that the best way to meet environmental objectives while increasing the use of domestic energy resources was to encourage the replacement of old dirty power plants with cleaner new ones. For this reason they opposed adding further restrictions to new sources. With one exception, the regulations circulated within the agency gave unlimited stack height

---

50. Memorandum, Doug Carter (Division of Stationary Source Enforcement, Office of Enforcement) to Robert Duprey (Office of Enforcement), "Good Engineering Practice—Tall Stacks," July 10, 1974, quoted in memorandum, Robert Duprey to Richard Wilson (director, DSSE), July 25, 1974. Ayres claims that at about this time EPA documents started appearing on his doorstep in plain paper bags (personal interview, September 20, 1978).

credit to all sources with NSPS controls. That exception—for coal plants—required case-by-case analysis of BACT. But the regulations allowed the EPA to consider cost in this review, which meant that scrubbing would not be required in all cases. The NRDC believed that the EPA was not being tough enough on coal-burning plants and that the agency was unwisely forgoing siting restrictions that would give added impetus to technology forcing.

THE CONTEMPT SUIT. In the spring of 1975 both the NRDC and the state of Georgia asked the Fifth Circuit to force the EPA to announce a final policy on stack height. Georgia wanted the EPA to approve its SIP, which had been hanging in limbo for over a year. The NRDC wanted to make sure the EPA did not make further concessions in interagency review and hoped to force the EPA to get tougher with new sources. These suits were not entirely unwelcome in the EPA, which was facing substantial opposition from other federal agencies. Almost everyone wanted the issue resolved quickly.

OGC attorneys soon realized that the EPA was in a ticklish situation with the court. It had failed to respond promptly to the original remand and had issued a variety of statements implying that it would not comply with the letter of the court decision. Not only did it have no final regulations, but the regulations in interagency review allowed many sources unlimited stack height. Most embarrassing of all was the lengthy report agency engineers had prepared for the court. As mentioned above, that report included the assumption that several sources with stacks below good engineering practice height would eventually raise their stacks and get credit for these increases. By the time the OGC learned that the report was based on the OAQPS's original policy preferences, it was too late to redo the requisite dispersion modeling.

EPA attorneys considered two options for dealing with these problems. The first was to admit that the report gave credit for good engineering practice stack height, to defend this policy approach, and to explain that the court's original "no dispersion" ruling made little sense. One attorney who favored this direct approach warned:

> Both the introduction and conclusion to the Reply [to the NRDC's critique of the EPA's report] distort the EPA findings of April 7, 1974 [the report on the Georgia SIP], and are nonresponsive at best (or fraudulent, at worst) with respect to the court's February, 1974, remand order.... In my judgment, EPA should just "come clean" and admit that the emission limitations don't meet national standards absent stack height credit, that emission limitations

without the credit are totally impracticable, and that certain stack height credit is entirely justifiable.[51]

The OGC, however, rejected this "come clean" approach as too risky. If the court rejected the EPA's attempt to revise the original decision, it might insist on the measures advocated by the NRDC—which the OGC termed "draconian." If the EPA avoided confrontation it might be able to slip by with a more moderate position.

The option the OGC eventually chose was to hide the good engineering practice assumption contained in the report by using a complicated "equity" argument. The OGC attorney arguing the case before the Fifth Circuit explained the agency's position in a candid internal memo:

Although the Fifth Circuit opinion tended strongly to reject any approach that would permit reliance on tall stacks (including good engineering practice stack heights) EPA's analysis of the Georgia Plan factored in 2 1/2 times stack height for all sources which began increased stack height after the Georgia Plan was submitted in early 1972 and prior to EPA's court-ordered reassessment of the Plan. Fortuitously, all such construction had commenced prior to the date of the Court's decision on February 8, 1974. As a result, in a classic boot strap move, we argued (in papers filed with the Court and at oral argument) that, as a matter of equity, sources that had, in good faith, begun increased stack construction prior to the date of the first judicial announcement on the subject of dispersion technology (February 8, 1974) should be credited with that stack height—the 2 1/2 times standard which comported with historical practice.[52]

The NRDC protested that the EPA was misleading the court. But the EPA promised to give credit only to sources that had contracted for stack height increases with the expectation that such increases would comply with the law.

EPA lawyers left the hearing confident that the judges would accept its "bootstrap" argument, but obsessed with "the need to maintain the good standing of the Agency before the Court."[53] The court instructed the EPA to publish final regulations forthwith and promised to scrutinize them carefully. While the OGC had been particularly worried about how the court would react to its policy on new sources, the court had

51. Letter, Thomas Ries (Region IV) to G. William Frick (deputy general counsel), July 3, 1975.

52. Memorandum, Jerome Ostrov (OGC) to Robert Zener (general counsel), "Comments on OAWM's December 3, 1975 'Policy Guidelines for Stack Height Increases,'" December 4, 1975.

53. Memorandum, Jerome Ostrov (OGC) to Roger Strelow, September 9, 1975.

not said a word about the issue during the hearing. Nevertheless, OGC attorneys warned that if the agency did anything that would make the court think it had tried to circumvent its order, "the fragile house of cards that we have presented to the Court could easily come tumbling down." The need to appease the Fifth Circuit had clearly taken precedence over all policy considerations.

The stack height guidelines that the EPA finally published in February 1976 bore the marks of these years of litigation in the Fifth Circuit.[54] First, to escape the interagency review that threatened both to delay response to the court and to weaken the EPA's growing commitment to scrubbers, the agency published the rules as "legal interpretations and guidelines," rather than as formal regulations requiring rulemaking under the Administrative Procedures Act. Second, the guidelines denied existing sources any credit for stack height increases completed after 1972 unless the sources applied BACT. The only exception to this was the one growing out of the EPA's "bootstrap" equity argument: sources that increased their stack height between 1972 (the date of the EPA's approval of state plans) and 1974 (the date of the first *NRDC* decision) could get credit for those increases up to a maximum of two and one-half times building height.

Third, while the NRDC lost its battle against unlimited stack height for new sources complying with NSPS limitations as well as its fight in favor of case-by-case BACT for coal plants, it succeeded in putting strict limits on the EPA's definition of good engineering practice for new sources that had no applicable NSPS. The rules defined good engineering practice as an absolute limit of two and one-half times building height, leaving no room for case-by-case determination of local downwash, high terrain, or unfavorable weather conditions. This applied even to sources that had previously received permits from the states allowing taller stacks on the basis of individualized determinations. The NRDC's complaints to the court about the looseness of the OAQPS definition of good engineering practice had borne fruit. The EPA turned the original engineering rule of thumb into an absolute limit—a limit the agency did not dare to exceed even on equity grounds.

The Fifth Circuit put its official blessing on these guidelines in April 1976, just as Congress was considering amendments to the act. The court said nothing about the legitimacy of good engineering practice or

54. 41 Fed. Reg. 7450 (1976).

about the stack height appropriate for new sources. It devoted its opinion solely to the question of whether the EPA could "grandfather" stack extensions begun or contracted for before the court's original decision. While admitting that the NRDC's objections to the EPA's report on the Georgia SIP were "serious," it declined to "apply our February, 1974 decision retroactively." The court then meekly dismissed the NRDC's objection to the use of the "two and one-half times" rule for these grandfathered sources, explaining "we cannot say that the 2.5 rule is an arbitrary one."[55] Whether the court recognized that explicit analysis of either the new-source issue or the justification for the "two and one-half times" rule would expose the weaknesses of its original decision or whether it simply ignored these seemingly technical matters are questions to which the court's opinion gives no answers.

The EPA had extricated itself from a difficult situation. It had saved its reputation with the court, prevented the NRDC from imposing harsh restrictions on new sources, and even used the court decision to circumvent interagency review. Yet the agency was stuck with complicated regulations that made little intrinsic sense. Those sources that had moved quickly to cure extremely localized problems got relief. Those who had not, did not. The "two and one-half times" rule of thumb, originally deduced from a "study of the height of disturbances over a ridge in connection with an investigation into the disaster of an airship,"[56] became a hard-and-fast rule governing control requirements and siting decisions for many sources. Wanting to call a halt to the stack height controversy, the EPA officially recommended to Congress that it retain these guidelines. But many people within the agency were discontent. The same was true of almost everyone outside the EPA.

Stack Height Rules after 1977

In 1977 Congress passed legislation "intended to ratify the general thrust, if not the specific holdings," of the several court decisions on dispersion.[57] While the 1977 amendments accepted the FEA-EPA compromise on intermittent control systems, they made significant changes in the EPA's stack height policy. Congress responded to environmentalists'

---

55. *NRDC* v. *EPA*, 529 F.2d 755 at 760.
56. EPA, OAQPS, "Draft Technical Support Document for Determination of Good Engineering Practice Stack Height," July 31, 1978, p. 7.
57. *Clean Air Act Amendments of 1977*, H. Rept. 95-294, p. 91.

complaints by limiting all new sources and all but a handful of existing smelters and power plants to good engineering practice stack height credit. But it also authorized existing sources to increase their stacks to good engineering practice height and gave the EPA additional flexibility to determine that height.

The new section of the act on stack height (section 123) at first glance seems to replace the EPA's patchwork guidelines with a simple, rational rule. It states that no sources (except specially designated smelters and power plants) can receive credit for "so much of the stack height of the sources as exceeds good engineering practice," defined as

> the height necessary to insure that emissions from the stack do not result in excessive concentrations of any air pollutant in the immediate vicinity of the source as a result of atmospheric downwash, eddies and wakes which may be created by the source itself, nearby structures or nearby terrain obstacles (as determined by the Administrator). For purposes of this section such height shall not exceed two and a half times the height of such source unless the owner or operator of the source demonstrates, after notice and opportunity for public hearing, to the satisfaction of the Administrator, that a greater height is necessary as provided under the preceding sentence.

The act also required the EPA to publish regulations implementing this provision by February 1978. However, the EPA did not even propose stack height regulations until January 1979.[58] Soon thereafter it changed its mind, deciding the proposed regulations would allow excessive pollution increases.[59] By the time the Reagan administration took office, the EPA still had no valid regulation. In 1981 the Sierra Club took the agency to court, and the D.C. Circuit Court put the EPA on a schedule for producing the regulations.[60] After making a second proposal in October 1981, the EPA finally promulgated stack height rules in February 1982.[61] The NRDC and the Sierra Club promptly asked the D.C. Circuit to overturn these regulations as impermissibly lenient.[62]

Why did this process take so long? It was not because the issues received little attention; the opposite is more true. The fundamental problem has been that the provision in effect requires the EPA to address an extremely complex and controversial energy and environmental issue

58. 44 Fed. Reg. 2608 (1979).

59. 11 *Environment Reporter—Current Developments* 665.

60. 12 *Environment Reporter—Current Developments* 558.

61. 46 Fed. Reg. 49814 (1981); 47 Fed. Reg. 5864 (1982).

62. *Natural Resources Defense Council* v. *Environmental Protection Agency*, No. 82-1384 (D.C. Cir.), reported in 12 *Environment Reporter—Current Developments* 1643. By mid-1983 the court had not responded.

by relying on a slippery engineering concept. As each side increased its efforts to use the amendments to its advantage, the concept of good engineering practice slowly crumbled, leaving the EPA with a shaky foundation for any decision it made.

On the surface the new legislation seemed to resolve the stack height controversy. The House report gave the EPA further direction, specifying for example that it must give a narrow interpretation to the phrase "nearby structures or nearby terrain obstacles."[63] But a number of troublesome questions have arisen nonetheless. The issues the EPA had to resolve before publishing final rules included, among others, the following: What is an "excessive concentration"? Is it a violation of a national standard, or some lower concentration that could possibly do some harm? Can the EPA consider nearby terrain features that do not cause downwash but experience high ambient concentrations because they are directly hit by the source's plume? What exactly are "downwash, eddies, and wakes"? Can the EPA prevent sources from building "fat stacks" that increase plume rise and thus dispersion? Should the EPA demand that sources with stack heights less than two and one-half times building height demonstrate that they need this height to avoid downwash? And, last but hardly least, what does such a "demonstration" entail? The act assumes that many of these determinations are essentially technical ones. But they are not. In each instance the agency must try to balance a wide array of environmental, energy, and economic considerations.

Environmentalists argue that in making these policy determinations the EPA should be guided by what they see as the overriding purpose of section 123, limiting total emissions by restricting stack height credit. This puts environmentalists in the paradoxical position of downplaying the importance of local air quality. The NRDC, for example, complained:

> The point of amending the law was to prevent operators from escaping emission controls by using tall stacks and other dispersion enhancing techniques. EPA seems to have become fixed on the concept chosen to achieve this end—"good engineering practice"—as if preventing atmospheric downwash, not limiting emissions, were the purpose of enacting section 123.[64]

Conversely, industry has jealously guarded what it interprets as its right to correct localized pollution problems by increasing stack height.

63. *Clean Air Act Amendments of 1977*, H. Rept. 95-294, p. 93.
64. NRDC, "Comments on Proposed Regulatory Revisions: 1977 Clean Air Amendment for Stack Heights," p. 5, contained in EPA docket on stack height regulations.

Some polluters have searched aggressively for excessive concentrations that would justify taller stacks. While industry argues that any pollution level above the primary standards should be considered an excessive concentration, environmental groups claim that concentrations are not excessive until they reach about 150 percent of the national standards and that the EPA should ignore highly localized "hot spots."

The essential problem the EPA faces is that Congress tried to use the concept of good engineering practice both to limit total emissions and to prevent high local pollution levels. The original engineering-based purpose of the concept was to ensure that stacks are *tall* enough to avoid local pollution problems. When the EPA and then Congress became concerned about the atmospheric loading problem, they transformed good engineering practice into a mechanism for ensuring that the stacks used in dispersion modeling are *short* enough to force sources to reduce their emissions. Good engineering practice is both a tool for meeting the original goals of the Clean Air Act (attainment of national standards) and a stopgap measure for dealing with the environmental problems that escape the ambient air quality approach of the act.

By pointing in two directions at the same time, section 123 of the act confers considerable discretion on administrators—a fact that before 1980 pleased its sponsors and thereafter tormented them. Increasingly concerned about the problem of acid rain and convinced that midwestern utilities should sharply reduce their sulfur dioxide emissions, President Carter's appointees moved gradually toward greater restrictions on stack height credit. Under the Reagan administration the EPA quickly marched in the other direction. The final rules announced in 1982 allow all sources to increase their stack height to good engineering practice (generally defined as two and one-half times building height) without any demonstration that stack height increases are needed to avoid downwash. Their definitions of "excessive concentration" and "demonstration" are relatively lenient. The regulations specifically allow sources to channel all their emissions through one stack to increase plume temperature, plume rise, and, thus, dispersion of pollutants. Moreover, the EPA's rules offer sources "impaction credit," which allows them to raise their stacks above good engineering practice height to avoid having their plume strike surrounding high terrain. While admitting that "section 123 does not mention impaction," the agency "considers impaction to be enough like downwash that the same rationale should apply. GEP stack height should include credit needed to avoid high concentrations caused by impaction."[65]

The EPA estimated that the rules proposed in 1979 would reduce sulfur dioxide emissions by 973,000 tons and that those published in 1982 will produce reductions of less than 200,000 tons. Although industry offered few complaints about the final regulations, environmentalists labeled them "an example of the worst in federal regulation writing."[66]

The Search for an Alternative

As they grow more frustrated with the EPA's failure to write stack height rules that deal adequately with the problem of atmospheric loading, environmental groups, congressmen, state officials, and academic observers have looked for more direct methods of limiting sulfur emissions. Ironically, some of the recent proposals for combating acid rain and related environmental problems were first put forth in the early 1970s by the Nixon administration and the EPA, but received little support from congressmen and environmental groups who vigorously sought to limit use of dispersion enhancement. One example of this is a national emission standard for existing sources, an approach first advocated by the National Air Pollution Control Administration in the late 1960s. Another is the emission tax.

As early as 1971 a variety of agency officials, interest group representatives, and economists pointed out that the EPA could deal with the problems of atmospheric loading, long distance transport, and synergistic pollutants by supplementing its enforcement of state plans with an emission tax on sulfur dioxide. President Nixon proposed such a tax in his 1971 message on the environment. The Council on Environmental Quality endorsed his plan, and EPA Administrator Train later proposed a similar tax. While they were considering amendments to the Clean Air Act, both the House and Senate committees heard favorable testimony on the sulfur tax from environmental groups and a number of economists.

---

65. 47 Fed. Reg. 5866 (1982). The regulations followed the 1979 proposal by using this variation of the "two and one-half times" formula: good engineering practice equals building height plus one and one-half times the lesser of the building height and building width.

66. 12 *Environment Reporter—Current Developments* 978.

A variety of other organizations, including the National Academy of Sciences, the National Association of Manufacturers, the Sierra Club, and the National Audubon Society, have also voiced support for this two-pronged approach to the sulfur dioxide and sulfate problem.[67]

Those who advocate the use of a sulfur dioxide tax to supplement the Clean Air Act's ambient air approach include a surprising number of those normally opposed to effluent fees. The EPA, usually a proponent of "command and control" regulation, stated in 1975 that "the unique characteristics of the sulfate problem . . . make such a tax disincentive worthy of serious consideration."[68] One reason for this is that atmospheric loading is a national (or at least regional) problem. This means that the law or the agency could set uniform national (or regional) charges rather than try to set local tax rates on the basis of estimated local damage functions. Second, since there are no measurable health or welfare thresholds for sulfates or acid rain, the agency would not need to keep readjusting the level of taxation to get the "right" pollution level. The EPA has never attempted to do more than minimize total sulfur dioxide emissions or discourage emission increases.[69] A sulfur dioxide tax would achieve much the same results while allowing industry more flexibility in siting new plants and distributing low-sulfur fuel. Third, compared to other criteria pollutants, sulfur dioxide stack emissions are relatively easy to monitor. The EPA is considering requiring in-stack monitors for all major emitters of sulfur dioxide. These factors all contribute to making an emission tax less administratively cumbersome than stack height regulations.

Despite these advantages and this widespread support for experimentation with regulatory alternatives, both the House and Senate committees opposed emission charges altogether. The possibility of using a tax or any other scheme relying on economic incentives to supplement the

67. Frederick R. Anderson and others, *Environmental Improvement through Economic Incentives* (Resources for the Future, 1977), pp. 51–54, 149–50; 4 *Environment Reporter—Current Developments* 857; *Clean Air Amendments—1975*, Hearings before the Subcommittee on Health and the Environment of the House Committee on Interstate and Foreign Commerce, 94 Cong. 1 sess. (GPO, 1975), pp. 709–17; Allen V. Kneese and Charles L. Schultze, *Pollution, Prices, and Public Policy* (Brookings Institution, 1975), pp. 99–101; and Charles L. Schultze, *The Public Use of Private Interest* (Brookings Institution, 1977), pp. 48–51.

68. EPA, "Position Paper on Atmospheric Sulfates," p. 69.

69. See EPA, "National Strategy for Control of Sulfur Oxides"; and A. Michael Spence and Martin L. Weitzman, "Regulatory Strategies for Pollution Control," in Ann F. Friedlaender, ed., *Approaches to Controlling Air Pollution* (MIT Press, 1978), p. 199.

national ambient air quality standards received no mention in committee reports or on the floor. Court decisions and resulting agency action on dispersion patched up the ambient air scheme of the 1970 act, thereby reducing the pressure for innovation. Congress tinkered with the solutions proposed by the EPA and the courts without seriously examining the inherent weaknesses of the regulatory scheme that had created the problem in the first place. The successors to Senator Muskie and Representative Rogers have yet to confront the fundamental issues skirted during the 1970s.

The Courts Muddle Through

In the dispersion enhancement cases, the courts, led by the Fifth Circuit, relied on a highly questionable legal analysis to address a serious environmental problem that threatened to slip through the regulatory net created by the 1970 Clean Air Act. As with PSD, both the EPA and Congress in time accepted "the general thrust if not the specific holdings" of the court decisions. Limits on the use of dispersion enhancement techniques have become important—although cumbersome and ultimately inadequate—tools in the battle against acid rain and the health threat posed by long distance transport of sulfur dioxide, nitrogen oxides, and particulate matter. While the court decisions on dispersion in effect required the EPA to add a second goal (limiting total emissions) to its original goal of meeting national air quality standards, they did not force the agency to construct a new regulatory program. The EPA already recognized the importance of limiting the substitution of dispersion enhancement for constant controls. In short, the NRDC decision and its progeny prodded an agency beset by conflicting political pressures and nearly immobilized by its analysis of complex policy options to write regulations closing a loophole in the 1970 act. Yet these court decisions were far from an unalloyed blessing for the EPA or its environmental protection programs.

The dispersion cases present graphic examples of three attributes of judicial review praised by those who favor judicial activism. First, while the president and Congress engaged in a partisan, crisis-oriented battle over environmental and energy policies in the hectic months after the 1973 oil embargo, the courts took a more long-range perspective on the issues before them. Not under pressure to show that they were doing something to respond to the energy crisis, the courts forcefully reminded the EPA of the importance of protecting the environment against the adverse effects of increased reliance on domestic fuels. The courts' actions not only helped the EPA to construct a coherent policy to replace its series of tentative, ad hoc decisions on use of dispersion, but provided the groundwork for a compromise between environmental and energy agencies. In 1977, when cooler heads prevailed, both Congress and the new president accepted this compromise. Thus the nonpolitical courts apparently corrected the faults of the political process.

Second, the court decisions strengthened the bargaining power of environmental groups in the long and complex negotiations over stack height regulations. While many industry groups and federal agencies hostile to environmental regulation followed closely the EPA's development of stack height rules, the NRDC was the only group familiar with the details of the controversy pushing the EPA to be tougher with polluters. The NRDC's presence not only helped the EPA resist pressure for weaker regulation, but also prevented the EPA's engineers from using a good engineering practice formula that would have required source-by-source negotiations over allowable stack height. The environmentalists realized what the EPA's engineers probably did not: in these discussions industry would usually be the only private party involved and would frequently get its way. Thus the court decisions not only added balance to the representation of interests in the writing of general stack height limits, but helped to defeat a definition of good engineering practice that could have led to industry dominance.

Third, the court decisions helped political executives gain control over lower levels of the bureaucracy. For years—even after the Fifth Circuit decision—the OAQPS continued to view stack height regulations primarily as a way to elevate local "hot spots" and to include in agency regulations concepts that maximized their discretion. If it had not been for the contempt proceedings initiated by the NRDC, it is unlikely that agency political executives would have taken control of rulemaking or would have recognized the policy implications of the concepts used by agency technocrats. The need to appease the courts led the EPA both to restrict the application of good engineering practice and to use the simple "two and one-half times" rule to define it. The courts thus helped the EPA's generalists to see the environmental forest through the engineering trees.

Counterbalancing these advantages of court intervention are three corresponding liabilities. First, the courts ended the political stalemate over dispersion only by entering the political thicket themselves. By reading the preferences of Muskie and Rogers into the 1970 act, the courts stacked the political deck against the White House, the FEA, and those congressmen (sometimes constituting a majority in the House) who supported increased use of dispersion. While the debate over this issue was especially heated in the months after the embargo, it has not disappeared. The conflict between domestic energy use and protection of air quality remains a real and a heated one. "Correcting" the political process is inseparable from changing who wins and who loses.

Second, if the courts strengthened the position of environmental groups and political executives in the bargaining over stack height limits, they did so only by announcing an extreme "no dispersion" rule that revealed their primitive understanding of the issues before them. The EPA—especially its OAQPS—tried for years to evade the courts' impractical solution, which even the NRDC did not accept entirely. The NRDC decision and subsequent contempt proceedings encouraged the EPA to hide the extent to which it gave sources credit for stack height and the extent to which dispersion through use of smokestacks is an integral part of any control strategy. Consequently, the guidelines the EPA published in 1976 (which were never submitted to the public for formal comment) were technically arbitrary, seriously inequitable, and riddled with perplexing exemptions. This led Congress to write new stack height rules, attempting to give them the intellectual coherence the EPA's guidelines lacked. Yet by retaining the courts' general "no dispersion" policy while seeking to avoid its harsh implications, Congress came back to the same concept, good engineering practice, which had previously caused so many problems. The debate over dispersion has once again focused on engineering questions because the fact that limiting dispersion requires making political, not technical, choices was ignored by the courts and hidden by the congressmen who reaped political advantage from the court decisions. This added to the difficulty of resolving the questions before the EPA.

Third, while the court decisions closed a loophole in the 1970 act, they concomitantly led environmental advocates in the EPA, Congress, and private groups to pin their hopes on an indirect and ineffective method for dealing with the atmospheric loading problem. The court decisions gave environmentalists a quick and easy way to prop up the ambient air approach of the act. With this stopgap measure in place, they failed to address the more fundamental inadequacies of the statute. They turned their backs on innovative suggestions such as the Nixon administration's proposal to supplement the act's emphasis on local air quality with a tax to discourage emission increases. Some environmentalists, discouraged with the cumbersome ambient air quality approach and the agency's stack height regulations, have rediscovered these alternatives. But adding new pollution control requirements is far harder in the 1980s than it was in the 1970s.

The courts, hailed by some as the most rational of the three branches of American government, produced these consequences by issuing an extreme opinion, the implications of which it most likely did not understand, and by denying that it was making a fundamental policy choice. It was the extreme nature of the Fifth Circuit's "no dispersion" rule that increased the bargaining power of the NRDC and allowed the EPA and its congressional patrons to prevail in 1974. Far from guiding government action, the court's opinions became political resources used by various combatants in battles about which the courts knew little. The EPA first used the Fifth Circuit decision as a pawn in its fight with the administration, and then the NRDC used the decision against the EPA. Congressional sponsors of the 1977 amendments used the court decisions to put statutory limits on dispersion, but later saw industry use their definition of good engineering practice to justify stack height increases. The court decisions helped the EPA and Congress to "muddle through" on this issue—with all the debits and credits that term implies. In using the courts' awkward rulings to their advantage, the EPA, congressional supporters of stricter environmental regulation, and public interest groups all became captives of the court decisions and of the ambient air quality approach of the Clean Air Act.

CHAPTER SIX

Variances: The Fruits of Judicial Distrust

In 1973 the Natural Resources Defense Council (NRDC) filed suit against the Environmental Protection Agency in six federal courts of appeal to force the agency to disapprove the variance provisions included in a large number of state implementation plans (SIPs).[1] The NRDC contended that the states might use these variance provisions to delay pollution cleanup and thus make a mockery of the Clean Air Act's deadlines. The EPA replied that it had approved variance mechanisms with the understanding that specific variances would become part of a state plan only when approved by the EPA as legal plan revisions. It would not approve variances that would lead to postdeadline violations of national air quality standards. In essence the issue before the courts was whether to trust the EPA to supervise the granting of variances by the states.

The courts split into two camps on this issue. The differences in the two positions reflect the conflicting assumptions of the "old" and the "new" administrative law: the former assumes that the agency in question is conscientiously pursuing its statutory mission and checks to see that

1. *Natural Resources Defense Council* v. *Environmental Protection Agency,* 478 F.2d 875 (1st Cir. 1973); *Natural Resources Defense Council* v. *Environmental Protection Agency,* 494 F.2d 519 (2d Cir. 1974); *Natural Resources Defense Council* v. *Environmental Protection Agency,* 489 F.2d 390 (5th Cir. 1974); *Natural Resources Defense Council* v. *Environmental Protection Agency,* 483 F.2d 690 (8th Cir. 1973); and *Natural Resources Defense Council* v. *Environmental Protection Agency,* 507 F.2d 905 (9th Cir. 1974). In *Natural Resources Defense Council* v. *Environmental Protection Agency,* 481 F.2d 116 (10th Cir. 1973), the court denied the NRDC standing. The Supreme Court ruled on the issue in *Train* v. *Natural Resources Defense Council,* 421 U.S. 60 (1975).

it has not overstepped its statutory limits; the latter questions whether the agency has been sufficiently aggressive and often insists upon judicially prescribed measures to increase the agency's effectiveness in achieving the goals set by Congress.

The first court to decide the NRDC case on variances, the First Circuit, shared the environmental group's suspicion of the agency. It ruled that while the EPA could allow states to grant variances before the 1975 deadline, it could not condone postdeadline variances. Conceding that the 1970 act did not explicitly disallow post-1975 variances, the court nonetheless found that "the existence of open-ended exemptions" conflicted with the purpose of the act, which was to reduce pollution levels as quickly as possible. The Second and Eighth Circuits, and to some extent the Fifth, followed the lead of the First.

The other courts that decided the case on the merits sided with the EPA. The Ninth Circuit and later the Supreme Court found that the statute nowhere prohibits the use of variances. Moreover, the act entitles the states to grant variances that do not contribute to violations of national standards. The Supreme Court assumed that the EPA was both willing and able to decide whether state actions would endanger the environmental goals established by Congress.

While the court decisions on prevention of significant deterioration (PSD) and dispersion added new objectives to the EPA's regulatory effort, the variance cases addressed the questions of *how* the EPA should pursue goals clearly defined in the 1970 act. Since the First Circuit's decision was the prevailing ruling on the variance question for the two years preceding the Supreme Court's 1975 decision, these cases provide an opportunity to compare the consequences of decisions based on the new and the old administrative law. Did the First Circuit's ruling provide an effective method for ensuring that the standards were met? Has the use of variances since the 1975 Supreme Court decision impeded efforts to meet national air quality standards? Since the variance cases focus on the means the EPA used to achieve ends clearly specified by Congress, evaluating the performance of the courts is simpler here than for the PSD and dispersion issues.

Hindsight shows that insofar as the decisions of the First, Second, Fifth, and Eighth Circuits affected the programs of the EPA and the states, they caused confusion, delay, and animosity between state and federal administrators. The courts that favored the NRDC actually hurt the EPA's enforcement efforts.

The obstacles confronting enforcement officials attempting to bring polluters into compliance with the act were far greater than any of the courts realized. Variances and extended compliance schedules were important components of control agencies' efforts to commit major polluters to schedules that would eventually bring them into compliance with state implementation plans. Without legal authority to issue variances (under whatever name), pollution control agencies could not negotiate with polluters. Rather than shut down, those noncomplying sources that could not get variances simply ignored SIP regulations. The courts did not recognize this irony because they made no effort to learn about the realities of the enforcement process or to monitor the consequences of their decisions. While the Supreme Court's decisions mitigated this difficulty to some extent, the legalizing of the variance issue continued to hurt enforcement efforts until the passage of the 1977 amendments. To see how this happened one must review the dilemmas of the enforcement process as well as the variance litigation itself.

The Litigation

The SIPs submitted by the states in early 1972 combined existing state regulations with provisions taken from the EPA's 1971 guidelines and from model state codes. Almost every SIP followed the standard state practice of allowing the air pollution agency, a special review board, or the governor to exempt specific sources from generally applicable regulations. The Rhode Island SIP, for example, allowed the state to grant variances to those sources that could show that enforcement of the plan would cause "undue hardship on such person without a corresponding benefit or advantage." The Georgia SIP allowed the Department of Public Health to issue variances where "strict compliance would result in substantial curtailment or closing down of one or more businesses, plants or operations."[2] These provisions are typical not just of SIPs, but of state health and safety regulations in general.

The Office of Air Quality Planning and Standards (OAQPS) engineers charged with reviewing the state plans at first ignored this problem but

2. The Rhode Island SIP is quoted in NRDC v. EPA at 884 (1st Cir. 1973); the Georgia SIP is in Train v. NRDC at 69. For a list of state variance provisions, see Implementation of the Clean Air Act Amendments of 1970, Hearings before the Subcommittee on Air and Water Pollution of the Senate Committee on Public Works, 92 Cong. 2 sess. (Government Printing Office, 1973), pp. 117–30.

then informed the states that the EPA would treat all variances as plan "revisions."[3] Section 110(a)(3) of the act requires the EPA to approve all revisions that "have been adopted by the state after notice and public hearing," and that provide "for the attainment of such primary standards as expeditiously as practicable but . . . in no case later than three years from the date of such plan." The EPA intended to use standard modeling techniques to review variance requests. A variance that did not receive EPA approval would not legally amend the SIP and thus would not protect the source against federal, state, or citizen suit enforcement.

The EPA defended this variance policy as consistent with the act's emphasis on allowing the states to choose any pollution control mix adequate to meet national standards. The policy also allowed the states to adjust SIP regulations in light of new information. The agency even saw an environmental advantage in the variance mechanism: it encouraged states to set emission limitations more stringent than required to meet national standards, pointing out that they could later relax regulations that caused special hardship.[4]

The NRDC at first voiced its agreement with the EPA's policy, but soon thereafter challenged the variance provisions of almost every state plan in its series of multi-issue suits against the EPA.[5] The NRDC argued that the act provides two methods for delaying plan requirements—section 110(e) "extensions" and section 110(f) "postponements"—and that Congress intended these provisions to be exclusive. Section 110(e) allows the EPA to grant two-year extensions of the 1975 deadline if it finds that requisite control technology does not exist to allow a particular control region to meet the primary standard before 1977. The states had to request these extensions when they submitted their original plans. Only a few states requested extensions for stationary sources.

Section 110(f) allows the EPA to grant one-year postponements to sources that the states determine are unable to comply with SIP requirements and are "essential to national security or to the public health and welfare." Before granting such a postponement the EPA must hold a formal hearing. The EPA argued that section 110(f) was too cumbersome to use except when an essential facility would contribute to a violation

3. 36 Fed. Reg. 15486 (1971), secs. 51.6, 51.15, and 51.32(f).
4. Memorandum, Rodney Snow (OGC) to Paul Defalco (Region IX), December 7, 1971.
5. The NRDC first stated its approval of this policy in *Implementation of the Clean Air Act Amendments of 1970*, Hearings, p. 45. The NRDC's change of heart is another indication of the extent to which one's stand on the issue is determined by one's opinion of the EPA, not by one's reading of the statute.

of a health-based air quality standard. But the NRDC claimed that Congress intended section 110(f) to be the *sole* mechanism for changing individual emission limitations after 1972. The revision section of the act, it maintained, applies only to categories of sources, and should be used only to strengthen SIPs approved by the EPA but later found to be inadequate.

Why did the NRDC advocate this reading of the statute? Certainly not because the legislative history of the act compelled such an interpretation of "postponement" and "revision." As the Supreme Court's opinion explains, the legislative history on the subject is highly ambiguous. Moreover, in 1977 Congress claimed that the EPA's original reading of the act was correct. Rather, the NRDC had larger policy considerations in mind.

Most obviously, the NRDC hoped to lock into each state plan the "overkill" that the states had included in their SIPs before they appreciated the cost of pollution control. In addition, the NRDC feared that variance requests would make enforcement more difficult. Sources would use variances to get individualized emission limitations. This would require control agencies and citizens acting under section 304 to study the details of a long series of variance provisions before they could take enforcement action. To make matters worse, the variance option would encourage sources to hire sophisticated dispersion modelers to argue that they could increase their emissions without violating national standards. Review of modeling studies would absorb scarce control agency resources. Enforcement officials would inevitably wait until the revision process had ended before initiating enforcement actions. Given the complexity of modeling, this could produce years of delay. Nor did the NRDC trust the EPA to disapprove variance requests based on questionable modeling analysis. In sum, the NRDC claimed that the EPA's variance policy represented a return to the discredited approach of resting enforcement on the discovery of actual violations of air quality standards.

The NRDC presented all these arguments to the circuit courts. The government, in contrast, eschewed policy debate, relying instead on stock procedural arguments and on a brief explanation of why its reading of the statute was sufficiently reasonable to withstand judicial review. While the NRDC devoted a great deal of attention to the case, the Office of General Counsel (OGC) and Department of Justice attorneys who presented the EPA's case viewed the dispute as minor compared to the scores of other Clean Air Act cases in the courts. The OGC and the

Department of Justice neither understood the potential consequences of an NRDC victory nor foresaw legal defeat for the agency. It was not until they found themselves in the Supreme Court that the government's lawyers supplemented their legal arguments with explanations of the policy implications of the lower courts' decisions.[6]

The First Circuit, the first court to address the variance issue, spent little time considering the intrinsic meaning of "postponement" or "revision," but proceeded immediately to the issue of congressional intent. According to the court, Congress's overriding purpose was to ensure the rapid attainment of the primary standards, a goal which "could too easily be frustrated by the existence of open-ended exemptions." To follow the EPA's policy of allowing polluters to "raise and perhaps litigate" the issue of whether their emissions were contributing to violations of national air quality standards would be "to invite protracted delay." The court concluded—without any reference to legislative history—that "we think Congress meant [section 110(f)] to be the exclusive mechanism for hardship relief after the mandatory attainment dates."[7] In effect the court announced that it did not trust the agency's judgment on how to achieve rapid attainment of the national standards.

The First Circuit did not completely accept the NRDC's argument. It discovered two exceptions to the general rule against variances. First, "some flexibility may be allowed for mechanical breakdown and acts of God." The court gave no statutory explanation for these short-term exemptions. The court's second exception shows even more clearly that it was engaging in creative statute reading. Noting that Congress had given the states three years to meet the primary standards, it allowed the EPA to approve variances before 1975. This three-year "grace period" was "a necessary adjunct to the statutory scheme, which anticipates greater flexibility during the pre-attainment period." It made the following pragmatic argument:

> We can see value in permitting a state to impose strict emission limitations now, subject to individual exemptions if practicability warrants; otherwise it may be forced to adopt less stringent limitations in order to accommodate those who, notwithstanding reasonable efforts, are as yet unable to comply.[8]

The Supreme Court understandably characterized the First Circuit's

6. Government briefs in *NRDC v. EPA* (1st Cir. 1973) and *Train v. NRDC*.
7. *NRDC v. EPA* at 886 (1st Cir. 1973).
8. Ibid. at 887.

solution to the variance issue as "Solomonesque" and "quite candidly a judicial creation."[9]

Later in 1973 the Eighth Circuit announced its agreement with the First. The Second Circuit followed suit in early 1974. The Fifth Circuit also overturned the EPA's variance policy, but rejected the First Circuit's arguments and its two exceptions. The Fifth Circuit based its decision on the difference between a revision and a postponement: "a revision is a change in a generally applicable requirement; a postponement or variance is a change in the application of a requirement to a particular party. The distinction between the two is familiar and clear."[10] While the EPA could approve requests for changes in "generally applicable requirements" that protect national standards, all SIP changes applying to individual sources would have to go through the elaborate section 110(f) process. The NRDC was pleased with the decision since it doubted that states could relax many "generally applicable requirements" without causing standard violations in some areas.

The EPA decided to use the Fifth Circuit ruling to obtain Supreme Court review of the entire variance issue. While the agency had previously decided it could tolerate the First Circuit's ruling, the Fifth Circuit's decision compounded the programmatic and political troubles produced by the 1973 oil embargo. When the Ninth Circuit upheld the agency's original position in late 1974, the EPA was in an even better position to recoup its earlier losses.

In 1975 the Supreme Court upheld the EPA's original variance policy in its entirety. The Court first rejected the statutory interpretations of the First and Fifth Circuits and then deferred to the agency's expertise in deciding whether its variance procedures were adequate to safeguard the act's goals. The Court stressed that section 110(a)(3) instructs the administrator to approve "any revision" of a SIP that complies with section 110(a)(2). It dismissed the Fifth Circuit's distinction between general rules and individual applications, noting that

> normal usage would suggest that a postponement is a deferral of the effective date of a requirement which remains a part of the applicable plan, whereas a revision is a change in the plan itself which deletes or modifies the requirement.[11]

While the function of section 110(a)(3) is to allow the states to adjust

9. *Train* v. NRDC at 73.
10. NRDC v. *EPA* at 401 (5th Cir. 1974).
11. *Train* v. NRDC at 89.

their pollution "mix" within the bounds of the national standards, the purpose of subsection (f) is to provide a "safety valve by which may be accorded, under certain carefully specified circumstances, exceptions to the national standards themselves." Variances that do not threaten national standards, whether individualized or general, need not go through the section 110(f) process.

More important, the Supreme Court rejected the First Circuit's assertions that rapid achievement of the national standards is the only important goal of the Clean Air Act, and that the courts are better able to establish mechanisms for achieving this goal than is the EPA. The Court pointed out that Congress also announced the goal of returning responsibility for pollution control to the states. Denying the states the opportunity to revise their SIPs would lock them into their provisional choices and thus deny them the preeminence the act accords them. In response to the First Circuit's claim that such a bow to the states would cause endless delay, the Supreme Court simply noted that the expert agency charged with administering the act had denied that this would be a serious problem.

None of the variance decisions were dictated by the clear wording of the law. The former set of courts, seeing themselves as the protectors of unorganized breathers, feared that the federal regulators would cave in to the states and industry. The latter two courts saw themselves as protectors of the states and sources that the EPA regulates and assumed the EPA would adequately protect breathers. Each reading of the law, in short, rested on a different view of the administrative process.

Gaining Compliance: The Grim Realities

Despite their differences, all the courts hearing the NRDC's suit shared two basic unstated assumptions. The first was that state plans included specific regulations carefully chosen by the states to meet the national standards. The second was that polluters would obey these regulations unless they received or hoped to receive a variance. Both assumptions were incorrect.

Rather than carefully weighing the societal implications of various pollution control options, the states rushed to submit SIPs that would receive federal approval. Many of the SIPs submitted in 1972 contained hopelessly ambiguous regulations. Others included sweeping provisions that ignored critical differences among industries—to say nothing of differences among individual facilities. Some SIPs contained requirements such as the blanket "no visible emission" rule for incinerators, power plants, and steel mills. These provisions later proved both impractical and extremely expensive.

These characteristics of the original SIPs compounded the inherent difficulty of forcing private parties to spend billions of dollars to comply with government regulations. As the EPA and state agencies soon learned, compliance with SIP regulations was hardly an automatic consequence of their promulgation. Most polluters ignored the law until threatened with enforcement action. It took years of concerted effort by state and federal enforcement officials to induce the thousands of major pollution sources subject to the SIPs to comply with their emission limitations.

The EPA claimed that 70 percent of all major air pollution sources had complied with their SIP requirements by mid-1975. Yet it admitted that many of the nation's largest polluters were among the delinquent 30 percent. According to EPA figures, in 1975 over 60 percent of the nation's coal-burning power plants, nearly 70 percent of all steel mills and smelters, almost half of the country's pulp and paper mills, over 80 percent of municipal incinerators, and two-thirds of all federal facilities had yet to comply with state plans. These SIP violations contributed to violations of health-based standards in over half of the nation's air quality control regions.[12]

In retrospect one can see that the circuits that ruled against the EPA were right to worry about regulatory delay. But hindsight also indicates the folly of freezing the original regulations in order to avoid this delay. Effective enforcement of SIP requirements, the EPA soon learned, requires making regulatory demands that appear reasonable to state officials, to judges hearing enforcement cases, to local citizens and congressmen, and to polluters themselves. To reduce the intransigence of polluters—who usually escaped punishment for their lack of cooperation—and to stem the growing political opposition to pollution control efforts, the EPA encouraged the states to replace infeasible regulations with achievable, affordable ones and to extend the compliance schedule of sources that could not install necessary control equipment by 1975. Variances provided a tool both for improving the quality of the state plans and

12. EPA, Office of Air Quality Planning and Standards, *State Air Pollution Implementation Plan Progress Report, January 1 to June 30, 1975* (EPA, September 1975), pp. 1–31; and *Congressional Record* (June 8, 1977), p. 18035.

for offering polluters a deal that would get them started down the road to compliance. While the Supreme Court was wrong to assume that the EPA had air pollution well under control, the courts it overruled were equally wrong in their assessment of how the agency could minimize delay.

SIP Inadequacies

In 1971–72 few state air pollution control agencies had either the time or the expertise to perform careful economic, engineering, and air quality analysis for the thousands of sources subject to regulation. Consequently they took a number of shortcuts.

Many of the regulations included in SIPs were those previously in effect in the states. For areas that might violate national standards, most states followed the EPA's advice of basing emission limitations on crude worst-case analysis. For example, most states established sulfur dioxide regulations by estimating the percentage reduction in ambient pollution levels necessary to reach the secondary standards in the most polluted areas of the state and then requiring all sources in nonattainment areas— or even in the entire state—to roll back their emissions by that percentage. Use of rollback analysis rather than dispersion modeling made most SIP regulations more stringent than necessary to meet the minimum requirements of the Clean Air Act. For particulate matter most states relied on either a blanket opacity regulation (such as no visible emissions or no emissions of greater than 20 percent opacity) or included in their SIP a process weight formula setting a maximum emission level on the basis of raw material input levels. These opacity and process weight regulations applied uniformly to steel mills, power plants, incinerators, and all forms of manufacturing.

Given the crudeness of these regulations, it is not surprising that the states insisted upon using variances to fit emission limitations to individual sources. From the states' point of view, setting tough standards that could later be relaxed had a special advantage: it put the burden on polluters to show why the general regulation was too stringent. The EPA encouraged the states to start with stringent rules that they could later modify,[13] rather than to propose regulations of questionable adequacy

---

13. 37 Fed. Reg. 10845–46 (1972); and EPA, Office of Planning and Management, "General Report of the Air Compliance Review Group" (EPA, January 1975), chap. IV.

that the EPA might have to amend. The EPA was well aware that it did not have the time or the experience to suggest more suitable alternatives.[14]

The compliance schedules included in these original SIPs were even cruder than the standards for ultimate compliance. Rather than specifying a timetable for compliance by each source as required by section 110, most states either made their regulations effective immediately or told sources to comply by 1975. Immediate compliance was impossible for most sources since installation of control equipment can take months. Conversely, requiring compliance by 1975 left sources without enforceable interim control requirements. This meant that control agencies would have to wait until 1975 to see if these sources complied, and only then begin enforcement action against the stragglers. Realizing that states could not possibly devise source-specific compliance schedules by early 1972, the EPA gave the states until February 1973 to produce the schedules. Yet even then only six states produced a full array of schedules. Twenty states failed to respond at all. Some states included schedules extending past 1975. The EPA attempted to propose timetables for sources that lacked approvable state-written schedules. While its enforcement office gave top priority to this effort, 4,000 major sources remained without schedules by late 1974. Enforcement could not begin until scheduling was completed.

As the EPA and state agencies struggled to write source-specific emission limitations and compliance schedules, they confronted three especially difficult problems. The first was the ambiguity of the original SIPs. Many regulations included phrases such as "to the extent possible," "reasonably available controls," and "taking reasonable precautions." Others failed to specify the test method to be used. The EPA, the states, and polluters spent years arguing about what SIPs meant.

The second problem was that many SIPs demanded emission reduction far in excess of that achievable through application of state-of-the-art control equipment. The feasibility controversy took several forms. The EPA claimed that scrubbers constituted a feasible and reliable method for reducing sulfur dioxide emissions from power plants. Power companies, however, disputed this and pressured the agency to allow them to use dispersion enhancement techniques instead. In the case of smelters, the EPA agreed with industry that state-of-the-art controls would not be sufficient to meet national standards. But it disagreed with both

14. 38 Fed. Reg. 16144 (1973).

industry and the states on the extent of control necessary to meet primary standards, the amount of reduction achievable through currently available technology, and the obligation of industry to develop new technology. Many of the regulations set by the states for steel mills were neither achievable without shutdown nor necessary for attainment of national standards. This was especially true of the strict limits placed on fugitive emissions (emissions not released through smokestacks), which are as hard to control as they are to measure. In other cases SIP regulations could be met by relatively new sources or by firms in a strong financial position, but not by marginal firms with old facilities. Many New England pulp and paper mills, for example, could not afford to comply with the many air and water pollution rules that applied to them.

In a few instances state agencies wrote regulations that they knew would force sources to discontinue operation. For example, some states wrote zero emission standards for municipal incinerators in order to compel cities to use sanitary landfills. Usually, though, the state wrote the regulation requiring shutdown without understanding its implications, and later decided to relax it. The EPA looked favorably on these revisions, especially in attainment areas. While many environmental groups and a number of EPA officials firmly believed that the government should shut down sources contributing to air quality standard violations regardless of economic consequences, few took such a position on sources in relatively clean areas. There was general agreement among all participants that at least in attainment areas SIPs should be revised or interpreted to reflect available pollution control technology.

The third problem confronting control agencies was the low-sulfur fuel shortage. When most states included stringent sulfur dioxide standards in their SIPs, they expected that most utilities could comply simply by switching from high-sulfur to low-sulfur coal or from coal to oil. The EPA at first encouraged massive fuel switching. By the time the states had submitted their original plans, however, the agency warned:

> The aggregate emission control requirements of the 55 State plans will create such a great demand for clean fuels, emission control equipment, and other items that attainment of the primary standards in many urban areas in significantly less time than 3 years generally will not be feasible. . . . It appears that all State plans can be completely implemented by 1975 only with a major short term shift to naturally clean fuels. Unfortunately, these naturally clean fuels are not likely to be available in quantities necessary to meet the projected demand.[15]

15. 37 Fed. Reg. 10843 (1972).

The EPA's 1973 clean fuels policy attempted to induce some states to *relax* their SIPs in order to make low-sulfur fuel available for areas still exceeding the health-based sulfur dioxide standards. But while low-sulfur fuel remained relatively inexpensive few states responded to the EPA's request.[16]

This changed in the fall of 1973. The near-term shortage of low-sulfur oil forced the EPA and the states to permit utilities to burn more coal to avert curtailment of service. As oil prices shot up, the states took a second look at their stringent sulfur dioxide regulations. With consumers complaining about their rising electricity bills, state legislatures ordered state air agencies to eliminate the "overkill" included in the original plans. The Nixon administration and the FEA encouraged the states to revise their plans, tried to force the EPA to approve these relaxations, and supported amendments to the Clean Air Act authorizing the EPA to *order* the states to eliminate sulfur dioxide overkill.[17]

Thus the SIPs the EPA approved in 1972 were little more than rough first efforts to define reasonable, workable emission limitations and compliance schedules. The original plans' failure to match emission limitations with the characteristics of individual sources, their high cost, and their heavy reliance on low-sulfur fuels all led to demands for SIP revisions. Even if gaining compliance with SIP requirements had been a simple matter, many environmental advocates inside the EPA and out would have favored amending the SIPs.

Obstacles to Enforcement

Forcing thousands of private sources to comply with emission limitations is not an easy job even when the applicable regulations are unambiguous and unchanging. While the next chapter explains in detail the problems of enforcement under the Clean Air Act, the following paragraphs summarize three obstacles to federal enforcement that created special problems in the mid-1970s: shortages of experienced enforcement personnel; the 1970 act's failure to include credible sanctions for noncompliance; and the growing political opposition to environmental regulation.

16. *Coal Policy Issues,* Hearings before the Senate Committee on Interior and Insular Affairs, 93 Cong. 1 sess. (GPO, 1973), pp. 238–45.

17. See *Administration's Proposal for Relaxation of Air Pollution Standards,* Hearings before the Senate Committee on Public Works, 93 Cong. 1 sess. (GPO, 1973), especially the testimony of John Love.

Before 1971 the EPA and its predecessor agencies had engaged in only one enforcement action against a source of air pollution. Before it could mount a serious enforcement effort the agency had to compile an inventory of major polluters, discover which of these had complied with SIP regulations, write compliance orders for those in violation, and threaten the uncooperative with sanctions. Just building a list of 20,000 major facilities and their characteristics is a large undertaking.[18] Moreover, sources' emissions are hard to measure accurately and vary almost constantly. Even with the greatly expanded staff available by 1980, the EPA could inspect only 10 percent of all major sources per year. At this rate it would take ten years to check the compliance status of all major sources—by which time the sources inspected first would most likely be out of compliance.

Performing all the tasks necessary for enforcing environmental laws takes more than warm bodies and raw data. It requires an experienced staff of engineers who can accurately predict the emission reductions achieved by various control devices and who can provide expert testimony that will hold up in court. It requires lawyers who not only understand the basics of pollution control, but who can deftly negotiate with polluters and win cases in court. The EPA has spent many years accumulating the information and the expertise it needs to carry out an aggressive enforcement program. This apparatus was hardly in place by the 1975 deadline.

Both because the states originally had more experienced personnel than did the EPA and because Congress expected the states to take responsibility for enforcing their own SIPs, the EPA's enforcement program has relied heavily on state agencies. While this dual enforcement system has allowed the EPA to learn from state officials, it has had serious shortcomings. The priorities of state agencies often conflict with those of the federal government. The states frequently resent interference by those whom they consider insensitive to local problems and object to the detailed reporting requirements of the federal government. While such tension often characterizes the relations between the upper and lower levels of a bureaucracy, they become particularly severe when, as here, the "street-level" enforcement officials are not directly under the control of those directing the national enforcement effort.

Compounding this administrative difficulty was the failure of the 1970 act to give the EPA credible sanctions to use against first-time offenders.

18. EPA, "General Report of the Air Compliance Review Group," pp. IV-1 to IV-5.

The agency did not receive authority until 1977 to impose administrative penalties or to ask courts to assess civil penalties for past violations. Since winning a criminal conviction against a polluter is extremely difficult, the worst that could happen to a source that refused to cooperate with the EPA would be a court injunction prohibiting it from exceeding its emission limitations in the future. Most district court judges have studiously avoided taking actions that could close down local businesses, preferring instead to put violators on new compliance schedules. Not only do sources losing court battles receive no penalties for past violations, but they also get plenty of time to come into compliance. The 1970 act's lack of civil penalties, combined with the attitudes of most federal judges, have produced the very sort of litigation-related delay that the First Circuit's variance decision tried to eliminate.

Finally, it did not take the EPA long to realize that efforts to close down major industrial facilities that employ thousands of workers and provide goods and services for millions of consumers would invite political reprisal. While the legislative history of the act repeatedly stated that noncomplying sources should be closed down, EPA officials realized that most congressmen had not appreciated the significance of this command. Congressional opposition to the EPA mounted as environmental protection measures began to inflict economic pain. The energy crisis, inflation, and the recession of 1974 added to this political opposition. The EPA did not want to use its scarce political capital shutting down small sources in attainment areas. It chose its enforcement cases carefully to appear reasonable to Congress and the public.

As a consequence of all these factors, noncompliance with SIP regulations remained the norm for many years. With everyone a sinner in the eyes of the law, there was little stigma associated with violating air pollution regulations. This reduced the extent of voluntary compliance, the mainstay of most enforcement programs, even further. Enforcement of SIP regulations was a painfully slow process.

The EPA's Enforcement Strategy

The EPA slowly formulated an enforcement strategy between 1972 and 1975. This informal policy left a great deal of discretion in the hands of enforcement personnel in the regional offices. Stated in summary form, the EPA's strategy replaced the goals of achieving complete compliance with SIP regulations and attaining the national primary standards by the 1975 deadline with the goal of negotiating agreements with all major sources that committed them to installing all reasonably available control equipment (or contracting to buy available low-sulfur fuel) as soon as possible. In effect the EPA offered polluters a deal: the agency would lower its demands if they would comply without a long struggle. The mechanism the EPA used to effect this deal was the administrative order mentioned in the enforcement section of the Clean Air Act. Between 1972 and 1977 the EPA wrote hundreds of administrative orders that informally rewrote state plans by specifying compliance schedules.

Four characteristics distinguish the enforcement order strategy from the compliance process formally established by the act. First, rather than focusing on emissions, which are hard to measure, the EPA focused on the easily monitored steps of installing control equipment and contracting for low-sulfur fuel. Once a source had installed technological controls, the EPA would consider the source in compliance unless it received firm evidence to the contrary. While realizing that the effectiveness of control equipment is highly dependent on operating levels and on proper maintenance, the EPA preferred to use its scarce resources to convince sources to take the step of installing equipment rather than to conduct inspections and stack tests. Although the agency usually informed sources that they remained liable for equipment malfunctions, polluters realized that neither the EPA nor the courts would punish firms that made good-faith efforts to install controls the EPA itself had deemed suitable.

Second, although the EPA spent a good deal of time and effort defending its legal authority to enforce infeasible regulations, it did not demand that sources install controls beyond those it considered "reasonably available." Usually this meant controls that were both commercially available and affordable. With the exception of a few marginally profitable older plants with very poor pollution records, the EPA never tried to shut down major facilities. Where infeasible regulations were on the books, the EPA engineers based their recommendations for enforcement orders on engineering manuals, consultants' reports, and their own assessment of the peculiarities of individual facilities. When there was serious doubt about a firm's ability to pay for controls the EPA deemed reasonably available, the agency would either give the firm a long time to comply or allow the source to cut a few corners by installing controls of marginal effectiveness. The EPA was tougher on sources in nonattainment areas than those in attainment regions. But even in nonattainment areas the agency looked for measures that would not require shutdown.

The third characteristic follows from the second: compliance schedules often ran past the 1975 deadline. Time was one of the EPA's best bargaining chips. The agency extended compliance schedules in return for the source's commitment to start installing controls. As the deadline approached, it made less and less sense to demand that sources meet it. Just ordering equipment, waiting for delivery, and installing controls can take months or even years. The EPA allowed the compliance schedules for some "problem sources" to extend into the 1980s as long as the sources agreed to meet enforceable increments of progress along the way. Most environmental groups, including the NRDC, accepted this practice, objecting only to those few compliance schedules that lasted a decade or more.

Finally, the EPA did not impose its enforcement order unilaterally but negotiated with the source to find a solution agreeable to both. The following description of the states' negotiations with those seeking permits applies equally well to the EPA's enforcement order negotiations:

> [The] process becomes a bargaining situation in which both sides face steadily increasing costs the longer it takes to reach an agreement, especially if court action ensues. Yet, the possible gains from delay and/or reduced requirements mean that some firms may choose to be noncooperative. In deciding how to respond, the agency must trade the time and manpower costs of a tough stance and the gains in increased cleanup that toughness might achieve, against the value of a quick agreement that frees its limited resources for other tasks.[19]

The results of this process depend on a number of factors, including the skill of the players, the political clout of the source, the enforcement resources of the regional office, the seriousness of the violation, the financial situation of the source, the past success of the regional office in winning court cases, and the effectiveness of the state's enforcement program.

The EPA preferred to conclude these negotiations by having the source sign a consent order specifying both a compliance schedule and a fine for failure to comply with it. The EPA would thus in effect be able to collect civil penalties if the source deviated from the order. Before 1977 most sources refused to sign consent orders, agreeing only to follow the

19. Marc J. Roberts and Susan O. Farrell, "The Political Economy of Implementation: The Clean Air Act and Stationary Sources," in Ann F. Friedlaender, ed., *Approaches to Controlling Air Pollution* (MIT Press, 1978), p. 162.

schedules contained in the EPA's enforcement orders. Since the EPA could enforce such orders only by going to court and since most courts would only put offending sources on new schedules, the bargaining process continued long after the EPA issued its first set of orders. Large or troublesome sources would often receive a number of enforcement orders.

The EPA expected the states to follow much the same strategy and relied on them to do the bulk of the negotiating. But here the agency faced a problem: how could it adequately supervise the states' negotiations? The EPA's guidelines for the states emphasized terms such as "reasonable" and "as expeditiously as possible." This meant that the orders should be as good as the EPA could have gotten if it had done the bargaining. But the EPA could never know what it would have gotten without doing the actual negotiating. Moreover, it was obviously advantageous for the EPA to tolerate somewhat more lenient state-negotiated orders rather than to spend its own resources renegotiating them. The EPA had enough to do just going after sources that the states ignored. Overseeing the adequacy of state efforts was thus a highly uncertain science.

While the technical personnel who came to the EPA from the National Air Pollution Control Administration consistently supported this "reasonably available control technology" approach, many other EPA officials agreed to the strategy only when it became clear that a hard-line position would not work. Worried about being labeled ineffective, wary of court suits brought by environmentalists, and suspicious of those who predicted high compliance costs, the EPA at first disapproved compliance schedules submitted by the states that extended past 1975.[20] But by 1973 even the aggressive Office of Enforcement conceded that it needed authority to negotiate postdeadline compliance schedules. When the OGC argued that such orders would violate the act, the Office of Enforcement replied that issuing long-term orders was well within its inherent "prosecutorial discretion."

Although the Office of Enforcement became the leading proponent of the EPA's enforcement order strategy, it continued to disagree with the OAQPS about its implementation. One key difference between the offices concerned the question of whether to encourage the states to revise their SIPs to reflect the changes made by the administrative orders. The

20. EPA, Enforcement Guideline S-6, "Evaluation of Individual Source Compliance Schedules" (November 23, 1972).

VARIANCES 173

Office of Enforcement generally opposed revisions. The young, aggressive lawyers in that office believed in technology forcing and wanted to keep pressure on polluters to achieve greater reductions in the future. Moreover, the officials responsible for negotiating these orders believed that having infeasible regulations on the books scared polluters and increased the EPA's bargaining power. They also feared that revising SIPs would invite industry to file a torrent of section 307 challenges. Conversely, the OAQPS advocated encouraging the states to revise their SIPs to eliminate requirements more stringent than could be met through reasonably available control technology—at least in attainment areas. The OAQPS warned that keeping infeasible regulations made the EPA look unreasonable to the public. It also saw that the dual system of enforcement orders and SIPs would reduce the importance of the office that approves formal emission limitations. The *NRDC* decision aided enforcement attorneys in their dispute with the OAQPS.

Everyone familiar with the EPA's enforcement program recognized that its use of administrative orders constituted, as one environmental law book put it, "a variance mechanism excusing widespread noncompliance."[21] Environmental groups occasionally complained about the lack of public hearings on enforcement orders and about a few particularly lengthy schedules that they claimed served mainly to prevent citizens from suing polluters under section 304. Yet the EPA succeeded in putting thousands of sources on schedules eventually leading to compliance with SIP limitations. With some problem sources the EPA got half a loaf instead of forcing a confrontation that would have hardened industry resistance and weakened the agency's political support. Given the advantages, the complaint that the strategy might be illegal appeared minor.

The Many Uses of Variances

Part of the confusion over the legality of variances resulted from disagreement about the meaning of the term. As late as 1976 the EPA admitted it had never clearly defined the term "variance."[22] The EPA and the states used many forms of exemptions to deal with the diverse problems they faced. The circuit courts that heard the *NRDC* cases

21. William H. Rodgers, Jr., *Handbook on Environmental Law* (West, 1977), p. 345.
22. 41 Fed. Reg. 18510 (1976).

generally assumed that "if you have seen one variance you have seen them all," and attempted to write a simple, uniform rule to govern the granting of all variances. To appreciate this diversity, it is useful to discuss the many ways the EPA and the states used variances in their enforcement programs. Table 6-1 summarizes the uses of variances and the courts' reactions.

First, many states used variances to ease sources into compliance during the 1973–75 period. As the Supreme Court pointed out, some states preferred to set tough, immediately effective regulations that they would relax only upon the showing of some special hardship. Several state air agencies had no legal authority to issue enforcement orders and thus no choice but to use variances to establish individual compliance schedules. Many EPA enforcement orders fell within this category. While the First Circuit allowed the states to grant this form of variance, the Fifth Circuit did not.

A second use of variances was to cope with the emergency created by the 1973 oil embargo. The EPA approved many variances that postponed scheduled switches to lower-sulfur fuel. The EPA and the states also allowed some sources whose oil supplies were disrupted to increase their emissions. While these variances fell within the three-year grace period established by the First Circuit, the logic behind them had nothing to do with easing sources into compliance. Some involved temporary fuel switching; others represented the beginning of state efforts to remove sulfur dioxide overkill.

Table 6-1. *Courts' Reactions to the Uses of Variances by the Environmental Protection Agency and the States*

Purpose of variance	Used after 1975 deadline	Allowed violation of national air quality standards	Condoned by courts		
			First Circuit	Fifth Circuit	Supreme Court
Ease source into 1975 compliance	No	Yes	Yes	No	Yes
Cope with oil embargo	No	Yes	Yes	No	Yes
Eliminate overkill	Yes	No	No	a	Yes
Establish post-1975 enforcement schedule	Yes	Yes	No	No	No
Deal with short-term emergencies	Yes	Yes	Yes	...	...

a. Depends on whether revision applies to a few sources or a "category."

A third use of variances was to effect a long-term reduction in SIP overkill. The EPA preferred to call these "revisions." It generally required these relaxations, most of which applied to the regulation of sulfur in fuel, to expire after two or three years. This gave the agency a chance to check that its models had correctly predicted that no violation of national air quality standards would occur. While the EPA at first purposely blurred the distinction between these revisions and the type of variances condoned by the First Circuit, it expected many revisions to extend well beyond 1975. The Supreme Court required the EPA to approve state-submitted revisions that do not threaten national standards.

A fourth use of variances was to establish compliance schedules extending beyond 1975. As the above description of the EPA's enforcement order strategy indicates, these schedules fit into three subcategories: (1) those that would eventually bring the source into compliance with its SIP limitations; (2) those that would not bring the source into compliance with its legal emission limitation but would lead to the attainment of national standards; and (3) those that could require the source to install control equipment but would lead neither to complete compliance nor to attainment. No court condoned granting post-1975 variances in nonattainment areas; but none of them explicitly denied that the states or the EPA could use their enforcement discretion to authorize postdeadline extensions.

Finally, the states have often granted short-term variances to sources that experience emergencies such as fire, strike, equipment malfunction, or unforeseen delays in delivery of equipment or conforming fuel. The EPA has had trouble defining what constitutes a legitimate emergency, since emergencies by their very nature are difficult to foresee and categorize. Yet the agency has never objected to the emergency variance provisions in SIPs or to the states' use of these exemptions. The First Circuit allowed states to grant variances in response to "acts of God." The Fifth Circuit and the Supreme Court ignored the problem.

The Consequences of the Variance Decisions

The EPA's policy on variances went through several stages. The agency first attempted to ignore the courts and pursue its original policy. Then, just as the NRDC and several circuit courts were insisting that the EPA comply with the First Circuit's demands, the agency came under intense political pressure to approve a large number of variances for sulfur in fuel. During this second period the EPA did everything it could to cope with the energy crisis in a way that would not lead Congress to gut the Clean Air Act. The legislation Congress finally passed in 1974 did nothing to resolve the variance issue, but only provided further evidence of the political stalemate on the sulfur dioxide issue. The EPA's variance policy entered a third phase in mid-1974 when the NRDC's threat to bring contempt motions against the agency led it to write new guidelines for the states. These guidelines, carefully designed to please the court while preserving flexibility for the EPA and the states, infuriated many state and local officials. The EPA later tried to repair this damage by conceding that the states could write post-1975 enforcement orders—which angered the NRDC. After the Supreme Court announced its 1975 decision, the EPA entered a fourth phase, writing new regulations on revisions after considerable delay. In 1976 the EPA published final regulations that were later ratified by the 1977 amendments. The variance decisions and their consequences provide vivid examples of how administrative agencies can evade court orders as well as how court decisions can increase the bargaining power of successful litigants.

Ignoring the Courts

The EPA spent no more time responding to the First Circuit's order than it had preparing its argument before that court. Technically the decision applied only to two states, Massachusetts and Rhode Island. EPA program officials saw no urgency in responding to a court order that showed little appreciation for the agency's practical problems. After waiting three months, the EPA disapproved the two challenged SIP provisions. The Federal Register notice carefully avoided any mention of revisions, leaving the EPA's previous regulations on that subject intact.[23] The air program office contended that the action raised "no important policy issues." While the First Circuit took "a somewhat more restrictive view of Section 110 than EPA's current legal and policy position," an action memo concluded, its ruling "does not appear to be an unworkable approach."[24]

Shortly after publishing the notice, the EPA indicated its intention to approve long-term SIP relaxations. The regional office directly affected

23. 38 Fed. Reg. 18879 (1973).
24. EPA, action memorandum on Rhode Island and Massachusetts SIPs, June 1973.

by the First Circuit decision threw out all variance requests for non-attainment areas, but continued to review relaxations requested for attainment areas. The OAQPS started to write general guidelines for evaluation of revision requests. This process bogged down, though, when the Office of Enforcement claimed the OAQPS was making it too easy for states to receive SIP relaxations. Yet even the Office of Enforcement did not object to all revisions. It told the regional offices that headquarters would automatically approve all "simple" compliance schedules (those to end before 1975), but would require the states to provide extensive air quality monitoring data before approving a "complex compliance schedule revision" (one "which permanently relaxes an emission limitation beyond the attainment date").[25] Asked to explain how EPA could justify approving post-1975 revisions, the agency's general counsel responded:

> Had the court been faced with an implementation plan designed solely for maintenance of a standard, we believe that it could not have come to the same restrictive conclusion.[26]

In other words, the EPA would not change the policy that the First Circuit had explicitly rejected.

Maintaining this position grew increasingly difficult. In July the Eighth Circuit followed the First. More courtroom defeats loomed on the horizon. Meanwhile, the Nixon administration had introduced legislation authorizing the EPA to order states to relax SIPs inconsistent with its clean fuels policy. While the EPA did not want this authority, the Federal Energy Administration (FEA) used the First Circuit decision to show that unless the act were amended, the states could not comply with the clean fuels policy even if they desired to. The Department of Justice agreed with the FEA's legal interpretations.[27] Thus, by reducing the EPA's flexibility, the NRDC's victories played into the hands of those who sought to weaken the act.

Coping with the Crisis

In October 1973 the states began to flood the EPA with variances for sulfur in fuel. The EPA had little choice but to approve most of these;

25. Memorandum, Alan Kirk (acting assistant administrator for enforcement and general counsel) to regional administrators, July 2, 1973.
26. Letter, William Frick (OGC) to Diana Dutton (Region VI), August 31, 1973.
27. Letter from Assistant Attorney General Wallace Johnson to John Love (FEA), September 13, 1973.

utilities would burn whatever fuel they had regardless of what the EPA said. The agency tried to limit these variances to a few months since this would keep the variances within the First Circuit's grace period and would avoid setting long-term policy in a crisis atmosphere. The EPA preferred to wait until spring to assess the damage done to its programs by the embargo and increased energy costs. The EPA's congressional allies adopted a similar strategy, keeping permanent amendments to the Clean Air Act out of the Energy Supply and Environmental Coordination Act and discouraging the EPA from doing anything that would make the Clean Air Act appear unworkable.

Viewed in this light, the February 1974 decision of the Fifth Circuit was an environmental disaster. That court required the EPA to go through the clumsy section 110(f) process before it could approve any variances for an industrial source. This policy would either have prevented the agency from approving SIP relaxations or would have forced the states to submit requests for wholesale relaxation in order to deal with local fuel shortages. Fearing that the Second Circuit might follow this precedent, the EPA promised that it would issue regulations consistent with the First Circuit's decision.[28] The agency also appealed this portion of the Fifth Circuit decision to the Supreme Court. Chief Justice Warren E. Burger immediately stayed the Fifth Circuit's decision, preventing it from having any direct effect on agency policy.

Meanwhile Congress debated the Nixon administration's emergency energy legislation, but failed to resolve the major policy issues confronting the EPA. The sections of the Energy Supply and Environmental Coordination Act relating to variances and revisions reflected the general political stalemate on the fossil fuel controversy, as had Congress's handling of the dispersion enhancement issue.[29] The act contained only those provisions that Senator Muskie, the EPA, and the Republican administration agreed were absolutely necessary for dealing with the near-term shortage of low-sulfur fuel. The act allowed the EPA to relax temporarily controls on sources unable to get low-sulfur fuel even if this would cause violations of air quality standards. It also authorized the EPA to extend compliance schedules through 1979 for sources converting

28. Letter, Michael James (OGC) to Henry Bourguignon (Department of Justice), February 21, 1974.

29. For a review of the Energy Supply and Environmental Coordination Act, see William F. Pedersen, Jr., "Coal Conversion and Air Pollution: What the Energy Supply and Environmental Coordination Act of 1974 Provides," 4 *Environmental Law Reporter* 50101 (1974).

to coal, provided these extensions would not contribute to violations of primary standards. The Muskie forces presented these provisions on fuel-burning sources as special exemptions that affirmed the stringency of the 1970 act. The FEA and the administration viewed them as explicit confirmation of the EPA's authority to cope with the energy crisis, not as an admission that the EPA could not approve revisions to other categories of sources.

The changes wrought in the revision section of the Clean Air Act in 1974 reveal Congress's inability to resolve the variance issue. The original legislation proposed by Nixon and passed by both the House and the Senate required the EPA to identify those SIPs that included substantial sulfur dioxide overkill and to *order* the states to relax them. After Nixon vetoed the bill containing this provision, the Senate changed its position slightly, allowing the EPA to *recommend* relaxation of state sulfur-in-fuel regulations. The House retained its previous language.[30] The clear assumption behind all these provisions was that any state could revise its SIP as long as the EPA determined that no national standard violation would result.

In the final conference on the Energy Supply and Environmental Coordination Act, the Senate prevailed on the revision issue. Sulfur-in-fuel revisions remained voluntary for the states. Without explanation, however, the conference committee also made one seemingly minor alteration in the language of the new paragraph of section 110(a)(3), adding the italicized phrase:

> Any plan revision which is submitted by the State shall, after public notice and opportunity for public hearing, be approved by the Administrator *if the revision relates only to fuel burning stationary sources (or persons supplying fuel to such sources),* and the plan as revised complies with paragraph (2) of this subsection.

This novel phrase arguably implied that the EPA could not approve nonfuel revisions even if they complied with section 110(a)(2). Yet if this section of the Energy Supply and Environmental Coordination Act reveals any congressional intent at all, it is only the intent of the few conferees and staff members who drafted the final version of the legislation.[31]

30. *A Legislative History of the Energy Supply and Environmental Coordination Act of 1974*, prepared for the Senate Committee on Public Works, 94 Cong. 2 sess. (GPO, 1976), pp. 135–36, 763–64, 1228.

31. Ironically, the Supreme Court ignored this section of the statute. See *Train v. NRDC* at 75.

The EPA expected that Congress would pass comprehensive Clean Air Act amendments in 1975 to resolve the issues left hanging in 1974. But Senator Muskie was in no hurry to act. In fact, when Administrator Train told the Senate committee that the EPA wanted new legislation to confirm its authority to issue post-1975 enforcement orders, Muskie encouraged him to look for loopholes in the 1970 act. The senator observed, "I think to the extent that we can live within the present law at the Federal and State level it is useful to understand what the possibilities for flexibility are."[32] Thus while Muskie and his allies had tried in 1974 to circumscribe the EPA's authority to approve variances, by 1975 they were attempting to do just the opposite. Muskie did not intend to open the act to amendment until just the right political moment. This left the job of devising a variance policy to the EPA.

The Variance Regulations and Their Hostile Reception

Several factors prompted the EPA to begin drafting regulations on the availability of revisions and variances in the spring of 1974. The passage of the Energy Supply and Environmental Coordination Act required the EPA to explain how it would review sulfur-in-coal revision requests. In addition, the NRDC threatened to bring contempt motions against the EPA if it continued to ignore the First and Eighth Circuit decisions.[33] The OGC had also promised the Second Circuit it would initiate regulations carrying out the First Circuit's commands. It hesitated to go before the Supreme Court without having responded to any of the lower court decisions.

The job of writing regulations that would please the NRDC, the Supreme Court, and agency program officials fell to the OGC. The EPA proposed the regulations written by OGC attorneys in September 1974.[34] Although the EPA never formally promulgated final regulations, it followed the policy announced in the proposal until the Supreme Court issued the 1975 *Train* decision.[35] The proposed regulations were a

32. *Clean Air Act Oversight,* Hearings before the Subcommittee on Environmental Pollution of the Senate Committee on Public Works, 93 Cong. 2 sess. (GPO, 1974), p. 1121.

33. Letter, Richard Ayres (NRDC) to Alan Kirk (general counsel), May 2, 1974. The OGC was in constant contact with the NRDC on this issue. Two letters, Michael James (OGC) to Richard Ayres (NRDC), June 21, 1974, and Ayres to James, June 28, 1974, describe these contacts.

34. 39 Fed. Reg. 34533 (1974).

35. 40 Fed. Reg. 14876 (1975) and 40 Fed. Reg. 22587 (1975) refer to the September 1974 proposal as "existing regulations."

masterpiece of circumlocution and carefully disguised ambiguity. They were addressed to two different audiences: the NRDC and the courts on the one hand and the states, industry, and EPA officials on the other. Unfortunately, the subtlety of the wording of the regulations escaped some participants.

The regulations contained two key sections. The first gave the states the following instructions on what constitutes an adequate SIP:

> Enabling authority relating to the issuance of enforcement orders, variances, or other State-initiated measures designed to defer compliance with a plan requirement which is necessary for attainment of a national standard shall specifically provide for consistency with the following requirements.
>
> (1) . . . a plan requirement necessary for attainment of primary standards may not be deferred beyond the primary standards attainment date and a plan requirement for attainment of secondary standards may not be deferred beyond the secondary standards attainment date.

The second section noted that "state plans generally are not consistent with the Clean Air Act" in this respect. It disapproved all state plans

> to the extent that their enabling authority and regulations permit the deferral of compliance with applicable plan requirements beyond the statutory attainment dates specified in the Clean Air Act.[36]

The proposal looks like a simple, direct response to the First Circuit's decision—until one considers the implications of the precise wording.

The first curious aspect of the regulation is the phrase "plan requirement which is necessary for attainment of a national standard." Read in one way, this language distinguishes requirements that are part of a state's strategy for meeting the primary standards from the more stringent requirements designed to attain secondary standards. But one could easily interpret "plan requirement necessary for attainment" to exclude requirements found at any time not to be necessary for attainment of a standard. By this interpretation, overkill is not necessary for attainment of national standards. The regulation thus leaves unanswered the key question of whether states can change their minds about what steps are necessary for attainment of national standards. Not by accident did the regulations fail to mention when the states could apply for plan revisions.

The second curious aspect of the regulations is the use of the terms "enforcement orders" and "enabling authority." While the courts spoke only of variances, the regulations prohibit states from including in their SIPs legal authority to issue postattainment enforcement orders. Why did the EPA, which increasingly encouraged states to issue such orders,

36. 39 Fed. Reg. 34535 (1974).

go further than required by the courts? Apparently the OGC feared that "in view of the strong opinion of the First Circuit," the agency had no choice but to include enforcement orders in its prohibition.[37] But it managed to preserve two loopholes. First, its regulations made no mention of *federal* enforcement orders. Second, the regulations do not prohibit the states from issuing such enforcement orders, but only from including in their SIPs formal authority to do so. This left the states free to employ what the EPA later called their "inherent enforcement authority."

Read in this way, these regulations constituted a victory for those states and industries that sought SIP relaxations and extended compliance schedules. The regulation (1) held open the possibility that states could revise regulations not necessary for meeting the national standards; (2) put no restrictions on EPA enforcement orders; and (3) allowed states to issue enforcement orders as long as they did not mention this in their SIPs. The OGC attorneys who drafted these regulations understood these subtleties. Unfortunately, most states and sources—and even many EPA regional officials—did not.

While industry reacted bitterly to what they saw as overly restrictive regulations written in response to a court decision "initiated by a single organization which represents only a small segment of the public,"[38] the loudest complaints come from state and local air pollution agencies. Their primary concern was the apparent ban on post-1975 variances and administrative orders. Many states were in the middle of major efforts to negotiate compliance schedules with the largest polluters. Most of these schedules lasted longer than the nine months remaining before the mid-1975 deadline. State officials viewed the EPA's regulations as hypocritical as well as disruptive. The day before the EPA proposed these regulations it had signed a consent order with Philadelphia Electric Company giving the utility until 1978 to install a scrubber needed to comply with SIP requirements. By the end of November 1974 the EPA had stated publicly that it intended to issue a large number of enforcement

37. Memorandum, Richard Stoll (OGC) to Alan Kirk (general counsel), October 17, 1974. An OGC attorney had previously advised, "Enforcement orders must be restricted so as not to prevent circumvention of 110(f) . . . in view of the court's acknowledgement of these procedures as a means of changing plan requirements." Letter, William Frick (OGC) to Jean Schueneman (OAQPS), August 24, 1973.

38. Comments of Bethlehem Steel on 39 Fed. Reg. 34533 (on file at the EPA). The American Iron and Steel Institute, Baltimore Gas and Electric, the Tennessee Valley Authority, and a coalition of midwestern utilities offered similar complaints.

orders that would protect sources against enforcement suits and had issued twenty-five compliance orders, some extending to 1985.[39] The EPA seemed to be telling the states, "Do as we say and not as we do."

To make matters worse, the EPA regional offices were giving the states conflicting signals. Some told state agencies they simply could not issue post-1975 orders. Some informed the states that while they could issue such orders, the EPA could not approve them. Other regions either ignored the issue or told the states to ignore the regulations. In the words of an internal EPA report, each regional office "appears to be striking out in its own direction."[40] As the weeks passed EPA headquarters began to realize that it had failed to communicate its intentions to the regions and the states.

The proposed regulations ultimately produced three unfortunate results. The first and most obvious was heightened animosity between the partners in the national enforcement program, the EPA and the state agencies. The states viewed the proposals as just one more example of the EPA's arrogance, incompetence, and detachment from reality. During this period the EPA was trying to convince the states to help it administer several new and controversial programs, including prevention of significant deterioration, indirect source review, and transportation control plans. Now the EPA was making it more difficult for them to perform their basic function. The head of Colorado's air agency complained, "The variance procedure starting this July is going to be in a state of total confusion with the introduction of EPA compliance orders." The director of the West Virginia air program lost his temper at a meeting with EPA enforcement officials and then told the Muskie subcommittee:

> EPA has ruled that these [post-1975] schedules are not "approvable" and is strongly pushing that EPA issue "friendly" "consent orders" or "enforcement orders" which will, in effect, duplicate the compliance schedules West Virginia has filed with the Administrator. . . . Quite frankly, it is confusing as to how EPA can take this action and make it lawful and the same action by a state, filed under the requirements of its plan, is unlawful.[41]

The second consequence was that some states stopped issuing enforcement orders until they received assurances that the EPA would not object. Some state officials were genuinely concerned about the possibility

39. 5 *Environment Reporter—Current Developments* 1097–98, 1130–31, 1232–34. The state of Pennsylvania signed an identical order with Philadelphia Electric, stating that the order was issued "in lieu of variances."
40. EPA, "General Report of the Air Compliance Review Group," p. IV-20.
41. *Clean Air Act Oversight,* Hearings, pp. 301, 305.

that their actions might be illegal. Others acted out of pique, showing the EPA that it could not get along without the states. But the major reason for the states' slowdown of their enforcement efforts was their reluctance to spend time negotiating orders that EPA enforcement officials would later rule invalid. This put the EPA on the defensive. Regional officials tried to assure the states that they could safely disregard official agency statements on the inviolability of the 1975 deadline.

The third consequence of the September proposal was that the states that continued to issue post-1975 enforcement orders hesitated to inform the EPA of their activities. The EPA could not disapprove orders it did not know existed. The EPA had always had difficulty getting the states to submit copies of their orders; it now became even harder to do so. This meant that the EPA could neither review the states' orders for consistency nor coordinate its enforcement program with the states. If the states were reluctant to talk to the regions, the regions were equally reluctant to tell headquarters what they knew about the states' activities. No administrative level cared to admit what it was doing.[42] Thus, rather than increasing EPA supervision of the states, the NRDC decisions served to reduce the flow of information to and through the EPA. The agency's enforcement program suffered as a result.

In early 1975 enforcement officials in Washington decided that something had to be done to address these problems. They advocated publishing guidelines explaining to the states that the proposed regulations allowed them to write post-1975 enforcement orders and encouraging the states to submit their orders to the EPA for review. In April 1975, shortly before the Supreme Court announced the *Train* decision, the EPA proposed a second set of enforcement regulations announcing that "it was not the intention of the Administrator to restrict a State from taking such enforcement action."[43]

The EPA explained that it recognized the "inherent enforcement authority residing in the State" and laid out procedural and substantive requirements that, if followed, would give the source "some assurance that its conscientious compliance efforts, in response to a State issued enforcement order, will be relatively free from Federal challenge." The procedural requirements included providing members of the public with

42. EPA, "General Report of the Air Compliance Review Group," pp. IV-16 to IV-31. The review group found that "knowledge of a source's compliance status increased as the review group went from the Federal to the State to the local level" (p. III-10).

43. 40 Fed. Reg. 14876 (1975).

notice and "opportunity to comment and request a public hearing." The substantive requirements were much more vague: states must demand that sources achieve compliance "as expeditiously as possible," that they install "appropriate interim control measures," and that they meet "appropriate increments of progress." The EPA knew it could not police these guidelines, but it hoped that they would encourage the states to continue issuing enforcement orders, to involve the general public, and to communicate with the EPA.

The major opposition to these regulations came not from environmental groups or from Congress, but from state agencies and regional offices, which thought the hearing requirement would take too much time. Realizing it had little leverage against the states, the EPA backed down on the hearing requirement. In all other respects the proposed enforcement regulations served as rough guidelines for EPA and state enforcement officials until 1977. Yet the EPA never formally adopted the proposed rules, and the OGC continued to express qualms about their legality.[44]

In 1975, 1976, and 1977 the EPA asked Congress to ratify the policy contained in this second set of proposed regulations. While Senator Muskie and others recognized the difficult position the EPA was in, they let the agency muddle along as it had been doing rather than open the act to amendment. The EPA spent considerable effort during those years trying to cut its previous enforcement losses.

The Aftermath of the Train Decision

Shortly after the EPA announced its new enforcement policy, the Supreme Court upheld the agency's initial policy on revisions. The decision seemed to come just when the EPA needed it most: the First Circuit's grace period would end within a few months. Yet, as the EPA soon realized, the Supreme Court's decision was both too little and too late. It was too little because it ignored the crucial question of postdeadline enforcement orders. The previous court decisions had forced the EPA to issue guidelines on postdeadline variances and enforcement orders, and the Supreme Court's decision gave the agency no authority to alter them. The decision came too late because it left the EPA without revision guidelines just when many sources wanted to use revision requests to

44. 40 Fed. Reg. 21046 (1975).

delay complying with SIP limitations. For two years court orders had inhibited the EPA from developing a clear policy on what sources had to do to qualify for revisions. When the Supreme Court ruled that the states are *entitled* to revisions that allow attainment and maintenance of national air quality standards, many sources broke off negotiations with enforcement officials, hoping to substitute plan revisions for extended compliance orders. This added yet another obstacle to enforcement of SIP regulations.[45]

Once again the EPA undertook the task of defining approvable SIP revisions. In writing new guidelines the EPA walked a tightrope between making its requirements too strict and making them too loose. On the one hand, the more lenient the guidelines, the greater the risk of ambient standard violations. SIP relaxations would also compound the atmospheric loading problem and slow enforcement by encouraging more sources to apply for revisions. Environmental groups forcefully pointed out all these dangers.

On the other hand, if the EPA made its requirements too demanding, sources would refrain from seeking revisions—which are susceptible to EPA control—and would instead increase pressure on the states to grant less restrictive compliance orders—which are much harder for the EPA to oversee. States that thought the EPA was being unreasonable could simply refrain from asking the agency to approve state-issued variances. To make matters worse, strict requirements would hamper the EPA's effort to redirect low-sulfur fuel to areas needing it most and would absorb scarce state and EPA resources. The cost of extensive modeling and monitoring requirements would put an especially heavy burden on small sources.

While the EPA recognized the urgency of publishing revision guidelines, it could not reach internal agreement on them until early 1976.[46] Even then it avoided many of the hardest issues by leaving significant discretion

45. In a June 6, 1975, memorandum, Acting Assistant Administrator for Enforcement Richard Johnson told Assistant Administrator Roger Strelow, "The toll on our enforcement program of further delay could be particularly severe. Already sources in several regions have refused to continue negotiations for consent orders, expressing in doing so their intent to apply for a variance that would obviate the need for such an order. . . . Until a variance request is formally disapproved, or until EPA formally promulgates approval criteria which would render a variance request unapprovable, it may be very difficult to proceed with enforcement."

46. The EPA announced its intention to formulate such guidelines on May 23, 1975 (40 Fed. Reg. 22587). They were proposed on December 16, 1975 (40 Fed. Reg. 58317) and promulgated on May 5, 1976 (41 Fed. Reg. 18510).

in the hands of its regional offices. The EPA required the states to provide detailed air quality monitoring data for the area affected by the proposed revision and to produce dispersion modeling estimates of the potential impact of emission increases. But it allowed the regional offices to define the "affected area" to which these requirements applied. Noting that small sources in rural areas should not be subjected to the same level of scrutiny as large sources in urban areas, the agency announced that "the areas considered in different control strategy demonstrations would therefore vary widely depending on many considerations." After mentioning a few of these relevant circumstances, the EPA concluded, "It is impossible to specify uniform standards by which demonstration will be evaluated by EPA."

These regulations drew predictable criticisms from environmental groups and state agencies. The NRDC, which had always feared that the EPA would not carefully scrutinize variance requests, described the EPA's policy as "maximizing its discretion by vague general regulation (or no regulation at all)."[47] State and local officials, in contrast, claimed that the regulations were unnecessarily rigid. One local California air pollution agency, for example, saw the regulations as another illustration

> that the Federal government is too much involved with setting procedures to protect air quality by uncertain means (mathematical models) against some insignificant (very small) sources among unknown phenomenon (all oxidant and particulate sources) without corresponding benefits for local government or local air quality.[48]

The state of Wisconsin warned that strict revision requirements could have perverse results:

> By treating "variances" as plan revisions we are establishing a very time-consuming and expensive procedure for processing them. By definition this procedure is only applicable in attainment areas. At the same time the problem sources located in non-attainment areas can be handled on an informal basis with no procedural controls. We fear that the elaborate procedures will require a concentration of staff time and monies, both for EPA and Wisconsin in the attainment areas. This effort would better be spent in the non-attainment areas.[49]

These comments indicate that there was not a unitary "pro-environmental" position on the revision issue.

---

47. Comments on December 16, 1975, proposal submitted by the NRDC (on file at the EPA).
48. Ibid., from Yolo Salona Air Pollution Control District.
49. Ibid., from State of Wisconsin.

In writing revision guidelines the EPA discovered the inherent difficulty of controlling the behavior of polluters, state officials, and lower levels of the federal bureaucracy. The tougher it made its formal review, the stronger became incentives to resolve controversies in informal proceedings, the less cooperation it received from lower-level enforcement officials, and the more effort it spent reviewing a few revision requests. More lenient review both allowed a greater number of formal SIP relaxations and encouraged sources to stall while seeking SIP revisions. The EPA had little choice but to trust its regional offices to use their knowledge of local circumstances to avoid these dual dangers. The EPA's approach contrasts sharply with that of the First Circuit, which tried to use clear, uniform rules to control the behavior of bureaucrats whom it did not trust.

The Contrast between Congress and the Courts

In amending the Clean Air Act in 1977 Congress indicated that it too had qualms about the EPA's use of variances and enforcement orders. Congress's solution to the problem was far different from that of the circuit courts that ruled against the EPA. The contrast between the actions of Congress and the courts serves to highlight the judiciary's limited ability to control the behavior of large bureaucracies.

The 1977 amendments—in contrast to the Energy Supply and Environmental Coordination Act—directly confronted the revision issue and explicitly condoned the EPA's original policy. The House report confirmed "the correctness of the Supreme Court's opinion in the *Train* case." But neither house took nearly so sanguine a view of the EPA's use of extended compliance orders. While the House report claimed that the EPA's administrative orders were "of questionable legal validity," the Senate report bluntly announced, "This procedure has no basis in law."[50] Of course, the EPA had long recognized this and had requested legal authority to write realistic compliance schedules.

Rather than either prohibit all postdeadline extensions or give the EPA a blank check to determine when sources must comply with state plans, the authors of the amendments attempted "to strike a middle

50. *Clean Air Act Amendments of 1977*, H. Rept. 95-294, 95 Cong. 1 sess. (GPO, 1977), pp. 55, 57; and *Clean Air Amendments of 1977*, S. Rept. 95-127, 95 Cong. 1 sess. (GPO, 1977), p. 45.

course on the question of how and to what extent continued non-compliance with the State implementation plan requirements may be permitted." The House report explained its dissatisfaction both with the approach suggested by the NRDC and with that used by the EPA in this way:

> On the one hand, the committee recognized that the single one-year limitation and formal procedures of the section 110(f) postponement provision were too restrictive. On the other hand, the committee did not favor continued use of the section 113(a) enforcement order as a means for permitting delayed compliance schedules for several reasons. First, as construed and applied by EPA, the section 113(a) delays are not limited to any particular date or time period. Second, the Administrator under section 113(a) can grant lengthy delays without the consent or approval of the State, despite the apparent inconsistency between such a unilateral Federal extension authority and the policy and language of section 116 of the act. Third, section 113(a) does not require the holding of a public hearing prior to issuing an enforcement order.[51]

Consequently Congress put strict limits on the use of administrative orders, but provided the EPA with other means for dealing with the problems that occasioned their use in the first place.

The amendments limited the EPA's enforcement discretion by prohibiting it from issuing unilateral administrative orders and requiring it to file suit whenever it finds a violation of the act. The amendments also invalidated most of the agency's administrative orders extending past 1979. In addition, the new section 120 requires the EPA to assess noncompliance penalties against all sources that exceed their emission limitations after 1979.

At the same time, the 1977 amendments gave the agency a number of tools for dealing with those sources that had not yet complied with SIP limitations. Under section 113(d) the EPA could issue a delayed compliance order to any source unable to comply immediately with SIP regulations. A delayed compliance order could extend compliance no later than July 1979. Before issuing one, the EPA had to publish the proposed order in the Federal Register, conduct a public hearing, gain the approval of the state, and publish a final order that included interim control measures. This put a time limit on the use of administrative orders and added procedural requirements designed to involve both the public and the states in the deadline extension process.

Congress also recognized that a few categories of problem sources would be unable to comply even by the mid-1979 deadline without

51. *Clean Air Act Amendments of 1977*, H. Rept. 95-294, p. 56.

shutting down. For these sources the 1977 amendments created special exemptions. Some coal-burning power plants received extensions to 1980 and a few others to 1985. The amendments authorized the EPA to issue nonferrous smelter orders extending compliance for these troublesome sources for up to ten years.

Just as important, the amendments strengthened the EPA's capacity to force polluters to comply with SIP regulations. The agency finally received legal authority to ask courts to impose civil penalties for past SIP violations. This makes it much riskier for sources to sit back and wait for the EPA to initiate enforcement action. The threat of civil penalties also increases the EPA's bargaining power in negotiations over consent decrees. With these new penalties the EPA need not trade extended compliance schedules for mere promises of cooperation. By imposing harsh no-growth sanctions in nonattainment areas, the amendments also increase the states' incentives to force sources in these areas to reduce their emissions.

The EPA still has a great deal of trouble bringing the worst polluters into compliance with their SIP limitations. Enforcement remains a slow and often frustrating process for an important minority of facilities. There can be no doubt, though, that the 1977 amendments aided the EPA in its enforcement efforts and made the enforcement process more visible to the public. In this the actions of Congress stand in marked contrast to those of the courts that decided the variance cases.

Judicial Capacity and the Variance Issue

The courts that ruled in favor of the NRDC in the variance cases sought to reduce delay in the enforcement process and to promote expeditious attainment of the national ambient air quality standards. To the extent that the decisions affected the EPA's actions, they produced just the opposite result. Once the EPA found it could no longer simply ignore the NRDC decisions, the agency and the states circumvented the court rulings by substituting informal enforcement orders for formal variances. This reduced the extent of oversight both by the general public—which had no opportunity to comment on de facto SIP revisions—and by the EPA—which had great difficulty explaining its intentions to the states. The states, irritated by EPA regulations designed to appease the NRDC and the courts, responded by reducing their enforcement efforts and refusing to coordinate their enforcement programs with the EPA's. When the Supreme Court finally confirmed the EPA's authority to approve revisions consistent with attainment of national standards, the agency was left without revision guidelines just as the rapid approach of the statutory deadline was creating a torrent of revision requests. Delay in the writing of revision guidelines caused further delay in the enforcement process.

The variance cases illustrate three institutional weaknesses of courts. First, the courts were woefully uninformed about the informal constraints on the EPA's enforcement program. Neither the EPA nor the NRDC explained to the circuit courts the inadequacies of the original SIPs, the consequences of the oil embargo, or the reasons why the EPA had to rely heavily on cooperation from the states and from polluters themselves. The NRDC had no incentives to divulge these facts. Moreover, the cases were first argued long before the EPA had had much experience with enforcement. To make matters worse, the Department of Justice and OGC lawyers who argued the EPA's case in the circuit courts were far removed from the regional office's enforcement personnel. Enforcement officials not only had trouble explaining their position to other branches of the agency, but hesitated to admit openly that the SIPs were full of holes or that the EPA had resigned itself to issuing lenient section 113(a) orders. A candid description of EPA's enforcement conundrum would have weakened the agency's bargaining position with industry and would have invited further attacks by environmental groups on its use of extended compliance schedules. The adversarial process failed to provide all the information the courts needed to design a workable solution to the problem before them.

The second weakness of the courts was their need to rely on a simple rule to address a complex problem. Sources requested variances for many reasons. Some simply did not want to spend the requisite money on control equipment; others could not get low-sulfur fuel after 1973; a few could not comply without shutting down; many did not learn about control requirements until the date for compliance had passed; others hesitated to spend large amounts of money on controls not necessary for meeting national standards. The First Circuit's "no variances after 1975" rule lumped together sources that contributed to ambient standard violations with those who did not, those who needed a few months to comply with those who needed years, those who could comply without reducing operations with those who could not, and those who preferred to cooperate with the EPA with those who had no intention of meeting their SIP limitations. A more effective rule would have been a far more complex one—one closer to the collection of enforcement provisions in the 1977 amendments than the order issued by the First Circuit. Yet even if the courts had known enough about the SIP compliance problem to formulate such a rule, they would have had greater difficulty explaining why the statute required such interpretations and even more difficulty trying to monitor the EPA's compliance with it.

Finally, the consequences of the variance cases show that the greater the burdens placed on the EPA in its formal dealing with states and sources, the greater the agency's incentives to develop informal agreements that appear more reasonable to lower-level bureaucrats. To prevent this the courts must scrutinize not just the hundreds of enforcement orders issued by the EPA, but the even larger number of cases in which the EPA took no official action whatsoever. This would require the courts to build a bureaucracy nearly the size of the EPA's. While the courts can force agencies to write regulations, they have far more difficulty compelling them to take the hundreds of steps necessary to make sure that private parties comply with these regulations.

While the new administrative law questions the dedication of administrative agencies to their statutory mission, in the end the courts must rely on these very agencies to execute the law faithfully. The courts succeeded in instituting a prevention of significant deterioration program and in limiting the use of dispersion techniques because most EPA officials agreed that these policies were reasonable ones. The courts failed to speed up the EPA's enforcement effort because EPA enforcement officials believed—with good reason— that the expedient offered by the courts was both unreasonably harsh and unrealistically inflexible. Before being overturned by the Supreme Court, the variance decisions stood as roadblocks to bureaucratic enforcement efforts, not as spurs to more effective administrative action.

CHAPTER SEVEN

Enforcement: The Triumph of Equity

The position of the Government ... was that, upon the basis of the violation as found by the EPA and the non-compliance by the Town, the Government was ipso facto *... entitled to an order of enforcement. We think this was too rigid a position and that proof of relevant circumstances was admissible in support of what we consider to be the Court's duty, in the exercise of its equitable powers, to fashion its decree in such a way as to deal fairly with the case.*

—U.S. v. *Town of North Hempstead,* 1979

CONGRESSMEN and environmentalists who criticized the Environmental Protection Agency's use of administrative orders before 1977 often claimed that the EPA would have been more successful in forcing polluters to comply with emission limitations had the agency filed more enforcement suits under section 113 of the Clean Air Act. Responding to this criticism, Congress added to the 1977 amendments a section requiring the EPA to initiate litigation in federal district court against all sources not in compliance with state implementation plans (SIPs) by 1979.

Yet the EPA originally adopted its administrative order strategy because it considered litigation an extremely risky and burdensome undertaking. Agency lawyers with experience in arguing environmental cases before federal district courts warned that since judges seldom impose credible sanctions on local polluters, the meager benefits of filing suit do not come close to equaling the large administrative costs of the enterprise. The EPA has filed many enforcement suits since 1977, but it has tried hard to settle these cases through consent decrees, even if this has required making concessions to polluters on schedules, extent of control, and civil penalties.

Has court action in enforcement proceedings impeded the EPA's efforts to force polluters to comply with the act, or is this an excuse used by bureaucrats to hide their timidity and ineffectiveness? Studies of other regulatory programs indicate that delay and the "balancing of equities" to favor local business firms is a common feature of enforcement through the courts.[1] But several federal courts have indicated that achieving health-based air quality standards is so important that the EPA and the courts must deal harshly with violators. "Sources of pollutants," the First Circuit stated in its decision on variances, "should either meet the standard of the law, or be closed down."[2] It is possible, therefore, that while the procedural safeguards provided defendants in court suits make court-based enforcement slow, the courts have used their discretion where possible to insist that polluters comply with the act.

Estimating the effect of court decisions on the enforcement process is not an easy task. The courts have handed down a large number of decisions influencing enforcement. Most of these rulings involve particular, often unusual, fact patterns. Moreover, while thousands of sources remain out of compliance with SIP limitations, only a handful of cases have actually gone to trial. Many more judges have helped resolve enforcement cases in pretrial conferences and in their responses to requests for summary judgment. Few of these actions are formally reported, and they, too, revolve around the idiosyncrasies of individual cases.

This does not mean that these court actions do not have a substantial impact on the EPA's entire enforcement effort. The EPA cannot impose sanctions on violators without the approval of the judiciary. Consequently, the agency's ability to force polluters to install pollution controls ultimately rests on the threat of judicially mandated fines and compliance schedules. One of the major determinants of the EPA's success in the cases that never reach court is polluters' perceptions of the likelihood that the courts will take action against them. Both the EPA and pollution sources look to past judicial action on enforcement to help them guess how the courts will react to future cases.

Taken as a whole, court decisions on enforcement contrast sharply with those on prevention of significant deterioration, dispersion, and variance. In interpreting the enforcement sections of the Clean Air Act,

---

1. See, for example, William A. Irwin, Edward I. Selig, and others, *Enforcement of Federal and State Water Pollution Controls: A Report to the National Commission on Water Quality* (Environmental Law Institute, 1975), especially pp. 208–09; and Philip G. Schrag, "On Her Majesty's Secret Service: Protecting the Consumer in New York City," 80 *Yale Law Journal* 1529 (1971).

2. *Natural Resources Defense Council* v. *Environmental Protection Agency,* 478 F.2d 875 at 886 (1st Cir. 1973).

reviewing the validity of individual SIP requirements, and setting penalties for those who violate regulations, the federal courts have significantly impeded the EPA's efforts to bring polluters into compliance with the act. First, federal courts have insisted upon extremely restrictive readings of the enforcement provisions of the act. They have been as niggardly in granting the agency tools with which to implement the law as they have been enthusiastic about expanding the environmental goals the EPA must pursue. Court decisions on the EPA's enforcement authority have brought enforcement of some regulations to a screeching halt. Other decisions have inhibited the EPA from bringing suit while a legal cloud hangs over its enforcement authority.

Second, the courts have interpreted the Clean Air Act to require that the EPA do far more than show that the polluter in question has violated a legal emission limitation. The courts have demanded that the EPA also prove that the violation contributes to a significant health hazard and that the source can comply with the regulations by installing commercially available, affordable controls. These requirements reduce the number of cases the EPA can pursue in court, increase the uncertainty of litigation, and thus make the agency more eager to reach agreement with the polluter before going to trial.

Third, by avoiding decision in enforcement cases altogether, many federal district court judges have added to regulatory delay and have encouraged the EPA to make further concessions to polluters. While a few judges (notably those in western states) have shown open hostility to the EPA, most district court judges simply do not want to hear complex air pollution cases that clog their dockets and force them to make hard choices between pollution control and local prosperity. They often rely on procedural or jurisdictional arguments to put off decisions on the merits and at times instruct both parties to reach agreement among themselves. Ironically, the complexity that so often intimidates trial judges results from judicial demands that the EPA produce detailed evidence on feasibility, health effects, and other factors relevant to the balancing of equities.

The Enforcement Process

To appreciate the import of judicial activity on the SIP enforcement process, it is necessary to examine the many administrative steps that precede judicial resolution of a section 113 case. The authors of the 1970 act claimed that section 113 created a streamlined enforcement mechanism to replace the cumbersome and ineffective conference procedure established by the 1967 act. Under section 113, once the EPA discovers a violation of a SIP it must issue a notice of violation to the source. If the violation persists for more than thirty days the administrator can either file a civil suit for "appropriate relief, including permanent or temporary injunctions," or issue an administrative order to the source. If the EPA issues an order, it must grant the source an opportunity to confer with the administrator and must "specify a time for compliance which the Administrator determines is reasonable, taking into account the seriousness of the violation and any good faith efforts to comply with applicable requirements." If a source violates an order, the EPA can bring a subsequent civil action.

Since SIPs should include specific, numerical emission limitations for each source, it would seem that the act established a simple, efficient enforcement process. Yet every step in the enforcement process has turned out to be much more difficult and time consuming than any of the sponsors of the 1970 act ever imagined. Most of the EPA's enforcement resources are devoted to carrying out the supposedly simple steps that precede the filing of a court case.[3]

Defining and Detecting a Violation

Before the EPA can initiate any form of enforcement action it must compile a list of major polluters and establish a specific emission limitation for each facility. It took the EPA and the states several years to gather this information and to decide exactly how SIP regulations apply to

3. Since enforcement policy is hardly ever codified in regulations or formal statements, this chapter relies heavily on interviews with enforcement officials in the Environmental Protection Agency's Division of Stationary Source Enforcement in Washington, D.C., and in the following regional offices: Boston, New York, Philadelphia, Chicago, Denver, and San Francisco. I have avoided direct quotations, since many officials spoke candidly with me with the understanding that I would write nothing that would prejudice pending cases. The same applies to agency files on individual cases, which I perused in some regional offices. Other important sources for this chapter include Irwin, Selig, and others, *Enforcement of Federal and State Water Pollution Controls;* EPA, Office of Enforcement, "General Enforcement Procedural Guidelines" (on file in Division of Stationary Source Enforcement, Office of Enforcement, EPA); Memorandum, Assistant Administrator Marvin Durning to regional administrators, "Civil Penalty Policy—Certain Air and Water Act Violators," April 11, 1978; and the exchange between Charles Corkin II and Leslie Carothers in 1 *Harvard Environmental Law Review* 333 (1976).

particular sources. Unfortunately, SIP revision is a never-ending process. The Clean Air Act's reliance on an air quality management approach rather than an emission-based regulatory scheme increases the delay in establishing those source-specific emission limitations that are the sine qua non of enforcement.

The enforcement process begins in earnest when the EPA receives data indicating that a particular source has exceeded its emission limitation. Using authority granted by section 114 of the act, the EPA requires major sources to submit periodic reports on their production and emission rates. State air agencies must inspect each major source at least once per year to retain federal grants. The EPA audits the states' reports by inspecting 5 to 10 percent of the major sources in each state. It also conducts special "case development" inspections of sources with a history of noncompliance. Regional offices feed all this information into a computerized compliance data system, which reports the compliance status of each major source in the country.

Even with this elaborate system, though, many SIP violations escape detection. Yearly inspections cannot uncover episodic equipment malfunctions and production rate increases. Clever polluters can increase their emissions at times when inspectors are unlikely to visit. Investigations by the EPA and the General Accounting Office indicate that almost 25 percent of the sources registered as "in compliance" by the compliance data system actually exceeded their legal emission limitation.[4]

When an EPA regional office receives evidence suggesting that a source is out of compliance, it can either ask the state agency to handle the case or deal with the source itself. The EPA takes only cases that are particularly complex, that the state has failed to resolve, or that the state has avoided for political reasons. If the EPA tackles the case, it must wait for a regional office engineer to visit the source and complete a trip report recording his findings. This report combines the inspector's observations with engineering rules of thumb to compare the source's actual emissions with its legally allowable emissions. Since elaborate stack testing is done for only the largest sources, the engineering sections of the regional enforcement office must rely on extrapolations and judgment calls about opacity and fugitive emission levels. It can take this section of the EPA weeks to decide whether a SIP violation has in fact occurred. In a borderline case the EPA will request additional information from the source.

4. General Accounting Office, "Improvements Needed in Controlling Major Air Pollution Sources," Report CED-78-165 (Government Printing Office, 1979), pp. 8–9.

Only when the engineers are convinced that they can prove a source is in violation will they ask enforcement lawyers to issue a notice of violation. These lawyers must then decide whether the engineers have correctly interpreted the regulation, whether the violation is serious enough to merit attention, whether the state should be given another chance to take charge, and whether the EPA needs more evidence. While the EPA officially accepts the legal doctrine that it *must* issue a notice of violation as soon as it receives evidence of a violation, it frequently ignores this "nondiscretionary duty" in practice.[5]

Even in a simple case months can elapse between the time the EPA notes a possible violation and issues a notice. In complex, controversial cases, where the evidence is ambiguous or where the EPA and the state disagree on the meaning of the regulation, delay is even longer. Yet the EPA can neither file suit nor issue an administrative order until it finds a second violation thirty days or more after the first. If the source has not come into compliance by this time, most likely its problem is a serious one.

Negotiating a Compliance Schedule

Before the EPA can take further action against a source, it must hold a conference with the source to present its evidence on the alleged violation and to discuss possible cures. The EPA uses this meeting to open negotiations with the source on possible compliance schedules. Before 1977 these negotiations almost always culminated in a section 113(a) administrative order. Since the 1977 amendments deprived the EPA of authority to issue these orders, the agency now tries to convince sources to sign consent agreements specifying both interim compliance measures and penalties for failure to meet them. Because the conference follows fast on the heels of issuance of the notice of violation, the EPA will often delay sending the notice until its engineers and lawyers are prepared for these negotiations. For most large problem sources the conference is only the beginning of negotiations that can take months or even years.

What do the EPA and the source bargain about? Occasionally there is remaining ambiguity in the regulation, which leads to dispute over the extent of the violation. More frequently negotiations center on four other issues. The first is timing. The EPA always gives the source enough

5. The key case is *Wisconsin's Environmental Decade* v. *Wisconsin Power,* 395 F. Supp. 313 (W.D. Wis. 1975).

time to receive and install requisite control equipment. It usually allows firms in financial trouble to phase in expensive controls. In a few instances the agency permits a firm to operate a facility that violates SIP regulations while it constructs a replacement facility. The EPA and the source usually disagree on how long each of these steps will take.

The second issue is the type of controls the source must install. While the EPA insists that a polluter bears responsibility for installing control equipment that does not bring it into compliance, by issuing an administrative order or signing a consent agreement the agency gives its tacit approval to the plan followed by the source. Both sets of negotiators realize that the EPA will not take punitive action against a source that makes good-faith efforts to comply with its schedule. The EPA usually insists upon conservative estimates of the reduction produced by control equipment. But if enforcement officials believe that the source cannot afford the best controls, they allow the firm to purchase equipment of marginal effectiveness. The EPA and the source argue both about the effectiveness of various control measures and the firm's ability to pay for them.

The 1977 amendments added a third bargaining issue, civil penalties. Most agreements between the EPA and polluters now include provisions limiting the sources' liability for past violations, specifying additional controls to be installed in lieu of civil penalties, and providing stipulated penalties for failure to meet interim compliance requirements contained in the agreement. While the prospect of being assessed civil penalties for past violations brings some sources to the bargaining table, the penalty issue also increases the complexity of negotiations. Often this part of the bargaining process continues long after both sides have agreed on a compliance schedule.

Finally, enforcement negotiations often meld with efforts to revise SIP regulations. The EPA gives no formal recognition to revision applications until they have received final approval. But enforcement officials at the state and federal levels seldom insist that an enforcement order include control requirements that will soon become superfluous. In fact, the EPA may even suggest revisions, hoping to trade this concession for the source's signature on a consent agreement. This means that negotiations expand to include the regional office's air branch and the state air agency. This requires enforcement officials to wait for dispersion modelers to conclude their air quality assessment before finishing the negotiations.

A regional office can usually complete negotiations with a relatively small source within a few months. The regions now have authority to conclude such agreements after only pro forma review by headquarters. For sources such as coal-burning power plants, smelters, steel mills, refineries, municipal incinerators, and federal facilities, however, the process takes far longer and involves more extensive headquarters review. Often negotiators must wait for the completion of technical reports on the effectiveness of various control measures, the accuracy of monitoring devices, the financial condition of the firm, and the time required to construct replacement facilities.

The specificity of major consent decrees explains why they take so long to negotiate. The 1979 agreement between the EPA and U.S. Steel governing four of that firm's Pittsburgh facilities, for example, was eighty-two pages long (not including technical appendixes) and took years to negotiate. It included such arcane provisions as the following:

> Defendant may install a three or four sided unevacuated doghouse enclosing each vessel at each BOP shop. If Defendant installs a four sided doghouse, it shall be equipped with door seals of similar design to those seals which Defendant has installed at vessel "U" at its Fairfield, Alabama works. . . . Defendant shall complete any installation by July 1, 1980. Defendant may attempt to demonstrate to the Plaintiff and the Intervenors by August 31, 1980, that it has achieved compliance at each shop with the emission limitations in paragraph 4(a), in accordance with the test procedures in Appendix 1.[6]

These consent agreements are really new SIPs that provide the specificity lacking in the old ones.

After a source signs a consent agreement it frequently asks the EPA to accept modifications as it learns more about the cost and effectiveness of various control measures. The EPA often enters into further negotiations. In part this is because the agency, like the source, is in the process of learning about pollution control and will accept changes it considers reasonable. In part, too, the EPA wishes to avoid the alternative to renegotiation—filing suit against the source. As one EPA engineer who helped reach an agreement with steel companies remarked, "The negotiations never end."

Filing Suit

Before it can file suit in federal court, the EPA must explain the issues arising in the case to the Department of Justice and the local U.S.

---

6. Quoted from the EPA's consent agreement with U.S. Steel, 1979–80 (on file in the EPA's Region III office). The EPA later amended the consent decree, eventually going to Congress to receive authority to allow the compliance schedule to extend past 1982.

attorney and must convince them to pursue the case. These non-EPA attorneys seldom are well versed in the technical details of air pollution control. Moreover, they hesitate to bring cases they might not win and insist upon being prepared to answer any question the judge might ask. This means that the EPA spends a great deal of time answering the inquiries of government lawyers before the case ever gets on a court docket. While the EPA blames the Department of Justice for delaying litigation, Justice responds that if the EPA cannot convince its own lawyers that the case has prosecutorial merit, then it can never win the case in district court.[7]

When the EPA asks Justice to forward a proposed suit to the U.S. attorney for the district in which the violation has occurred, it must include a litigation report. This report has become a focal point of controversy between the EPA and Justice. It generally includes the following information: the EPA's interpretation of the regulation; the evidence of violation; possible defenses the sources could raise and the EPA's response to them; suggestions on the relief a court could order; and an evaluation of harm caused by the violation. This report must survive extensive review, first within the regional office and then at EPA headquarters before going to Justice.

Review of this litigation report becomes a tug-of-war between upper-level officials who want as much information, analysis, and predictability as possible and regional enforcement officials who do not have time to perform all these tasks, who want to argue cases in court but lack trial experience, and who resent what they regard as the excessive caution of the Justice Department and their superiors in the EPA. The cases the regional offices refer to headquarters usually involve especially uncooperative firms or particularly serious violations. Regional officials see no need to explain their prosecutorial merit. Moreover, they insist that the Clean Air Act does not require the EPA to prove that a SIP violation has caused a violation of a national air quality standard or to tell the judge how a source can comply with its emission limitation. While regional offices do not object to discussing these matters briefly in the litigation report, they resent spending weeks collecting detailed information on issues they consider legally irrelevant. The Justice Department and EPA headquarters reply that district court judges always ask for

---

7. Donald Horowitz, *The Jurocracy: Government Lawyers, Agency Programs, and Judicial Decisions* (Lexington Books, 1977) provides a general review of relations between the Department of Justice and agency attorneys.

this information and will not impose sanctions on polluters until the EPA presents an airtight case on each issue.

Thus in the writing and review of the litigation report one begins to see the effect of prior court action. Both the EPA and Justice try to anticipate how the courts will react to Clean Air Act cases. The more information they think the courts will require and the more they expect district court judges to favor polluters, the more demanding they will be of lower-level enforcement officials. And the harder it becomes for regional office personnel to convince others to file suit, the more likely they will be to make concessions necessary to reach agreement with polluters. The bureaucratic politics of filing suit gives added significance to the courts' rulings on the consideration of feasibility in enforcement proceedings, which will be examined later in this chapter.

The Court Case

After the EPA files suit against a source, the case will usually sit on the district court's docket for several months. Not only are court dockets long, but criminal cases take precedence over civil ones. This does not mean that nothing happens before the trial date. Both sides file requests for summary judgment, and each responds to the petitions of the other. Both engage in extensive discovery proceedings, trying to put on the record any information that could possibly strengthen their case. The more issues the judge allows the parties to raise, the costlier this stage of litigation becomes.

While the case is pending before the court, the defendant tries to raise as many issues as possible and to convince the court to dismiss the case. Sources often claim, for example, that the regulation in question was improperly promulgated, that the EPA misinterpreted it, that the judge should stay enforcement while the state decides whether to revise its SIP, and even that the EPA cannot legally compel a source to comply with a SIP requirement not essential to the attainment of national standards. While the Clean Air Act specifically prohibits district courts from hearing any legal argument in an enforcement proceeding that could have been raised in earlier challenges to SIP regulations, the line between contesting the validity of a regulation and contesting the EPA's application of the regulation to a particular source is a fine one. If a court stays enforcement for what the EPA considers improper reasons, the agency must decide whether to go through the long process of appealing the ruling or to correct the problem the court perceived. Usually the source continues to exceed its emission limitations while the EPA appeals. Some sources have adeptly used these preliminary motions to avoid trial and sanctions.

The EPA responds to these moves by asking the judge to confine pretrial fact finding and the trial to the question of whether the source has violated the SIP. If the judge agrees with the EPA, the only matter before the court is whether the judge should issue a prohibitory (or preventive) injunction. This form of injunction simply commands the source to cease exceeding its emission limitation and subjects the firm to substantial fines if it is subsequently found in violation.

As the quotation at the beginning of this chapter indicates, however, judges seldom take such a narrow view of their responsibilities. They almost always allow litigants to present any information that will help the courts frame mandatory (or regulatory) injunctions.[8] These orders, like EPA administrative orders, set out detailed compliance schedules. When judges consider issuing mandatory injunctions, the EPA and the source must present detailed expert testimony explaining to the judge all the issues discussed in previous negotiations.

To avoid losing a case, the EPA must prepare for the worst. It must find and coach experts who will testify that the EPA correctly monitored the source's emissions, that the environmental effects of the violation are significant, that adequate controls can be installed at this site, and that the source can afford requisite pollution control expenditures. To reinforce its credibility with the court, the EPA tries to use experts who have no affiliation with the agency. Agency lawyers not only have to refute the sophisticated arguments of the source's experts, but must also explain the rudiments of pollution control and of the Clean Air Act to the judge—who most likely has never before encountered such a case.

Most judges hold at least one pretrial conference with the EPA and the defendant. Here both sides learn how the judge views the case. District court judges vary greatly in their receptivity to air pollution cases. Some use the pretrial conference to instruct the source to comply with the EPA's demands. Others tell the litigants they had better negotiate a settlement before the trial date. A few have told government lawyers that they simply do not intend to put people out of work. EPA attorneys quickly learn which judges to avoid.

Typically the EPA and the source continue negotiating while the case

8. Owen M. Fiss, *Injunctions* (Foundation Press, 1972), p. 1.

sits on the court docket. The closer the case gets to trial and the clearer the judge's position becomes, the more likely settlement becomes. For this reason, only a handful of Clean Air Act cases have yet gone to trial, and even fewer of these trials have reached completion.

The few trials conducted have lasted for as short a time as a few hours and for as long as several days. The trial involving West Penn Power's coal-burning generator in the Pittsburgh area (described below) took three days in October, three in November, and five in February. Extended trials can tie up a large proportion of a regional office's enforcement resources for months. As the EPA pursues such hard cases as steel mills with hundreds of emission points, trials could become longer and more complex than ever.

The judge need not issue an order immediately after the trial concludes. It can take weeks for him to do so. In addition, most injunctions allow polluters to request amendments to the order if they cannot meet the court's schedule. Some judges hold periodic conferences to assess the source's progress and issue numerous modifications to the original order. A few have appointed special masters to see that sources come into compliance. Some have even allowed sources to raise additional defenses in contempt proceedings after failing to meet court deadlines.[9] At times it seems that the courts' involvement in Clean Air Act cases, like the EPA's negotiations with noncomplying sources, never ends.

Litigation and Negotiation

On the basis of this description of the enforcement process one can establish several propositions that explain why the EPA prefers to reach agreement with sources rather than go through litigation. These help explain the consequences of court decisions on enforcement issues.

The first proposition is that detecting violations and negotiating agreements with the many polluters that exceed SIP emission limitations is itself a time-consuming process. Because there are always more sources

9. For example, *U.S.* v. *Town of North Hempstead,* 610 F.2d 1025 (2d Cir. 1979); *Town of Greenwich* v. *Department of Transportation,* 14 *Environment Reporter Cases* 1177 (D. Conn. 1980); and *Pennsylvania Department of Environmental Resources* v. *Pennsylvania Power Co.,* 337 A.2d 823 (Pa. Sup. Ct. 1975). Also see Comment, "Defense to Orders and Actions of the Pennsylvania Department of Environmental Resources," 80 *Dickinson Law Review* 265 (1976); Note, "Enforcement of Environmental Consent Orders in Pennsylvania," 39 *University of Pittsburgh Law Review* 340 (1977); and William H. Rodgers, Jr., *Handbook on Environmental Law* (West, 1977), p. 267.

to tackle than the EPA has time for, it can address only the most serious problems.

The second proposition is that filing and arguing a court case is an especially resource-intensive enterprise for the EPA. Bringing a case requires the regional office to convince EPA headquarters, the Department of Justice, and the local U.S. attorney that the case has "prosecutorial merit" and will produce a courtroom victory. The EPA must explain the issues to each of these organizations—none of which are familiar with those problems faced daily by the regional office—and must respond to any arguments they raise.

Third, litigation is risky for the EPA. If it loses one of the few cases it brings in federal district court, it has not only wasted precious enforcement resources, but has weakened its bargaining position in the vast majority of cases that never go to court. The agency's losses encourage noncomplying sources to hold out for better deals in informal negotiation.

The fourth proposition is that even if the EPA wins a formal victory in court, it may gain little if the court refuses to impose penalties or to put the source on a strict compliance schedule. If judges show leniency on penalties and schedules, the EPA may be better off making concessions to sources before devoting resources to litigation.

Fifth, the cases that reach court are unusual ones that the EPA has been unable to settle. Its evidence may be especially weak or its reading of the SIP especially strict. More likely the costs of compliance are so great that the expense of litigation for the source is insignificant by comparison. This means that the sources that come to court are at one and the same time the worst polluters and the biggest employers in the area. The hard cases come to court and set precedents that influence negotiations over more routine violations.

The Patterns of Judicial Action

In hearing suits against alleged violators of the Clean Air Act and cases brought by polluters to stay further EPA enforcement action, the courts play two roles. First, they are the ultimate enforcers of the law. During the first decade of the Clean Air Act's history, only the courts could impose fines, criminal penalties, or other punitive sanctions. While the EPA can now assess noncompliance penalties equal to the economic savings realized by those exceeding their emission limitations, its authority to do so is carefully circumscribed by court review.[10] The courts have jealously guarded their prerogative to take punitive action against those who violate the law.

The second role of the courts in enforcement proceedings is protecting the legal rights of private parties threatened by agency action. Polluters subject to the act can challenge the procedures used to write and approve the SIP; claim that the SIP violates the substantive requirements of the act; question whether the EPA has authority to enforce the regulation; argue that the SIP constitutes an unconstitutional taking of property; refute the EPA's evidence that a violation has occurred; dispute the EPA's interpretation of the regulation; or argue that the compliance schedule designed by the EPA is infeasible and thus invalid. While most district courts have refused to entertain preenforcement suits raising challenges polluters should have made earlier in section 307 cases, they almost always give polluters an opportunity to present these arguments once the EPA files an enforcement suit. The courts view enforcement proceedings as an opportunity to ensure that justice is done in the individual case and that the EPA has not overstepped its legal authority.

It is no accident that the judiciary is asked to play the dual role of enforcer of the law and protector of those subject to the demands of the law. Placing authority to impose sanctions in the hands of those sensitive to the possible abuse of governmental power is a method by which limited, constitutional government protects private parties from excessive government intrusion. Yet these two roles pull the courts in opposite directions. In their enforcer role the courts are called upon to make sure the goals of the Clean Air Act—especially attainment of the national air quality standards—are achieved promptly. In their protector role the courts are called upon to add balance to the regulatory scheme and to give the benefit of the doubt to private parties. Thus the courts must decide when to help the agency carry out its environmental protection mission and when to restrain it.

10. The EPA did not promulgate noncompliance penalty rules until 1980. 45 Fed. Reg. 50086 (1980). It made little effort to impose penalties until the rules received judicial approval in *Duquesne Light Co. v. Environmental Protection Agency,* 18 *Environment Reporter Cases* 1489 (D.C. Cir. 1983). While economists have hailed noncompliance penalties as a major step forward in environmental enforcement (for example, William Drayton, "Economic Law Enforcement," 4 *Harvard Environmental Law Review* 1 [1980]), most enforcement officials are skeptical. They claim that the rules are so complex, the opportunity for hearings and judicial review so easy to invoke, and the number of sources involved so large, that methodical application of the penalties will be nearly impossible.

In making this judgment, have the courts "leaned" toward stringency or toward leniency?[11] Those who included the citizen suit provision in the 1970 act expected the courts to be aggressive enforcers. After reading the court's decisions on prevention of significant deterioration, dispersion, and variances, one would expect them to show a preference for achieving the "overriding purpose" of cleaning up the air. But in enforcement cases the courts have not leaned in the direction of stringency. On the contrary, they have resolved doubts about the EPA's enforcement authority to the benefit of polluters and have demanded that regulators consider compliance costs and other mitigating factors. This inclination toward leniency shows itself not just in written opinions, but in many other forms, including rulings on preliminary motions and comments at pretrial conferences, which only those directly involved in the case observe. There is evidence of this orientation in the courts' interpretations of the EPA's enforcement authority, in their handling of the feasibility issue, and in their application of the Supreme Court's doctrines on feasibility.

Circumscribing Enforcement Authority

On several occasions the courts—particularly the Supreme Court—have relied on questionable readings of the act and its legislative history to prevent the EPA from taking effective enforcement action against those clearly violating valid regulations. These judicial opinions artificially sever regulatory means from regulatory goals. Their consequences have proven greater than predicted by the deciding court. The two leading examples of this type of decision are the Supreme Court's opinions on federal enforcement of hazardous pollutant standards and on state enforcement against federal facilities.

Section 112 of the act establishes special procedures for control of pollutants that "may cause, or contribute to, an increase in mortality or an increase in serious irreversible or incapacitating reversible illness." It directs the EPA to set and enforce uniform national emission standards for these pollutants, thus bypassing the indirect state-run program used to control less hazardous "criteria" pollutants. To underscore the seriousness of these emissions, section 112 makes violation of national emission standards for hazardous pollutants a criminal offense.

11. I have borrowed the metaphor of an agency "leaning" toward either stringency or leniency from Robert A. Kagan, *Regulatory Justice: Implementing a Wage-Price Freeze* (Russell Sage Foundation, 1978).

While the authors of the 1970 act expected the EPA to set emission standards for several hazardous pollutants shortly after passage of the act, the EPA was slow to issue regulations. On several occasions the federal courts, responding to suits brought by environmental groups, ordered the EPA to publish standards for pollutants the agency admitted were hazardous.

In one such case the D.C. District Court instructed the EPA to write regulations for asbestos.[12] The EPA proposed a "no visible emission" standard for asbestos released during the demolition of buildings. When the wrecking industry complained that this would make demolition of old buildings impossible, the EPA amended its rule to require only that wreckers wet buildings before tearing them down.[13] But when the EPA brought suit against several demolition companies for violating the wetting rule, the defendants claimed that the regulation was invalid since wetting is a "work practice," not an "emission standard."[14] While this controversy was before the courts, Congress approved an EPA-sponsored amendment confirming the administrator's authority to set work practice standards when numerical emission standards are not practical. The Senate committee stated, "This limited provision would fully authorize the present EPA regulations governing asbestos."[15]

Shortly after passage of the 1977 amendments the Supreme Court overturned the conviction of the demolition companies who had ignored the EPA's wetting requirement. In its *Adamo Wrecking* decision the Court ruled that a "work practice rule" is not an "emission standard." Justice William H. Rehnquist justified this narrow definition by pointing to the criminal sanctions imposed on those who violate the regulation. "Where there is an ambiguity in a criminal statute," Rehnquist explained, "doubts are resolved in favor of the defendant."[16] Not only did the Court show no deference to the agency's interpretation of the act, but it denied that Congress intended to include "work practices" in its definition of "emission standards." Indeed, the Court read the 1977

12. *Environmental Defense Fund* v. *Ruckelshaus*, 3 *Environmental Law Reporter* 20173 (D.D.C. 1973).

13. 36 Fed. Reg. 23240 (1971); 38 Fed. Reg. 8820 (1973).

14. *U.S.* v. *Adamo Wrecking Co.*, 545 F.2d 1 (6th Cir. 1976).

15. *Clean Air Amendments of 1977*, S. Rept. 95-127, 95 Cong. 1 sess. (GPO, 1977), p. 44; *Clean Air Amendments of 1977*, Conf. Rept. 95-564, 95 Cong. 1 sess. (GPO, 1977), pp. 21, 131–32.

16. *Adamo Wrecking Co.* v. *U.S.*, 434 U.S. 275 at 285 (quoting *U.S.* v. *Bass*, 404 U.S. 336 at 348 [1971]) and 289 (1978).

amendments to support its argument that the two are distinct. Thus the Court used Congress's effort to overrule the lower court's decision as evidence that the lower court had decided the case properly.

This reading of the 1977 amendments would have had no practical significance (other than absolving those who had violated the regulation before August 1977) if they had been carefully drafted. Unfortunately, while the amendments changed section 112(a) to allow the EPA to *promulgate* work practice rules, they did not change section 112(c), which grants the EPA authority to *enforce* the promulgated regulations. So, under the Court's reading of the statute, the EPA could promulgate a wetting requirement, but not enforce it. This perverse result led Justice John Paul Stevens to complain in his dissenting opinion:

> The Court's holding today has effectively made the asbestos regulation, and any other work-practice rule as well, unenforceable. Ironically, therefore, the 1977 Amendments, which were intended to lift the cloud over the Administrator's authority, have actually made his exercise of that authority ineffectual. This is the kind of consequence a court risks when it substitutes its reading of a complex statute for that of the Administrator charged with the responsibility of enforcing it.[17]

The EPA rules on asbestos (as well as hazardous emission regulations for vinyl chloride, which were also the product of litigation by environmental groups) remained in limbo until Congress passed further amendments to the act.[18] Thus, while the courts have forced the EPA to regulate hazardous pollutants, they have made it difficult for the agency to gain compliance with its rules.

In its rulings on state regulation of pollution from federal facilities, the Supreme Court demonstrated a similar inclination to interpret the enforcement provisions of the Clean Air Act narrowly, refusing to assume that the statute authorized means necessary for achieving stated ends. This legal controversy arose when several states tried to force the Tennessee Valley Authority, by far the largest polluter in the Southeast, to comply with permit requirements included in their SIPs. A firmly established rule of constitutional law states that federal instrumentalities are exempt from state regulations unless Congress provides a "clear

---

17. Ibid. at 306.
18. 92 Stat. 3458, Health Services Research, Health Statistics, and Health Care Technology Act of 1978, sec. 13(b). The effect of the *Adamo* ruling on vinyl chloride regulation is examined in David D. Doniger, *Law and Policy of Toxic Substances Control: A Case Study of Vinyl Chloride* (Johns Hopkins University Press for Resources for the Future, 1978), pp. 68–69.

statement" to the contrary.[19] Noting that in the past federal facilities had been slow to comply with pollution limitations, in section 118 of the 1970 legislation Congress required "each department, agency, and instrumentality of the executive, legislative, and judicial branches of the Federal Government" to "comply with Federal, State, interstate, and local requirements respecting control and abatement of air pollution to the same extent that any person is subject to such requirements." While the EPA and the states believed that this language provided a "clear statement" that federal facilities must comply with all SIP regulations, the TVA and the Department of Justice argued that it did not.

The circuit courts disagreed on whether federal agencies must obtain permits from the states. The Sixth Circuit found that section 118 refers only to "substantive" regulation, not to "procedural" requirements such as obtaining a permit.[20] The court turned a deaf ear on the claims of Alabama and Kentucky that permits are the heart of the SIP enforcement process. Shortly thereafter, the Fifth Circuit rejected the Sixth Circuit's argument, which it described as an attempt "to avoid the impact of Section 118 by engrafting upon it a substantive procedural overlay."[21] Finding no reason to impose such a distinction on the wording of the section, the Fifth Circuit ruled that when Congress granted the states authority to regulate federal facilities, it also delegated authority to use all appropriate regulatory tools. With this legal support the EPA encouraged the states adversely affected by the Sixth Circuit decision to appeal to the Supreme Court.

When the Supreme Court examined the issue, it found that section 118 "discloses no clear declaration or implication of congressional intent" to submit federal facilities to "the enforcement mechanisms of state plans." The Court dismissed Kentucky's claim that it would be "utterly meaningless" to require federal facilities to comply with state regulations without at the same time granting the state an "administrative means of implementing and enforcing its standards against federal facilities." The justices justified this restriction of state authority by claiming that state enforcement is superfluous. Enforcement by the EPA, they indicated, is sufficient for accomplishing the goal set out in section 118. The Court noted that the EPA had recently

19. Laurence H. Tribe, *American Constitutional Law* (Foundation Press, 1978), pp. 242–44.

20. *Kentucky ex. rel. Hancock v. Ruckelshaus,* 497 F.2d 1172 (6th Cir. 1974).

21. *Alabama v. Seeber,* 502 F.2d 1238 at 1245 (5th Cir. 1974).

promulgated guidelines for compliance by federal agencies with stationary source air pollution standards . . . which will lead to federal agencies' entering "consent agreements which are exactly identical in every respect to what a [state] compliance schedule would have been."[22]

The possibility of federal enforcement was the trump card that allowed the Court to restrict the states without appearing to reduce section 118 to a nullity.

Congress quickly overturned this reading of section 118. In 1976, shortly before the Supreme Court handed down its decision, the House Commerce Committee's report on proposed amendments to the act stated that section 118 "declared the clear and unequivocal policy" that all federal facilities must "comply with all substantive and procedural requirements of Federal, State, interstate, and local law."[23] The 1976 Senate report stated that the courts that prohibited state enforcement "misconstrued the original intent."[24] After the Supreme Court's decision, the new House report added, "In the committee's view the language of existing law should have been sufficient to insure Federal compliance in all of the aforementioned situations. . . . The new section 113 of the bill is intended to overturn the *Hancock* case."[25] This section of the bill passed without any debate in either house.

Not only was the Supreme Court's reading of Congress's intent repudiated by both houses, but its assertion that federal enforcement against federal facilities would be an adequate substitute for state enforcement was without foundation. Until passage of the 1977 amendments all efforts to force federal facilities to comply with SIP emission limitations failed. The Department of Justice refused to file suit against any federal facilities, including the TVA. Justice argued that one federal agency cannot sue another, and that the president, not the courts, should resolve all disputes within the executive branch. With the president and the Office of Management and Budget reluctant to insist that the TVA and other installations spend more money on pollution control and with the states unable to take action against them, compliance by federal

22. *Hancock* v. *Train*, 426 U.S. 167 at 183–84 and 199 (1976) (citing transcript of oral argument).

23. *Clean Air Act Amendments of 1976*, H. Rept. 94-1175, 94 Cong. 2 sess. (GPO, 1976), pp. 170–75.

24. *Clean Air Amendments of 1976*, S. Rept. 94-717, 94 Cong. 2 sess. (GPO, 1976), p. 45.

25. *Clean Air Act Amendments of 1977*, H. Rept. 95-294, 95 Cong. 1 sess. (GPO, 1977), p. 199.

facilities lagged far behind that of comparable private facilities. In fact, by the end of 1975 only 35 percent of federal facilities had complied with all SIP requirements.[26] While the EPA has continued to fight with the Department of Justice on the federal facilities issue, the threat of state action under the 1977 amendments has led many federal facilities to comply with SIPs in recent years.[27] If the Court had understood the institutional constraints on the EPA's enforcement program, it might not have felt so free to ignore Congress's protestations about the original purpose of section 118.

While these illustrations of the courts' tendency to reduce the EPA's enforcement authority are graphic, they are not aberrational. Circuit courts have also made it difficult for the EPA to force the states to comply with transportation control plans, which themselves were the product of court decisions (see chapter 9). District court decisions have restricted the EPA's authority to press charges against smelters and utilities. In the hazardous emission and federal facilities cases Congress eventually overturned the courts' decisions. But on other issues Congress has proved either unable or unwilling to return to the EPA the authority the courts took away. This is particularly true in the dispute over the economic and technological feasibility of SIP control requirements.

The Feasibility Cases

While the EPA struggled to establish a stationary source enforcement program in the first half of the 1970s, the federal courts were explaining when and how the EPA must consider economic and technological feasibility. These decisions had a major effect on the EPA's enforcement program, first delaying enforcement against some of the nation's worst polluters and then adding to the difficulty of bringing suit against all sources of pollution. The agency is still grappling with the legacy of these rulings.

Most federal health and safety regulations specify that regulations promulgated under them must be "feasible" or "reasonable," but the

---

26. *Congressional Record* (June 8, 1977), p. 18035, reporting information compiled by the EPA's Compliance Data System.

27. The EPA eventually circumvented Justice's opposition to an enforcement suit against the TVA by joining a section 304 suit brought by environmental groups. Once the TVA's governing board changed following the election of President Carter, the EPA and the TVA reached an agreement. The EPA and Justice continued to disagree on whether the TVA should pay civil penalties.

Clean Air Act does not. As discussed in chapter 2, the authors of the 1970 act rejected an "available technology" approach in favor of a "technology-forcing" health-based regulatory scheme. The act not only based new-car emission standards on the percentage reduction needed to produce safe air quality, but was passed without a provision in the House bill requiring the EPA to give "due consideration to the technological feasibility" of SIP regulations when enforcing the act. In explaining the operation of the citizen suit provision included in the final bill, the Senate report stated:

> An alleged violation of an emission control standard, emission requirement, or a provision in an implementation plan, would not require reanalysis of technological or other considerations at the enforcement stage. These matters would have been settled in the administrative procedure leading to an implementation plan or emission control provision.[28]

The report emphasized the "health, not technology" thrust of the act by proclaiming:

> The health of people is more important than the question of whether the early achievement of ambient air quality standards protective of health is technically feasible. . . . Therefore, the Committee determined that existing sources of pollutants either should meet the standard of the law or be closed down.[29]

Thus the structure and legislative history of the 1970 act seemed to make the feasibility of control measures irrelevant in the eyes of the law.

Despite this the courts have consistently maintained that the EPA must at some stage in the administrative process consider the feasibility of control measures needed to meet SIP requirements. While it took nearly four years of litigation for the Supreme Court to resolve the issue of *when* the EPA and the courts should consider feasibility, no court hearing industry challenges questioned the assertion that polluters have the right to raise the defense of economic or technological infeasibility at some time. Because the courts never explained why control requirements must be "feasible," they never managed to define that vague term.

The feasibility dispute began in 1972 shortly after the EPA approved the SIPs submitted by the states. A number of utilities, steel companies,

---

28. *A Legislative History of the Clean Air Amendments of 1970,* prepared for the Senate Committee on Public Works, 93 Cong. 2 sess. (GPO, 1974), pp. 436.

29. Ibid., pp. 402–03. For a thorough review of the legislative history of this aspect of the act and its relevance to litigation, see Samuel A. Bleicher, "Economic and Technological Feasibility in Clean Air Act Enforcement Against Stationary Sources," 89 *Harvard Law Review* 316 (1975).

and smelters claimed that the EPA violated the act and denied them due process of law by failing to hold hearings on the feasibility of complying with state plans. The three circuit courts that ruled on these challenges—not by chance those with jurisdiction over the heavily polluted Midwest—all remanded the SIPs to the EPA with instructions to review their feasibility. The Fourth Circuit ruled that the EPA must either hold its own hearing or review the record compiled by the state.[30] The Third Circuit stipulated that unless the EPA held its own feasibility hearings it could not bring enforcement action until polluters had a chance to present their claims to state agencies and state courts.[31] The Sixth Circuit was even more explicit, finding "the Agency's argument that technological infeasibility, high cost-benefit [sic], and resource unavailability are irrelevant under the 1970 Amendments, devoid of merit."[32] This court vacated the agency's approval of the Ohio SIP, ruling both that it must consider industry's evidence on the feasibility of controls and that infeasibility constitutes a defense in enforcement proceedings.

The EPA complied with the procedural commands of the circuit courts and reapproved each of the remanded SIPs. The agency claimed that scrubbers provided utilities with an affordable mechanism for meeting sulfur dioxide limitations. While admitting that Pennsylvania's regulations for smelters were technologically infeasible, it continued to deny that it could disapprove a SIP on this basis. The EPA's actions precipitated a second round of industry challenges, which eventually found their way to the Supreme Court.

The Third Circuit continued to maintain that the EPA could not approve infeasible SIP regulations. While conceding that "the Act does not expressly empower the agency to disapprove a plan where restrictions are too narrow to be practicable," the court argued that Congress would have made its intent more evident had it expected the EPA to enforce infeasible requirements that might not be needed to meet national air quality standards.[33] In a later case the Third Circuit went even further, questioning the EPA's finding that flue gas scrubbers are feasible. The

30. *Appalachian Power Co.* v. *Environmental Protection Agency,* 477 F.2d 495 (4th Cir. 1973).

31. *Duquesne Light Co.* v. *Environmental Protection Agency,* 481 F.2d 1 (3d Cir. 1973).

32. *Buckeye Power Co.* v. *Environmental Protection Agency,* 481 F.2d 162 at 169 (6th Cir. 1973).

33. *St. Joe Minerals Corp.* v. *Environmental Protection Agency,* 508 F.2d 743 at 748 (3d Cir. 1975).

agency again reviewed Pennsylvania's SIP, and the court responded with its *third* remand.[34]

Chastened by this succession of judicial losses, the EPA made two concessions to circuit courts hearing later feasibility cases. The first was that the agency would not bring enforcement action against a source whose SIP regulation had been invalidated by a state court. The EPA insisted that the federal government should leave the feasibility issue to the states, and that it would allow state processes to work themselves out. The second concession was that it would consider the feasibility of control measures when writing section 113(a) administrative orders, and that it expected courts to do the same in issuing injunctions under section 113.

The EPA's new tactic produced short-term benefits. Both the Seventh and the Eighth Circuits rejected the argument that the EPA must disapprove infeasible regulations. Both also alluded to the EPA's concessions. The Eighth Circuit hinted that since polluters could not pursue claims of infeasibility when challenging the validity of SIP regulations, they could raise this defense in enforcement proceedings.[35] The Seventh Circuit stated that

> arguments concerning technology and economic impact may be presented to the Administrator prior to the date on which a compliance order issued pursuant to Section 113(a)(4) takes effect, and may be raised in the course of enforcement proceedings under Section 113(b).[36]

The court also noted that polluters "have a right to challenge the reasonableness of state plans in the state courts." If the EPA cannot approve a SIP as modified by a state court, it must propose a plan of its own. These two apparent victories later came back to haunt the EPA.

In 1976, four years after the filing of the first feasibility challenge, the Supreme Court took a major step toward resolving the issue. In *Union Electric Co.* v. *Environmental Protection Agency,* Justice Thurgood Marshall, writing for a unanimous Court, appeared to take a strongly pro-environmental position. He stated, "Congress intended claims of economic and technological infeasibility to be wholly foreign to the

---

34. *Duquesne Light Co.* v. *Environmental Protection Agency,* 522 F.2d 1186 (3d Cir. 1975).

35. *Union Electric Co.* v. *Environmental Protection Agency,* 515 F.2d 206 (8th Cir. 1975).

36. *Indiana and Michigan Electric Co.* v. *Environmental Protection Agency,* 509 F.2d 839 at 847 (7th Cir. 1975).

Administrator's consideration of a state implementation plan."[37] He argued that the courts that had come to the opposite conclusion had twisted the meaning of statutory terms and misused legislative history. While Justice Lewis F. Powell warned that "the shutdown of an urban area's electrical system could have an even more serious impact on the health of the public than that created by a decline in ambient air quality" and predicted that "Congress, if fully aware of this draconian possibility, would strike a different balance," he went along with the rest of the Court in finding that the EPA cannot consider feasibility in reviewing plans submitted by the states.

However, the Court stopped well short of endorsing the doctrine that the EPA and district courts must shut down sources that fail to comply with their emission limitations. Justice Marshall identified several possible safety valves in addition to revisions, two-year extensions, and one-year postponements (all under subsections of section 110). First, a source "may be able to take its claims of economic or technological infeasibility to the state courts." The Court offered no explanation of when state courts could honor these claims or whether the EPA had to follow their determinations. Second, the Court recognized that the EPA can consider feasibility in issuing administrative orders under section 113(a). Third, and most important, the Court raised the possibility that federal courts can consider feasibility in enforcement proceedings. While claiming "we do not address this question here," the Court referred the reader to a footnote in the EPA's brief that stated, "Presumably, a court, too, in exercising its equitable power to fashion the 'appropriate relief' could consider economic and technological factors."[38] Since it is district courts that grant this relief, presumably they would be the ones to decide the meaning of feasibility.

Thus, after spending four years battling with industry on the feasibility issue, the EPA won only a modest victory in the Supreme Court. To be sure, the *Union Electric* decision removed the cloud hanging over those SIPs remanded by the circuit courts. This allowed the enforcement process to begin in several highly polluted areas. Yet the combination

37. *Union Electric Co.* v. *Environmental Protection Agency*, 427 U.S. 246 at 256 (1976).

38. Government brief in *Union Electric*, p. 36, note 34, and *Union Electric* at 268, note 18. The Court refused to decide whether the due process clause "demands that at some time it [the source] be afforded the opportunity to raise before a court claims of economic or technological impossibility." (At 269, note 19.) See the reference to this dictum in the *West Penn Power* case, discussed below.

of the EPA's representations to the circuit courts and the comments in *Union Electric* increased the likelihood that state court decisions over-turning SIP regulations could disrupt EPA enforcement efforts and suggested that district courts retain authority to decide what controls are feasible and reasonable.

It is not at all clear that the EPA is better off with *Union Electric* than it would have been with the circuit court decisions that required the agency to consider feasibility when approving SIPs submitted by the states. Consideration of feasibility in enforcement proceedings creates two difficulties. First, if the EPA or a district court finds a regulation infeasible in a particular case, they have no opportunity to redistribute the cleanup burden to other sources. In contrast, if the agency were to invalidate a SIP regulation on this ground it would need to insist on such redistribution to ensure the attainment of national standards. Second, under the *Union Electric* scheme the EPA must devote enforce-ment resources to fighting the feasibility battle time and time again, often before district court judges distrustful of the agency. To make matters worse, the EPA must do more than show that the control measures in question are generally available and affordable, as it must do before promulgating new source performance standards. It must demonstrate that the requisite control equipment can be installed at a particular facility and that the firm in question (not just most firms in the industry) can afford the expenditure. This puts a heavy burden on EPA enforcement officials and inhibits them from filing court suits.

Application by Lower Courts

While courts differ considerably in their handling of Clean Air Act cases, almost all district court judges have required the EPA to demon-strate the economic and technological feasibility of possible control measures, and most have deferred to state court decisions on the validity and meaning of SIP regulations. Even those courts that have shown most sympathy for environmental causes have held that courts must use their equity power to fashion reasonable compliance schedules instead of issuing prohibitory injunctions.

For example, in allowing environmental groups to use section 304 to bring enforcement action against a utility for violating an admittedly impractical "no visible emission" regulation, the D.C. District Court noted:

In formulating equitable relief the Court must always exercise discretion and balanced judgment. . . . The Court might for example, upon finding of prior good faith efforts at compliance by the source, place it on a tight schedule with shutdown specifically ordered if compliance had not been effected by a date certain. Whether such an extension of the original SIP requirements may be permitted will depend on the circumstances of each case, again with the public health criteria of the Act as primary guidelines. It may also of course be relevant to consider what relief plaintiffs actually seek.[39]

As the quotation at the beginning of this chapter indicates, the normally pro-environmentalist Second Circuit Court has announced a similar position. In fact, no federal court has disputed this "equitable" approach to defining relief under the Clean Air Act.

This interpretation of the act leaves district courts free to define feasible control measures. Some judges accept the EPA's suggestions as long as the agency can convince the court that its schedule will not put people out of work or disrupt municipal services. More frequently judges split the difference between the schedule the EPA claims is reasonable and the one the source claims is feasible. Occasionally courts have become involved in the minute details of source compliance, amending and reamending their orders to meet changing circumstances.[40]

District courts have also relied upon *Union Electric* to justify continuing deference to state courts and state agencies. Although the Supreme Court's *Train* decision held that requests for revisions have no legal importance until approved by the EPA (see pp. 161–62), the D.C. District Court stated that "the Court will naturally take into account the probability that approval of the new regulation is imminent."[41] Since EPA approval of revisions is based on the air quality impact of the source, this question becomes a major issue in enforcement litigation.

Some judges have gone even further in forcing the EPA to defer to the states. One district court ruled that the EPA *must* accept the state's determination of what controls are feasible.[42] Another prohibited a

39. *Friends of the Earth* v. *Potomac Electric Power Co.*, 419 F. Supp. 528 at 535 (D.D.C. 1976).

40. This happened in the *North Hempstead* case, leading the Second Circuit to complain, "The delays in this case are unconscionable and the confusion defies description. The burden of all this delay and confusion falls most heavily on those affected for all these years by the stench and noisome vapors emanating from the landfill." *U.S* v. *Town of North Hempstead* at 1031. Also see *Town of Greenwich* v. *Department of Transportation* and *Pennsylvania Department of Environmental Resources* v. *Pennsylvania Power Co.*

41. *Friends of the Earth* v. *Potomac Electric Power Co.* at 535.

42. *Kennecott Copper Corp.* v. *Train*, 424 F. Supp. 1217 (D. Nev. 1976).

federal grand jury from meeting to consider an indictment against a polluter who was being charged by the state.[43] Yet another declined to issue an injunction against a source that had signed—but violated—a consent decree under the supervision of a state court.[44] Most important, the federal courts have generally refused to hear enforcement cases brought by the EPA until state courts have resolved controversies over the validity and meaning of SIP provisions.[45]

No case better illustrates the opening the Supreme Court decision gave to district court judges who wish to avoid imposing sanctions on polluters than a second suit brought by the Union Electric Company of St. Louis. In the first round of litigation the district court issued a stay of enforcement, the Eighth Circuit reversed the district court, and the Supreme Court upheld the circuit in 1976. By 1978 the utility was still violating its SIP regulations, and the district court judge issued a second stay of enforcement, this time because the state air quality commission had tabled but not disapproved the utility's request for a plan revision. The court concluded that "under its general equitable powers" it had "authority to stay an enforcement proceeding to prevent irreparable harm while the plaintiff seeks in good faith a variance under State procedures."[46] The Eighth Circuit overruled the district court once again, but it stressed that once the EPA filed suit, Union Electric could again raise the infeasibility defense.[47] Given his past performance, it is unlikely that the district court judge will insist upon harsh penalties or a tight compliance schedule for the utility.

When it comes to imposing sanctions on private parties, the federal courts have abandoned the "lean" toward stringency evidenced in the decisions on prevention of significant deterioration, dispersion, and variances. They have instead ruled in favor of polluters in resolving doubts not just about the adequacy of evidence but about the meaning of the Clean Air Act. Such decisions make the EPA think twice about

43. *U.S.* v. *Interlake*, 429 F. Supp. 193 (N.D. Ill. 1977).

44. Ruling of Judge Holder, Southern District of Indiana, *U.S.* v. *Barmett of Indiana* (1978).

45. *Sierra Club* v. *Indiana-Kentucky Electric Co.*, 16 *Environment Reporter Cases* 1511 (S.D. Ind. 1981). Also see *Ohio Environmental Council* v. *U.S. District Court*, 10 *Environment Reporter Cases* 1934 (6th Cir. 1977).

46. *Union Electric Co.* v. *Environmental Protection Agency*, 450 F. Supp. 805 at 815 (E.D. Mo. 1978).

47. *Union Electric Co.* v. *Environmental Protection Agency*, 593 F.2d 299 (8th Cir. 1979).

bringing polluters to court rather than striking a bargain with them. Moreover, the legal doctrines announced by appellate courts have given district courts broad discretion to define the relevant issues in enforcement proceedings. This means that the EPA must prepare an elaborate litigation report on all matters that could possibly interest the judge. While many district court judges listen sympathetically to the EPA's enforcement cases, others do not. "A judge who does not want to enforce a regulation," one experienced EPA enforcement official complained, "can always come up with some reason why it doesn't apply." The decisions described above provide ample evidence for this claim.

Consequences for Compliance

The EPA and state agencies have succeeded in inducing a large number of sources of pollution to install control equipment adequate to meet SIP requirements. In 1979 the EPA claimed that 90 percent of all major sources (those with a potential to emit at least one hundred tons per year) had either complied with the law or were on schedules that would bring them into compliance. Between 1972 and 1978 particulate emissions dropped by more than 40 percent and sulfur dioxide emissions by almost 10 percent. This has improved air quality, especially in heavily polluted urban areas.

Yet noncompliance with SIP requirements remains widespread, especially for large "problem" sources. A large number of the sources that missed the 1975 deadline eventually came into compliance by 1979, as required by the 1977 amendments. But the sources still exceeding their legal limitations include not just the 8 to 10 percent officially listed as in violation, but the equal number of sources—about 1,200—that are meeting schedules that will not bring them into full compliance for many years. In addition, the General Accounting Office estimates that almost 25 percent of the sources regarded by the EPA as in final compliance actually are exceeding their emission limitations.

Most important, those violating the act tend to be the biggest polluters. Ten percent of all sulfur dioxide emissions come from twenty-eight nonferrous smelters; only half of these had complied with SIP regulations by 1980. Two-thirds of total sulfur emissions come from oil- and coal-burning utilities, of which 20 percent have yet to comply with the law on sulfur dioxide emissions. And these figures do not include Ohio's utilities, which produce over 10 percent of the nation's sulfur dioxide pollution but were without valid emission limitations for many years. The record of integrated iron and steel facilities is even worse: only 13 percent had complied with SIP regulations a decade after passage of the Clean Air Act.[48]

The courts do not bear sole responsibility for this widespread non-compliance. The authors of the 1970 act seriously underestimated the economic consequences of cleanup, the speed with which polluters could devise and install controls, and the ability of the EPA and state agencies to pursue violators. Moreover, not until the late 1970s did the EPA begin to file large numbers of enforcement actions in federal court. Between 1972 and 1977 the EPA issued 2,431 notices of violation and administrative orders under the act, but filed only 42 court cases. By contrast, in 1978 it requested the Department of Justice to file 144 cases and in 1979, 76 more. By 1979 one-third of these cases had been settled, one-third remained in the Department of Justice, and one-third were on court dockets.[49] The EPA's experience in recent years indicates that filing suit can at times produce settlements with previously intransigent polluters. While the EPA's post-1977 litigational strategy has borne fruit, court actions on enforcement discouraged the agency from pursuing this approach before passage of the 1977 amendments and they still impede enforcement against many problem sources.

Ordinary Pollution Sources

Most facilities emitting air pollution can comply with SIP requirements by installing state-of-the-art controls such as electrostatic precipitators, bag houses, and hoods to capture fugitive emissions or by switching to lower-sulfur fuel. Few such sources remained in violation of the act by 1980. Court action affected these sources in two ways. First, by discouraging the EPA from filing suit against polluters shortly after issuing an administrative order, the courts contributed to temporary regulatory delay. Second, they have made it difficult for the EPA to take

48. Statistics on emission levels and compliance rates can be found in Council on Environmental Quality, *Environmental Quality—1978* (GPO, 1978), pp. 71–76, and *Environmental Quality—1980* (GPO, 1980), pp. 170, 180–83.

49. Testimony of Assistant Administrator Marvin Durning, *Enforcement of Environmental Regulations,* Hearings before the Subcommittee on Environmental Pollution of the Senate Committee on Public Works and Environment, 96 Cong. 1 sess. (GPO, 1979), pp. 136–53; and GAO, "Improvements Needed in Controlling Major Air Pollution Sources."

action against sources that have the support of a state or are in weak financial condition.

Given the hazards of litigation, the administrative order strategy the EPA pursued in the mid-1970s made good sense (see chapter 6). But it did not produce speedy compliance. With the courts refusing to take a hard-line, comply-or-shut-down position, the EPA lost a key regulatory tool, what one experienced state official has called the "shock value" of a few well-publicized forced closures.[50] Moreover, a polluter willing to call the EPA's bluff could probably have escaped punishment. An internal EPA report explained why the agency was seldom willing to seek judicial sanctions for failure to comply with an administrative order:

> The only advantage of a civil action is that a court order results with contempt provisions if a party fails to comply with the order. However, in many instances a judge may subsequently decide that even though he ordered a source to comply by a certain date, the technology needed is not presently available. Thus even if it is possible to get a satisfactory civil action, it may not be possible to make the terms stick.[51]

While most sources tried to comply with the EPA's administrative orders, some waited until the agency took further action. By 1977 the EPA could threaten sources with civil penalties and noncompliance penalties if they refused to obey the newly established delayed compliance orders. For most small sources the threat of these sanctions far outweighed the benefits of continuing noncompliance. They realized that even equity-balancing judges would not let them avoid installation of state-of-the-art control equipment and might impose further penalties. In these instances the regulatory delay caused by anticipation of court leniency ended by 1979.

There are two exceptions to this generalization. The first is sources that receive some sort of reprieve from state agencies, review boards, or courts. As explained above, the federal courts have frequently prevented the EPA from taking enforcement action while polluters are pursuing appeals in state agencies and state courts. The other exception involves sources in financial trouble. Knowing that district court judges hesitate to take actions that will force local businesses to close their doors and that the 1977 amendments allow courts to consider the "economic impact of the penalty on the business" when imposing civil penalties,

---

50. David P. Currie, "Enforcement Under the Illinois Pollution Law," 70 *Northwestern University Law Review* 389 at 425 (1975).

51. EPA, "Report of the Air Compliance Review Group," p. IV-50.

economically marginal facilities are in a relatively strong position to resist EPA demands to comply with SIP limitations.[52] Two examples of sources in this category are pulp and paper mills in the Northeast and incinerators run by financially strapped municipalities. The EPA does not anticipate success in gaining compliance from these sources in the near future.

A final word should be said about the consequences that court doctrines on enforcement have had for citizen suits brought against polluters. One purpose of section 304 was to allow citizens to supplement EPA enforcement efforts when the agency cannot or does not act. Given the widespread noncompliance in the 1970s, one would expect environmental groups to have filed a large number of such suits. But they did not. One reason for this was that enforcement cases became too complex for environmental groups to pursue. While they might be able to prove that a violation had occurred, they usually could not prove the feasibility of requisite controls, show that the firm could afford them, propose a reasonable construction schedule, or determine the air quality impact of the violation. Consequently, most environmental groups decided to leave enforcement to the EPA.

Nonferrous Smelters

No industrial facilities have been more successful in using litigation to avoid adding pollution controls than lead, copper, and zinc smelters. About two dozen such facilities located in western states account for one-tenth of the nation's sulfur dioxide emissions. The EPA has admitted that smelters face especially severe control problems. Although the agency has ruled that "double-acid" treatment plants constitute available technology for new plants, it has agreed to allow existing facilities to employ "single-acid" controls provided they use intermittent control systems (ICS) to avoid air quality violations and they actively search for new control technologies. Congress endorsed this general strategy in 1977. Confronting stiff opposition from the smelting industry, the EPA did

---

52. The EPA's civil penalty policy allows penalties to be reduced or even dropped against such economically marginal firms. (Memorandum from assistant administrator for enforcement to regional administrators, "Civil Penalty Policy—Certain Air and Water Violations," April 11, 1978, pp. 16–17.) For an example of the courts' reluctance to impose penalties under the 1977 amendments even where a clear violation has occurred, see *Alabama Air Pollution Control Commission* v. *Republic Steel*, 646 F.2d 210 (5th Cir. 1981).

not publish the smelter regulations required by the act until 1980. These rules were subsequently overturned by the D.C. Circuit as too strict, leaving the EPA once again without enforceable rules and smelters still without controls necessary to meet national standards.[53]

The key to the smelting industry's success has been its ability to convince state governments to propose SIP regulations weaker than those endorsed by the EPA and to convince federal district courts to invalidate the more stringent EPA rules. Smelting firms such as Anaconda, Kennecott Copper, ASARCO, and the Bunker Hill Company have unusual political influence at the state and local levels because they employ large numbers of people in states with small populations. The shutdown of a smelter can turn cities such as McGill, Nevada, and Kellogg, Idaho, into ghost towns. With the price of copper dropping and American smelters facing keen competition from abroad, industry has been able to make this threat a credible one.

Litigation over SIP requirements for smelters began in 1972 when the EPA disapproved the states' proposed regulations because they relied too heavily on ICS and tall stacks. The smelters challenged the EPA's reading of section 110, the validity of its ambient sulfur dioxide standards, and the procedures used to formulate federal SIP regulations. The EPA received its first in a series of district court losses when a judge in Denver ordered it to hold an adjudicatory hearing and write an environmental impact statement before setting an emission standard for an Anaconda smelter. The court charged that the EPA's use of informal rulemaking was "totalitarian rather than democratic." A year later the Tenth Circuit overturned the district court.[54] This set a pattern often repeated in smelter litigation: a district court issues a decision preventing the EPA from proceeding further with enforcement, and the circuit court takes a year or more to overturn the lower court decision. The EPA eventually wins the case, but the polluter wins delay.

The EPA spent 1973 and 1974 negotiating with the states on smelter requirements and waiting for the courts and Congress to resolve the ICS

53. 45 Fed. Reg. 42514 (1980); and *Kennecott Copper Corp.* v. *Environmental Protection Agency,* 17 *Environment Reporter Cases* 1833 (D.C. Cir. 1982). For a history of the EPA's smelter regulations, see 44 Fed. Reg. 6284 (1979). For a review of the compliance record of smelters, see *Clean Air Act,* Hearings before the Subcommittee on Health and the Environment of the House Committee on Energy and Commerce, 97 Cong. 1 sess. (GPO, 1982), pt. 2, pp. 283–485.

54. *Anaconda Co.* v. *Ruckelshaus,* 352 F. Supp. 697 at 704 (D. Colo. 1972); *Anaconda Co.* v. *Ruckelshaus,* 482 F.2d 1301 (10th Cir. 1973).

issue. After rejecting more lenient state plans, in 1975 the EPA settled on the three-pronged control strategy described above. While some smelters, notably those in Arizona, began construction of single-acid plants, others chose to continue litigating instead.

The most extreme case of court-aided delay involves Kennecott Copper's McGill smelter. Kennecott first challenged the EPA's regulation in the Ninth Circuit, claiming it should be allowed to rely completely on ICS to meet national standards. In late 1975 the circuit court dismissed this challenge.[55] The EPA soon thereafter requested that Kennecott submit a schedule for expeditious compliance. Meanwhile Kennecott informed the Nevada state air agency that it could not afford to install *any* constant controls since the facility was operating at a loss. The state agreed that the EPA's plan was economically infeasible and approved a one-year variance. When the EPA refused to approve this variance, Kennecott filed suit in the federal district court in Nevada to force the EPA to revise the Nevada plan.

Relying on statements in *Union Electric*, the judge ruled "that the State of Nevada was the proper authority to make such a finding and that it is binding on the Administrator of the EPA."[56] The court enjoined the EPA from enforcing its regulation. This stay of enforcement lasted until April 1978, when the Ninth Circuit finally overturned the district court on jurisdictional grounds.[57] In ruling that only a circuit court hearing a section 307 suit could decide whether the EPA had properly disregarded the state's finding on the infeasibility of the control measure in question, the appellate court left Kennecott free to file another suit against the EPA when the agency formally disapproved the state's request for a revision. Shortly before the EPA disapproved the 1976 variance,[58] Nevada submitted a second proposed revision, giving Kennecott yet another opportunity to challenge the EPA in court. The McGill smelter still operates without controls.[59]

Litigation over the Bunker Hill Company's Idaho smelter (which eventually did shut down) produced similar delay and set a precedent that could cause major difficulties for the EPA in the future. The agency

55. *Kennecott Copper Corp.* v. *Train*, 526 F.2d 1149 (9th Cir. 1975).

56. *Kennecott Copper Corp.* v. *Train*, 424 F. Supp. 1217 at 1231 (D. Nev. 1976).

57. *Kennecott Copper Corp.* v. *Costle*, 572 F.2d 1349 (9th Cir. 1978).

58. 44 Fed. Reg. 15735 (1979).

59. While this litigation was before the Ninth Circuit, Congress granted special relief to the McGill smelter. This provision of the 1977 amendments is explained in *Congressional Record* (June 8, 1977), pp. 18045–46 (statement of Senator Howard W. Cannon).

claimed that the smelter could achieve an 82 percent sulfur dioxide reduction and promulgated regulations accordingly. The state of Idaho and Bunker Hill claimed only 72 percent reduction was feasible. They challenged the EPA's SIP regulations in the Ninth Circuit and won.[60] After two years of litigation, during which time the court made numerous requests for additional evidence, the court ruled that the regulation was invalid because the EPA had not proved that the controls it required were feasible.

The *Bunker Hill* decision, issued shortly before Congress passed the 1977 amendments, drew a sharp response from Senator Muskie. In his explanation of the conference committee's report, Muskie announced that the sections of the amendments relating to smelters "overrule the recent decision of the Ninth Circuit in *Bunker Hill* in which the court suggests that the burden in such matters would be on the EPA."[61] Rather, Muskie explained, smelters must prove that constant controls are infeasible before they can receive permission to use ICS. But when the EPA asked the Ninth Circuit to alter its decision in light of the 1977 amendments, the court refused, claiming that it had made no ruling on where the burden of proof lies.[62]

The EPA faced similar difficulties in other states. In Arizona the smelters' challenge to the agency's sulfur dioxide regulations has remained in limbo for several years pending review of the SIP regulations by the Ninth Circuit and promulgation and judicial review of final nonferrous smelter orders under the new amendments.[63] Several Arizona smelters have installed single-acid plants, but some have no sulfur dioxide controls. These smelters contribute to frequent violations of primary ambient air quality standards for sulfur dioxide and particulate matter. Moreover, two of these smelters (Phelps Dodge at Douglas and Magma at San Manuel) produce over one-third of the sulfur dioxide emitted west of the Continental Divide. Yet a series of actions by the courts, the states, and Congress have prevented the EPA from taking enforcement action. At one facility, for example, a federal district court prohibited the EPA from ordering the smelter to install a monitor in the facility's stack.

60. *Bunker Hill Co.* v. *Environmental Protection Agency*, 572 F.2d 1286 (9th Cir. 1977).

61. *Congressional Record* (August 4, 1977), p. 26844.

62. *Bunker Hill Co.* v. *Environmental Protection Agency*, 572 F.2d 1305 (9th Cir. 1977).

63. 43 Fed. Reg. 755 (1978) (history of Arizona smelter regulations); 45 Fed. Reg. 42514 (1980) (nonferrous smelter order regulation).

After waiting almost three years before issuing a decision, the Ninth Circuit upheld this ruling.[64]

The smelter cases show how polluters can avoid installing controls when they can count on sympathetic treatment in state agencies and federal district courts. While the circuits have often overturned the lower courts, the appeal process can take months or even years, during which time enforcement is effectively stayed. Moreover, since it is these same district courts that assess civil penalties, it is highly unlikely that smelters will ever be forced to pay fines for failure to comply with regulations first invalidated by the district courts.

The courts do not bear sole responsibility for smelters' poor compliance record. Western states have often done all they could to avoid imposing burdens on these important employers. Smelters face unusually difficult compliance problems. In the early 1970s the EPA seriously underestimated the costs of compliance for smelters, thus playing into the hands of those who claimed that the agency was excessively zealous. The special compliance extension granted to smelters by the 1977 amendments both required the EPA to begin another lengthy round of regulation writing and encouraged smelters to hope for similar legislative reprieves in the future. But the courts abetted polluters' efforts to delay complying with the emission limitations set by the EPA and gave smelters additional opportunities to appeal to other forums.

Midwestern Utilities

Nearly one-third of the sulfur dioxide emitted east of the Mississippi comes from Ohio, Indiana, and Illinois.[65] Most of this pollution comes from coal-burning power plants. Yet a decade after passage of the 1970 act the EPA had barely begun to enforce SIP emission limitations applicable to these polluters. Midwestern utilities have proved nearly as skillful at combining litigation with appeals to state governments and Congress as have smelters.

Soon after the EPA approved state plans in 1972, utilities filed a flood of section 307 challenges. The feasibility rulings of the Third, Fourth, and Sixth Circuits, discussed at length above, invalidated the EPA's

64. *ASARCO* v. *Environmental Protection Agency*, 616 F.2d 1153 (9th Cir. 1980); and *Clean Air Act*, Hearings, pt. 2, pp. 296–97, 431–36.

65. *Acid Rain*, Hearings before the Senate Committee on Environment and Public Works, 97 Cong. 1 sess. (GPO, 1981), p. 267.

approval of the plans of Ohio, Kentucky, Virginia, West Virginia, Maryland, and Pennsylvania. These decisions had three consequences. First, they left the EPA without enforceable regulations for several years—especially in Pennsylvania, where the Third Circuit remanded the EPA's approval of the state's plan on three occasions. Second, after the EPA responded to the *Buckeye Power* decision by removing its approval of the plan submitted by Ohio, the state withdrew its plan. This left Ohio without valid regulations and precipitated a long series of EPA actions and court challenges. Third, to stop the courts from invalidating other SIPs, the EPA promised the Seventh and Eighth Circuits that it would not try to enforce regulations invalidated by state courts. When courts in Indiana and Illinois overturned sulfur dioxide rules in those states, the EPA felt compelled to let the state courts resolve the issue before initiating enforcement action.

OHIO. In 1972 Ohio had submitted an ambitious SIP to the EPA. But by the time of the *Buckeye* decision in 1973, state officials had changed their minds on the advisability of stringent sulfur dioxide controls. Utilities and coal interests presented evidence showing that such controls would cost consumers tens of millions of dollars and could severely damage the local coal industry. In addition, before the state had resubmitted a plan, John Rhodes, one of the EPA's strongest opponents in state government, replaced Governor John Gilligan, who had shown greater support for environmental programs. The state of Ohio proved unable to agree on any sulfur dioxide control plan it could submit to the EPA. The agency approved the state's control strategy for particulate matter, but by late 1974 it realized that Ohio would not have a plan for sulfur dioxide until the EPA wrote one itself.[66]

Devising a control strategy was a long and difficult task for the EPA —one the agency hopes never to undertake again. The EPA, unlike the states, cannot legally build "overkill" into its SIP. This means it must use dispersion modeling to calculate for each sulfur dioxide source the maximum emission level compatible with attaining national standards. The EPA began work on the Ohio SIP in early 1975 and finally promulgated a plan in August 1976.

When the EPA announced its plan, every investor-owned utility in the state, along with thirty-three other corporations, filed suit in the

66. Paul Anderson, "Implementing Air Pollution Control Policy: The Sulfur Dioxide Emission Limitation Program in Ohio," in Michael Steinman, ed., *Energy and Environmental Issues: The Making and Implementing of Public Policy* (Lexington Books, 1979).

Sixth Circuit. The court instructed the EPA not to begin enforcing the regulations until the court resolved the case. The complex litigation dragged on for almost two years. Meanwhile the EPA reexamined some of its modeling and made many changes in its control strategy. The Sixth Circuit eventually upheld most of the SIP in its lengthy and detailed 1978 Cleveland Electric decisions.[67] Ohio's utilities, following the strategy of prolonging litigation for as long as possible, appealed to the Supreme Court, but lost.[68] In the companion case to Cleveland Electric, however, the Sixth Circuit overturned the EPA's regulations for two Ohio counties.[69] The court ruled that the EPA had failed to justify the conservative assumptions it included in its dispersion model. The EPA finally issued substitute regulations for these counties in December 1979. But courtroom victories by industry once again stalled enforcement.[70]

As a consequence of the Buckeye remand, the EPA's difficulty in writing Ohio's sulfur dioxide control plan, and the litigation over the validity of that plan, the EPA could not begin enforcement activity against most Ohio utilities until 1979. By then the agency faced additional problems. Claiming the EPA's regulations would ruin Ohio's high-sulfur coal industry, Ohio coal companies and unions called upon the EPA to invoke section 125 of the new amendments, the "local coal" provision. Sponsored by Ohio Senator Howard Metzenbaum, section 125 requires the EPA to hold hearings to determine if SIP requirements will cause "significant local or regional economic disruption or unemployment" as a result of utilities switching to coal mined outside the state. If it makes such a finding, the EPA must order utilities to burn local coal and meet SIP requirements through scrubbing. A major political battle raged on the issue of local coal and expensive scrubbing—a controversy made all the more difficult for the EPA because the Carter administration viewed Ohio as critical to the president's success in the 1980 election.[71] The EPA could not enforce SIP regulations until it resolved the "local coal"

67. Cleveland Electric Illuminating Co. v. Environmental Protection Agency, 572 F.2d 1150 (6th Cir. 1978).

68. Cert. denied, 416 U.S. 911 (1978).

69. Cincinnati Gas and Electric Co. v. Environmental Protection Agency, 578 F.2d 660 (6th Cir. 1978).

70. PPG Industries v. Costle, 630 F.2d 462 (6th Cir. 1980).

71. For a history of the "local coal" amendment and the EPA's handling of it, see Bruce A. Ackerman and William T. Hassler, Clean Coal/Dirty Air (Yale University Press, 1981), pp. 44–48; Dick Kirschten, "Coal Politics with an Eastern Tilt May Boost Carter Stock in Key States," National Journal (September 13, 1980), p. 1519; 44 Fed. Reg. 52030 (1979); 45 Fed. Reg. 9101 (1980); and 45 Fed. Reg 21345 (1980).

issue. The agency's failure to publish final stack height regulations added further uncertainty to the picture (see chapter 5). Enforcement against Ohio utilities exceeding their sulfur dioxide limitations will not begin in earnest until the courts review and uphold the EPA's action on both these difficult issues. Enforcement officials have put this part of their program on the back burner.

ILLINOIS AND INDIANA. The EPA's problems in Illinois and Indiana started when utilities in those two states initiated the litigation culminating in the Seventh Circuit's *Indiana and Michigan Electric* ruling, and they grew worse as state courts refused to uphold the SIPs earlier approved by the EPA. When the EPA promised the Seventh Circuit that it would either wait for state courts to validate state plans or propose plans of its own, it had no idea how long it would take state courts to resolve the issues before them or how difficult it would be to promulgate federal SIPs.

In Illinois a state appellate court first overturned the plan written by the Pollution Control Board in 1974, claiming that the board had failed to prove that the sulfur dioxide and particulate controls it required were economically and technologically feasible. The state supreme court upheld the lower court.[72] The board then reaffirmed its plan. This led to another round of challenges, with the state courts again remanding the regulations, this time complaining that the board had failed to consider use of ICS.[73] By 1980 the state did not yet have a judicially approved plan. The EPA notified Illinois of the deficiency of its plan, but attempted neither to enforce the existing plan nor to write its own.[74]

In Indiana a similar pattern emerged. In 1975 a state court invalidated Indiana's plan for sulfur dioxide control. When the EPA issued a notice of violation to a facility violating the regulations in question, the firm asked the Seventh Circuit to stay enforcement in conformance with its opinion in *Indiana and Michigan*. The EPA again promised to delay enforcement until the state appellate court reviewed the lower court decision. The Seventh Circuit issued a stay of enforcement. To the EPA's surprise, the state appellate court agreed with the lower court.[75] While at least fifteen major sources of sulfur dioxide are exceeding the SIP

72. *Commonwealth Edison Co.* v. *Pollution Control Board*, 323 N.E.2d 84 (Ill. App. Ct. 1974); *Commonwealth Edison Co.* v. *Pollution Control Board*, 343 N.E.2d 459 (Ill. Sup. Ct. 1976).

73. *Ashland Chemical* v. *Pollution Control Board*, 381 N.E.2d 56 (Ill. App. Ct. 1978).

74. 41 Fed. Reg. 32304 (1976); 44 Fed. Reg. 40724 (1979).

75. *Indiana Environmental Management Board* v. *Indiana-Kentucky Electric Corp.*, 393 N.E.2d 213 (Ind. Ct. App. 1979).

regulations in question, the EPA has not taken action against them. The agency has been no more willing to write its own plan for Indiana than for Illinois.[76]

Many EPA enforcement officials argue that the agency should disregard its 1975 promise not to bring enforcement actions against sources whose SIP regulations have been invalidated by state courts. The Office of General Counsel and the Department of Justice have blocked such a move, however, arguing that doing so would weaken the EPA's credibility with the federal courts. It could also lead to another series of court battles culminating in a disastrous defeat for the EPA. If the EPA forces the state court issue and loses, they contend, sources in other states will increase their efforts to convince state courts to invalidate SIP provisions. This could throw the EPA's entire enforcement program into disarray.

The two federal courts that have heard citizen suits seeking enforcement of the Illinois and Indiana SIPs have split on this issue. In 1980 a federal district court judge in Chicago ruled that the attorney general of Illinois could bring a citizen suit against an Illinois utility despite the fact that state courts had invalidated the SIP regulation in question.[77] The next year a federal district court judge in Indiana summarily dismissed a Sierra Club suit seeking to enforce Indiana's SIP.[78] EPA has yet to take action under either of these SIPs, and judicial resolution of the issue is not in sight.

In all three states the legacy of the original feasibility cases has been stalled enforcement. The legal challenges of 1972–74 gave polluters time to build political support to block regulatory action in Ohio. When combined with the EPA's representations to the circuit courts and the Supreme Court's dicta in *Union Electric,* these challenges also gave state courts de facto veto power over federal as well as state enforcement. The federal courts again proved an important element in the coalition delaying enforcement against some of the worst polluters in the country.

Other Problem Sources

Not all problem sources have evaded federal and state enforcement. In 1978 the EPA won the first major enforcement case to go to trial

76. These events are described in *Enforcement of Environmental Regulations,* Hearings, p. 324.

77. *Illinois v. Commonwealth Edison Co.,* 490 F. Supp. 1145 (N.D. Ill, 1980). Commonwealth Edison subsequently negotiated an agreement with the EPA and the state of Illinois to install pollution controls. 13 *Environment Reporter—Current Developments* 380.

78. *Sierra Club v. Indiana-Kentucky Electric Co.*

under the Clean Air Act. In that case the district court judge ordered the West Penn Power Company to begin installing a scrubber at its coal-burning generating station near Pittsburgh. Reviewing the facts of this case illustrates both the difficulties the EPA's enforcement program has faced in the past and the reasons why bringing other large problem sources into compliance will continue to be a slow process.

Not by accident did the EPA make West Penn the first case it pursued through the entire judicial obstacle course. The utility's Mitchell unit is located in a metropolitan area that continues to exceed the national primary standards for both sulfur dioxide and particulate matter. While Pennsylvania's SIP requires the unit to burn coal emitting no more than 0.6 pounds of sulfur per million British thermal units (Btu) of heat output, the power plant has continued to emit at least 3.16 pounds of sulfur per million Btu. The state of Pennsylvania has supported the EPA's efforts to force West Penn to lower its emissions. West Penn Power came as close as any to being a perfect case for the EPA.[79]

For years West Penn tried to convince the courts and the state to change the SIP regulation applicable to the Mitchell plant. Although it failed to challenge the EPA's initial approval of the SIP regulation, it applied for a variance from the state. The Pennsylvania variance board issued West Penn a variance lasting until June 1976 on the condition that the company eventually install scrubbers at Mitchell. Insisting that it be allowed to use low-sulfur fuel and taller smokestacks rather than install scrubbers, West Penn appealed this decision to the Pennsylvania Environmental Hearing Board, which upheld the variance board. Meanwhile, in September 1973, the EPA issued a notice of violation to West Penn. This prompted West Penn to ask the local federal judge to instruct the EPA and Pennsylvania to accept its tall stack proposal. When the district court ruled that section 307 precluded review of the SIP at that time, West Penn appealed to the Third Circuit. In July 1975 the circuit issued a lengthy opinion denying the appeal, but suggesting that the utility either raise its claim in a state court or present its argument to the district court once the EPA brought an enforcement suit.

In 1976, encouraged by the Third Circuit's decisions in *St. Joe*

---

79. This discussion is based on documents from the following cases: *West Penn Power Co. v. Train*, 522 F.2d 302 (3d Cir. 1975); *West Penn Power Co. v. Train*, 538 F.2d 1020 (3d Cir. 1976); and *U.S. v. West Penn Power Co.*, 460 F. Supp. 1305 (W.D. Penn. 1978). I also conducted personal interviews with several officials in the EPA's Region III who participated in this litigation.

Minerals and *Duquesne Light,* West Penn filed another challenge to Pennsylvania's SIP, this time asserting that its emission limitation was economically and technologically infeasible. The circuit court waited for the Supreme Court to issue its *Union Electric* decision and then dismissed West Penn's challenge. But the court indicated that it intended to preserve West Penn's right to receive "meaningful judicial consideration of its feasibility contentions." Citing *Union Electric's* statement that feasibility considerations are appropriate in the EPA's fashioning of section 113(a) orders, the court suggested that West Penn could challenge an EPA compliance order under the Administrative Procedures Act. The utility thus lost another legal battle, but gained still another chance to seek judicial relief. By this time the sulfur content of the coal burned by the Mitchell plant was up to 4.51 pounds per million Btu.

The company continued to fight its emission limitation, appealing the Third Circuit decision to the Supreme Court and filing another variance request with the state board. In October 1977, after it became clear West Penn would lose in these forums, the EPA filed a section 113 suit against West Penn, asking the district court to issue preliminary and permanent injunctions and to impose civil penalties. Four years after the issuance of the notice of violation, West Penn was finally the defendant.

While the EPA considered the district court judge hearing its case to be unusually knowledgeable and friendly to its cause, it failed to persuade the judge to limit his task to deciding whether a violation had occurred and ordering West Penn to comply. The court denied the EPA's request to bar West Penn from raising a feasibility defense, explaining:

> To make sure that defendant's rights to due process are being respected, the court has heard lengthy testimony, expert and otherwise, as to the technological and economic infeasibility of installing scrubbers to reduce the SO_2 emissions at this plant [and] the use of so called "Tall Stacks." . . . We have done so in compliance with what we regard as the determination of this Circuit in *West Penn Power Co.* v. *Train,* supra, and the use of such defense in enforcement proceedings as suggested by the U.S. Supreme Court in *Union Electric Co.* v. *E.P.A.*[80]

The judge also overruled the EPA's objection to the utility's discussion of the air quality impact of its violation of the SIP regulation.

The court held eleven days of hearings on the case during the fall and winter of 1977–78. The EPA relied heavily on the testimony of contractors it had hired to prove the reliability of scrubbers, the technical

---

80. *U.S.* v. *West Penn Power Co.* at 1314.

feasibility of installing a scrubber at the facility, the ability of the firm to pay for the scrubber, the inevitability of primary standard violations if it did not substantially reduce its emissions, and the reasonableness of the EPA's proposed construction schedule. West Penn countered with its own experts on each issue. The judge's final opinion reviewed all this evidence, discussing the success of scrubbers at nearby plants, the difficulties of retrofitting the Mitchell unit, and even the willingness of local residents to tolerate traffic resulting from trucks removing sludge from the scrubber. The court also evaluated the financial strength of West Penn Power, the utility's chances of raising money to pay for scrubbers, and the likelihood of its receiving a rate increase from the Public Utilities Commission. On top of this, the court investigated the EPA's dispersion modeling and the possible consequences of stack height increases at Mitchell. After considering all these factors, the judge decided that West Penn should either install scrubbers or close down the Mitchell plant.

Although he concluded that "there are no equities in defendant's favor," the judge found the EPA's twenty-seven-month construction schedule "too stringent" and established his own thirty-six-month timetable, complete with requirements for monthly reports to the court. This continuing judicial oversight left the door open for the utility to request additional extensions of time. Moreover, the court put off imposing civil penalties until the final disposition of the case. The EPA eventually agreed to waive civil penalties in return for West Penn Power's commitment to install a scrubber more effective than the one required by the Pennsylvania SIP. After months of additional litigation in state court over where West Penn could dispose of the sludge, the utility finally constructed the scrubber.

The *West Penn Power* decision was a major victory for the EPA, but not a cheap one. The case showed other polluters that the EPA could and would pursue successful enforcement litigation against those who ignore their SIP limitations. But for several months the case absorbed a large percentage of regional enforcement resources. Moreover, the EPA spent hundreds of thousands of dollars on consultants in order to ensure a courtroom victory. Most important, the West Penn case confirmed the court's authority to inquire into a large number of factors other than whether a violation has occurred. EPA officials worry that both federal judges and U.S. attorneys will expect the agency to match this level of expert testimony and prosecutorial thoroughness in all enforcement cases.

In 1978 the EPA began a major enforcement offensive against problem sources violating SIP regulations. Its first target was the steel industry. After several years of work the EPA signed consent agreements with many of the major integrated steel mills in the country. This involved, among other things, getting special legislation through Congress authorizing lengthy compliance schedules. The EPA expected to move on to smelters and coal-burning power plants. Continuing controversy over SIP requirements, uncertainty over congressional action, turmoil caused by the Reagan administration's constant reorganizing of the Office of Enforcement, and severe budget cuts have all prevented the EPA from moving expeditiously against these noncomplying sources.[81] They will, no doubt, continue to violate their emission limitations for many years.

While the *West Penn* case may show sources with "no equities in their favor" that they must comply with SIP regulations, most problem sources do not fit into this category. Some can meet SIP requirements only by installing innovative technology. Many are in financial trouble. A few can count on more sympathetic treatment from state governments and federal district courts than West Penn received. With these "equities" in their favor, polluters may continue to delay complying. Knowing that it can litigate only a few cases at a time, the EPA must choose either to put many of these cases at the bottom of its list of priorities or make additional concessions on timing, extent of controls, civil penalties, or SIP revisions. Although the agency made significant progress in the late 1970s in forcing utilities and steel mills to sign consent decrees that will eventually bring them into compliance with state plans, many of the hardest cases remain.

The Ambivalence of the Courts

It should come as no great surprise that the courts, which are charged with protecting the legal rights of private citizens, have contributed to delay in the enforcement process. Nor is it clear that court doctrines

81. "Special Report: EPA's First Years under Reagan Marked by Friction with Congress, Criticism over Budget, New Direction," 13 *Environment Reporter—Current Developments* 1272; and 13 *Environment Reporter—Current Developments* 429, 493.

on the balancing of equities have produced bad policy results. In some cases the costs imposed on a community by forcing local employers to comply with the law may dwarf the environmental benefits that might accrue to it. Both Congress and the EPA have recognized this possibility and have moderated the initial deadlines of the Clean Air Act for several categories of sources. Yet the courts' leniency in enforcement cases contrasts markedly with their insistence in other cases that the EPA comply with the letter of the law. Moreover, as this chapter has suggested, the consequences of the courts' actions in enforcement cases are greater than the courts realize. The ripples that emanate from court decisions involving particular polluters become waves by the time they reach crucial stages of the administrative process.

What accounts for the different approach of the courts toward enforcement and toward general policy issues? One factor is the narrow focus of the cases brought before the courts. In cases such as those on prevention of significant deterioration, dispersion, and transportation controls, the courts have asked whether the law mandates these actions, not whether these programs are worth the cost. Likewise, in the cases examined in this chapter the courts have asked whether the agency followed the letter of the law at each step of the enforcement process and have disregarded the administrative and environmental costs of their rulings. In the federal facilities case the courts went remarkably far in disassociating regulatory means from statutory goals, overlooking clear evidence that Congress intended to delegate authority commensurate with the ends it established. In short, the legal process separates discussion of goals from consideration of administrative resources, sometimes aiding those who wish to expand government programs and sometimes helping those who wish to stop the government from acting.

A second factor is the contrast in perspective of trial judges and appellate judges. Appellate judges tend to be more interested in abstract legal and policy questions, more receptive to legal doctrines currently in vogue in the academic legal community (such as preventing agency "capture"), and less knowledgeable about or tied to local affairs. This is especially true of the D.C. Circuit, which hears the most far-reaching cases and is located in that most peculiar political community, Washington, D.C. Trial judges are not only more deeply involved in the political and economic life of their states, but also spend much of their time resolving concrete controversies rather than abstract questions. A district court judge hearing an enforcement case can see the cost of environmental regulation more clearly than a circuit court judge contemplating the wisdom of technology forcing. Conversely, the trial judge who hears the pleas of local businesses may overlook the problems pollution causes for local asthmatics—who seldom intervene in enforcement cases—or the extent to which local facilities export their pollution to other states.

A third and related factor is that of responsibility. It is one thing to be responsible for initiating an aggressive government program and quite another to bear responsibility for putting someone in jail or putting many people out of work. In general, the closer officials come to the odious task of imposing penalties, the more they look for loopholes. Moreover, the further along one gets in the administrative process, the clearer it becomes that "compliance" is not a state that is easy to define or achieve. Courts often try to avoid the complex tasks of specifying the steps private parties must take and monitoring their subsequent actions.

The courts are hardly alone in their ambivalence toward enforcement of environmental regulations. Congress has retained the ambitious goals of the 1970 act, but has often backed down when it comes to forcing individual sources to comply. Indeed, one could argue that in performing their task of balancing equities the courts are responding to congressional demands. Nor does the EPA want to impose harsh sanctions on most polluters. Not only do regional enforcement officials have sympathy for the economic plight of the region in which they live, but the agency as a whole tries to avoid taking steps that bring political reprisal. In the words of one enforcement official, "Enforcement is a political process, and this is a hell of a political agency." In general the EPA does not object to the strategy of getting as much pollution control as possible from sources without shutting them down. Its only disagreements with most judges come on the questions of what a particular source can achieve, how much evidence the EPA must present to the court, and the possible shock value of a few shutdowns.

The regulatory safety valves employed by the courts and to some extent condoned by other institutions have several unfortunate policy consequences. First, the ability of a firm to obtain a reprieve may depend on its ability to exert pressure on state agencies, on the attitudes of the particular judge it faces, and on its willingness to take risks—rather than on the seriousness of the environmental harm it causes or the relative cost of cleanup at its facility. Second, since de facto rewriting of SIPs comes at the end of the administrative process, little attempt is made to redistribute the burden taken off the shoulders of sources that receive reprieves. Third, to the extent that Congress and control agencies do attempt to compensate for this environmental loss, they tend to increase controls for sources that have relatively weak political support and for which enforcement is comparatively easy—that is, new sources. Since 1970 controls on existing sources have grown weaker and controls on new sources have become ever more stringent. The courts' rulings on prevention of significant deterioration and enforcement have contributed to this trend.

Those who criticize administrative agencies for political timidity and lack of follow-through often call upon the courts to add toughness to federal regulation. Theodore Lowi, for example, claims that judges armed with specific standards can make "unsentimental decisions about how to employ coercion."[82] But most people also expect judges to make sure that the resolution of each individual case seems reasonable and fair. This is why most judges insist on balancing equities rather than requiring strict compliance with the law. Clean Air Act enforcement decisions and their consequences suggest that the courts have yet to find a legal synthesis satisfying litigants' demands for both consistent striving toward the substantive goals of the act and responsiveness to the peculiar exigencies of individual circumstances.

82. Theodore J. Lowi, *The End of Liberalism: Ideology, Politics, and the Crisis of Public Authority* (Norton, 1969), p. 85.

CHAPTER EIGHT

Air Quality Standards in the Courts

Scientists and doctors have told us that there is no threshold, that any air pollution is harmful. The Clean Air Act is based on the assumption, although we knew at the time it was inaccurate, that there is a threshold.
—Senator Edmund S. Muskie, 1977

The legislative history of the Act also shows the Administrator may not consider economic and technological feasibility in setting air quality standards; [this] was . . . the result of a deliberate decision by Congress to subordinate such concerns to the achievement of health goals.
—Judge J. Skelly Wright in *Lead Industries Assoc. v. EPA,* 1980

HEALTH-BASED ambient air quality standards form the cornerstone of regulation of air pollution under the Clean Air Act. Yet the act itself gives the Environmental Protection Agency little guidance on how to set these standards. Section 108 instructs the EPA to write a criteria document for each pollutant that is emitted by numerous sources and endangers the public health. Criteria documents must contain "the latest scientific knowledge useful in indicating the kind and extent of all identifiable effects on public health or welfare." Section 109 requires the EPA to establish primary air quality standards that, "allowing an adequate margin of safety, are requisite to protect the public health" and secondary standards to "protect the public welfare from any known or anticipated adverse effects." The dangers of this broad grant of discretion are readily apparent. If the EPA sets excessively stringent standards, billions of dollars of unnecessary control costs will be imposed on the economy. If standards are too lenient, then the health of thousands of individuals will suffer.

Not surprisingly, the courts have attempted to circumscribe the EPA's discretion in this area. They have added new procedural requirements to "notice and comment" rulemaking under the Administrative Procedures Act. They have insisted that the EPA present elaborate technical explanations for its standards, that it make these justifications available for public comment, and that it respond to all legitimate criticisms of its proposals. To ensure that the EPA has acted competently and fairly, the courts themselves have taken a hard look at the basis for the agency's standards. In addition, they have opened their doors to "nondiscretionary duty" cases, ordering the EPA to set standards for previously unregulated pollutants. No court decisions better illustrate the new administrative law's willingness to investigate complex technical issues and its commitment to protecting the public from government inaction than those involving the setting of national ambient air quality standards.

These decisions have received praise from the EPA, Congress, legal commentators, the National Academy of Sciences, and even environmental and industry litigants. Despite their different perspectives and objectives, all these groups seem to agree that the courts have succeeded in upgrading the scientific competence of federal regulators. While the EPA's standards continue to incite controversy, close judicial scrutiny is now an integral part of the decisionmaking process. In the words of William H. Rodgers, Jr., "The hard look doctrine plays no favorites; it is advanced as enthusiastically by industry as it is by environmentalists. Its acceptance is deep."[1]

Two cases decided in the early 1970s are often cited to confirm the benefits of close judicial scrutiny of EPA decisions on air quality standards. In the first, *Kennecott Copper Corp.* v. *Environmental Protection Agency,* the D.C. Circuit Court of Appeals ruled that while the EPA had complied with the minimal notice and comment rulemaking procedures of the Administrative Procedures Act, the court could not approve the challenged secondary standard for sulfur dioxide until the EPA put forth a more substantial explanation for the standard.[2] When the agency took a second look, it found that in rushing to meet the deadlines of the act

1. "A Hard Look at *Vermont Yankee:* Environmental Law Under Close Scrutiny," 67 *Georgetown Law Journal* 699 at 706 (1979). Among the works praising these court decisions are the following: National Academy of Sciences, *Decisionmaking in the Environmental Protection Agency* (NAS, 1977); William F. Pedersen, Jr., "Formal Records and Informal Rulemaking," 85 *Yale Law Journal* 38 (1975); Richard B. Stewart, "The Development of Administrative and Quasi-Constitutional Law in Judicial Review of Environmental Decisionmaking: Lessons from the Clean Air Act," 62 *Iowa Law Review* 713 (1977); and *Clean Air Act Amendments of 1977,* H. Rept. 95-294, 95 Cong. 1 sess. (Government Printing Office, 1977), pp. 318–25.

2. *Kennecott Copper Corp.* v. *Environmental Protection Agency,* 462 F.2d 846 (D.C. Cir. 1972).

it had misinterpreted the one study that might have supported its standard. It eventually dropped the standard altogether.[3]

In the second case, *Natural Resources Defense Council* v. *Environmental Protection Agency*, the same court ruled that once the EPA had determined that airborne lead endangers the public health, it had no choice but to regulate the major source of that pollutant, leaded gasoline.[4] EPA scientists had previously concluded that combustion of leaded gasoline contributes to lead poisoning among inner-city children. But opposition from the lead industry and the White House had prevented the EPA from ordering a reduction in the lead content of gasoline. Once the court issued its order, the EPA followed the advice of its technical staff and ordered a phased reduction of lead in gasoline. Subsequent research has confirmed the danger of this form of pollution.

In both these cases court decisions forced the EPA to base its actions on scientific evidence, not political pressure or an untutored zeal for protecting the environment. To guard against further embarrassing reversals the EPA has adopted an elaborate record-building process, replete with multiple opportunities for public comment and review of scientific evidence by panels of technical specialists. The agency now spends years developing the criteria documents on which air quality standards are based.

As convincing as it seems at first, the argument that the courts have improved the EPA's standards by forcing it to upgrade its technical analysis suffers from two serious flaws. First, several factors other than fear of court reversal help explain the transformation of the EPA's

3. The Office of General Counsel attorney charged with constructing an explanation for the court gave the following report to his superiors: "We were at first struck by the lack of written data supporting the levels set forth in the standards. As we went deeper into the matter it became more and more apparent that to some extent, the lack of documentation was due to lack of supporting data. . . . There appears to be no doubt that the secondary standard for SO_x was incorrectly established." (Memorandum, Robert Baum to John Quarles, March 27, 1972.) After long negotiations with the Office of Management and Budget and the Department of Agriculture, the EPA revoked the standard. 38 Fed. Reg. 11355 (1973) and 38 Fed. Reg. 25678 (1973).

4. *Natural Resources Defense Council* v. *Environmental Protection Agency*, No. 72-2233 (D.C. Cir., October 28, 1973). The D.C. Circuit never published its decision in this case, but members of the panel discussed the ruling in *Ethyl Corp.* v. *Environmental Protection Agency*, 541 F.2d 1 (D.C. Cir. 1976). John Quarles discusses the impact of this ruling in *Cleaning Up America: An Insider's View of the Environmental Protection Agency* (Houghton Mifflin, 1976), chap. 7. Subsequent episodes of the lengthy story of the courts and airborne lead are discussed below.

standard-setting process in the 1970s. The 1970 Clean Air Act required the EPA to set six sets of air quality standards by April 1971. Not only was this a monumental task for a fledgling agency, but few private parties offered comments on the EPA's criteria documents or its proposed standards. Industry and environmental groups did not yet understand how these standards would affect them. The EPA acted the only way it could—quickly and informally.

All this changed as the regulatory consequences of these first air quality standards became clear. Industries hard hit by state implementation plan (SIP) regulations soon discovered the thinness of the EPA's evidence and complained loudly to the EPA, Congress, the states, and the press. Congress asked the National Academy of Sciences (NAS) to reexamine the standards. While the NAS did not recommend specific changes in existing standards, it underscored the need for more research and called on the EPA to begin a long-term reassessment of all its standards.[5] This time industry and environmentalists were prepared for battle. Moreover, by the mid-1970s the EPA was well aware both of the importance of selling its regulatory programs to Congress, the states, and the public and of the harm faulty research could do to its image as a public health agency.[6] Thus the courts were but one of many audiences to whom the EPA addressed its analysis. To attribute all changes within the EPA to court actions is to engage in *post hoc, ergo propter hoc* analysis.

5. National Academy of Sciences–National Academy of Engineering, *Air Quality and Automobile Emission Control*, prepared for the Senate Committee on Public Works, 93 Cong. 2 sess. (GPO, 1974), vol. 1, pp. 1, 6, 20–21.

6. The EPA's image—and its research program—suffered greatly from the controversy over its Community Health and Environmental Surveillance System (CHESS) study. In 1974 the EPA claimed the study provided support for its sulfur dioxide standards and for its policies on tall stacks and prevention of significant deterioration. But newspaper articles charged that EPA officials had distorted research findings to produce conclusions satisfactory to regulators. While the congressional committees that investigated these charges cleared EPA officials of willful misconduct, a report by a panel of prominent research scientists commissioned by the House found that the EPA had used shoddy research methods, that it had seriously "overinterpreted" the evidence, and that the findings of this major research project were almost totally unreliable. See "The Environmental Protection Agency's Research Program with Special Emphasis on the Community Health and Environmental Surveillance System (CHESS): An Investigative Report," Committee Print, House Committee on Science and Technology, prepared for the Subcommittee on Special Studies, Investigation and Oversight and the Subcommittee on Environment and the Atmosphere of the House Committee on Science and Technology, 94 Cong. 2 sess. (GPO, 1976); and Richard J. Tobin, *The Social Gamble: Determining Acceptable Levels of Air Quality* (Lexington Books, 1979), pp. 102–06, 139–43.

The second problem with the argument cited above is the way it frames the question it proceeds to answer. Asking whether the courts have improved the standard-setting process implies that this job is essentially a technical task, not a political one. That observers should take this view is not surprising since the Clean Air Act itself presents standard setting as a scientific investigation of the location of health effect "thresholds." A threshold is the concentration at which sensitive individuals begin to suffer adverse health effects as a consequence of exposure to pollution. By ordering the EPA to set national primary standards at these thresholds, the act seems to make standard setting a job for medical experts.

Few scientists now believe it is possible to identify nonzero health effect thresholds for most pollutants. Almost any nonzero concentration of a pollutant will affect some sensitive individuals (however few) in a way that some doctors will consider adverse (however minor). In the words of the 1974 NAS study mentioned above:

> In no case is there evidence that the threshold levels have a clear physiological meaning, in the sense that there are genuine adverse health effects at or above some level of pollution, but no effects at all below that level. On the contrary, evidence indicates that the amount of health damage varies with the upward and downward variations in the concentration of the pollutant, with no sharp lower limit.[7]

By 1977 even the House subcommittee chaired by Representative Rogers conceded, "The 'safe threshold' concept is, at best, a necessary myth to permit the setting of some standards,"[8] and Senator Muskie stated: "When we set the standards, we understood that below the standards . . . there would still be health effects. The standard we picked was simply the best judgment we had on the basis of the available evidence as to what the unacceptable health effects in terms of the country as a whole would be."[9]

Consequently, each time the EPA publishes or revises a standard, it must make a *policy* choice about what constitutes an "acceptable" health risk. Standard setting is a political process, both in the sense that the EPA must make a policy choice not dictated by medical evidence and in the sense that many political forces seek to influence its decision. For

7. NAS–NAE, *Air Quality and Automobile Emission Control,* vol. 1, p. 17.
8. *Clean Air Act Amendments of 1977,* H. Rept. 95-294, p. 111.
9. *Clean Air Act Amendments of 1977,* Hearings before the Subcommittee on Environmental Pollution of the Senate Committee on Environment and Public Works, 95 Cong. 1 sess. (GPO, 1977), pt. 3, p. 8.

this reason, an assessment of the consequences of court actions must consider not just whether the courts have improved the EPA's technical competence, but also how they have influenced the agency's concept of its statutory mandate and how they have affected the balance of power among competing interests. The second half of this chapter addresses these questions by looking at the EPA's choice of the two primary standards announced between 1971 and 1982. First, however, will be examined the reasons why science alone cannot answer the questions regulators confront and how Congress, the EPA, and the courts have responded to the collapse of the threshold myth.

Legal Standards and Medical Evidence

"One of the nice things about the environmental standard setting business," one EPA scientist noted at a meeting of the agency's Science Advisory Board, "is that you are always setting the standard at a level where the data is lousy."[10] While the EPA is often blamed for relying on questionable research and for using unsubstantiated assumptions, the act gives it little choice but to base standards on extrapolations from incomplete evidence. The EPA must make critical decisions not only about the reliability of various medical studies, but also about the significance of these findings for setting standards.

Reliability and Research Design

The Clean Air Act requires that national primary standards be based on "the latest scientific knowledge," that they "protect the public health," and that they include a "margin of safety." The 1970 Senate report further explained that "ambient air quality is sufficient to protect the health of such persons whenever there is an *absence of adverse effect* on the health of a statistically related sample of persons in *sensitive* groups from exposure to the ambient air."[11] This means that as soon as the EPA finds clear evidence that some sensitive individuals experience

10. Statement of Roger Cortesi (Office of Research and Development), transcript of meeting of Science Advisory Board Panel on Photochemical Oxidants, November 10, 1977, p. 135 (contained in EPA docket on revision of ozone standard).

11. *A Legislative History of the Clean Air Amendments of 1970*, prepared for the Senate Committee on Public Works, 93 Cong. 2 sess. (GPO, 1974), p. 410 (emphasis added).

adverse health effects at a certain level, it must search for studies that suggest that health effects start at even lower concentrations. The lower the pollution level examined, the more subtle the health effect and the smaller the percentage of subjects affected. The act and its legislative history thus ensure that standard setting will take place on the frontiers of scientific research.

Exacerbating this fundamental problem are a number of practical difficulties that constantly vex those who design research projects to aid standard setters. Regulators need information on the effects of pollutants on sensitive individuals who are exposed to the pollutants for many years and experience a variety of additional environmental stresses. Yet regulators cannot delay decisionmaking while researchers conduct studies lasting ten, twenty, or fifty years. Moreover, ethical constraints prevent researchers from exposing sensitive individuals to potentially dangerous pollution levels. It would be unseemly—to say the least—for a public health agency to expose a million people to a suspected carcinogen to see how many eventually die from cancer. In addition, financial constraints prevent researchers from studying large numbers of human subjects under carefully controlled conditions while reproducing the many stresses of everyday life. Consequently, standard setters must rely on three types of indirect evidence, each of which has its own peculiar shortcomings.

CLINICAL STUDIES. The evidence most favored by scientists and regulators comes from clinical studies in which carefully observed subjects are exposed to varying pollution concentrations. Most such studies examine only a handful of subjects (rarely as many as twenty), none of whom are particularly sensitive to the pollutant. Moreover, clinical studies expose these subjects to the pollutant for only a short period of time. To make their findings useful to regulators, researchers must extrapolate from short-run to long-run exposures, from healthy to sensitive individuals, and from exposure to one pollutant to exposure to several (possibly synergistic) pollutants. These extrapolations seldom amount to much more than educated guesses. To make this extrapolation more accurate, some studies use experimental regimes designed to simulate real-world conditions. Yet these regimes themselves invite controversy over whether the analogy used is an appropriate one. To make matters worse, given the small number of subjects involved in clinical studies, their results are often not statistically significant. This raises the question of whether regulators should use studies—and extrapolations based on these studies—that do not meet the standards of certainty usually employed by research scientists.

EPIDEMIOLOGICAL STUDIES. One way to avoid these problems is to conduct epidemiological studies that compare the mortality and morbidity rates of populations residing or working in areas with different pollution levels. Epidemiological studies examine a large number of subjects, including the most sensitive sectors of the populations. These populations have been exposed to pollution for years and experienced all the other stresses of daily life. Epidemiological studies suffer from a number of infirmities, however. The following quotation from a report commissioned by the House to study the EPA's epidemiological research program offers a succinct summary of the hazards of this form of analysis:

> Exposure to suspect pollutants is not controlled in population studies. Indeed with current technologies, it is not possible to be sure that the correct pollutant is even being measured. . . .
>
> The health measurements are often subjective responses to a questionnaire or interview. . . . Even objective endpoints respond to uncontrolled events like an undetected influenza epidemic or high pollen count.
>
> Whether the health measurement is subjective or objective, the response is often affected by factors (covariates) associated with the subject studied and unrelated to pollutant exposure. Whether the individual smokes or is subjected to cigarette smoke at home or work is a covariate of dominant importance in pollution studies. . . . Occupation, age, sex, race, immunity to influenza, allergy, access to air-conditioning and countless other covariates complicate the interpretation of epidemiologic data. . . .
>
> The epidemiologist has little control over the subjects studied. He cannot assign them at random to reside in polluted communities of interest. Thus, a clean town may contain many asthmatics because asthmatics have wisely chosen to live there rather than in a more polluted community. This fundamental problem of self-selection must qualify any conclusions obtained from non-randomized population studies: it may be possible to demonstrate temporal or spatial associations between health and pollution measurements, but a causal relationship cannot be inferred on the basis of a single epidemiologic study.[12]

In short, while epidemiological studies address the questions confronting regulators more directly than do clinical studies, they are subject to even more attacks on their reliability.

ANIMAL STUDIES. When clinical and epidemiological evidence is inconclusive, regulators often rely on toxicological evidence produced in studies of laboratory animals. Animal studies have many advantages.

---

12. "The Environmental Protection Agency's Research Program," pp. 57–58.

Ethical considerations usually do not constrain exposure levels. Since animals are not covered by minimum wage laws, a large number can be included in experiments. Also, since animals such as rats and mice have relatively short life spans, researchers can test the effects of lifetime exposures to various pollution levels. But extrapolation from toxicological evidence is more difficult than from clinical evidence. The ongoing debate over proof of carcinogeneity raises the difficult issues of the accuracy of extrapolation from high doses to low doses and from animals to humans. By using different conversion models one can come up with human equivalences that differ by as much as a millionfold. Such a range of errors hardly breeds confidence in standard setting.[13]

Given the nature of the evidence on the health effects of air pollutants, it is not surprising that scientists give conflicting advice to regulators. To some extent disputes over the accuracy and reliability of experimental evidence result from the differing perspectives of various research disciplines. Those who do clinical work, for example, tend to distrust epidemiological studies. Epidemiologists claim that other types of studies overlook critical evidence and insist upon too high a level of proof. Even within a discipline or subdiscipline reasonable experts disagree. This can reflect different political views: those who consider themselves environmentalists emphasize the strengths of studies whose weaknesses are pointed out by those more sympathetic to industry's position. For almost every key study one can discover a range of scientific opinion on its reliability. Regulators often find themselves in the unenviable position of having to arbitrate disputes among noted specialists.

The Significance of Evidence: Defining "Acceptable Risk"

In setting air quality standards under section 109 regulators must also address a second set of issues that are even less amenable to scientific proof. Because the evidence provided by scientific studies seldom indicates sharp discontinuities between adverse and benign physiological changes or sensitive and healthy individuals, regulators must draw lines to determine what constitutes "acceptable risk." The Clean Air Act, based as it is on the concept of health effect thresholds, does not appear to permit the agency to make such policy choices. But by ignoring this

13. See James P. Leape, "Quantitative Risk Assessment in Regulation of Environmental Carcinogens," 4 *Harvard Environmental Law Review* 86 at 103 (1980) and references cited therein.

problem the act does not cause it to disappear. The EPA must make at least four types of policy choices that define acceptable risk.

The first and most obvious policy issue arising under the act is what constitutes an "adverse" health effect. Almost any amount of pollution will cause some change in the human body. Some pollutants cause minor discomfort (such as eye irritation) without impairing basic body functions. Others reduce the body's ability to perform certain functions but do not cause overt symptoms. For example, small amounts of lead in the blood inhibit formation of a precursor of hemoglobin, yet do not reduce the blood's ability to carry oxygen from the lungs to the rest of the body under normal circumstances. Is minor discomfort an adverse effect? How about a physiological change that reduces the body's ability to survive only when coupled with unusual stress? Physicians often disagree on these issues. While regulators must learn from medical science about the possible long-term consequences of these physiological changes, medical science itself cannot provide answers to the questions of what constitutes adequate bodily well-being, tolerable discomfort, or acceptable security.

Second, individuals vary tremendously in their sensitivity to environmental stress. Pregnant women, asthmatics, heavy smokers, the elderly, and those with heart conditions are especially vulnerable to air pollution. These groups can overlap, producing subgroups that experience adverse health effects from pollution even when it dips below natural background levels. As one physician on the EPA's Science Advisory Board put it, "If you have a big enough population, someone is going to freak out at some incredibly low level."[14] If one does not set the standard to protect the most sensitive individual in the country, where does one draw the line? At the most sensitive 1 percent? The most sensitive 0.1 percent? Just as the act and its legislative history are silent on the question of what constitutes an adverse effect, they do little to define the sensitive group that a standard must protect.

Third, the health consequences of exposure to one air pollutant often depend on the subject's exposure to other forms of pollution. For example, lead enters the body both through ingestion and respiration. Many inner-city children have dangerously high levels of lead in their blood as a result of eating lead-based paint. Thus any contribution of lead from the air may adversely affect their health. There is a similar

14. Transcript of Science Advisory Board Panel on Airborne Lead, January 31, 1977, p. 175 (EPA docket on lead, sec. II A-F1).

pattern with pollutants that appear in only one medium. In its explanation of its ozone standard the EPA stated:

> Air pollution is one of the many stresses which can precipitate an asthma attack or worsen the disease state in persons with chronic cardio-pulmonary disease. Other factors that can precipitate attacks include respiratory infection, passage of cold fronts, seasonal pollens, extreme heat or cold, or emotional disturbances.[15]

Unless regulators set standards at zero in an effort to eliminate totally the health risk created by pollution, they must build into their analysis assumptions that limit the exposure of sensitive individuals to additional stress. In doing so regulators in effect decide how much risk should be addressed through control of air pollution, how much through control of water quality, housing conditions, food quality, and climate—and how much need not be addressed at all.

Finally, no matter how low a standard is set, there is always a possibility that adverse effects may, for some as yet unknown reason, appear at even lower levels. The "margin of safety" wording of section 109 attempts to address this problem. Some physicians claim that prudent medical practices require reducing exposure levels to 1 percent of the level at which adverse effects are observed. Such rules of thumb do not reflect medical findings, however, but only the approach of certain physicians to dealing with uncertainty.[16] The political nature of standard setting is especially evident when it comes to establishing a margin of safety. Even the EPA, which has clung tenaciously to a purely technical view of standard setting, admits that this part of the process requires a policy choice.

Separatists and Advocates

Just as research scientists often disagree about the reliability of various studies, they likewise come to divergent conclusions on the role scientists should play in defining acceptable risk. On this issue scientists tend to fall into two broad categories, which I shall term "separatists" and "advocates." The first group denies that science can provide definitive

15. 44 Fed. Reg. 8215 (1979).

16. See the exchange between Samuel Epstein and other members of the Science Advisory Board, transcript of SAB Panel on Airborne Lead, pp. 1-175 and 2-154. Epstein argued that standard medical practices require setting the standard at a level equal to one one-hundredth of the demonstrated effects level. Other members of the panel disputed this claim.

answers to the four questions just discussed and tries to limit the role
of scientists to making evidence available to political decisionmakers,
explaining the reliability of this evidence, offering "best guess" estimates
of where various health effects begin, and attempting to quantify the
risk associated with setting standards at various levels. The "advocates,"
in contrast, believe that scientists should do more than describe risks;
they should make recommendations consistent with the mission of their
profession, the protection of public health.

The separatists draw a sharp line (in theory, if not always in practice)
between scientific and political decisions. Partly to protect the autonomy
and integrity of scientific research, they object to the threshold approach
of the Clean Air Act, which obscures the political aspect of standard
setting and threatens to entangle research scientists in divisive political
controversies. According to the report prepared by the National Academy
of Sciences in 1974:

> There is no escape from a reasoned judgment, containing an unavoidable
> subjective element, as to the level at which the possible benefits from reducing
> pollution further no longer justify the high probable costs of bringing about
> such further reduction.[17]

Consequently, they argue, the law should be changed to recognize the
political nature of standard setting. In the words of a later NAS report:

> Legal language that is rigid and categorical serves little useful purpose, in the
> face of the scientific uncertainty and ambiguity. The concept of "reasonable
> safety" or "acceptable risk" needs to be considered as a replacement for "no
> adverse health effect" in the assessment of air pollutants.
>
> What constitutes an "adverse" effect needs to be defined. . . . Inherent in
> this is the need to define what is an acceptable risk.[18]

Working under present legislation, these separatists try to impress on
administrators the fact that political executives bear final responsibility
for determining what constitutes an adverse effect, how many people
deserve protection, and what constitutes an adequate margin of safety.

The advocates are far less modest. They view the Clean Air Act as a
mandate to protect the public health to the maximum extent possible.
If there are no absolutely safe levels of air pollution, the public should
be made aware of this, and steps should be taken to lower pollution
levels as quickly as possible. The only legitimate constraint on the

17. NAS–NAE, *Air Quality and Automobile Emission Control*, vol. 1, p. 18.
18. National Academy of Sciences, *Health Effects of Sulfur Oxides* (National Academy
Press, 1978), p. 16.

lowering of standards is the need to provide some evidence that adverse effects occur at that level. If this means that each air quality standard will eventually reach zero or background levels, so much the better. The 1974 NAS report cited above noted that a minority of members on the committee "take the view that all pollution is bad and should be eliminated."[19] Advocates tend to transfer their role as private physician to the public realm: the job of the physician is to tell patients to stop doing things that are harmful to them, whatever the cost. While the patient may not always take the doctor's advice, the doctor has not done his duty unless he warns—or even scares—his patient. Most advocates not only view this as their responsibility under the act, but strongly support retention of the "health only" focus of the statutes.[20]

Not surprisingly, the advocates are usually strong defenders of the reliability of studies showing health effects associated with low pollution concentrations. This is consistent with their reading of the statute and their conception of their professional mission: health standards should reflect the *possibility* that concentrations above the level of the standards could harm public health. The position of the separatists on the issue of the reliability of evidence is not nearly so easy to describe. Some clearly believe that the costs of regulation are so high that standard setters should use only studies that produce statistically significant results and have no major flaws. Others are much less demanding. Some separatists are as committed to the protection of the public health as are most advocates, but limit their advocacy to explaining to decisionmakers the possible risks associated with low-level pollution concentration.

Thus handing the job of setting air quality standards to "experts" seldom resolves controversy. Given the range of scientific opinion on both the reliability and significance of health evidence, it is almost always possible for interest groups, industry and environmentalists alike, to find respected, honest scientists who support their position.

19. NAS–NAE, *Air Quality and Automobile Emission Control*, vol. 1, p. 58.

20. For a vivid contrast between these two approaches, see the exchange among Stephen Horvath, Jay Nadel, and Marvin Schneiderman (advocates) and Benjamin Ferris, Jr., (separatist) in *Health Standards for Air Pollutants*, Hearing before the Subcommittee on Health and the Environment of the House Committee on Energy and Commerce, 97 Cong. 1 sess. (GPO, 1982), pp. 2–54. Steven Kelman has found the approach of the "advocates" prevalent in the Occupational Safety and Health Administration. "Occupational Health and Safety Administration," in James Q. Wilson, ed., *The Politics of Regulation* (Basic Books, 1980).

Paradoxes from Capitol Hill

Did Congress endorse the position of the public health advocates when it passed the 1970 act and the 1977 amendments? Or did it simply fail to understand that clear thresholds do not exist and that science cannot offer regulators definitive advice on where to set air quality standards? Answering this question requires distinguishing between the events of 1970 and those of 1977, as well as between the views of committee members and those of congressmen less familiar with air pollution issues.

The issue of how the EPA should set air quality standards received amazingly little attention in 1970. For years Congress had debated *whether* the federal government should establish mandatory standards. By 1970 everyone seemed to agree that it should. The debate then shifted to the question of *when* the states must attain these national standards. The Nixon administration wanted to allow federal administrators to set compliance dates, but Senator Muskie and his allies insisted upon explicit statutory deadlines. The only differences between the sections of the Nixon and Muskie bills that explained how the EPA should set these standards was that the Muskie bill established separate primary (health) and secondary (welfare) standards and added a clause requiring standards to incorporate a margin of safety. There was virtually no discussion of these changes either on the floor or in the press.

There are several explanations for Congress's apparent failure to confront the issue of how the EPA should set national standards. Health is a popular issue; every congressman wants to let his constituents know that he yields to no one in his efforts to protect the public health. So potent a symbol is health that few politicians ever go beyond the symbolism. For years advocates of stronger air pollution regulation had pushed the Department of Health, Education, and Welfare to define "safe" air pollution levels. They thought this would create irresistible pressure for the federal government to reduce pollution concentrations to those "safe" levels.[21] Moreover, turning the job of defining adequate

21. The Clean Air Act of 1963 required the Department of Health, Education, and Welfare to compile and publish criteria documents "reflecting accurately the latest scientific knowledge useful in indicating the kind and extent of such effects which may be expected from the presence of such pollution agents (or combination of agents) in the air in varying

standards over to "experts" relieves congressmen of the burden of resolving difficult controversies.

In 1970 National Air Pollution Control Administration chief John Middleton warned the Muskie committee not to equate national standards with "no-effect" pollution levels. He testified:

> To identify a no-known-effects level is something that would be, in my opinion, not only extremely difficult but very likely not possible. . . . The knowledge that we have shows that there is not any single level where something either begins or stops. . . . As science progresses, it is very likely we are going to find still other body chemical systems that are being affected, so the no-effect level always corresponds, you might say, to the limitations of scientific knowledge in this area.[22]

Years later Senator Muskie claimed that the sponsors of the 1970 act recognized the futility of searching for no-effect levels. Yet the 1970 Senate report stated that the primary standards must guarantee an "absence of adverse effects" among members of sensitive groups.

Why did the Senate committee insist upon a definition of national standards at odds with what it knew about the medical evidence on air pollution? Senator Muskie has claimed that the restrictive language of the act and the Senate report was designed to protect the EPA from court challenges, industry pressure, and, most important, Nixon administration efforts to water down Congress's programs. A less stringent statutory command would have produced long debates over the cost of regulation and thus interminable delay.[23]

The words of section 109 and its legislative history, though, did far more than insulate the EPA from outside pressure. In effect they instructed the EPA to strike while the iron was hot, to set very demanding standards while political support for pollution control was strong. The Senate

---

quantities." The 1967 act added, without explanation, that the secretary of HEW should recommend "such criteria of air quality as in his judgment may be requisite for the protection of the public health and welfare." National Air Pollution Control Administration officials warned that this bizarre use of the term "criteria" confused scientific description and political prescription. Until 1970, though, this confusion had little practical significance. The National Air Pollution Control Administration issued only one criteria document before 1970. In 1969, after an extended political battle, HEW withheld its recommendation on a "safe" level of sulfur oxides. Richard Tobin provides a detailed and perceptive review of these events in *The Social Gamble*, pp. 33–67.

22. *Air Pollution—1970*, Hearings before the Subcommittee on Air and Water Pollution of the Senate Committee on Public Works, 91 Cong. 2 sess. (GPO, 1970), pp. 1184–85.

23. Richard B. Stewart, "Ambient Standard Setting," paper prepared for National Academy of Sciences, *Decisionmaking in the Environmental Protection Agency* (on file at National Academy of Sciences), p. 9.

committee left nothing to chance—and little to agency discretion. The Senate report, for example, endorsed specific standards for photochemical oxidants and carbon monoxides and used them to justify the act's controversial "technology-forcing" automobile emission limitations.[24] Put bluntly, Muskie and his staff insisted that the EPA set standards stringent enough to keep constant pressure on major polluters.

Thus, if only the congressional "insiders" are considered, one can find clear support for the position taken by public health advocates. But these insiders certainly did not advertise the implications of their position. Moreover, while the Muskie and Rogers committees continued to insist that the EPA set "precautionary" standards and to resist efforts to introduce cost-benefit analysis, they drew back from the advocates' position that national standards should eventually approach zero. This was far too big a step for practical politicians.

In 1977 the question of how the EPA should set national standards received more attention than it did in 1970. Once again Congress as a whole followed the lead of its committees. But this time it took a firm stand—on both sides of the issue. On the one hand, Congress repulsed attempts to discard the "health only" approach of the 1970 act or to increase the evidentiary burden of proof on the EPA. The 1977 amendments revised section 108 to allow the administrator to regulate any pollutants which "in his judgment, cause or contribute to air pollution which may reasonably be anticipated to endanger public health or welfare." The House report stated that inclusion of this language was intended to emphasize the precautionary nature of primary standards.[25]

On the other hand, Congress passed an extensive program for prevention of significant deterioration (PSD), the purpose of which was

24. *A Legislative History of the Clean Air Amendments of 1970*, pp. 423–28. The Senate report stated that on the basis of criteria documents recently completed by the National Air Pollution Control Administration, "The ambient standard necessary to protect the public health from carbon monoxide is 8–10 parts per million (ppm) ... for photochemical oxidants (hydrocarbons) is 0.06 ppm ... for nitrogen oxides is anticipated to be about 0.10 ppm" (p. 425). These numbers came from a paper written by a National Air Pollution Control Administration official, hastily thrown together for a meeting of the Air Pollution Control Association in June 1970. The Senate committee used this paper to justify the 90 percent auto emission reduction requirement—even though the official, Delbert Barth, repeatedly warned that his findings were only preliminary. Delbert Barth, "Federal Motor Vehicle Emission Goals for CO, HC, and NO_x Based on Desired Air Quality Levels," 20 *Journal of Air Pollution Control Association* 519 (1970); and Paul B. Downing and Gordon Brady, "Implementing the Clean Air Act: A Case Study of Oxidant Control in Los Angeles," 18 *Natural Resources Journal* 237 at 243–44 (1978).

25. *Clean Air Act Amendments of 1977*, H. Rept. 95-294, p. 49.

to protect the public against possible health effects of criteria pollutants at concentrations well below the national standards. The House report admitted that "the 'safe threshold' concept is, at best, a necessary myth." But it rejected the advocates' alternative of dropping national standards to zero, remarking only that "obviously, this no-risk philosophy ignores all economic and social consequences and is impractical."[26] The practical solution, of course, was a PSD program that established additional air quality standards for areas with pollution levels below the precautionary national standards.

This two-pronged response to the problem of standard setting pleased environmental advocates who sought to keep existing standards intact, to preserve the idea that every citizen has a legal right to breathe safe air, and to keep air in rural areas even cleaner than required by national standards. The EPA supported PSD as well as the revision of section 108. Although these changes protected the EPA's autonomy, they simultaneously undermined its rationale for setting standards without regard to control costs. The clear implication of PSD is that national standards should *not* reflect a "no-risk philosophy"; the EPA should not "ignore all economic and social consequences" in its choice of standards. But Congress gave no indication of what risk is acceptable and even seemed to bar the agency from considering the nonhealth consequences of its standards.[27] With its congressional supporters playing both ends against the middle, the EPA ended up, not surprisingly, caught in the middle.

The Bureaucratic Politics of Standard Setting

As noted earlier, the standard-setting process within the EPA changed dramatically during the 1970s. When the EPA set standards for its original six criteria pollutants in 1971, a handful of agency officials reviewed the few health studies available on each, considered in brief intra-agency discussions whether the effects noted were adverse, and

26. Ibid., p. 127.
27. In 1981–82 some business lobbyists argued for revising sec. 109 to require the EPA to consider cost in standard setting. These recommendations received little support in either house. The Senate subcommittee unanimously defeated a measure to change methods for setting primary standards and defeated by a 10–4 vote a proposal to allow the EPA to consider costs in setting secondary standards. 12 *Environment Reporter— Current Developments* 891.

issued the standards with a minimum of explanation.[28] The standards were very close to those endorsed by the Senate report. In recent years standard setting has become more complex and more institutionalized. EPA officials, interest groups, and independent scientists spend years debating each proposed revision and new standard. The EPA offers extensive, sophisticated documentation for its proposed and final standards. Yet the EPA has retained the "health-only" threshold approach to standard setting, which almost all scientists agree is seriously flawed. This raises two questions: why has the EPA clung to the threshold approach, and how does it set standards within this framework?

The agency has at times come perilously close to abandoning the entire threshold concept. In defending its airborne lead standard, the EPA explained:

> Investigation of the effects typically reveals that there is no clear threshold above which there are "adverse effects" and below which there are none. . . . Pollutant effects typically exist as a continuum, ranging from very serious effects at high pollutant concentrations down to the "no-effect" level, which may exist only at a zero-concentration level for some pollutants.[29]

Similarly, the EPA's 1979 ozone criteria document concluded that "it is most unlikely that a discrete threshold pollutant concentration can be established even for a single population segment and a single biomedical indicator."[30]

The EPA has drawn a surprising policy conclusion from these medical findings, however. In announcing its 1979 ozone standard it stated:

> Adverse health effect thresholds for sensitive persons are difficult or impossible to determine experimentally, while the threshold for healthy persons or animals is not likely to be predictive of the response of more sensitive groups. In this notice of rulemaking EPA uses the terminology "probable effects level" to refer to the level that *in its best judgment* is most likely to be the adverse health effect threshold concentration. It is the fact that the adverse health effect threshold concentration is actually unknown that necessitates the margin of safety required by the Act.[31]

In other words, the uncertainty over where thresholds fall requires an ultimately unexplainable exercise of judgment by the administrator.

What type of judgment does the EPA refer to here? Rather than admit

28. 36 Fed. Reg. 8186 (1971).

29. Brief for the United States at 63 in *Lead Industries Assoc.* v. *Environmental Protection Agency*, 647 F.2d 1130 (D.C. Cir. 1980).

30. EPA, Environmental Criteria and Assessment Office, *Air Quality Criteria for Ozone and Other Photochemical Oxidants* (EPA, April 1978), p. 4.

31. 44 Fed. Reg. 8203 (1979) (emphasis added).

that the disappearance of thresholds requires regulators to make a political judgment about acceptable risk, the EPA has continued to justify its standards in terms of its scientific judgment about the probable location of the elusive threshold. Such determinations as what constitutes an adverse health effect and what percentage of the population deserves protection become matters to be decided on the basis of prudent public health practice. The EPA thus manages to get the best of both worlds: standard setting is not a political act, but a technical task that must be performed by an expert agency; yet the uncertainty of the task frees the agency from the dictates of scientific evidence and its political executives from responsibility for the economic and social consequences of its determinations.

That the EPA should take this position is not surprising. This elusive threshold approach not only maintains the autonomy of the bureaucracy, but strengthens its image as a public health agency and pleases its congressional patrons. Presenting national standards as absolutely necessary to the protection of public health adds to the moral force behind emission limitations based on these standards. It allows the EPA to escape from the demand that each and every action be justified on the basis of economic analysis. It also allows the agency to convince the courts that it is faithfully executing rather than distorting the law. There is only one problem: this approach requires the EPA to use its "expert judgment" to estimate the location of a threshold that the EPA itself concedes does not exist. The logic of bureaucracy is not always the logic of science.[32]

How does the EPA use the discretion it has fought to protect? Figure 8-1 indicates the steps the agency goes through before announcing a standard. Three aspects of this process deserve special attention.

---

32. The contradictory nature of the EPA's position becomes most apparent when one compares its treatment of criteria and hazardous pollutants. Sec. 112 requires the EPA to establish federal emission limits for hazardous pollutants that cause debilitating illness or death. To emphasize the need for strict control of these sources, the 1970 Senate report stated that the EPA could set emission limits at zero.

Among the hazardous pollutants the EPA must regulate are carcinogens. While the EPA has conceded that most carcinogens probably have no thresholds, it has backed away from setting emission standards at zero. More surprisingly, it has read sec. 112 to allow it to consider cost in setting emission limitations. This means that the EPA takes cost into consideration in regulating hazardous pollutants, but not in regulating less dangerous pollutants—even though no thresholds exist for either. 44 Fed. Reg. 58642 (1979).

Bureaucratic politics helps explain this anomaly. With criteria pollutants the EPA can consider cost in writing and enforcing SIPs. It has no such flexibility under sec. 112.

Figure 8-1. *The Standard-setting Process in the Environmental Protection Agency*

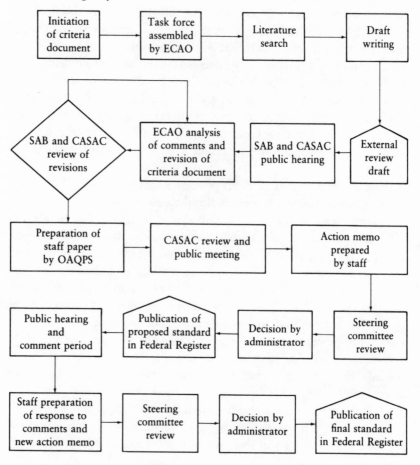

First, the EPA devotes far more attention to surveying the scientific literature on the effects of pollution, subjecting its findings to peer group review, and writing the criteria document than to other stages of the process. The 1977 amendments require the EPA to submit its criteria document to the Clean Air Scientific Advisory Committee (CASAC), which supplements review by the EPA's Science Advisory Board (SAB). The SAB and CASAC almost always require the EPA to revise its criteria document several times. Both the lead and ozone criteria documents, for example, went through three separate drafts and three rounds of review by the CASAC and SAB. Realizing that comments offered before the EPA formally proposes a standard are more effective than those submitted later in the process, interest groups now offer voluminous comments on draft criteria documents. In 1978 the EPA created a special office, the Environmental Criteria and Assessment Office (ECAO), within the Office of Research and Development (ORD) to coordinate the increasingly burdensome job of compiling a criteria document.

Second, the task force responsible for preparing alternatives for consideration by the agency's political executives is dominated by the ECAO and the Strategies and Air Standards Division of the Office of Air Quality Planning Standards (OAQPS), both of which are located in Durham, North Carolina. As the ECAO nears completion of its criteria document, the OAQPS begins work on a staff paper that summarizes pivotal studies and presents the questions that must be addressed by political executives. The ECAO and OAQPS work together closely, usually with little guidance from above. The staff paper they produce goes to the director of the OAQPS, who turns it into a draft action memo. Once the OAQPS can produce an action memo that the assistant administrator for air programs can support, it goes to the EPA's steering committee for review by the administrator and all the agency's assistant administrators. If the steering committee can agree, a proposed standard is published in the Federal Register, the agency invites comments on it, and the OAQPS begins work on a second action memo, this one for promulgation of a final standard.

Third, decisions on standards usually receive serious attention from all political executives within the EPA. Setting national standards is one of the agency's most important, most controversial, and most visible jobs. In the end the decision on the level for a standard is made by the administrator of the EPA. Explaining why the administrator chose a particular standard is as much a job for a psychologist as for a political scientist or a physician. It is possible, though, to identify the points of view that the administrator usually hears from within the agency. Typically agency officials divide into three camps on standards: the advocates, the regulators, and the economists.

Many officials within the EPA share the position of the public health advocates described above. According to this view, since all pollution is potentially harmful, especially to the most vulnerable members of society, pollution levels should be kept as low as possible. The EPA should set standards as stringent as possible without inviting crippling retaliation from Congress, the scientific community, or others upon whom it is dependent. This viewpoint is not confined to one office or one profession within the EPA; indeed, it comes close to representing the reigning ideology of the organization. Often the most zealous proponents of this position are physicians and researchers commissioned by the agency to perform research or hired as consultants. In addition, attorneys in the Office of General Counsel (OGC) have strongly supported the advocate position, arguing not just that this is what the law demands, but also that for policy reasons the EPA should back down only on deadlines, not on its ultimate public health goals. At critical junctures some political executives have also joined the advocate camp.

Agency engineers and regional officials charged with turning air quality standards into control strategies frequently adopt a different position. Tension between these regulators and the advocates becomes most obvious when the EPA must decide whether to regulate a new pollutant. While the advocates generally favor setting clear air quality goals by invoking section 109, the regulators are all too aware of the resources consumed in the standard-setting and -implementation process. The OAQPS has resisted efforts to add new criteria pollutants or to revise existing standards. It has not wanted to oversee the wholesale revision of more than fifty SIPs.

After the EPA decides to add or revise an air quality standard, the regulators tend to support standards slightly more stringent than those requiring use of commercially available control equipment by polluters in major metropolitan areas. If a standard is restrictive enough to require such controls in most such areas, then control agencies need not perform complex modeling to specify emission limitations. Any gap between the reduction achieved by these controls and the reductions required for attainment of standards will further the technology-forcing goal of the act. Yet if this gap is so large that attainment seems practically impossible, then control programs may suffer from lack of credibility and urgency. In short, the regulators seek to use national standards as carrots that can be kept just out of reach—but not too distant to be seen.

Finally, the EPA's economists, most of whom are located in the Office of Planning and Evaluation (OPE) under the control of the assistant administrator for planning and management, are in the anomalous position of having to defend the economic reasonableness of standards that the agency claims cannot be set on the basis of cost. By executive order, the EPA must prepare cost estimates for all major regulatory actions. The OPE must carry the ball for the EPA in negotiations with other agencies, which frequently claim that the EPA's standards will bankrupt the nation. Not surprisingly, the OPE tends to recommend that the administrator make concessions to those who complain about the high costs of the standards. As criticism of excessive regulation has mounted, interagency review has grown more intense, and cost-benefit, cost-effectiveness, and risk assessment analyses have become more sophisticated, the OPE's participation in the standard-setting process has expanded.

There is, in short, no simple answer to the question of how the EPA sets air quality standards. Medical evidence cannot offer definitive guidance. Congress has given the agency contradictory signals on how to cope with the task of defining significant risk. The EPA itself has refused to deal with the problem in a forthright manner, hiding its policy choices behind its interpretation of scientific evidence. Standard setting inevitably becomes a political battle, pitting the EPA against those who seek to reduce its autonomy and three factions within the agency against one another. It is into this tangled thicket that the courts have ventured.

The Court Decisions

The federal courts have issued a large number of decisions directly affecting the setting of national air quality standards. The subjects of these decisions fall into four broad categories: nondiscretionary duties; rulemaking procedures; consideration of nonmedical factors; and review of the reasonableness of standards.

Nondiscretionary Duties

As explained in chapters 1 and 3, the federal courts greatly expanded the concept of nondiscretionary or mandatory duties in the late 1960s and early 1970s. The Clean Air Act's citizen suit provision gave legislative approval to the courts' practices. In the mid-1970s environmental groups won a number of courtroom victories under section 112 of the act, which requires the EPA to set emission limitations for hazardous

262 REGULATION AND THE COURTS

pollutants.[33] After it found that several pollutants, including asbestos, mercury, and beryllium, are hazardous, the EPA failed to set emission limitations. The district courts hearing cases brought by environmentalists put the EPA on schedules for regulating these pollutants, giving the victorious litigants a major role in determining how and when the EPA regulates hazardous pollutants.

Even where the act seemed to give the administrator discretion to decide which pollutants to regulate, the federal courts have forced the EPA to enlarge its regulatory program. Nowhere is the expansion of mandatory duties clearer than under section 109, which requires the administrator to establish national standards for each pollutant (a) that adversely affects public health, (b) that is emitted by numerous sources, and (c) "for which he plans to issue air quality criteria under this section." The EPA claimed that the third requirement gives the administrator a choice about whether to regulate a pollutant meeting the first two requirements. But the courts disagreed.

The key ruling on this issue came when the EPA determined that lead meets the first two conditions, but decided that the usual regulatory scheme was not an effective method for controlling pollutants that enter the body through ingestion as well as inhalation. The Natural Resources Defense Council (NRDC) challenged the EPA's decision not to issue a national air quality standard, and won. According to the Second Circuit,

> while the literal language of Section 108(a)(1)(c) is somewhat ambiguous, this ambiguity is resolved when this section is placed in the context of the Act as a whole and in its legislative history.... The structure of the Clean Air Act as amended in 1970, its legislative history, and the judicial gloss placed upon the Act leave no room for an interpretation which makes the issuance of air quality standards for lead under Section 108 discretionary. The Congress sought to eliminate, not perpetuate the opportunity for administrative foot-dragging.[34]

33. For example, *Environmental Defense Fund* v. *Ruckelshaus*, 3 *Environmental Law Reporter* 20173 (D.D.C. 1973). Also see David D. Doniger, *The Law and Policy of Toxic Substances Control: A Case Study of Vinyl Chloride* (Johns Hopkins University Press for Resources for the Future, 1978), pp. 66–86, for a description of how the threat of court suit produced regulations on vinyl chloride. Suits by the Environmental Defense Fund and the Natural Resources Defense Council finally led the EPA to propose a generic carcinogen policy to avoid time-consuming, pollutant-by-pollutant regulation. 44 Fed. Reg. 58642 (1979).

34. *Natural Resources Defense Council* v. *Train*, 545 F.2d 320 at 327–28 (2d Cir. 1976). Also see *Natural Resources Defense Council* v. *Train*, 411 F. Supp. 864 (S.D.N.Y. 1976).

In effect, the court's conception of the judiciary's role in pushing a lethargic agency to protect individuals' health led it to brand standard setting under section 109 as a mandatory duty. After losing this case, the EPA conceded the point.

Rulemaking Procedures

The court decisions that have received most attention in the legal literature are those involving rulemaking procedures.[35] When the EPA set its first national standards in 1971, it followed the minimal requirements of the Clean Air Act and the Administrative Procedures Act by proposing a standard in the Federal Register, accepting comments on this proposal, and publishing a final standard along with a very brief statement of its reasons for taking this action. Shortly thereafter the Court of Appeals for the D.C. Circuit announced that this procedure did not provide the courts with enough information to evaluate the reasonableness of the EPA's standards. Without requiring the agency to conduct trial-like hearings, the courts ordered it to comply with a set of procedures designed to increase public participation and to provide courts with an administrative record to review. Congress included these so-called "paper hearing" requirements in the 1977 amendments.[36]

The procedures developed by the courts contain four essential elements. First, when the EPA proposes a standard, it must make available to the public the data upon which it relied and the technical methodology it used to reason from the data to the standard. Second, the preambles to the proposal and the promulgation must include a detailed explanation of the agency's decision. These explanations must be written so that laymen can understand them. Third, the agency must respond to all "significant" comments on the proposal before issuing its final rule. Fourth, all this material—data, methodology, explanation, comments, and responses—constitutes the record that the court will examine in

35. The major decisions on procedures are the following: *Kennecott Copper Corp.* v. *Environmental Protection Agency,* 462 F.2d 846 (D.C. Cir. 1972); *International Harvester* v. *Ruckelshaus,* 478 F.2d 615 (D.C. Cir. 1973); *Portland Cement Assoc.* v. *Ruckelshaus,* 486 F.2d 375 (D.C. Cir. 1973); and *Essex Chemical Corp.* v. *Ruckelshaus,* 486 F.2d 427 (D.C. Cir. 1973).

36. William Pedersen summarizes these developments in "Formal Records and Informal Rulemaking." These procedures are now contained in sec. 307(d) of the Clean Air Act. They are explained in *Clean Air Act Amendments of 1977,* H. Rept. 95-294, pp. 318-25.

reviewing the standard. Objections not raised during the comment period cannot be raised in court.

The courts have emphasized that the adequacy of the specific procedures used by the EPA depends on how well they illuminate the policy issues before the agency. Cross-examination, for example, is not required in standard setting since it is unlikely to elicit the type of information standard setters require. This means that to evaluate the EPA's procedures, the courts must in effect judge the adequacy of the support for the standard itself. In deciding whether the EPA's explanations are reasonable or whether the agency has responded to all significant comments, the court must take what Judge Harold Leventhal has called a "hard look" at the substantive issues at hand. In short, the procedures established by the courts are not a simple checklist of formalities but rather are instruments of closer judicial scrutiny of the reasonableness of agency decisions.

Consideration of Cost

In reviewing the reasonableness of the EPA's standards, the courts must decide whether the agency has taken into account the proper policy factors. This means that the courts must enter the highly charged debate over whether and how the EPA can consider the control costs of the standards it announces.

For many years the courts carefully skirted this issue. However, in 1980 the D.C. Circuit removed all doubt about where it stood on this issue. Judge J. Skelly Wright's opinion announced that "the legislative history of the Act also shows the Administrator *may not* consider economic and technological feasibility in setting air quality standards."[37] The court even denied the EPA authority to consider costs in setting a margin of safety. To substantiate these claims, Judge Wright relied on the many statements of the House and Senate committees indicating that national standards should be "precautionary," based on the need to protect sensitive individuals rather than on cost-benefit analysis. He ignored the fact that the collapse of the threshold concept gives the EPA no choice but to define acceptable risks and that Congress rejected a no-

---

37. *Lead Industries Assoc.* v. *EPA* at 1149 (emphasis added). The D.C. Circuit later reaffirmed this position in *American Petroleum Institute* v. *Costle*, 665 F.2d 1176 (D.C. Cir. 1981).

risk approach to standard setting when it passed its program for prevention of significant deterioration.

The D.C. Circuit's reading of the Clean Air Act has clearly been affected by its belief that the courts should show special solicitude for protection of public health. In a previous case on regulation of airborne lead, Judge Wright noted that his conclusions followed not just from the language of the act and the legislative history,

> but from the nature of the Administrator's charge: to protect the public from danger. Regulators such as the Administrator must be accorded flexibility, a flexibility that recognizes the *special judicial interest in favor of protection of the health and welfare of people*, even in areas where certainty does not exist.[38]

If citizens have a constitutionally protected interest in, or a right to, safe air, then the cost of guaranteeing that right is irrelevant. Such absolutism is inherent in the nature of rights. This view of the courts' role both protects the agency against industry pressure and puts a "heavy burden" on the agency to show why it has not eliminated all possible health risks.[39]

Reviewing the Facts: Leaning toward Stringency

In case after case the courts have held that reviewing judges must scrutinize the EPA's arguments and evidence to make sure that they support the action taken. In light of the debate among experts about the reliability and significance of health evidence, one must wonder how judges can distinguish reasonable actions from arbitrary and capricious ones. Describing how courts make this determination is an extremely difficult task. The courts have reviewed only a handful of standards under the Clean Air Act.[40] The facts of each case are so different that the courts' analysis of them defies easy generalization.

Amid this swirl of scientific disputes and airy discussions of "scope of review," one fact stands out: after remanding the secondary sulfur

38. *Ethyl Corp.* v. *EPA* at 24 (emphasis added).

39. *Environmental Defense Fund* v. *Environmental Protection Agency*, 598 F.2d 62 at 88 (D.C. Cir. 1978). In this case the court upheld the EPA's regulations on PCB, a likely carcinogen. The court notes other cases in which this "heavy burden" has led judges to order the EPA to initiate action against possible carcinogens.

40. These cases are the secondary standard for sulfur dioxide (*Kennecott Copper*), the standard used to justify EPA's leaded gas regulations (*Ethyl Corp.*), the primary lead standard (*Lead Industries Assoc.*), and the ozone standard (*API* v. *Costle*).

dioxide standard—for which the EPA could discover no supporting evidence—the courts have upheld each standard challenged by industry. In doing so the courts have indicated that those who challenge EPA standards as too stringent carry an extremely heavy burden of proof. The D.C. Circuit has bent over backward to find justifications for the EPA's standards. It has even supplied missing links in the agency's analysis. The courts' leniency in reviewing the adequacy of the EPA's evidence comports not just with their reluctance to find an agency's treatment of the facts arbitrary and capricious, but also with their general prescription that when in doubt the EPA should decide health-related matters by erring on the side of overprotection.

The strength of this presumption in favor of stringent standards is revealed by a close look at the case in which it was firmly established. In *Ethyl Corporation* v. *Environmental Protection Agency* the lead industry challenged the EPA's decision to phase out lead in gasoline, a decision resulting from the preceding *NRDC* case. The first panel of the D.C. Circuit to hear the case agreed with industry's claim that the evidence did not support the EPA's standard. The full Circuit Court later reversed this ruling in a highly unusual 5-4 *en banc* decision.[41] This opinion, which is frequently cited in standard-setting cases, dramatically illustrates the character of the D.C. Circuit's review of the EPA's standards.

The EPA, industry, and environmental groups all agreed that a level of 40 micrograms of lead per deciliter of blood should be considered hazardous to health. The two points of contention were whether a significant number of Americans have blood lead levels above 40 micrograms, and whether there is a correlation between lead levels in blood and in the air. Judge Malcolm R. Wilkey, who wrote the initial majority opinion and the dissent in the *en banc* decision, found the EPA's evidence on both issues inadequate. Judge Wright, dissenting at first and prevailing in the end, upheld the agency on both counts.

Judge Wilkey was particularly upset with the EPA's frequent but inconsistent use of the only major analysis of lead exposure in the general

41. After the original panel remanded the standard to the EPA in January 1975, the full court called for a rehearing. Meanwhile the 1976 House report severely criticized the original decision. The 1977 House report praised the court's final decision. *Clean Air Act Amendments of 1977*, H. Rept. 95-294, pp. 43–51. For a trenchant analysis of the *Ethyl* decision, see Thomas Drechsler, "Public Health Endangerment and Standards of Proof: *Ethyl Corp.* v. *EPA*," 6 *Environmental Affairs* 227 (1977).

population, the so-called Seven Cities Study sponsored by the EPA and several other agencies. The study reported that 99.85 percent of the urban population has blood lead levels within the range deemed safe by the EPA. Claiming that this study was methodologically flawed, the EPA relied instead on evidence showing elevated blood levels among occupational groups exposed to unusually high levels of automobile exhaust. According to Judge Wilkey, the methodological flaws the EPA used to discredit this part of the study had nothing to do with its finding on urban blood levels. Wilkey also complained that the EPA failed to explain why it relied more heavily on evidence relating to occupational subgroups than evidence gathered in a population survey. In his words, "The Administrator chose among the available data without any explanation as to . . . why he was relying upon certain studies and rejecting others. . . . This is not a case of a 'clear error of judgment'; it is rather a case of a clear absence of judgment."[42]

Wilkey likewise rejected the EPA's argument on the relation between air lead and blood lead levels. The Seven Cities Study found (1) while *air* lead levels are higher in the New York area than in the Philadelphia area, *blood* lead levels are generally higher in Philadelphia than New York; and (2) within these two metropolitan areas, both blood lead levels and air lead levels are lower in the suburbs than in the urban core. The EPA considered the urban-suburban contrast significant, but dismissed the intercity blood level comparisons as biased by dietary differences. Wilkey offered harsh criticism of what he saw as a "selective approach to the evidence."[43] While admitting that the D.C. Circuit had forced the EPA to rely on scanty evidence by insisting that it reach a decision on lead within thirty days, Wilkey rejected the regulations as "a blind stab through a curtain of ignorance, inflicting anguish, but in our judgment not rationally solving any problem."[44]

Judge Wright, in contrast, attempted to construct a step-by-step justification for the EPA's regulation, offering a stirring tribute to the need for "precautionary" health standards. On the issue of the blood lead levels of the urban population, Wright first condoned the EPA's rejection of the Seven Cities Study. Then, disregarding the dictates of previous case law, he went outside the record to find a medical text that supported his (and the EPA's) assertion that "studies of occupational

42. *Ethyl Corp.* v. *EPA* at 104.
43. Ibid. at 106.
44. Ibid. at 111.

groups are often particularly valuable in acting as an early warning system of possible effects on the public at large." From this he drew the surprising inference that high blood levels in these groups could indicate high blood levels in the population at large.[45] He did not explain the logical connection between these statements.

On the second issue, the correlation between air lead levels and blood lead levels, Wright had no objection to EPA's reliance on intrametropolitan differences and dismissal of intermetropolitan contrasts. Moreover, he accepted as reasonable an EPA hypothesis that airborne lead falls to the ground near highways and is ingested by young children.[46] Thus, throughout his decision Wright remained faithful to his position that in environmental policy, where judgment is necessarily more "speculative" than in other areas, the court will not demand findings "of the sort familiar from the world of adjudication." The court's review should be highly deferential since the EPA shares in the "special judicial interest in favor of protection of the health and welfare of people."[47]

In the *Ethyl* decision the D.C. Circuit informed the EPA that it could use "suggestive" evidence and even a "hypothesis" to justify costly health-based standards. While Judge Wright often buttressed his argument with reference to the norm of judicial restraint in the traditional administrative law, his line of analysis indicated that this deference could disappear if the agency appeared to lose its public health zeal. For if the EPA has a mandatory duty to set standards for dangerous pollutants, it likewise has a duty to ensure that the standards are sufficiently protective of the public's judicially guarded interest in health.

Review of the variety of court decisions on standards raises the question of how these rulings have interacted with the many other factors that affect the EPA's decisions on standards. Has court scrutiny, as environmental groups at first feared, made the agency more cautious and allowed undue influence by industry, which can finance massive technical analyses and prolonged court suits? Or have the courts' commands on mandatory duties, disregard for cost, and the need for precautionary standards induced the EPA to strengthen its standards?

The airborne lead standard the EPA announced in 1978 and the revised ozone standard it promulgated in 1979—the only two standards it produced between 1971 and 1982—provide illuminating before-and-

45. Ibid. at 41.
46. Ibid. at 44.
47. Ibid. at 23–24.

after contrasts that help one assess the influence of the courts. In the case of lead, the agency first opposed setting a standard, then indicated it would set a standard so lenient that only one area in the entire country would violate it. After receiving heavy criticism from the SAB and threat of suit by environmental groups, the EPA experienced a stunning change of heart. It eventually set a standard that pleased environmentalists but infuriated industry. The revision of the ozone standard provides an equally useful contrast between standard setting in 1971 and the process in 1979, when the agency relaxed its previous standard by 50 percent.

Airborne Lead: The Advocates Get Their Standard

Between 1972 and 1981 hardly a day went by when the EPA was not involved in litigation over regulation of airborne lead. In fact, most of the pivotal cases discussed above relate directly to this issue: the 1973 NRDC case ordering the EPA to take action under section 211; the Ethyl decisions reviewing the resulting regulations; the 1976 NRDC cases requiring the EPA to set a standard for lead; and the Lead Industries Assoc. v. EPA decision, which upheld the EPA's "health only" interpretation of the Clean Air Act. In these cases the EPA slowly learned what it could expect from the courts.

Throughout this struggle over the lead standard, the EPA was caught between two contending forces. On one side, the lead industry vigorously resisted all efforts to impose restrictions on the use of lead. At times it enlisted influential senators and White House officials to aid its cause. On the other side was the NRDC, which pushed the EPA first to regulate lead in gasoline, then to set a stringent ambient standard, and later to speed up the process of writing SIPs.

The EPA had considered setting a lead standard in 1971, but declined to do so for two reasons. First, it doubted it had sufficient scientific evidence on the effects of lead to fend off the inevitable industry attack. Second, and more important, the OAQPS preferred to control the two major sources of airborne lead (leaded gasoline and lead smelters) directly, using provisions of the act authorizing regulation of fuel additives and of all pollutants controlled by new source performance standards. While the EPA was worried about lead poisoning, especially among inner-city children, it wanted to proceed slowly and carefully. The events following the Second Circuit's 1976 "nondiscretionary duty" decision

(*NRDC* v. *Train*) convinced the NRDC that the EPA was reacting far too slowly and the lead industry that the EPA was not very careful.[48]

The EPA's About-face

The EPA's Office of Research and Development started work on the lead criteria document in October 1976, shortly after the Second Circuit announced the *NRDC* v. *EPA* decision. The ORD, which had not produced a criteria document since 1971, put together a small task force that hastily wrote one. Not surprisingly, the task force overlooked several important recent studies. To make matters worse, the criteria document— supposedly a descriptive report—included a recommendation on where to set the lead standard. While the EPA had previously claimed that ambient concentrations above 2 micrograms per cubic meter endangered the public health (a claim upheld by the D.C. Circuit in the *Ethyl* case), the first draft of the criteria document suggested that the EPA set a standard of 5 micrograms per cubic meter. The NRDC and its allies suspected that the EPA was not only incompetent, but was intent upon making a mockery of the *NRDC* decision.[49]

When the EPA submitted its draft criteria document to the SAB, the review procedures mandated by the courts began to have an effect on the agency. Each member of the SAB sharply criticized the document, focusing on its failure to mention key studies and its endorsement of an extremely lenient standard. EPA representatives offered embarrassed apologies. The NRDC's attorney threatened to take the EPA back to court. The SAB recommended that the EPA hire consultants and rewrite the document in its entirety.

Prodded by the NRDC to follow these recommendations, the ORD

48. The EPA's original control strategy for lead is discussed in briefing memo, John Middleton to William Ruckelshaus, January 21, 1971. The following discussion of the lead standard relies on the court decisions already cited and on the following sources: EPA, *Air Quality Criteria for Lead* (EPA, 1977); the proposed standard, 42 Fed. Reg. 63076 (1977); the promulgation, 43 Fed. Reg. 46246 (1978); the briefs for the Lead Industries Association and the EPA in *Lead Industries Assoc.* v. *EPA;* the appendix of documents submitted by the Lead Industries Association; the EPA docket on the standard; and personal interviews with many of those who participated in the standard-setting process.

49. The 2 micrograms per cubic meter standard appeared in "EPA's Position on the Health Effects of Airborne Lead" (EPA, November 29, 1972) and in its 1973 regulations on fuel additives, 38 Fed. Reg. 33734 (1973). Environmental groups claim that Administrator Train told them that if he established a standard, it would be at 2 micrograms.

eventually created an entirely new task force, devoted more resources to the task, and hired a number of respected researchers as consultants. When the SAB reviewed a second draft of the criteria document, it praised the improvements but made further suggestions. Several months later the ORD produced a version that its former critics on the SAB hailed as "a most admirable document."[50] Satisfied that the EPA was finally acting in good faith, the NRDC agreed to a modification of the court order giving the EPA more time to propose its standard.[51]

With changes in the criteria document came changes in the standard supported by the agency. On the day the EPA published its criteria document it also proposed a standard of 1.5 micrograms per cubic meter. With minor changes, it eventually promulgated this standard. The NRDC did not challenge this decision, but the lead industry howled. Congressmen from lead-producing districts demanded that the EPA set a more lenient standard. The Lead Industries Association appealed first to the D.C. Circuit and then to the Supreme Court—but to no avail. The EPA's restrictive standard survived judicial review.

The Ambiguous Evidence

What caused the EPA's dramatic turnabout on the lead standard? The lead industry has offered a simple political explanation: David Hawkins left the NRDC to become the EPA's assistant administrator for air programs. The NRDC and most EPA officials give a far different reason: the review process educated the EPA about the health effects of elevated blood lead levels. Science, not politics, they claim, caused the shift.

Although Assistant Administrator Hawkins definitely favored a stringent lead standard and his subordinates were generally aware of his preference, support for the standard of 1.5 micrograms per cubic meter originated not in his office, but in the ORD. Research scientists within the ORD and those hired as consultants developed a rough consensus on that figure. In the words of one ORD participant, "We settled with some peace of mind on 1.5 micrograms. There was a subjective feeling that everything pointed there." According to another, there was a "remarkable convergence on the whole as well as the parts of the

50. Samuel Epstein, meeting of Science Advisory Board Panel on Airborne Lead, October 7, 1977 (transcript contained in EPA docket).
51. 8 *Environment Reporter—Current Developments* 586.

analysis." Embarrassed by their previous mistakes and surprised by the new evidence on health effects of lead exposure, the ORD and OAQPS embraced a standard below the previous 2 micrograms. As one participant put it, the EPA was determined "to do it right this time."

If the "technical education" explanation for the EPA's change of heart is superior to the "political pressure" explanation, it is not sufficient by itself. The reason for this is that medical evidence, taken alone, cannot point to a specific standard. Standard setters must add their own policy choices to this evidence to arrive at a standard. In the case of lead the EPA had to address four critical policy questions: (1) what constitutes an adverse health effect; (2) how to estimate the ratio between blood lead and air lead levels; (3) how to treat the nonair sources of body lead; and (4) what percentage of the sensitive population to protect.

Examination of how the EPA arrived at the figures that produced a standard of 1.5 micrograms per cubic meter shows that the key to the EPA's turnabout was not so much the new evidence provided by medical research as its acceptance of the policy positions of those who presented this evidence. What is most striking about the agency's justification for its standard is the extent to which it reflects the conservative assumption of the public health advocates who gained access to the standard-setting process after the SAB's critical review of the first criteria document.

The most important choice made by the EPA—made early in the process and with almost no internal debate—was to retain the threshold analysis that had previously guided its standard setting. Ironically, while scientists are among the most vocal critics of the threshold concept, it was the physicians and medical researchers within the EPA and on the SAB who immediately plunged into addressing the four issues listed above. On each one they adopted estimates they considered precautionary.

SAFE BLOOD LEAD LEVEL. The most controversial of the four key determinations the EPA made in setting the lead standard was the blood lead level at which adverse health effects begin. The first criteria document claimed that adverse effects begin at 40 micrograms per deciliter of blood, the onset of anemia. While industry continued to support this threshold, the SAB, NRDC, and several independent researchers pushed the EPA to consider more recently obtained evidence showing that "subclinical" effects occur at blood lead levels far below 40 micrograms.

This new research showed that lead begins to affect the production of hemoglobin (the part of the red blood cell that transports oxygen) in a number of ways before blood lead levels reach 40 micrograms. At 10 micrograms lead inhibits the formation of a catalyst in the production of hemoglobin molecules. Somewhere between 15 and 20 micrograms, levels of free erythrocyte protoporphyrin (FEP) in the mitochondria rise, indicating further disruption of hemoglobin production. Far from clarifying the health effects issue, however, these new findings raised two additional questions: first, where precisely does each of these changes begin; and second, which of these various physiological changes are adverse?

The EPA had great difficulty resolving these questions. Its criteria document stated that while the first identifiable effects of lead are "relatively mild, nondebilitating symptoms," as blood levels rise health effects gradually "reach such magnitude that they are of clear-cut medical significance as indicators of undue lead exposure."[52] In its proposal the EPA used FEP elevation as the critical health effect and 15 micrograms per deciliter as the onset of FEP elevation. But it hedged its bet by stating that it was not suggesting that "individual blood lead levels" above 15 micrograms were necessarily "a significant risk to health." To back up its choice of 15 micrograms as the health effects threshold, it pointed out that using that level as a target mean blood lead level would keep 99.5 percent of all children between the ages of one and five below 30 micrograms per deciliter. Criticism received during the comment period on the use of FEP elevation as the crucial adverse health effect and the estimate of 15 micrograms as the point where FEP elevation begins caused the EPA to revert to its backup argument. The 15-microgram level became the target mean blood level that would keep 99.5 percent of the sensitive population below the 30-microgram level declared safe by the EPA.

This raises the obvious question of where the 30-microgram safety level came from. The EPA explained: "The maximum safe blood lead level should be somewhat lower than the threshold for a decline in hemoglobin levels" (40 micrograms per deciliter) and "at an even greater distance below the threshold for risks of nervous system deficits" (50 micrograms per deciliter). But why not 32, 35, or 38 micrograms? The only answer the agency offered was that the safe level "should be no higher than the blood lead range characterized as undue exposure by the Center for Disease Control of the Public Health Services."[53] This

52. EPA, *Air Quality Criteria for Lead,* p. 1-13.
53. 43 Fed. Reg. 46253 (1978).

organization had used 30 micrograms as a warning level in its screening of children for lead-based-paint poisoning. Thus, after a long debate over new evidence on the health effects of lead, the EPA deferred to another agency—which had set a safety level for lead in a different context.

The best explanation for the EPA's choice of the 30-microgram ceiling seems to be that EPA physicians and researchers who had previously accepted the 40-microgram threshold became worried when they learned that there were effects below this level that they had not previously recognized. "Prudent public health policy" and "sound principles of preventive medicine" (terms frequently repeated in EPA statements) seemed to require a corresponding tightening of the safety level. The 30-microgram figure was appealing because it was so salient: not only was it a round number 25 percent below the previously recognized threshold, but it would protect half the sensitive population from any rise in FEP levels. Everything seemed to point in the same direction. In short, the new evidence on the health effects of lead changed most EPA and SAB scientists' subjective impressions of what constituted a reasonably precautionary estimate of the safe blood lead level for children—without demanding this level as a matter of logic.

THE AIR LEAD–BLOOD LEAD CORRELATION. The second issue on which the EPA claimed to have new information was the relation between increases in air lead levels and increases in blood lead levels. There was even less agreement among scientists on this issue than on the question of what blood lead level is dangerous. Researchers could not even agree whether ingestion of lead particles in dirt constitutes a significant source of blood lead in children.

The EPA's first draft criteria document had used a ratio between blood lead and air lead of 1:1. Studies subsequently submitted to the ORD showed a broad band of ratios ranging from 1:1 to 2:1. The most accurate studies reported ratios of 1.7:1 and 1.8:1 at the ambient level of 1.5 micrograms per cubic meter.[54]

Not knowing how to choose among these numbers and at a loss to determine how much lead is transmitted to the blood through ingestion, the EPA opted for another good round number—2. Using a ratio of 2:1, the EPA argued, provided an additional margin of safety justified by the possible ingestion of lead in dirt by children. Once again, the EPA's technical staff felt comfortable with this precautionary stance.

54. Ibid., 46254.

NONAIR SOURCES OF LEAD. The two remaining determinations contained in the EPA's analysis were even less amenable to technical resolution and received less attention in the standard-setting process. Body lead comes from a number of different sources: food, water, lead-based paint, and air. Exposure to each of these sources varies so greatly that the EPA claimed "the implications of multiple sources of environmental lead are difficult to reconcile with the concept of a national ambient air quality standard." Even if air lead levels reach zero, some children will still have blood lead levels above 30 micrograms. Yet the EPA's threshold analysis required it to set a single nonair contribution figure for every child in the nation. This figure, as the EPA admitted, constituted a "policy choice reflecting how much of the lead pollution problem should be dealt with through control of air sources."[55]

In making this policy choice, the EPA refused to consider the relative costs of control programs in the various media and tried instead to find guidance in medical studies. It had two sets of studies of possible relevance. Isotope studies show that normally about two-thirds of blood lead comes from nonair sources. Other surveys show that when air lead levels are very low, blood lead levels remain in the range of 10.2 to 14.4 micrograms. The EPA rejected a nonair contribution of either 14.4 (the maximum) or 12.3 (the average of the range) in favor of 12.0, explaining, "If EPA were to use a larger estimate of non-air contribution to blood lead, the result would be an exceptionally stringent standard, which would not address the principal source of lead exposure."[56] The agency did not explain why it did not drop this figure to 10.0 (suggested by the isotope study), 10.2 (the lower end of the range of field studies), 11.0, or 11.5. The implication of its explanation is that these policy choices would result in a standard that EPA staff considered excessively lenient.

THE PERCENTAGE TO PROTECT. While the EPA and industry agreed that children between the ages of one and five constitute the sensitive population, at any given air lead level the blood lead levels of these children will vary greatly. The EPA estimated that when air lead levels are held constant children's blood lead levels fit a bell-shaped curve. This means that for any nonzero standard some children will exceed the safe blood lead level. Thus the EPA faced an awkward question: how many children should the standard protect?

The agency eventually chose a figure of 99.5 percent. Its only explanation was that such a percentage "is not excessive" given the fact

55. 42 Fed. Reg. 63080 (1977).
56. 43 Fed. Reg. 46254 (1978).

Table 8-1. *Calculations for Alternative Lead Standards*
Micrograms

Alternative approach	Lowest detectable adverse effect[a]	Maximum safe blood lead level[a]	Mean to protect 99.5 percent of sensitive population[a]	Blood:air ratio[b]	Nonair contribution[a]	Standard[c]
EPA proposal	15	...	...	2:1	12	$\frac{15-12}{2} = 1.5$
EPA promulgation	...	30	15	2:1	12	$\frac{15-12}{2} = 1.5$
Raise FEP threshold from proposal[d]	16	...	...	2:1	12	$\frac{16-12}{2} = 2.0$
Raise maximum safe blood level from promulgation	...	32	16	2:1	12	$\frac{16-12}{2} = 2.0$
Use average ratio found in field studies	...	30	15	1.5:1	12	$\frac{15-12}{1.5} = 2.0$
Reduce nonair contribution	...	30	15	2:1	11	$\frac{15-11}{2} = 2.0$

a. Per deciliter of blood.
b. The ratio of micrograms per deciliter of blood to micrograms per cubic meter of air.
c. Per cubic meter of air.
d. FEP = free erythrocyte protoporphyrin.

that 5 million children live in "central cities where lead exposures may be high."[57] Here the EPA had no choice but to trade off control costs and health benefits. But it did so without explicit analysis, basing its decision on what seemed right to those who performed the technical analysis on which it relied.

Table 8-1 shows how the EPA used the answers to these four policy questions to arrive at the proposed and final standard. It also shows that by relaxing slightly any one of the key parameters the agency could have arrived at a standard of 2 micrograms rather than 1.5. This fact became politically significant when the Office of Planning and Management released a study showing that raising the standard from 1.5 micrograms to 2 would reduce the cost of pollution control by one-third, or $200 million.

57. Ibid., 46253.

The Bureaucratic Process

Since the scientific evidence does not point to any particular standard, the reasons why the EPA settled on 1.5 micrograms per cubic meter must be found in the bureaucratic politics of standard setting. From January until December of 1977 ORD and OAQPS officials worked with the Science Advisory Board and the consultants hired at the SAB's recommendation to resolve disputes over the four issues discussed above. Under great pressure to produce a criteria document and to propose a standard before the NRDC dragged the agency back to court, staff members convened meeting after meeting (some lasting all night) to iron out disagreements among the recognized experts on each issue.

The political executives recently appointed by the Carter administration were busy finding their way around the agency and putting together a package of Clean Air Act amendments to send to Congress, and Assistant Administrator Hawkins seemed hesitant to appear to bias the process; thus technical personnel in the OAQPS and ORD in North Carolina were essentially on their own. Slowly a consensus developed on the 1.5-microgram standard. The action memo drafted by the OAQPS with the help of the ORD strongly recommended that the administrator propose this standard. Several times it noted that "slight numerical differences have a very large effect on the air standard." At each juncture the action memo recommended using a conservative estimate, claiming that the "margin of safety" language of the act required such caution.

The recommendation of the ORD and OAQPS sailed through the Steering Committee, and the EPA formally proposed the 1.5-microgram standard. During the comment period, however, the Office of Planning and Evaluation began to oppose the standard. According to its estimates, implementation of this standard could force as many as forty of the nation's sixty-one lead smelters to shut down, but would provide minimal additional health benefits compared to a standard requiring application of the best available control technology. To impress this fact upon political executives, the OPE sought to include in the action memo on the final standard a cost-effectiveness analysis comparing the marginal economic costs and health benefits of various possible standards.[58]

58. Memorandums, Michael James and James Cahan (OGC) to Joan Bernstein (general counsel), July 27, 1978; and William Drayton (Office of Planning and Management) to David Hawkins, August 25, 1978.

The OPE's proposed cost-effectiveness study sparked a heated internal debate over how the EPA could consider the economic costs of proposed standards and over how much weight must be given to the recommendations of the agency's technical staff. The Office of the General Counsel led the assault on the OPE's proposal. The head of the OGC's air regulation section warned that including such analysis in the action memo would create a "litigational risk that the standard will be reversed on appeal for improper consideration of economic factors." The danger of reversal would be especially great if the administrator rejected the recommendation of his technical staff "at this late date without a strong health-based rationale."

The OGC's argument went well beyond the issue of airborne lead. It claimed that the act precludes all consideration of cost (and, by implication, almost all participation by economists) in setting primary standards:

> They [EPA economists] argue that once a range of choices is arrived at by scientific analysis it is then permissible to consider economics in choosing a number or standard from that range. Such an interpretation is neither correct nor desirable. Although the legislative history here is sparse, the term "margin of safety" by its very nature means that at each step in the analytical process the decisionmaker, when faced with a range of alternatives, should choose from among the more conservative alternatives to insure that the public health will be protected. To do otherwise, and allow economics to result in a less protective choice, fails to provide the required margin of safety and is contra to Section 109.

Not content to present this legal argument alone, the OGC attorneys added the following appeal:

> There is more at stake here than whether the agency is potentially weakening its defense of the standard against challenges by environmental groups. Historically, EPA has contested vigorously all attempts to introduce economic considerations into the setting of ambient air quality standards. We have said that not only does the Act require that these standards be set only on the basis of health evidence, but that we believe this is entirely appropriate as a matter of public policy. . . . We have billed ourselves emphatically of late as a health protection agency. This is an instance where we really need to behave as if we believe our image-making.[59]

In short, the OGC embraced the policy position of the public health advocates and used the threat of court action to bolster its position.

The OGC eventually succeeded in keeping the cost-effectiveness

---

59. Memorandum, Michael James and James Cahan to Joan Bernstein, July 27, 1978.

analysis out of the action memo. This did not mean that Administrator Costle was unaware of the costs of various standards. By executive order the OPE must prepare cost estimates for various alternatives. An economic impact study was included in the packet provided to Costle. But the episode had a major effect on how the EPA's political executives, especially the administrator, viewed the question before them. Within the framework developed by their subordinates, these political executives faced three options: (1) approve the recommendation of those below; (2) amend this recommendation on the basis of their own reading of the health evidence; or (3) amend the recommendation on the basis of a surreptitious and legally and ethically questionable consideration of control costs. Given these choices, it is hardly surprising that Administrator Costle approved the 1.5-microgram standard.

While Costle's approval of the standard solidified the agency's opposition to any formal analysis of cost in the standard-setting process, it constituted a hollow victory for those seeking to reduce the amount of lead in the air. For on the day he announced the standard, Costle also indicated that he would probably support legislation to extend the three-year statutory deadline for meeting the standard. Smelters had already received compliance extensions for sulfur dioxide and would most likely require similar reprieves on lead to avoid shutdown. Thus the lead standard quickly became a long-range target rather than a binding requirement.[60]

When the D.C. Circuit rejected the Lead Industries Association's challenge to the EPA's lead standard, it praised the EPA's technical work, adopted the OGC's reading of section 109, approved the agency's use of multiple conservative assumptions, and showed obvious pique at industry's attempts to discredit the standard. Judge Wright, the author of the lengthy opinion, had long supported aggressive regulation of lead and seemed pleased with the new standard.

The resolution of the legal dispute over the lead standard has not

60. After the EPA proposed a standard of 1.5 micrograms, Administrator Costle came under attack from senators representing states with lead smelters. In its final standard the EPA made one change that produced a slight relaxation of the standard, shifting the average time for the standard from one month to three months. In announcing his decision, Costle promised to complete a study of the economic consequences of the standard and to ask for a statutory extension of the deadline if appropriate. Since the EPA did "not believe that a major disruption of this industry is an acceptable consequence," it would "explore every avenue to avoid such an impact while still protecting public health." 9 *Environment Reporter—Current Developments* 1091.

brought an end to controversy over regulation of that pollutant. OAQPS engineers, regional office personnel, and state agency officials have been extremely slow in writing SIPs to implement the standard. Not only were they entangled in the lengthy SIP revision process mandated by the 1977 amendments, but they saw little point in making lead regulation a priority while the lead in gasoline was being reduced and while politicians debated the smelter problem. Several months after the EPA announced its standard, the OGC warned that the NRDC was again threatening suit, this time under section 110.[61] The air quality standard for lead has done little thus far to improve air quality.

Implications

The lead case study leads to several propositions on the impact of the courts on standard setting. First, the long review process that has evolved partly in response to court decisions has increased the autonomy and the influence of the scientists responsible for writing the criteria document and making policy recommendations to agency political executives. If a rough consensus on where to set the standard emerges at early stages of this process, this recommendation will come before the administrator with substantial institutional momentum.

Second, if a consensus arises at this level, it will most likely reflect the policy positions of the public health advocates. This is so not just because these advocates are far more aggressive in advancing policy recommendations than their colleagues who try to separate scientific and policy issues, but also because agency lawyers have assured them that their policy positions are condoned—indeed mandated—by the statute. Professional norms, legal arguments, and the agency's conception of its mission all reinforce one another here.

Third, when political executives consider recommendations of their technical staff, they find it far easier to approve a stringent standard and to throw implementation issues into the lap of Congress and enforcement personnel than to risk adverse publicity about possible industry pressure or embarrassing court reversal on the grounds of improper consideration of cost. At least with the D.C. Circuit, it is always safer to err on the side of overprotection.

61. While lead SIPs were due in 1979, by 1982 only fifteen states had approved SIPs in place. The NRDC privately threatened suit in 1979 and publicly announced its threat in 1982. 13 *Environment Reporter—Current Developments* 14.

Finally, while the courts can tell the EPA when to set standards, they have a harder time forcing it to impose control strategies adequate to meet these standards. Not only is supervision of the SIP-writing process difficult for a court, but the stringency of the standards written under the auspices of the courts invites political opposition and regulatory uncertainty. One cannot help but wonder whether state and federal regulators have sometimes thought, "the NRDC and the courts have their standard, now let *them* enforce it."

Ozone: Protecting Agency Autonomy

In 1979 the EPA completed its first revision of an original national air quality standard, renaming the photochemical oxidant standard the ozone standard and relaxing it from a maximum hourly average of 0.08 to 0.12 part per million (ppm).[62] Although the EPA worked on the lead and ozone standards at about the same time, their development differs in three important ways. First, since the agency already had an ozone standard in place, impetus for change came from industry groups seeking to weaken the standard, not from environmentalists seeking to establish one. The American Petroleum Institute (API), which presented the EPA with an extensively documented petition to revise the standard, played a role on ozone similar to the NRDC's role on lead.

Second, while the SAB panel on lead attacked the EPA for overlooking relevant new data on low-level health effects, the SAB's panel on ozone criticized the EPA for relying on flawed studies suggesting health effects below 0.25 ppm. In part this reversal of roles resulted from the personalities involved: the SAB panel for ozone, unlike that for lead, was dominated by "separatists" who frowned upon the use of studies not meeting standard scientific levels of proof. In addition, all parties agreed that the health evidence on ozone was not nearly as extensive as that on lead.

62. 44 Fed. Reg. 8202 (1979). The analysis of the ozone standard relies on this and the following sources: EPA, *Air Quality Criteria for Ozone*; the proposal, 43 Fed. Reg. 26962 (1978); "Petition of American Petroleum Institute and Member Companies for Review and Revision," December 9, 1976; briefs of the EPA, NRDC, and API in *API* v. *Costle* and joint appendix for that litigation; EPA docket on ozone; Catherine G. Miller, "Case Study on the Revision of the National Ambient Air Quality Standard for Ozone," March 1980, prepared for Office of Planning and Evaluation, EPA; Lester B. Lave, ed., *Quantitative Risk Assessment in Regulation* (Brookings Institution, 1982); and personal interviews with several participants in the process.

Third, the ozone standard represented a victory for the forces of accommodation within the EPA, not for the public health advocates. The EPA found itself in agreement with neither environmentalists nor industry, but caught between the two. It also met strong opposition from cost-conscious White House aides. Both the API and the NRDC eventually challenged the ozone standard in court, attacking it from opposite points of view.

The EPA's revision of its photochemical oxidant standard illustrates the complex interrelation between standard setting on the one hand and SIP-writing and enforcement on the other. As early as 1973 the EPA knew that it had seriously misinterpreted the major study supporting its 1971 standard. Yet it made no attempt to amend the standard until 1976, when it began to reevaluate its entire mobile source program. It then took another two and a half years to decide on a new standard. Why did the EPA, after so much delay, crank up the revision process in 1976, and how did it pick a standard amid a mass of incomplete and contradictory medical evidence on the effects of ozone? Answering these questions is essential for understanding the subtle influence of court action on the ozone standard.

The Decision to Revise

In 1971 the EPA set a photochemical oxidant standard of 0.08 ppm, a level only slightly above natural background concentrations in some areas. Along with the carbon monoxide standard, the photochemical oxidant standard formed the keystone of the controversial transportation control plan strategy discussed in the next chapter. The chief justification for the 0.08 standard was a study that correlated oxidant levels with frequency of asthma attacks in Los Angeles. The EPA interpreted this study to show that asthma attacks become more frequent when oxidant levels reach 0.10 ppm. Adding a 20 percent margin of safety to this, the EPA arrived at the 0.08 figure. Shortly after announcing this standard, however, EPA officials realized they had misinterpreted the study and published a correction to the criteria document. A National Academy of Sciences study commissioned by Congress examined the oxidant standard in 1974 and found, "The technical data base for the oxidant standard was inadequate at the time the standard was set (1971) and remains inadequate, considering the implications for public health and the economic impact."[63]

63. NAS–NAE, *Air Quality and Automobile Emission Control*, vol. 1, pp. 49–50. The EPA had first proposed the 0.06 ppm standard endorsed by the 1970 Senate report.

As opposition to the EPA's oxidant control programs mounted, so did the cry for amending the 1971 standard. The EPA ignored these criticisms for several years, but in 1976 several factors combined to push the agency into action. Congress included in the 1976 version of its amendments to the act a provision requiring the EPA to revise each national air quality standard every five years. At the same time the American Petroleum Institute was completing a major study of the causes and effects of photochemical oxidants and was preparing a petition requesting the EPA to revise its standard. Finally, the EPA was reevaluating its entire mobile source control program. While these programs lay dormant the EPA could revise its standard without disrupting its regulatory effort.

Did the API petition and threat of court suit play a role analogous to the NRDC's legal action on the lead standard? Technically it did not. The EPA announced its decision to revise the standard several months before the API submitted its petition. The EPA and the API later signed a consent agreement establishing a schedule for completion of the revision. But each time the EPA fell behind on this schedule, the D.C. District Court granted it an extension.[64]

The EPA, of course, realized well before it began the revision process that the API stood a good chance of winning a court suit on this issue. The API's threatened legal action, though, was only one part of its assault on the ozone standard and the EPA's hydrocarbon control strategies. And the EPA was even more vulnerable elsewhere.

In early 1976 the director of the OAQPS toured the regional offices, searching for the reasons behind the collapse of the agency's transportation control plan. There he discovered

> the almost universal belief that a few hours of O_3 a year at levels two or three times the NAAQS was not a public health problem that deserved an urgent response. . . . State agency staffs point to millions of people exposed for years to levels three, four, or five times the NAAQS without apparent effect.[65]

Several states attacked this standard as based on flimsy evidence and, more important, as equal to or below natural background levels. The EPA moved the standard to the midpoint between its original standard and California's standard of 0.10 ppm. Downing and Brady, "Implementing the Clean Air Act," p. 245.

64. Memorandum, Bernard Steigerwald and Delbert Barth to Roger Strelow and Wilson Talley, "Revision of Air Quality Criteria Documents," August 26, 1976; 9 *Environment Reporter—Current Developments* 1245.

65. Memorandum, Bernard Steigerwald to Walter Barber, "Comments on SIPs for Ox and TSP," June 6, 1977, contained in EPA docket, pt. IV-D-146.

He warned that unless the EPA could convince the attentive public to take the standards for mobile source pollutants seriously, all regulatory efforts would fail. Thus the EPA had strong nonlegal reasons for beginning its reassessment of the original national standards with the weakest and most controversial one.

The Health Effects Controversy

The review procedures designed by the EPA and the courts ensured that the EPA would not make such glaring mistakes in revising the ozone standard as it had in 1971. The EPA produced three drafts of the criteria document, each of which was scrutinized by a panel of the SAB. The agency received and responded to hundreds of comments on its criteria document and proposed standard, producing a docket thousands of pages in length. The Regulatory Analysis Review Group offered extensive comments on the EPA's proposal and brought the standard to the attention of the Carter White House. Senator Muskie expressed his opposition to relaxation of the standard. Quiet, seat-of-the-pants decisionmaking was a thing of the past.

Despite this activity—or perhaps because of it—no consensus developed within the ORD, the OAQPS, or the SAB on where to set the standard. The SAB was highly critical of several key studies included in the first two draft criteria documents. The panel in fact never gave final approval to the criteria document published by the EPA. Several members, including the chairman of the panel, clearly believed that the document gave too much credence to studies indicating adverse health effects below 0.25 ppm.[66] The EPA nonetheless proposed a standard of 0.10 ppm and subsequently raised it only to 0.12.

According to the API, the EPA's disagreements with the SAB stemmed from the EPA's unwillingness to admit that scientific evidence did not support a standard consistent with its existing regulatory programs. Substantial evidence buttresses this "intransigent bureaucracy" explanation of the EPA's actions. Three times the EPA presented the SAB with evidence it claimed demonstrated adverse health effects at or below 0.15 ppm. Each time the SAB found the EPA's evidence seriously flawed. In its first meeting the SAB chastised the EPA for reviewing the findings of several key studies without explaining their methodological shortcom-

66. See, for example, the transcript of the February 23, 1978, meeting of the SAB panel on photochemical oxidants, pp. 101–02, 143–44; and Lave, *Quantitative Risk Assessment*, p. 97.

ings. In the second meeting the SAB warned the EPA against relying on the conclusions of two panels of experts specially selected by the EPA. After the EPA proposed its standard, several members of the SAB criticized its reliance on a study that had received little attention in previous drafts of the criteria document. Indeed, while the SAB consistently expressed skepticism about the reliability of studies showing effects in the range of 0.25 to 0.10 ppm, the EPA maintained that it could consider only standards between 0.08 and 0.15 ppm since "there does not appear to be any basis for setting the standard at a higher level."[67]

As compelling as this "intransigent bureaucracy" model may at first seem, it overstates the extent of agreement within the EPA. While no one within the EPA believed that the standard should go above 0.15 ppm, there was fierce disagreement about where within the 0.08 to 0.15 ppm range it should fall. Moreover, one of the principal reasons why the EPA insisted upon staying below 0.15 ppm and kept looking for studies showing health effects below this level was that agency officials believed they had a legal responsibility to set a precautionary standard and thus to search for evidence suggestive of low-level health effects.

The EPA's review of the literature on the health effects of ozone produced a number of studies, each of which had significant flaws, indicating health effects below 0.25 ppm. While several members of the SAB apparently thought that the EPA should disregard all studies with serious methodological weaknesses, EPA officials took the position that the accumulated weight of these studies showed that there must be some effects in the 0.15 to 0.25 ppm range. The different perspectives of SAB members and EPA officials were most evident in their treatment of the three studies the EPA stressed in its explanation of its standard.

The DeLucia and Adams study was the single most important clinical evidence relied upon by the EPA in its proposal and promulgation.[68] In their research DeLucia and Adams exposed six subjects to varying ozone levels, looking for changes in respiratory patterns and subjective discomfort (headache, chest tightness). Since all their subjects were healthy adults (including the two authors), the researchers had them exercise heavily (the equivalent of running six miles in an hour) to help reproduce

67. 42 Fed. Reg. 65264 (1977).

68. A. J. DeLucia and W. C. Adams, "Effects of O_3 Inhalation during Exercise on Pulmonary Function and Blood Biochemistry," *Journal of Applied Physiology*, vol. 43 (1977), pp. 75–81. 43 Fed. Reg. 26965 (1978) (proposal); 44 Fed. Reg. 8207–08 (1979) (promulgation).

the effects of ozone exposure on those with respiratory ailments. DeLucia and Adams reported a statistically significant change in pulmonary function at 0.30 ppm and a discernible but not statistically significant change at 0.15 ppm. At 0.15 ppm there was also an increase in subjective discomfort among some subjects. SAB members challenged the EPA's claim that the symptoms found at 0.15 ppm were adverse, that the exercise regime used by the researchers shed light on the possible effects of ozone on sensitive populations, and that evidence lacking statistical significance can still have regulatory significance. The EPA replied that studies such as this indicate possible effects of long-term exposure of sensitive populations to air pollution. As is the case with all suggestive evidence, the DeLucia and Adams study could neither be dismissed as useless nor hailed as proof that adverse health effects appear at 0.15 ppm.

A second controversial piece of evidence relied upon by the EPA was the analysis supplied by the Advisory Panel on the Health Effects of Photochemical Oxidants, commonly called the Shy Panel, after its chairman, Carl M. Shy. The OAQPS convened this panel early in 1977 to help it evaluate the evidence on ozone. The physicians placed on the panel by the OAQPS had all worked for or with the EPA previously. Shy, an employee of the EPA until 1973 and a professor at the University of North Carolina thereafter, had for years strenuously advocated stringent national standards. Before chairing this panel he had testified on behalf of the American Lung Association in support of retaining the existing ozone standard.

The OAQPS gave these physicians a list of possible effects of ozone exposure and asked them to estimate where these effects might begin for the most sensitive 0.5 percent of the population. For each ailment the estimates ranged between 0.15 and 0.25 ppm. The panel also offered a recommendation on where the EPA should set its standard. This conclusion reflects the "advocate" position of the panel's members:

> There appears to be a finite probability of health risk associated with population exposures to ozone concentrations above background, i.e., .05 to .06 ppm. . . . There is no compelling reason to suggest a change from the concentration defined by the existing primary air quality standard, namely, .08 ppm.[69]

69. Summary Statement of Shy Panel, June 7 and 8, 1977, contained in joint appendix to *API* v. *Costle*, vol. 1.

As the API often repeated, the answer you get to the question of where health effects begin usually depends on whom you ask.

When the EPA indicated that it might use these conclusions in setting a new standard, the SAB objected both to the panel's usurpation of the SAB's advisory functions and to the EPA's reliance on the unexplained, subjective impressions of a group of physicians handpicked by the agency. The EPA officials first agreed with the SAB and promised not to use the Shy Panel's report. But later the EPA added these conclusions to the list of evidence supporting its designation of the 0.25 to 0.15 ppm range as a "probable effects level." When the API cried foul, the EPA replied that it could not simply ignore the conclusions of respected health experts.

A similar dispute arose over the EPA's use of a decision analysis study begun but not completed by the OAQPS. Several young analysts in the OAQPS, dissatisfied with the agency's haphazard approach to the problem of risk assessment, suggested a method for eliciting from health experts their predictions about the possibility that sensitive individuals might experience adverse health effects at various ozone concentrations. They convened a panel of nine physicians (four of whom also served on the Shy Panel), asked them a series of questions on the health effects of ozone, and calculated the average of the responses. The OAQPS never completed the more elaborate analysis of this data that its sponsors had envisioned.

The SAB applauded the EPA's effort to experiment with risk assessment techniques, but concluded that this experiment was not designed well enough to provide reliable information for standard setting. The OAQPS, itself divided over the usefulness of the technique, agreed not to use the partial results of the program in its analysis of the health evidence. Once again, however, the EPA eventually used this evidence to buttress its claim that health effects begin at or near 0.15 ppm.[70]

Given this array of partially flawed studies, one can construct rationales for a variety of standards ranging from 0.25 ppm (the API's position) to 0.08 (the position of environmental groups). Table 8-2 summarizes these possible standards and their justifications. Thus once again the medical evidence failed to tell regulators where to set their standards. Understanding why the EPA acted as it did requires an investigation of the political aspects of the ozone controversy.

70. See Lave, *Quantitative Risk Assessment*, pp. 61–70.

Table 8-2. *Rationales for Alternative Ozone Standards*

Standard (parts per million)	Rationale
0.25	Studies of asthmatics show very small effect at this level and no effects below it.[a] All other studies too flawed to use (American Petroleum Institute position).
0.20	Same as above, but add 20 percent margin of safety (API fallback position).
0.16	Point where marginal cost per person-hour of unhealthy exposure increases rapidly (Council on Wage and Price Stability position).
0.15	Lowest level suggested by Shy and decision analysis panels when asked to make conservative, worst-case assumptions, which constitute a margin of safety. Results of study by DeLucia and Adams support a standard at this level, but are not statistically significant, so do not justify an additional margin of safety.[b]
0.12	Same as above, but add 20 percent margin of safety (EPA final position).
0.10	Studies criticized by Science Advisory Board show possible effects in 0.10 to 0.15 ppm range.[c] Use of 0.10 ppm assures adequate margin of safety (EPA position in proposal).
0.08	More speculative studies suggest effects could go down to zero.[d] Without clear evidence that 0.08 ppm is safe, no change should be made (position of Shy Panel and Natural Resources Defense Council).

a. Studies by Linn and others (1978), Hazucha (1973), Hackney and others (1975), and Schoettlin and Landau (1961), discussed in 44 Fed. Reg. 8208–09 (1979), and Environmental Protection Agency, Environmental Criteria and Assessment Office, *Air Quality Criteria for Ozone and Other Photochemical Oxidants* (EPA, April 1978), pp. 5–7. Full citations for these and other studies are provided in 44 Fed. Reg. 8220 (1979).

b. Discussed in 44 Fed. Reg. 8207–08 (1979).

c. Studies by von Nieding and others (1976) and Makino and Mizoguchi (1975), discussed in 44 Fed. Reg. 8209 (1979).

d. Studies by Kagawa and Toyama (1975), Wayne and others (1967), Durham (1974), and a variety of animal infection studies, discussed in 43 Fed. Reg. 26966 (1978), 44 Fed. Reg. 8209–10, and EPA, *Air Quality Criteria for Ozone*, pp. 7–11.

The Politics of Ozone

The long process of preparing a criteria document for ozone did not produce a consensus among the EPA's technical personnel as it did for lead. Instead, officials in the ORD and OAQPS presented as much information as possible to their superiors and quickly washed their hands of the matter. The ozone standard was chosen by the agency's political executives, not its technocrats.

The lack of a consensus on the ozone standard was a result of developments both in the scientific community and in the realm of regulation. The SAB's opposition to the approach of the EPA's advocates (exemplified by the Shy Panel) made divisions within the scientific community apparent to all. Moreover, the evidence on ozone was neither as extensive as that on lead nor as easily broken down into arguably technical components. Just as important, ORD and OAQPS officials realized that revision of the ozone standard had taken on symbolic significance and that their superiors had definite opinions on whether the standard should be relaxed. Intra-agency disputes emanating from the transportation control plan controversy (which had divided the EPA for years) would inevitably shatter any consensus developed within the bowels of the bureaucracy.

The EPA's political executives actively considered only three possible ozone standards: 0.08 ppm, 0.10 ppm, and 0.12 ppm. Its initial proposal, 0.10 ppm, was a compromise that gave the agency room to move in either direction after the close of the comment period. Its final standard represented a victory for the "economists" and "regulators," led by the assistant administrator for planning and management, William Drayton, and a defeat for the "advocates," led by Assistant Administrator Hawkins. At the same time it constituted a defeat for the staff of the Council on Wage and Price Stability, which conducted the review of the standard for the Regulatory Analysis Review Group and believed the EPA should go still higher. These events raise four questions about the politics of the ozone standard: What caused the divisions within the EPA? What led it to settle on 0.12 ppm? Why did the EPA never seriously consider moving above 0.12 ppm? How did it resist pressure from the Council on Wage and Price Stability (COWPS) and the White House to relax the standard further?

The contrasting perspectives of EPA's advocates, regulators, and economists were particularly apparent in the debate over ozone. Assistant Administrator Hawkins, fresh from leading the NRDC's litigation on transportation controls, maintained that the original standard should remain intact unless there emerged clear proof that concentrations above 0.08 ppm are safe. If the EPA relaxed the ozone standard in the absence of such convincing evidence, he warned, the agency would be forced to back down on other standards as well.[71]

The recently appointed head of the OAQPS, in contrast, saw the restrictive 0.08 ppm standard as detrimental to the EPA's control programs. Because many rural areas without significant hydrocarbon emissions exceed the standard, a relaxation would help get regulators

71. Miller, "Case Study of the Revision of the National Ambient Air Quality Standard for Ozone," pp. 106–45.

"out of the woods and into the cities." The action memo first drafted by the OAQPS explained:

> A change to 0.10 ppm would not result in a near term relaxation of the level of control efforts in heavily polluted urban areas or a reduction in the technology forcing impact of a restrictive standard. On the other hand, a 0.10 ppm standard would make attainment a realistic goal for many urban areas by 1987 and reduce the number of rural areas where mandatory controls might be required. This change would also improve the agency's credibility with the public and with state and local air pollution officials, and ultimately it will have a positive effect on overall hydrocarbon control efforts.[72]

State and local air pollution control officials likewise backed a standard in the 0.10 to 0.12 ppm range.

With the advocates and regulators at odds and with both the OGC and the ORD claiming they could defend any of the three standards under consideration, the agency's economists ultimately played a pivotal role in the EPA's decision. The Office of Planning and Management considered the costs of control below 0.12 ppm too large to justify the slight decrease in health risk achieved. As in the case of lead, it argued that the EPA could and should consider the cost of regulation in setting a reasonable margin of safety. Moreover, the Office of Planning and Management was responsible for countering the arguments of COWPS and its White House allies, who pressed the EPA to abandon its threshold approach and to raise the standard to 0.16 ppm. Assistant Administrator Drayton presented the 0.12 ppm relaxation as a way to appease COWPS, thus saving the EPA's threshold analysis while increasing the efficiency of its control efforts and enhancing the EPA's image as a reasonable regulator.

Undoubtedly the involvement of COWPS in the standard-setting process added impetus to the EPA's shift to 0.12 ppm. The ozone standard was one of the first rulemaking actions flagged for review by the newly created Regulatory Analysis Review Group. COWPS economists forcefully argued that the EPA's threshold analysis was inconsistent with what was known about the health effects of pollution. It presented an elaborate cost-effectiveness study that showed costs rising rapidly and benefits dropping dramatically at the 0.16 ppm level.[73]

72. Draft action memo, "Proposed Revision of the Existing National Ambient Air Quality Standard for Photochemical Oxidants" (contained in EPA docket, app. 52 of API comments on proposed standard).

73. "Environmental Protection Agency's Proposed Revisions to the National Ambient Air Quality Standard for Photochemical Oxidants," Report of the Regulatory Analysis

After the close of the public comment period the EPA and COWPS joined in several rounds of heated negotiations. When the EPA refused to go beyond 0.12 ppm, the COWPS staff contacted their superiors, Charles Schultze and Alfred Kahn, Carter's top economic advisers, who in turn conferred several times with Administrator Costle. After Costle indicated he would announce a standard of 0.12 ppm, Schultze and Kahn considered a last-minute appeal to the president. Having recently lost a similar appeal on OSHA's cotton dust standard (which they considered more unreasonable than the ozone standard), however, they decided to accept the 50 percent relaxation offered by the EPA.[74]

Why did the EPA, after rejecting the position of its advocates, draw the line at 0.12 ppm? Why was there no internal support for a greater relaxation? The answer most EPA officials give to this question is that the medical evidence pointed to health risks at about 0.15 ppm, and that the EPA had no choice but to add a margin of safety to this. But the EPA could easily have dismissed the studies showing health effects at 0.15 ppm. Or it could have ruled that since the range of 0.15 to 0.25 ppm is only a probable effects level, setting the standard at 0.15 ppm would offer a margin of safety. Yet the EPA never budged from the position that it must add a margin of safety to its determination of the threshold, and that the threshold is no higher than 0.15 ppm.

One possible explanation for the EPA's stubbornness was the fact that for months the ORD and OAQPS had argued with the SAB and the API over the validity of the studies showing effects at 0.15 ppm. The EPA had repeated its claims so often that they had become an article of faith. But this begs the question of why the EPA clung so tightly to these studies from the beginning. One factor at work seems to have been salience: several studies pointed to the same round number.

Another fact became more important as time went on. A number of major cities had ozone concentrations in the range of 0.12 to 0.15 ppm. A pervasive, if highly subjective, opinion developed within the EPA that the air in these cities simply could not be completely safe and that it

---

Review Group, submitted by the Council on Wage and Price Stability, October 16, 1978, pp. 23–26. Lawrence J. White, a principal author of the study, recounts the events surrounding preparation and submission of this report in *Reforming Regulation: Processes and Problems* (Prentice-Hall, 1981), pp. 48–69.

74. White, *Reforming Regulation,* pp. 66–69; Christopher C. DeMuth, "Constraining Regulatory Costs—Part I: The White House Review Programs," *Regulation,* vol. 4 (January–February 1980), p. 13.

would be shortsighted to abandon all efforts to improve air quality in these metropolitan areas. Once again the EPA's reading of its duty under section 109—that it cannot disregard "suggestive" evidence despite its flaws—meshed with its desire to retain regulatory control over the major determinants of air quality. While the EPA knew that many areas would never reach 0.12 ppm, it did not want to close down its control programs in regions attaining this level.

The prospects of judicial review, far from inhibiting the EPA from engaging in this self-protective activity, helped the agency to defend its position against attack by COWPS. Throughout its arduous negotiations with COWPS, the EPA insisted that it could not legally consider COWPS's analysis—however compelling it might be. COWPS had considered control costs in its study. The Clean Air Act did not allow this. Even if the EPA went along with COWPS, EPA lawyers argued, the D.C. Circuit would overturn the revision, embarrassing both the EPA and the administration.[75]

OGC attorneys also warned COWPS that attempts to appeal this decision to the president would invite angry suits by environmental groups. The EPA is the "expert agency" charged with making a technical decision on where to set air quality standards. COWPS and the White House were already involved in litigation over the propriety of their activity on strip mining regulations. The issue of ex parte communications from the White House would inevitably arise in litigation over ozone.[76] These arguments gave the EPA hope that it could protect its autonomy and may have influenced the decision of Schultze and Kahn to forgo further protest. Thus legal considerations, apparently irrelevant to most of the EPA's deliberations, reappeared in the final stages of the standard-setting process.

The response to the EPA's promulgation of the 0.12 ppm standard

75. 9 *Environment Reporter—Current Developments* 1340–41; personal interview with Jeffrey Cerar (OGC), April 1980; White, *Reforming Regulation*, pp. 56, 61, and 66–67.

76. For a summary of the legal arguments against White House involvement and a record of meetings between the EPA and White House officials, see the NRDC brief in *API* v. *Costle*, pp. 25–34. These issues are discussed in *Executive Branch Review of Environmental Regulations*, Hearings before the Subcommittee on Environmental Pollution of the Senate Committee on Environment and Public Works, 96 Cong. 1 sess. (GPO, 1979). After the ozone standard was promulgated, the D.C. District Court dismissed the EDF's suit on strip mining, and the D.C. Circuit Court condoned White House involvement in the setting of new source performance standards. *Sierra Club* v. *Costle* (D.C. Cir. 1981), 15 *Environment Reporter Cases* 2137.

was predictable. State and local air officials praised the change. Environmental groups, aided by reporters looking for a dramatic story, claimed the EPA had "caved in" to industry and White House pressure. Senator Muskie declared that the EPA had made the wrong decision and held hearings on executive branch involvement in EPA decisionmaking. The NRDC sued, claiming that the standard did not fully protect the most sensitive sector of the population and that COWPS and White House involvement after the close of the comment period was improper. The API sued, claiming that the EPA had failed to justify its standard and that it had improperly ignored the advice of the SAB. More than two years after announcement of the standard, the D.C. Circuit upheld the EPA on all the issues, noting that the EPA "may 'err' on the side of overprotection by setting a fully adequate margin of safety."[77]

Implications

If anticipation of judicial review influenced the EPA's choice of a new ozone standard, the effects were subtle. The API's original petition may have speeded up the revision process, but probably did not cause the EPA to choose ozone in starting its reanalysis of the 1971 standards. The rulemaking procedures developed by the court failed to produce a consensus and turned up so many partially flawed studies that EPA had a wide array of standards from which to choose. The agency's lawyers informed its political executives that they could defend any of the alternatives under consideration by the agency. Only at the very end of the process did legal arguments arise, as the EPA used the threat of litigation by environmental groups to strengthen its position against opposition from within the executive branch.

The courts helped the EPA protect its autonomy in another, probably more important, way as well. The EPA limited its alternatives to the 0.08 to 0.12 ppm range by continuing to employ threshold analysis. This form of analysis, intellectually weak as it is, had a powerful grip on the EPA's deliberations. The agency's commitment to threshold analysis not only allowed it to dismiss COWPS's arguments, but inhibited it from collecting information that would have helped it balance control costs against health risks. In a study conducted for the EPA, Catherine Miller of the Kennedy School of Government stated, "Conspicuous in

77. *API* v. *Costle* at 1186.

its absence from the criteria document is information on exposure, risk and cost. These topics are areas of research not undertaken by ORD for air pollutants. This is largely because of the EPA interpretation of the Clean Air Act."[78]

The EPA's interpretation of section 109 of the Clean Air Act was at least in part the product of previous court decisions and the OGC's reading of them. In the airborne lead controversy the EPA's public health advocates used legal arguments to enthrone the "health only" approach as basic agency policy. While the economists and regulators defeated the advocates in an internal dogfight over the ozone standard, the narrow range of options considered by the EPA reveals the extent of the advocates' previous victory.

Conclusions

Most writers who have evaluated the courts' performance in reviewing national air quality standards have praised the judiciary for improving the EPA's technical analysis and expanding public participation. They point to the contrast between the first and second round of EPA standard setting to show how court-mandated procedures have made the agency's deliberations more open and more sophisticated. This approach, however, overlooks two key attributes of standard setting. First, choosing an air quality standard is only the first step in a lengthy regulatory process. The experiences of the early 1970s taught the EPA that if it cannot convince others to take its standards seriously, then pollution control programs will founder. Second, since no pollution level is absolutely safe, the EPA must make a policy choice about acceptable risk when it sets primary standards. Consequently, in studying the impact of court decisions one must ask not just whether the courts have improved the EPA's technical competence, but also how they have affected its policy preferences. For this reason this chapter has focused on the politics of the standard-setting process.

The principal conclusion of this chapter is that the court decisions on standard setting have enhanced the position of public health advocates within the EPA and thus have helped to make air quality standards more stringent than they would otherwise be. They have done so in three

78. Miller, "Case Study of the Revision of the National Ambient Air Quality Standard for Ozone," p. 159.

ways. First, court decisions have contributed to the development of a massive data collection and analysis process that focuses on the question of where health effects begin in sensitive individuals. Expected to discover technical answers to the policy questions before them, the public health professionals charged with reviewing the medical evidence have generally inserted conservative, worst-case assumptions into their analysis. When these physicians and researchers can construct a consensus at lower levels of the bureaucracy, it is difficult for political executives to reject their recommendations.

Second, by stating emphatically that the EPA must disregard the costs of its standards, the courts have not only strengthened the position of advocates within the agency, but have also insulated the EPA from pressure exerted during interagency review. The threat of suit by environmental groups has helped hard-liners within the agency defeat efforts by its economists to use cost-effectiveness analysis in setting national standards and has allowed the EPA to tell cost-conscious White House aides, "Our hands are tied." While the courts have not barred direct contact between officials of the EPA and other elements of the executive branch even after the close of public comment period, their description of the task before the EPA has helped it to paint this involvement as somewhat illicit.

Third, the manifest unwillingness of the Court of Appeals for the D.C. Circuit to strike down standards as too stringent, along with its occasional charges of administrative laxity, has given the EPA political executives further incentives to "err on the side of overprotection." Not only are political executives first confronted with the recommendations of medical experts and then encouraged to defend the autonomy of their organization by resorting to arguments about administrative expertise, but they are also threatened with personally embarrassing and organizationally demoralizing charges of corruption and timidity if they fail to uphold the recommendations of those below them. Given the probability and the cost of being reversed by the D.C. Circuit for making standards too lenient, EPA political executives have chosen to announce stringent standards while backing down on enforcement deadlines. This has helped turn national standards into long-range goals, as opposed to legally binding requirements.

These conclusions might surprise some judges who have helped to develop the courts' doctrines on standard setting. Judge Leventhal, for example, once wrote, "In this area the courts find themselves rendering judgments not liked so much by environmentalist groups but sought by industry groups."[79] But in the lead and ozone cases and in the several cases involving hazardous pollutants, environmentalists have gained far more from court decisions than have industry groups. For while court-mandated procedures have increased industry's opportunities to criticize the EPA's evidence and analysis, the courts have defined the questions before the agency in a way that narrows the terms of the debate so as to aid substantially those favoring stringent standards.

This will come as no surprise to judges such as David L. Bazelon and J. Skelly Wright, who have for years viewed judicial scrutiny of environmental standards as a means of protecting the public's constitutionally based interest in a healthy environment and preventing industry from dominating the regulatory process. In a 1980 opinion attacking the EPA's decision to exempt very small emissions of the toxic substance polychlorinated biphenyl (PCB) from regulatory control, Judge Harry T. Edwards of the D.C. Circuit colorfully expressed that court's perception of the dangers of underregulation:

> Human beings have finally come to recognize that they must eliminate or control life threatening chemicals, such as PCBs, if the miracle of life is to continue and if earth is to remain a living planet. . . . Yet, we find that forty-six months after the effective date of an act designed to either totally ban or closely control the use of PCBs, 99% of the PCBs that were in use when the Act was passed are still in use in the United States. With information such as this in hand, timid souls have good reason to question the prospects for our continued survival, and cynics have just cause to sneer at the effectiveness of governmental regulation.[80]

Thus, when the D.C. Circuit sees bureaucratic slothfulness standing in the way of the survival of the species and the (constitutionally protected) right to life, it will act to increase the power of those groups that defend threatened individuals and the planet itself.

In short, the practical effect of the courts' apparently evenhanded procedures is far from politically neutral because their substantive pronouncements severely limit the issues that intervenors can discuss. While the courts claim to favor increased public participation, their decisions have discouraged effective participation by those (such as COWPS) who adhere to the belief that standard setting is a balancing act, not a search for a technically correct answer or an opportunity to

79. Harold Leventhal, "Remarks," 7 *Natural Resources Lawyer* 351 at 356 (1974).
80. *Environmental Defense Fund* v. *Environmental Protection Agency,* 636 F.2d 1267 at 1286–87 (D.C. Cir. 1980).

define a new environmental right. The courts, joined in their efforts by the EPA, environmental groups, and, perhaps most important, congressional committee members and their staff, have circumscribed the debate over national standards by claiming that Congress has already decided the most crucial of all policy issues, how administrators should define acceptable risk.

This chapter has not sought to evaluate the two contentions underlying the D.C. Circuit's review of air quality standards, namely, that the Constitution creates a special judicial interest in public health and that pollution threatens the survival of the human species. But the analysis above does suggest two serious shortcomings of the courts' analysis of the regulatory process.

First, while the courts have induced the EPA to announce stringent standards, it is doubtful that in doing so they have helped regulators achieve their ambitious goals. Indeed, by insisting upon a "health only" approach, the courts have helped reduce national standards to the status of long-term targets. Standards that seem excessively demanding to state and local administrators, congressmen and presidents, and members of the public directly affected by regulatory programs are harder to enforce than standards that seem more reasonable. Moreover, by denying the EPA discretion to decide how to regulate peculiar pollutants such as lead, court decisions have squandered valuable administrative time and political capital. By itself, announcing rights does not protect rights. Warnings about the imminent demise of the species do not improve the species' chances of survival if they contribute to the public's perception of the federal government as a bureaucratic Chicken Little.

Second, by ruling that the EPA cannot consider cost in standard setting the courts have preserved the myth of thresholds and have thus muddled the public debate over how to deal with the problem of risk. Regulators inevitably consider cost. But presently they cannot explain how they do so. The courts have told Congress that it decided the issue in this way even though Congress—at the urging of its environmental protection committees—endorsed two contradictory sets of positions. Thus, not only did the courts impute an intent to an ambivalent Congress, but they have done so in a way that camouflages the inevitability of political choice. Far from opening agency decisionmaking to public view, the courts have allowed and encouraged the EPA to sustain a myth and to keep secret its bureaucratic motives.

If the courts have had an unfortunate effect on standard setting, it is not because they have misinterpreted scientific evidence, but rather because they have been guided by an idea—a judicially protected, quasi-constitutional "right" to health—that is incompatible with the medical evidence on the effects of pollution. No amount of documentation, no number of "hard looks," no corps of science clerks will solve the courts' problem until judges reexamine the views on public health and the regulatory process that guide their laborious review of air quality standards.

CHAPTER NINE

The Rise and Fall of Transportation Controls

The foregoing order is technically in conformance with the statute but in some respects it ignores reality.
—Judge George E. MacKinnon in NRDC v. EPA, 1973

Unreasonable goals based on erroneous assumptions and scheduled within arbitrary deadlines do not enhance public understanding nor do they aid in getting the air cleaned up.
—Charles Barden, Texas Air Resources Control Board, 1975

THE federal courts presided over both the birth and the death of the programs designed by the Environmental Protection Agency to reduce automobile traffic in metropolitan areas. The 1970 Clean Air Act required state plans to contain all measures necessary for attaining national air quality standards, including "land-use and transportation controls." The EPA tried to avoid getting into the transportation planning business, but the court of appeals for the D.C. Circuit and a federal district court in California ordered the agency to comply with the letter of the law.[1] The previously timid bureaucracy responded to these court orders by proposing a large number of stringent transportation controls.

The EPA's regulations provoked a fire storm of criticism in the affected cities, state air agencies, the press, and Congress. No other controversy so damaged the EPA's public reputation as did its promulgation of transportation control plans. But the most crippling blows to the EPA's plans came from the courts themselves. Two circuits struck down EPA-written state implementation plans (SIPs) as technically deficient.[2] Three other circuits ruled that the EPA did not have authority to force the

1. *Natural Resources Defense Council* v. *Environmental Protection Agency*, 475 F.2d 968 (D.C. Cir. 1973); *City of Riverside* v. *Ruckelshaus*, 4 Environment Reporter Cases 1728 (C.D. Cal. 1972).
2. *South Terminal Corp.* v. *Environmental Protection Agency*, 504 F.2d 646 (1st Cir. 1974); *Texas* v. *Environmental Protection Agency*, 499 F.2d 289 (5th Cir. 1974).

states to comply with these plans.[3] The EPA's transportation control programs never recovered from these judicially imposed wounds.

It is hardly surprising that the EPA had great difficulty enforcing transportation controls adequate to attain national standards for carbon monoxide and ozone by 1975 or even 1977. Pollution levels in Los Angeles, New York, Denver, Boston, and other major metropolitan areas were so high that these cities could not meet air quality standards without imposing such unpopular measures as parking bans and surcharges, mandatory bus and carpool lanes, and gasoline rationing of up to 90 percent. The result of such restrictions (and, for some supporters, their purpose as well) would have been a fundamental shift in urban and suburban residential patterns. This has led some observers to describe the EPA's foray into transportation planning as an exercise in "lifestyle politics."[4] While most citizens favored forcing auto companies to clean up the air, very few were willing to reduce drastically their reliance on private automobiles in order to achieve air quality standards.

After encountering strong opposition from many quarters, the EPA and Congress all but abandoned federally mandated controls on the use of motor vehicles. In 1977 Congress prohibited the EPA from requiring SIPs to include indirect source review (ISR), the agency's name for programs to review the air quality impact of new highways, shopping centers, parking lots, and other structures that attract automobiles. Although the legislation passed in 1977 requires state plans to include transportation controls necessary to meet national standards by 1987 at the latest and imposes new sanctions on states that do not comply, the EPA has studiously avoided ordering states to institute restraints on vehicle use. The motto of the EPA's current efforts is "sell, not tell." The agency arrived at this position after discovering that when it issued commands, no one obeyed.

While those who have studied transportation control plans agree that the plans have failed miserably, they disagree on who should bear the blame.[5] The most common reaction to the plans was criticism of the

3. *Brown* v. *Environmental Protection Agency,* 521 F.2d 827 (9th Cir. 1975); *Maryland* v. *Environmental Protection Agency,* 530 F.2d 215 (4th Cir. 1975); *District of Columbia* v. *Train,* 521 F.2d 971 (D.C. Cir. 1975).

4. For example, Robert Sansom, *The New American Dream Machine: Toward a Simpler Lifestyle in an Environmental Age* (Doubleday, 1976).

5. There is a large secondary literature on transportation controls, including James E. Krier and Edmund Ursin, *Pollution and Policy: A Case Essay on California and Federal Experience with Motor Vehicle Air Pollution 1940–1975* (University of California Press,

EPA for proposing such drastic actions. According to former Deputy Administrator John Quarles,

> No one could believe that such a scheme was in the public interest. . . . To the more knowledgeable observers, we succeeded in explaining that this plan had been forced on EPA by the statutory terms of the Clean Air Act and the court order. To most of the general public, however, the plan was simply EPA's proposal.[6]

This perception of the EPA as an unthinking advocate of transportation controls grew stronger as the agency's transportation planning program became dominated by officials who intended to use the act to restructure urban transportation systems.

As Quarles and others point out, the EPA only reluctantly took on the task of promulgating transportation controls. Congress told it to perform this impossible task, although individual congressmen later complained about the EPA's actions. The "land-use and transportation controls" language was added to the Clean Air Act by the 1970 conference committee and slipped through Congress without debate. This phrase, when coupled with the deadlines in the legislation, gave the EPA little room to maneuver. To make matters worse, Congress failed to appropriate mass transit funds that could have provided alternative transportation for those currently relying on private autos. Congress willed the goal of clean air without providing the federal bureaucracy with either the money or the regulatory sanctions necessary for achieving it. Rather than correcting this imbalance between ends and means, most congressmen simply attacked those who followed Congress's orders.

A few commentators have also noted that the federal courts contributed to the EPA's problems by ordering it to formulate aggressive attainment plans and then, once the implications of the original orders became clear, refusing to help the EPA enforce them. While this is unquestionably true, the courts were not simply fickle. In the "action-forcing" decisions

---

1977); Eli Chernow, "Implementing the Clean Air Act in Los Angeles: The Duty to Achieve the Impossible," 4 *Ecology Law Quarterly* 537 (1975); Paul B. Downing and Gordon Brady, "Implementing the Clean Air Act: A Case Study of Oxidant Control in Los Angeles," 18 *Natural Resources Journal* 237 (1978); John Quarles, "The Transportation Control Plans—Federal Regulation's Collision with Reality," 2 *Harvard Environmental Law Review* 241 (1977); Robert J. Rauch, "EPA Regulation of 'Indirect Sources': A Skeptical View," 12 *Harvard Journal on Legislation* 111 (1974); and Thomas Keene, "The 1970 Clean Air Act and Transportation Control in Connecticut" (Senior Honors Thesis, Harvard College, 1978).

6. John Quarles, *Cleaning Up America: An Insider's View of the Environmental Protection Agency* (Houghton Mifflin, 1976), p. 202.

of 1972–73 the courts did not rely on ambiguous legislative history (as they did in the prevention of significant deterioration and dispersion cases), but only insisted that the EPA comply with the clear demands of the statute. When later asked to check the reasonableness of the technical analysis underlying the EPA's plans, the courts bent over backward to uphold the agency's actions. The Fifth Circuit announced that "necessity, which has mothered the EPA's invention of this [dispersion] model, also protects it from a judicial insistence on greater reliability."[7] The courts struck down those parts of the EPA's plans that were based on grossly inadequate data. In each instance the EPA subsequently admitted it had made serious mistakes.

In their third set of decisions the courts ruled that the federal government cannot order the states to carry out transportation controls written by the EPA. While these opinions have proven far more controversial than those reviewing the adequacy of the EPA's technical analysis, they are based on compelling constitutional arguments. The EPA's efforts to force state legislatures to spend money on mass transit improvements and to require state bureaucracies to administer EPA regulations presented a serious threat to traditional states' rights. Granting the EPA the authority it requested, the Ninth Circuit warned, "would reduce the states to puppets of a ventriloquist Congress."[8] If the courts gave conflicting signals to the EPA it was because they are responsible both for seeing that agencies carry out the laws passed by Congress and for protecting individuals and the states from unconstitutional or capricious intrusion by the federal government.

This does not mean that the courts had no choice but to play the dual role of obedient messenger and elder statesman in the transportation control tragedy. They could have read the Constitution so as to uphold the EPA's enforcement authority. They also could have relied on procedural arguments to refuse to hear the original "mandatory duty" suits that environmental groups brought against the EPA. The transportation control cases thus raise the question of whether it is better to have the courts force agencies to abide by statutory mandates or to require Congress to find other ways to keep administrators in line.

Two findings of this chapter bear upon this question. The first is that by serving as the proximate cause of agency action on transportation controls, the courts greatly enhanced the bureaucratic position of

7. *Texas* v. *EPA* at 301.
8. *Brown* v. *EPA* at 839.

politically naive and technically ignorant attorneys within the EPA. These lawyers refused to listen to the engineers who pointed out the technical shortcomings of the EPA's plans. They likewise turned a deaf ear upon those who warned that the EPA's efforts would not succeed unless the agency paid more attention to public opinion. The deeper agency lawyers sank into the transportation control bog the more dependent they became on court-based enforcement to extricate themselves. To shift metaphors, the courts became the *deus ex machina* to law school–trained playwrights who had written themselves into an unmanageable scene. The federal courts understandably refused to cooperate. Just as the original court orders occasioned the attorneys' rise to power within the EPA, the later decisions caused their fall.

Second, the "action-forcing" decisions of the courts have done little to force Congress to devise a transportation control policy that it is willing to stand behind. Rather than face hard choices, Congress has simply put off deadlines. The same problems that arose in 1975 will reappear in 1983 or 1987. Moreover, recognition that the courts will function as a safety valve when it comes to enforcement of EPA regulations has reduced Congress's incentives to establish realistic goals.

This chapter will document and expound upon these two findings as it describes the major technical and political aspects of transportation controls, the original "action-forcing" litigation, and the history of the EPA's programs to restrict the use of motor vehicles.

The Technical and Political Issues

In 1973 the EPA stated, "In requiring the States and EPA to impose transportation controls where they are needed to meet air quality standards, the Congress imposed a regulatory task whose difficulties and complexity are virtually unparalleled."[9] It had ample support for this assertion.

Before 1970 controlling pollution meant installing control equipment to reduce "end of the pipe" emissions. Most of those who debated the 1970 act shared this assumption about controls for motor vehicles as well as stationary sources. The major controversy over the 1970 legislation concerned the amount of emission reduction auto manufacturers

9. 38 Fed. Reg. 30630 (1973).

were to achieve. The Nixon administration proposed that new cars be required to reduce their emissions by 90 percent in 1980. The Muskie subcommittee, embracing "technology forcing," moved the deadline for 90 percent reductions to 1975. Both indicated that this technological fix, usually called the "Detroit strategy," would solve the nation's mobile source pollution problem.

Those who studied the structure of the 1970 act carefully, however, realized that this expedient would not be sufficient for meeting that statute's goals. The 90 percent figure came from a rather crude analysis put forth by the EPA estimating that the nation's most polluted cities must reduce ozone and carbon monoxide levels by 90 percent to achieve safe pollution levels.[10] By 1975 or even 1977, however, only a fraction of the cars on the road—the new models—would meet this stringent emission standard, even if Detroit complied fully with the law. In other words, the deadline for meeting air quality standards would come well before the Detroit strategy produced significant emission reduction. To make matters worse, even the cleaner new cars would not continue to meet the manufacturers' standards unless properly maintained. Achieving the deadlines for mobile source national air quality standards required not just compelling the auto companies to meet technology-forcing requirements, but also requiring private citizens to treat their new cars properly and reducing the emissions of the millions of older cars still on the road.

Members of the Senate committee and their staff were well aware of the problem created by the act's deadlines. They included in the legislation a little-noted provision requiring "periodic inspection and testing of motor vehicles to enforce compliance with applicable emission standards." More surprisingly, section 110 also stated that state plans must include not just "emission limitations, schedules, and timetables for compliance with such limitations," but also "such other measures as may be necessary to insure attainment and maintenance of such primary or secondary standards, including, but not limited to, land-use and transportation controls." The last five words appeared for the first time in the bill reported by the 1970 conference committee.

Two unusually blunt statements made by Senator Muskie and his

10. This is made clear in the 1970 Senate Public Works Committee report, contained in *A Legislative History of the Clean Air Amendments of 1970*, prepared for the Senate Committee on Public Works, 93 Cong. 2 sess. (Government Printing Office, 1974), pp. 425–27.

committee explained the implications of the transportation controls phrase. The Senate report stated:

> The Committee recognizes that during the next several years, the attainment of required ambient air quality in many of the metropolitan regions of this country will be impossible if the control of pollution from moving sources depends solely on emission controls. The Committee does not intend that these areas be exempt from meeting the standards. Some regions may have to establish new transportation programs and systems combined with traffic control regulations and restrictions in order to achieve ambient air quality standards for pollution agents associated with moving sources.
>
> The Committee realizes that changes or restrictions in transportation systems may impose severe hardship on municipalities and States.[11]

Senator Muskie's explanation of the conference committee's bill went even further:

> What is involved in these great urban areas, from the standpoint of air pollution, is the whole complex of residential patterns, employment patterns, and transportation patterns—the way in which people move around, go to their work, and live—and all of this ought to be subject to modification, and must be modified if the objective of clean air is to be achieved.[12]

The legislative history of the 1970 act thus left little doubt but that the Senate sponsors of the statute expected the EPA to effect major changes in the use of private automobiles.

Although these sections of the act and its legislative history made the EPA vulnerable to citizen suits, they did not indicate strong political support for transportation controls. Few congressmen were aware of the "land-use and transportation controls" language of the act—not to mention its broad-ranging implications.[13] Nonetheless, despite the gargantuan technical, administrative, and political obstacles the EPA confronted in implementing these controls, Congress did not remove the troublesome section of the act. Transportation controls continued to receive support from key sectors of Congress throughout the 1970s.

Technical Problems

Designing a control strategy adequate to meet ambient air quality standards requires a regulatory agency to make three types of technical assessments. First, it must determine existing air quality levels to estimate

11. Ibid., p. 413.
12. Ibid., p. 148.
13. See Quarles, "Transportation Control Plans," p. 261.

the extent of the pollution problem. Second, it must determine how large a reduction in emissions will produce the desired reduction in ambient levels. Third, it must define control measures that will achieve these emission reductions. Each of these steps proved even more difficult for mobile source pollutants than for those emitted by stationary sources.

The first difficulty the EPA faced in devising a transportation control program in the early 1970s was lack of data on emissions and ambient concentrations. In states other than California, monitoring data for hydrocarbon, ozone, and carbon monoxide was nearly nonexistent. Monitoring devices were often poorly located and frequently failed to operate properly. In the middle of the controversy over the Boston transportation control plan, for example, the EPA discovered that many of the socially disruptive controls it had required were based on readings from a single malfunctioning monitor. Even more embarrassing for the EPA was the discovery in the mid-1970s that rural areas without significant vehicular traffic frequently violate the primary standards for ozone. This suggested that even if major cities instituted the extreme measures required by the EPA, they would still fail to comply with the law. In short, the EPA began to construct a solution before it had any conception of the magnitude of the problem.

Second, it is even harder to relate emissions to air quality for pollutants from mobile sources than it is for those from stationary sources. Carbon monoxide is a highly localized pollutant. Elevated concentrations occur in "hot spots" such as busy intersections, but dissipate rapidly. Consequently, meeting the carbon monoxide standard requires a block-by-block control strategy with minutely detailed traffic restrictions. Photochemical oxidants (or ozone, as the regulated pollutant was called after 1979) pose just the opposite problem. Ozone is a *secondary* pollutant. Hydrocarbons and nitrogen oxides emitted by mobile and stationary sources react in a complex (and to some extent unknown) way to produce ozone and related pollutants. The rate of ozone formation depends on a large number of factors, including the levels of various types of hydrocarbons, temperature, humidity, and amount of sunlight.[14]

When the EPA issued instructions on how to achieve requisite ozone reductions it gave the states the option of using either a simple "rollback" model or a slightly more complicated formula described in appendix J

14. EPA, Environmental Criteria and Assessment Office, *Air Quality Criteria for Ozone and Other Photochemical Oxidants* (EPA, April 1978), pp. 19–115.

of its guidelines. Both methods of calculation treat ozone levels as a simple function of hydrocarbon emission. As early as 1971 the EPA admitted that the technical inadequacies of these formulas "clearly indicate the need for . . . a more comprehensive and definitive simulation model for NO_x, HC, and oxidants."[15] The EPA eventually discovered that as many as fifty or sixty factors affect ozone formation, that natural hydrocarbon emissions from vegetation contribute to the ozone problem, and, most important, that ozone, like sulfates, travels hundreds and even thousands of miles in the atmosphere. It also learned that long distance transport raises ozone concentrations above the primary standard almost everywhere east of the Mississippi, and that as much as 60 percent of Connecticut's ozone comes from the New York–New Jersey area. These findings obviously called into question the EPA's city-by-city control programs.

Third, to design control strategies, the EPA must relate emission reductions to concrete control measures. The EPA uses engineering manuals to estimate emission reductions for stationary sources. But estimating the emission reductions achieved by reducing available parking spaces or improving mass transit requires the agency to guess how such measures will affect the public's propensity to drive. Relating transportation control measures to reductions in vehicle miles traveled is a highly inexact art and one not familiar to EPA engineers. The EPA often overestimated the emission reduction achieved by control measures. Given this and other difficulties, it is not surprising that most of the technical personnel in the Office of Air Quality Planning and Standards (OAQPS) did not want to read the act literally or to draw a close analogy between stationary sources and transportation systems.

Administrative Problems

Even without these technical pitfalls, transportation controls would have overburdened the administrative resources of the EPA and state pollution control agencies. In part this results from the sheer size of the pollution problem. There are 20,000 major stationary sources in the country but tens of millions of cars and trucks. Sources that move around are harder to keep track of than those that stay put. Moreover, far more

15. EPA, Air Pollution Control Office, *Air Quality Criteria for Nitrogen Oxides*, no. AP-48 (EPA, January 1971).

areas exceed the carbon monoxide and ozone standards than exceed the standards for sulfur dioxide and particulate matter. By 1975 almost 90 percent of all air quality control regions were still violating the primary ozone standard, often by a large margin. For example, Los Angeles has experienced ozone levels of 0.41 part per million—over five times the national standard in effect in 1975. That year ten cities exceeded the primary standard by a factor of four and thirty-eight by a factor of two or more.[16] Clearly, reducing these levels to the national standards requires an enormous administrative effort.

The major administrative problem facing the EPA was not the quantity of sources to control or the extent of control required, but the nature of the requisite control strategies. Transportation policy is the province of state and local government, not of private industry. Independent transportation authorities often control key resources. States and localities in turn depend on the federal Department of Transportation for funding. While the EPA can threaten privately owned stationary sources with fines and jail sentences, transportation policies result from the interaction of a large variety of governmental units, none solely responsible for these policies and few subject to traditional legal sanctions.

To make matters worse, transportation planning requires expertise and a time frame foreign to the EPA and most state air agencies. EPA engineers knew about plume dispersion models and controls for industrial sources, not about highway use models or methods for improving mass transit. EPA lawyers work on a short time horizon that contrasts sharply with the decades it can take to plan and complete mass transit systems. Neither professional group is familiar with the diverse transportation problems of major urban areas. State agencies are in an even weaker position: they lack not just expertise, but statutory authority as well. To exert control over transportation policies they need new legislation, something state legislators almost never grant.

Political Problems

Given these administrative obstacles to implementation of transportation controls, the EPA desperately needed the political support of the

16. "Petition of American Petroleum Institute for Review and Revision," December 9, 1976, p. 22. The petition is reprinted in *Clean Air Act Amendments of 1977,* Hearings before the Subcommittee on Environmental Pollution of the Senate Committee on Environmental and Public Works, 95 Cong. 1 sess. (GPO, 1977), pt. 3, pp. 560–710.

driving public and of those state and local officials who shape transportation policy. This support never materalized. Reactions from state and local governments, Congress, and the states were overwhelmingly critical. While some EPA officials have claimed that this was the result of public misunderstanding, there are several more fundamental reasons why transportation controls lacked political support.

First, while the public usually blames businesses for stationary source pollution and fails to see that pollution controls result in higher prices, the costs of transportation controls fall unmistakably on average citizens. EPA plans struck at something very dear to most Americans: their freedom to live, work, and drive where they please.

Second, since transportation and land-use planning are primarily local responsibilities in the United States, the EPA's efforts to enter this territory were considered an affront to elected officials and an assault on the American political tradition of local control. Each step the EPA took to issue orders to local officials strengthened resistance to federal dictation. In some areas, candidates for state and local office saw the political advantage of running against a federal agency.

Third, the Clean Air Act was the outgrowth of a national consensus that the government should crack down on Detroit and private polluters. The transportation control section of the act quietly rode the coattails of this movement. Consequently, the controls proposed by the EPA appeared not as the product of a conscious national choice, but as the handiwork of overzealous bureaucrats. Congress was particularly appalled by the plans and anxious to deny that it had authorized them.

The deficiencies of the EPA's control strategies were cumulative. The more the agency leaned on state governments to administer its restrictions, the more state officials whipped up public opposition and the harder they looked for flaws in the EPA's analysis. As more information became available it became apparent that the strategies that threatened to create the greatest public inconvenience produced only minuscule reductions in pollution levels. For example, a long list of parking bans, parking surcharges, special bus lanes, and mandatory car pooling that the EPA proposed for Boston would have reduced levels by only 2.5 percent—far less than the 69 percent needed to reach the primary ozone standards.[17] Moreover, the EPA admitted that it had misinterpreted the health evidence supporting the ozone standard and in 1979 relaxed it (see chapter 8).

17. Quarles, "Transportation Control Plans," pp. 247–48.

Those who opposed transportation controls understandably used these findings to ridicule the EPA and its programs. This further eroded its credibility and political support.

The Side Benefits of Transportation Controls

Given the meager air quality benefits of transportation controls and their high costs, why did the EPA persist so long in supporting them? Why did Congress retain a significant portion of those programs in the 1977 amendments? To answer these questions one must consider the indirect benefits of transportation controls.

One key political consequence of these controls valued by environmental advocates in the EPA, Congress, and the public interest groups was that they helped keep pressure on the auto industry to meet emission standards for new cars. According to this view, if transportation controls had to absorb the slack created by Detroit's recalcitrance, those subject to them would oppose any backsliding on emission requirements.

Second, automobiles not only create air pollution, but also increase noise levels, require highways that can destroy neighborhoods, consume large amounts of gasoline, encourage suburban sprawl, and contribute to what some condemn as the "privatization" of American life. Reliance on the automobile creates a vicious cycle: highways drain money from mass transit, which makes everyone more dependent on private cars. The EPA claimed that its plans would break this cycle.[18] In fact, much of the internal disagreement over transportation control plans (TCPs) centered on the question of whether the agency should advocate what the former director of the OAQPS called "socially beneficial measures of marginal utility for air pollution control."[19] While his answer was "no," for several years the agency as a whole answered "yes."

Congressional supporters of the EPA's transportation control strategies saw them not just as tools for reducing the many bad effects of automobiles, but also as mechanisms for increasing their own control over policy matters within the jurisdiction of other subcommittees. This applies above all to Senator Muskie and his staff, who tried to use the EPA's programs to force the transportation and appropriations committees to spend more money on mass transit. The day after the EPA

18. 39 Fed. Reg. 30441 (1974).
19. Memorandum, Bernard Steigerwald (OAQPS) to Roger Strelow (assistant administrator), "Photochemical Oxidant Control Strategies," February 13, 1974.

announced its restrictive plan for Los Angeles, Senator Muskie introduced a bill to "bust" the highway trust to divert funds to mass transit. When a group of EPA officials met with Senate staffers to explain the frailties of their plans and the harm the controversy could do to the EPA's credibility, Muskie's chief aide, Leon Billings, responded that he expected a quid pro quo in return for relaxation of the EPA's proposals. One participant reported that Billings was "searching for a way to exact basic changes in the methods and patterns of metropolitan transportation and growth as the 'price' to be paid for short term alterations in the Clean Air Act."[20] In the battle between highway and mass transit forces the Clean Air Act gave the latter a lever for which they had high hopes.

Thus transportation controls were more than just half-baked environmental programs. They were pawns in complex political struggles between Detroit and Washington and between congressmen with conflicting views on the federal government's overall transportation policy. EPA political executives saw danger ahead and tried to skirt the issue. But with environmental groups eager to clamp down on the automobile, maintaining this position became nearly impossible.

The "Action-Forcing" Litigation

EPA officials were far from unsympathetic to the cause of those who had included the "land-use and transportation controls" language in the Clean Air Act. Many of the young environmental enthusiasts in the agency saw this section of the act as the "only land-use game in town." Before the court decision, two forces within the EPA held these transportation and land-use planning advocates in check. The OAQPS considered transportation control beyond its expertise and doubted that such measures would be needed once the Detroit strategy produced a significant reduction in new-car emissions. Joining the OAQPS in opposition to aggressive regulation of transportation was Administrator William Ruckelshaus, who did not want to squander political capital on a venture he viewed as futile.

The EPA took two preliminary steps on the transportation control issue. It commissioned studies of various control strategies and their air

20. Memorandum, Stephen Ells (Region I) to John McGlennon (Region I administrator), "Oxidant Transport Meeting and Its Implication for Our TCPs," November 4, 1974. Ells commented, "Now that's hard ball, and I admire him for it."

quality benefits and gave the states more time to comply with the act. In August 1971 the EPA granted blanket two-year extensions to all control regions that would not attain primary standards by 1975. It also gave the states until early 1973 to submit full-scale SIPs for ozone and carbon monoxide.

Environmental groups responded to these actions with two suits. The first, *City of Riverside* v. *Ruckelshaus,* was argued by a California public interest law firm that had previously received funds from the EPA to conduct a public education campaign on pollution control. California was one of the very few states to submit a control plan for mobile source pollutants in early 1972. The state admitted that its plan would not come close to attaining primary standards in heavily polluted areas such as Los Angeles and San Francisco. The EPA disapproved California's SIP, but failed to promulgate a substitute plan as required by the act. The federal district court for the Central District of California ordered the EPA to promulgate by January 15, 1973, a plan adequate to bring Los Angeles into compliance with the act by 1977. This meant that the EPA had to devise a strategy to cure the worst mobile source pollution problem in the country or face contempt of court. The *Riverside* case led Administrator Ruckelshaus to announce a plan that included reducing gasoline supplies in Los Angeles by 82 percent. This provoked predictable outrage.[21]

The second decision issued by the federal judiciary was that of the D.C. Circuit in *Natural Resources Defense Council* v. *Environmental Protection Agency.* This decision, announced in January 1973, represented the beginning of years of supervision of the EPA's transportation programs by the D.C. Circuit and nearly a decade of participation in EPA policymaking by the NRDC and its attorney, David Hawkins. The three-part court decision first ruled illegal the EPA's grant of a one-year extension for submission of state plans. Since the court did not issue its order until just one month before the EPA deadline, this part of the court order seemed superfluous. But in doing so the court committed itself to preventing the agency from delaying further and in effect gave the NRDC authority to negotiate scheduling with the EPA.

The court also instructed the EPA to rescind all the two-year extensions

21. There are several detailed descriptions of the TCP for Los Angeles. See Chernow, "Implementing the Clean Air Act in Los Angeles"; Krier and Ursin, *Pollution and Policy;* and Downing and Brady, "Implementing the Clean Air Act."

it had granted and to approve future extensions only if the states that requested them produced SIPs that would attain all national standards by 1975. The court did not explain why states should submit plans they did not believe could be carried out within this time frame. The Fifth Circuit later found section 110(e) "inherently ambiguous" and ruled that to require the states to submit plans they considered unworkable in order to qualify for extensions would be "pointless."[22] The EPA subsequently quietly promised to grant extensions to all states that produced plans with a 1975 attainment date. But few state officials wanted to take political heat for endorsing plans they considered unreasonable or to put themselves at the mercy of the EPA—or of the courts, which might again strike down extensions granted by the EPA. They preferred to let the EPA write and enforce its own plans.

In the third and final section of its order, the D.C. Circuit took note of the NRDC's claim that the EPA had not required state plans to include provisions ensuring the maintenance of national standards after 1975–77. Finding the record on this issue inconclusive, the court ordered the EPA to "review the maintenance provisions of all state implementation plans presently approved" and to disapprove those not including a plan for "maintenance of standards."[23]

While the first two parts of the D.C. Circuit decision, along with that of the California district court, played a major role in shaping the transportation control plans the EPA wrote for individual cities, the final command formed the cornerstone of the EPA's indirect source review. While both ISR and TCPs died, they succumbed to different diseases.

The Stillbirth of Indirect Source Review

Neither the Clean Air Act nor the *Riverside* or *NRDC* decisions mention regulation of what the EPA later dubbed "indirect sources," that is, facilities such as highways, parking lots, and shopping centers, which attract large numbers of motor vehicles. In fact, the only reference to maintenance programs during the *NRDC* litigation came in a footnote in the NRDC's brief suggesting that the EPA review such developments as the Hackensack (New Jersey) Meadowlands complex to make sure

22. *Texas* v. *EPA* at 313, note 44.
23. *NRDC* v. *EPA*, 475 F.2d 968 at 972.

they do not contribute to violations of national ambient air quality standards. The EPA's program to review the air quality impact of the construction of indirect sources grew out of negotiations between EPA attorneys and the NRDC on the meaning of the maintenance section of the D.C. Circuit's order.

The Development of Regulations

Shortly after the D.C. Circuit issued its *NRDC* decision, it became apparent that the Office of General Counsel (OGC) considered review of indirect sources (also called complex sources) good law and good policy. The lead OGC attorney reported, "We see no legal basis for resisting a suit to compel EPA to expand its current requirements to include complex sources" and reached an agreement with the NRDC on a schedule for developing regulations.[24]

The NRDC and OGC at first had grandiose plans for ISR, viewing it as a mechanism for state and federal review of all land use decisions that could affect air quality. According to guidelines issued in April 1973, indirect sources included not just shopping centers, highways, and parking lots, but "residential, commercial, industrial, and institutional developments," and "sewer, water, power, and gas lines, and other such facilities which will result in increased emissions from motor vehicles or other stationary sources."[25] As one commentator later noted, these guidelines constituted nothing short of "a directive to the states to institute statewide land use control."[26] Maintaining air quality standards for mobile source pollutants was the legal hook upon which environmental enthusiasts in the EPA hoped to hang extensive review of land use decisions.

The EPA soon learned that the original guidelines not only invaded traditional state and local prerogatives, but overestimated its ability to predict the air quality consequences of land use decisions. This led the EPA to reduce the scope of ISR. Its revised rules allowed the states to ignore the air quality impact of stationary sources that might locate near the facility under review. Moreover, they allowed the states to disregard

24. Memorandum, Robert Baum (OGC) to Robert Sansom (assistant administrator), "Complex Sources," March 26, 1973. Baum had made this point in an earlier memorandum to all regional counsels, "Legal Authority for Complex Sources," March 16, 1973.

25. 38 Fed. Reg. 6279 (1973).

26. Luke J. Danielson, "Control of Complex Emissions Sources—A Step Toward Land Use Planning," 4 *Ecology Law Quarterly* 693 at 699 (1975).

pollution emitted by traffic not having that facility as its origin or final destination. Most important, the revised guidelines allowed the states to set thresholds for determining which indirect sources to review. The EPA's retreat from comprehensive land use planning had already begun.

This retreat continued when all but a handful of states refused to submit ISR programs, forcing the EPA to propose a control program of its own. OAQPS modelers threw themselves into the difficult enterprise of constructing models to predict carbon monoxide levels near indirect sources, but they kept narrowing the scope of ISR to fit the boundaries of their technical expertise. Claiming it could not estimate the air quality impact of low-density facilities, the OAQPS subjected only large parking facilities, shopping centers, major highways, and airports to review. It set the threshold for parking facilities at 1,000 cars inside standard metropolitan statistical areas and at 2,000 cars outside these areas. Most important, the OAQPS explained that the complexity of ozone formation prevented it from predicting the effect that indirect sources would have on ozone concentrations.[27] The virtual elimination of ozone review was particularly galling to environmental groups. But they could not provide the technical sophistication the OAQPS claimed it lacked.

Constructing carbon monoxide dispersion models adequate to carry out these regulations took time. The EPA published final ISR regulations in February 1974, but did not explain how it would conduct the crucial modeling portion of review. Even the modeling guidelines the OAQPS issued in July 1974 failed to explain to the regional offices how they should account for such factors as meteorological conditions and terrain.[28] This delayed the implementation of ISR and caused confusion about when the D.C. Circuit should hear the growing number of legal challenges to the program. It also meant that the shape of ISR was determined by what the OAQPS believed it could achieve on a technical level.

Nothing illustrates the consequences of this form of policymaking better than the EPA's rules on "reasonable receptor sites." Since carbon monoxide is a highly localized pollutant, concentrations can vary greatly within a few hundred feet. This raised the question: where should

27. 38 Fed. Reg. 9599 (1973); 38 Fed. Reg. 15834 (1973); 38 Fed. Reg. 29893 (1973); and 39 Fed. Reg. 7270 (1974).

28. EPA, OAQPS, "Guidelines for the Review of the Impact of Indirect Sources on Ambient Air Quality," July 1, 1974; and Richard Lowerre, "Indirect Source Review: How to Roll with the Punches," case study prepared for the National Academy of Sciences, April 1976, pp. 32–37.

pollution levels be measured? Carbon monoxide levels are always high in the middle of parking lots and highways, but few people stand there for long. Thus, just as it makes little sense to prevent stationary sources from using smokestacks, it seems unreasonable to ban parking lots that produced a few carbon monoxide hot spots in areas where members of the public spend a few minutes at most. Defining "reasonable receptor sites" required drawing a number of arbitrary lines. Sidewalks became reasonable receptor sites, but not crosswalks.[29]

Those subject to these slowly emerging ISR rules found they could avoid causing violations at receptor sites by taking one of three measures. They could develop better traffic patterns to avoid the traffic jams that produce carbon monoxide hot spots. While making it easier for drivers to enter and leave parking lots and shopping centers may be a good idea, the supporters of ISR had originally wanted fewer such facilities, not easier access to them. Alternatively, developers could build in rural or suburban areas with low carbon monoxide levels. Or they could evade ISR altogether by building a larger number of smaller facilities that would not trigger review. The last two responses threatened to increase suburban sprawl—exactly the opposite of what the EPA intended. A report on the economic impact of ISR prepared for the EPA in 1974 concluded:

> The impact of ISR on location will generally be to reinforce existing trends of suburbanization. In the case of shopping centers, it was found that ISR and its attendant costs may provide developers with a marginal incentive to locate in suburban areas where air quality is relatively good and ISR-related costs would be minimized.[30]

To make matters worse, ISR might even increase total motor vehicle emissions by forcing motorists to drive farther to reach their destinations.

Not surprisingly, the original advocates of ISR slowly lost their enthusiasm for the program. The NRDC adopted a new "maintenance" project, arguing that the D.C. Circuit's ruling required the states to develop long-term (fifteen to twenty-five years) growth plans.[31] The OAQPS came to regret its expenditure of effort on ISR. The director of that office later commented,

> We dug our own hole by drawing too close an analogy between a traditional source and a highway. We gave headquarters too much information. CO

29. Lowerre, "Indirect Source Review," pp. 37–40.
30. Harbridge House Report on ISR, p. 1-10, quoted in ibid., p. 50.
31. The EPA reluctantly produced "maintenance plan" guidelines for the states in 41 Fed. Reg. 18382 (1976), but never sought to carry them out.

modeling was a technical challenge, and it got away from us. It was a hell of an interesting technical problem.[32]

Even the OGC attorneys eventually came to question the environmental benefits of ISR.[33]

The Political Backlash

The political costs of ISR grew nearly as quickly as its environmental benefits shrank. Intense opposition from Congress prevented the EPA from carrying out any form of indirect source review. ISR advocates had given no more thought to the political acceptability of the program than they had to its technical and administrative feasibility. The OGC and the NRDC used the D.C. Circuit's *NRDC* decision to avoid scrutiny from the EPA's political executives and other agencies. In late 1973, for example, the NRDC filed contempt motions against the EPA and the Office of Management and Budget to give the EPA a reason for circumventing potentially hostile, time-consuming interagency review.[34] But the NRDC and EPA had outsmarted themselves. By evading restraint from within the executive branch they precipitated strong opposition from Congress.

Shopping center developers spearheaded the attack on ISR. This relatively small and coherent group organized an effective lobbying effort that brought their complaints to the attention of the EPA, Congress, and the courts. The key to this group's success was the hostile reaction that greeted the plans the EPA announced in mid-1973 to reduce auto use in major cities. Many of these city-specific plans contained parking bans and surcharges. These quickly became the most despised elements of the EPA's control strategy. The shopping centers' opposition to ISR rode the wave of public opposition to restrictions on parking in general.

When Congress considered emergency energy legislation in late 1973, the opponents of transportation controls called for major cutbacks in the EPA's authority. With the House threatening to remove all control over parking from the EPA's jurisdiction, Senator Muskie and his staff looked for a way to head off permanent changes in the act. At a private

---

32. Personal interview with Bernard Steigerwald (OAQPS), November 8, 1978.

33. Personal interview with Robert Baum (formerly in OGC), September 7, 1978.

34. Memorandums, Michael James (OGC) to Alan Kirk (OGC), October 18, 1973; and Alan Kirk to Robert Sansom (assistant administrator), October 1973. Also see Lowerre, "Indirect Source Review," pp. 9, 66.

meeting with EPA Deputy Administrator John Quarles, Public Works Committee chairman Jennings Randolph, and ranking Republican Howard Baker, Muskie stated that if the EPA agreed to a one-year "voluntary" postponement of all parking-related restrictions he could convince the House to refrain from passing a permanent limit on EPA authority. Quarles convinced Administrator Russell Train to go along with this strategy.[35] The legislation Congress passed in early 1974 prohibited the EPA from imposing surcharges on parking, but merely authorized it to suspend other types of parking restrictions for a year. Although President Nixon vetoed this bill, an identical provision became part of the Energy Supply and Environmental Coordination Act in June 1974.

These developments in Congress complicated the litigation over ISR. When the EPA failed to promulgate final ISR regulations by December 15, 1973, the NRDC took the EPA back to court. The EPA asked the court to delay action while Congress considered the pending legislation, and the court granted a thirty-day extension. But when the legislation failed to pass, the NRDC again demanded final regulations. Meanwhile shopping center developers and others subject to ISR filed petitions for review in nearly every federal circuit court in the country. The OGC recommended promulgating the proposed regulations—despite congressional opposition—in order to satisfy the D.C. Circuit. Administrator Train prudently rejected the OGC's advice and followed through with his commitment to postpone the effective date of ISR.[36]

This did not end the cross-pressure the EPA was getting from Congress and the courts. As January 1975 approached, the NRDC once again dragged the EPA back to court. The D.C. Circuit stated it was "extremely concerned" that the EPA had not completed the technical appendixes necessary for administering ISR and demanded that the EPA explain the delay. Meanwhile the House Appropriations Committee passed a rider to an appropriations bill prohibiting the EPA from regulating parking in any way during the next fiscal year. The Muskie subcommittee, angered both by the jurisdictional imperialism of the Appropriations Committee and by the delay of ISR, tried to defeat this rider.[37] But it passed anyway.[38] Muskie's staff urged the EPA to ignore the restriction

35. 4 *Environment Reporter—Current Developments* 1553–54. These events are narrated in Quarles, "Transportation Control Plans," pp. 250–51.

36. 39 Fed. Reg. 1848 (1974); Memorandum, Richard Stoll (OGC) to Alan Kirk (OGC), "Indirect Source Issues," December 27, 1973.

37. 5 *Environment Reporter—Current Developments* 879.

38. Sec. 510 of Agriculture—Environmental and Consumer Protection Appropriation Act, 1975 (88 Stat. 1822).

included in the appropriations bill. The EPA again deferred the effective date of ISR, but bowed to the request of the Muskie subcommittee not to give official recognition to the action of the Appropriations Committee. The EPA attributed its decision to delay ISR to "public misunderstanding" of the issue.[39] The same thing happened again a year later. The NRDC filed suit to force the EPA to be ready to implement ISR as soon as the fiscal year ended. Congress passed another appropriations rider.[40] This time the EPA indefinitely suspended ISR.[41]

The NRDC finally conceded and devoted its efforts to lobbying Congress on the pending amendments. The D.C. Circuit, too, gave up, putting the four-year-old suit on the inactive docket. No doubt the judges were happy to get rid of a case that had produced scores of litigants, reams of regulation, and several pieces of legislation—but no environmental program. And in 1977 Congress put what appeared to be the final nail in ISR's coffin by prohibiting the EPA from conducting indirect source review (except for federally funded projects) and allowing the states to revoke their previously established ISR programs.[42]

Court action first allowed the EPA and NRDC lawyers to initiate and keep alive an ambitious ISR program. The objectives and scope of ISR then shrank as the OAQPS discovered the difficulty of modeling carbon monoxide and ozone. Despite support for ISR in the House and Senate subcommittees, the program eventually crumbled under intense pressure from Congress. Considering the fact that the EPA's proposed ISR regulations might have increased both suburban sprawl and total emissions, the agency's inability to stem the tide of congressional opposition was fortuitous. The courts contributed to this fiasco by helping the inexperienced attorneys in the OGC and NRDC ignore political and technical constraints that neither the EPA nor the courts could wish away.

39. 39 Fed. Reg. 45014 (1974).

40. Sec. 407 of Department of Housing and Urban Development—Independent Agencies Appropriation Act, 1976 (89 Stat. 581).

41. 40 Fed. Reg. 28064 (1975).

42. *Clean Air Amendments of 1977*, Conf. Rept. 95-564, 95 Cong. 1 sess. (GPO, 1977), pp. 126–27; *Clean Air Act Amendments of 1977*, H. Rept. 95-294, 95 Cong. 1 sess. (GPO, 1977), pp. 220–27. For a while it appeared that the courts would read the amendments so as to prohibit states that had voluntarily accepted ISR programs from getting rid of them. *Manchester Environmental Coalition* v. *Environmental Protection Agency*, 14 *Environment Reporter Cases* 1004 (2d Cir. 1979). A more recent decision of this court, however, greatly reduces the significance of the 1979 decision. *Connecticut Fund for the Environment, Inc.* v. *Environmental Protection Agency*, 16 *Environment Reporter Cases* 2185 (2d Cir. 1982).

TCPs: Lawyers, Engineers, and the Courts

In 1973 the EPA wrote comprehensive transportation control plans for twenty-five major metropolitan areas that could not attain primary standards for ozone and carbon monoxide without restricting the use of private automobiles. The plight of these attainment plans was in many ways similar to that of the ISR program. The EPA wrote the TCPs in response to the NRDC and Riverside decisions. Internal support for them came from the OGC and enforcement lawyers. The plans ran into heavy opposition in Congress. In the end they, like ISR, accomplished little, but substantially damaged the EPA's support in Congress, the states, and the public.

The TCP program differed from ISR in several important respects. First, the NRDC and Riverside decisions gave the EPA a more specific mandate on TCPs than on maintenance: the EPA or the states had to produce plans adequate to attain national standards for carbon monoxide by 1977 at the latest. Second, TCPs were of necessity far more comprehensive and draconian than ISR. They touched all aspects of transportation in major metropolitan areas, not just a few large parking facilities. The broad scope of TCPs meant that they imposed burdens on many private citizens, thus exacerbating the EPA's political difficulties. Moreover, the OAQPS could not limit the scope of TCPs to fit its technical competence. In particular, it could not ignore ozone. Third, because TCPs required changes in existing transportation patterns, they created major enforcement problems for the EPA. To enforce ISR the EPA could simply enjoin the construction of indirect sources that had not received permits. Enforcing TCPs, though, involved changing the driving patterns of millions of people.

Finally, while ISR was scheduled to take effect as soon as regulations were promulgated, the EPA had the option of phasing in TCP measures over the 1973–77 period. This provided the EPA and its congressional supporters with a convenient safety valve. They could put off the most extreme control strategies until later years and hope that new legislation would extend the act's deadlines. While Congress killed ISR in 1977, it merely gave the EPA and the states more time to implement attainment plans. No one expects cities such as Los Angeles and New York to institute all the measures contained in these plans even by the late 1980s. But the law still requires them to do so.

The courts played an even more central role in the rise and fall of TCPs than in the history of ISR. Agency lawyers who insisted that the EPA abide by the letter of the *NRDC* decision guided the development of most TCPs, generally without help from the OAQPS. A second round of court challenges then exposed the technical flaws of the plans written by these advocates without expertise. These court decisions gave those in the OAQPS who had protested the EPA's original actions a greater role in formulating its mobile source control strategy. The final blow to the attorneys came when the federal courts announced that they would not force the states to carry out the TCPs written by the EPA. It was at this point that the courts learned that the EPA expected *them* to help implement these controversial programs. They refused to cooperate. Soon thereafter the EPA abandoned its attempts to enforce the plans it had spent so much effort writing and defending. The rise and fall of TCPs coincided with the victories and defeats of the agency's lawyers.

The EPA's Political Dilemma

The *NRDC* and *Riverside* decisions created a dilemma for Administrator Ruckelshaus and his advisers. On the one hand, if they were laggard in following the courts' orders they would invite contempt motions, anger the congressional authors of the "land-use and transportation controls" section of the act, and make the EPA appear unwilling to serve as an advocate for clean air. On the other hand, if the EPA announced proposals that would meet national standards in cities like Los Angeles by 1977, it would look like an unthinking zealot and inspire both hostility and ridicule.

Ruckelshaus and his immediate successor, Acting Administrator Robert Fri, sought to avoid either of these consequences by coupling the proposal of attainment plans with a request to Congress for more time to meet the ambient ozone and carbon monoxide standards. In early 1973 Ruckelshaus flew to Los Angeles to announce an EPA plan that included a wide variety of traffic controls as well as gas rationing of up to 82 percent by the summer of 1977. He expressed "grave reservations" about whether this plan was workable. Shortly thereafter he appeared before the House and Senate subcommittees to recommend that cities like Los Angeles be given more time to comply with the act.

This strategy had several advantages. It kept the EPA out of legal trouble. "Faced with a choice between my freedom and your mobility,"

Ruckelshaus joked at the Los Angeles press conference, "my freedom wins."[43] It also helped to impress on the public the severity of the air pollution problem in many cities. And it drew Congress's attention to the need for amendment of the act.

As EPA officials soon learned, the strategy was also a risky one. The first risk was that the press and state officials would focus on the EPA's TCP and not on its legislative proposal. This danger quickly came to fruition as the EPA became every elected official's favorite whipping boy. The second risk was that Congress would fail to bail out the EPA. This too proved to be more than a remote possibility. In the spring of 1973 neither committee was willing to open the act to amendment. In June 1973, after Ruckelshaus had left the agency, Acting Administrator Fri had no choice but to announce nineteen additional TCPs, as required by the D.C. Circuit. Fri again asked for amendments and described parts of the plans as a "charade" included "solely to satisfy the court order."[44]

By this point Senator Muskie could no longer ignore the political opposition to the agency's plans. Rather than amend the act, Muskie sought to stifle the rebellion by proposing a National Academy of Sciences study of the oxidant problem to determine "the extent to which legislation may be needed to achieve the goals set in the Clean Air Act without disruption."[45] Arguing that the act's deadlines gave Congress several years to revise its 1970 legislation, Muskie was able to gather the support of TCP opponents for a stopgap measure.

This hardly solved the EPA's problem. It had committed itself to proposing and, if necessary, enforcing attainment TCPs. Yet its leaders had admitted that many of these plans were unwise and unworkable. The EPA's position became even more tenuous when Russell Train became the new administrator. While Fri had continued to call for amendment of the act, Train was understandably hesitant to antagonize the Muskie subcommittee or to make a request for relaxation of the act one of his first official actions. At his confirmation hearing, Train announced that Congress should not amend the act until the EPA saw how well TCPs worked.[46]

---

43. Sansom, *New American Dream Machine*, p. 163; also see Krier and Ursin, *Pollution and Policy*, pp. 224–26, and *New York Times*, January 16, 1973, p. 1.

44. *New York Times*, June 23, 1973, p. 6; also 4 *Environment Reporter—Current Developments* 266 and 586.

45. *Congressional Record* (June 29, 1973), p. 22297.

46. 4 *Environment Reporter—Current Developments* 586.

The political attack on the EPA and the Clean Air Act ignited by the 1973 oil embargo increased Train's resolve to save the act and some vestige of the TCP program. The Energy Supply and Environmental Coordination Act prevented the EPA from imposing parking surcharges and authorized it to "voluntarily" suspend the other parking restrictions in its TCPs. But it did not extend the deadlines or delete authority to promulgate or enforce TCPs. By the spring of 1974 the EPA still had legal responsibility for carrying out its TCPs. It did not want to appear to abandon environmental programs in the face of political pressure from Congress and the Nixon administration. The EPA's political executives had not escaped their initial dilemma.

The Exile of the Engineers

While this was occurring at the political level, the OAQPS was losing control over the content of the plans the EPA was proposing. The leaders of the OAQPS had always believed in engineering solutions (such as reducing new-car emissions and inspection and maintenance of in-use vehicles) to the mobile source pollution problem. A small transportation planning branch within the OAQPS sponsored studies on control strategies and wrote the original guidelines for the states, but played a relatively minor role in the drafting of the first TCPs announced in 1973.

In early 1974 Deputy Assistant Administrator Bernard Steigerwald, head of the OAQPS, mounted a counterattack against TCPs. Steigerwald asked Train and Assistant Administrator Roger Strelow to institute a "change in philosophy needed to put our strategy on a more sound technical basis."[47] He reported that new monitoring data provided convincing evidence of long distance oxidant transport, and that "neither Appendix J nor any other quantitative relationship between HC and Ox is technically defensible." He predicted that the EPA's proposed control strategies, including parking restrictions, mass transit improvements, and carpooling incentives, would achieve less than a 5 percent reduction in hydrocarbon emissions in most areas—far less than the margin of error of the agency's technical analysis. Steigerwald recommended that the agency abandon its efforts to relate hydrocarbon reductions to ozone levels, increase its efforts to control hydrocarbon from stationary sources,

47. Memorandum, Bernard Steigerwald (OAQPS) to Roger Strelow (assistant administrator), "Photochemical Oxidant Control Strategies," February 13, 1974.

and require cost-effective transportation controls only in a few cities with severe pollution problems. In effect the OAQPS claimed that the plans announced in response to court orders lacked technical justification and should be publicly renounced by the agency.

This proposal drew a predictably hostile response from the OGC and transportation planning advocates on the assistant administrator's staff.[48] The agency's political executives, forced to choose between these two factions, sided with the TCP advocates. Now was not the time, they decided, to repudiate previously announced environmental protection programs. Assistant Administrator Roger Strelow was particularly eager to see how far the EPA could push the states. He and Train not only directed the regional offices to proceed with their schedules on TCPs, but placed responsibility for writing and reviewing TCPs in the newly formed Office of Transportation and Land Use Planning directly under the control of the assistant administrator.[49] This office soon became a center of support for TCPs.

The decision to give the new transportation office primary responsibility for TCPs effectively removed the OAQPS from decisionmaking on transportation controls. As a consequence, few people in charge of the program had any technical familiarity with the intricacies of pollution monitoring, formation, or dispersion. This deficiency became apparent when the courts examined the EPA's justification for its plans. When they did, the balance of power swung back toward the engineers.

The TCP Advocates

If agency technical personnel disliked TCPs and its political executives were ambivalent at best, who within the EPA wrote and pushed the TCPs that got the agency into so much trouble? Starting in early 1974 the transportation office played a significant role in the TCP saga. Several regional offices also housed supporters of the program. But the most effective TCP advocates were lawyers in the OGC and the Office of Enforcement who viewed themselves as both guardians of the legal process and torchbearers of the agency's environmental mission. These

48. Memorandums, Joel Horowitz to the acting assistant administrator, March 1, 1974; Dave Hanson to Ed Tuerk, March 6, 1974; and D. P. Armstrong to Dave Hanson, August 1974.

49. Memorandum, Roger Strelow to regional administrators, "EPA Policy on Transportation Control Plans," April 9, 1974.

attorneys worked closely with their counterparts in the NRDC who had brought the original suit in the D.C. Circuit.[50]

Soon after the D.C. Circuit announced its 1973 decision, the OGC took responsibility for explaining to the regional offices what constituted an acceptable plan, setting deadlines for the production of the EPA proposals, and reviewing the adequacy of each TCP written by the regions. Working under the tight time schedule established in the NRDC case and lacking technical expertise and detailed knowledge of individual cities' transportation systems, the OGC resorted to a cookbook approach. It used the formula in appendix J of the EPA's 1971 guidelines for preparation of implementation plans to determine necessary emission reductions, and consultants' reports to estimate the results of various control strategies. Ironically, it also ignored both the OAQPS's warning about the inadequacies of appendix J and consultants' warnings that the emission reductions produced by various TCP measures would vary greatly from city to city.

Under this cookbook approach, each control measure was given an emission reduction number, and the numbers had to add up to the total emission reduction figure established for each city by appendix J. Control measures included: vehicle inspection and maintenance, parking bans and surcharges, mandatory bus and car pool lanes, auto-free zones, bridge and highway tolls, gasoline surcharges and rationing, selective driving bans, improved mass transit, staggered work hours, and mandatory four-day work weeks. When regional office personnel complained that many of these measures would be harsh and arbitrary, headquarters lawyers responded, "That's the law."

The OGC was clearly more concerned with appeasing the NRDC and the D.C. Circuit than with encouraging the states to go along with the TCP program. Nothing illustrates this better than its policy on extensions. As explained above, the D.C. Circuit told the EPA that it could not extend the deadline for primary standards to 1977 unless the state submitted a plan for meeting the primary standards by 1975. This meant that to apply for an extension a state had to endorse costly, controversial measures, some of which would be rendered superfluous by the infusion

50. The key supporters of TCPs within the EPA's Washington office were Dave Hanson (Office of Transportation and Land Use Planning), John Bonine (OGC), and Richard Penna (Office of Enforcement). They were joined by the NRDC's David Hawkins. The importance of this group is evident both from examination of agency documents and from interviews conducted with officials in Washington and the regional offices. Also see Sansom, *New American Dream Machine*, p. 35.

of new, cleaner cars during the 1975–77 period. While a few states indicated their willingness to phase in necessary controls over the 1973–77 period, they balked at submitting plans showing attainment by 1975. Rather than approve these plans and defend the action in court if challenged again, the OGC stood by the requirement that states submit plans for attainment by 1975. In several states this rigidity led to a breakdown of cooperation between the states and the EPA and forced the EPA to promulgate its own TCP.[51] Ironically, the EPA gave itself the two-year extension it would not grant the states.

Obeying the letter of the law was not the OGC's only objective. It also wanted to use transportation controls to achieve fundamental changes in urban transportation systems. In fact, while the EPA's political executives were trying to convince Congress that attainment plans would place intolerable burdens on some cities, TCP advocates in the OGC put off the effective date of the most extreme measures (such as gas rationing in Los Angeles) until the last possible moment, July 1977. They tried to protect the act by making immediately effective only those measures they considered reasonable. Of course their definition of reasonable control measures differed greatly from that of the OAQPS and most local officials. The only measures the OGC considered unreasonable were gas rationing and retrofitting of pre-1970 cars. Under the OGC's tutelage, the EPA announced that most cities could be expected to reduce the number of vehicle miles traveled by 10 percent by 1975 and 20 percent by 1977. The EPA even estimated that New York City could reduce this figure by 40 percent by 1977 by using "reasonable" controls.[52]

The key element in the control strategies proposed in 1973 was a combination of parking restrictions, mandatory bus and car pool lanes, and expansion of mass transit. TCP supporters in the EPA saw this as a quick and easy way to reduce dependence on the automobile. Parking bans and surcharges would discourage automobile use. Buses and car pools would provide alternative modes of transportation. The EPA envisioned revenues from parking surcharges being used to purchase new buses.[53] Increasingly these officials saw TCPs as an effort not just to appease the courts or to attain national air quality standards, but to create instant mass transit systems.

51. The clearest case of this was Massachusetts. See Michael Padnos and Edward I. Selig, "Transportation Controls in Boston: The Plan that Failed," prepared for the American Bar Foundation and National Academy of Sciences, June 30, 1976, pp. 23–27.
52. 38 Fed. Reg. 30629 (1973).
53. Ibid., 30628–30.

While the technical weaknesses of the agency's TCPs did not disturb OGC attorneys and their allies, they could not overlook the problem of enforcement. A few agency lawyers voiced doubt about the EPA's legal authority to impose surcharges on parking and gasoline or to interfere with local control over auto inspection and traffic management. The OGC replied that the Clean Air Act delegated to the EPA all authority necessary to meet air quality standards. In fact, the only measures the OGC would not include in federally promulgated SIPs were demands that the states spend more money on mass transit and that employers reduce their work hours.[54]

Even this expansive reading of the EPA's legal authority did not solve its key enforcement problem—its lack of an administrative apparatus extensive enough to carry out control strategies such as inspection and maintenance, parking bans, and bus lanes. TCP enthusiasts suggested a number of schemes for enforcing the federally promulgated plan, including using the National Guard and asking the Department of Justice to deputize thousands of federal marshals to enforce parking, traffic, and registration regulations. Recognizing the absurdity of creating a national police force to enforce pollution laws, the OGC searched for ways to require existing state agencies to implement federal plans. The solution it came up with was to treat state highways as air pollution "sources" and to issue enforcement orders to states that failed to carry out TCPs promulgated by the EPA. According to this argument, state officials who failed to institute necessary bus lanes, inspection and maintenance programs, parking restrictions, and even bicycle lanes had violated the act and thus become subject to criminal penalties and injunctive action. In effect the EPA would be asking the federal courts to compel the states to administer its programs. At times the EPA even claimed that it could order state legislators to adopt legislation essential to the operation of TCPs.[55]

While a few dissenters warned that the courts would never condone such an expansion of federal authority, the OGC, for several reasons, became firmly committed to advancing this argument. First, court-based

54. Memorandum, John Quarles to regional administrators, "Enforcement Considerations in Reviewing/Proposing State Transportation Control Strategies," March 28, 1973; Memorandum of law, John Bonine, "Legal Authority to Require State and Local Officials to Submit Compliance Schedules for Transportation Controls," April 18, 1973; Memorandum of law, John Bonine, "Transportation Controls, Legal Authority," May 9, 1973.

55. Memorandum, Alan Kirk (assistant administrator for enforcement and general counsel) to administrator, "Enforcement Policy for TCPs," July 24, 1974.

enforcement was the only hope the EPA had for implementing its TCPs. The OGC remained confident that the courts would continue to stand behind the environmental cause. Second, the argument that the EPA could treat state highway systems as if they were private stationary sources provided a convenient response to claims that the EPA lacked the expertise and the manpower to write and enforce complex transportation control measures. The agency need merely issue enforcement orders to compel the states to provide the necessary administrative details and enforcement personnel. Third, litigation in this area held out the exciting prospect of participating in pathbreaking constitutional decisions that would aid the federal government in its battle against the forces of degradation. Finally, some OGC attorneys believed that the only thing preventing local officials from cooperating fully with the EPA was the fear of political retribution. If these officials could put responsibility on the EPA, they might comply without being ordered to do so by federal courts.[56]

Subsequent events showed those who developed these arguments to be no better at predicting the reactions of judges than at estimating the political consequences of unilateral federal promulgation of ambitious TCPs. The EPA produced a flurry of TCPs in late 1973. Several regional administrators who announced these plans refused to say whether they would ever try to enforce them. The renewed public outcry led to congressional action prohibiting the EPA from placing surcharges on parking. The House passed, but a conference committee rejected, an amendment to the Clean Air Act that would have prevented the EPA from designating mandatory bus and car pool lanes. Meanwhile over 300 petitions for review piled up in federal courts throughout the country. There the EPA's plans did not fare well.

The Decline of TCPs

In the spring of 1974 the EPA faced the question of what to do with the many TCPs it had promulgated the previous year. The NRDC was already threatening further legal action against the state of New York for its failure to implement transportation control measures it had

56. Memorandum, John Bonine to Alan Kirk, "Legal Authority," April 18, 1973: "Since the major reason for California not to have submitted any adequate transportation plan up to this point may be that they are unwilling to take the political heat for it, a Federal requirement may result in voluntary compliance."

included in its SIP. The EPA knew it could be the NRDC's next target. Moreover, failure to follow through on its plans would make the agency look like a paper tiger, perhaps undermining enforcement efforts aimed at stationary sources. After winning major battles on prevention of significant deterioration and dispersion, the EPA's political executives decided to take a stab at implementing the plans produced by the OGC and the regional offices. Administrator Train told the regional administrators, "Aggressive enforcement should proceed."[57]

Realizing that it could not put all TCPs into effect at the same time and that the success of the first plans it tackled would in large measure determine the success of the entire TCP program, the EPA decided to focus on the Boston plan. The state of Massachusetts had been more cooperative than any other state. Moreover, while the pollution problem in Boston was severe, the EPA estimated that the city could attain primary standards without such drastic measures as gas rationing. Boston also has an extensive mass transit system. Partly as a result of these factors, the Boston regional office was more enthusiastic about TCPs than were most other regional offices. In fact Regional Administrator John McGlennon believed he had staked his reputation on the Boston TCP and wanted to show that the EPA meant business. Soon Washington as well staked its reputation on the Boston TCP. Boston became the laboratory in which the EPA tested its transportation plans.[58]

Enforcing the Boston plan was a frustrating experience. The best example of the difficulties the regional office faced involves a TCP regulation requiring all firms with fifty or more employees to reduce their available parking space by 25 percent. As part of its "get tough" approach, the EPA announced that it would send enforcement orders to 1,500 employers. Just before sending out these orders the regional office discovered that only about 300 firms fit the category governed by the control measure. Many of the 300 proved to be exempt for various reasons. Only seven or eight employers responded to the EPA's letter. The EPA could identify only twenty-five more to whom the regulation definitely applied. When the agency began preparing these few cases for

57. Memorandums, Administrator Train to regional administrators, "EPA Policy on Transportation Control Plans," July 22, 1974; and Roger Strelow to regional administrators, "EPA Policy on Transportation Control Plans," April 9, 1974.

58. Events in Boston are described in Padnos and Selig, "Transportation Controls in Boston," and in Quarles, "Transportation Control Plans." This section of the chapter also relies on interviews with regional staff members and on material retrieved from regional office files.

reference to the U.S. attorney, it discovered it did not have enough information to sustain its legal claims. Not one case reached the U.S. attorney.

The most damaging blow to the EPA's enforcement effort, though, came in the First Circuit. When the EPA promulgated its TCP for Boston, a number of private parties subject to it, including the South Terminal Corporation, which was building a new parking facility at Logan Airport, challenged both the EPA's legal authority to carry out various control strategies and its technical justifications for the entire TCP. The case dragged on for months while the court made numerous requests for additional technical information.

As the evidence emerged, Region I officials, like nearly everyone else, became increasingly appalled at the arbitrary assumptions and technical errors embedded in the plan. Not only had the EPA denied mistakenly that much of Boston's pollution comes from outside the area and relied on suspect rollback models, but it had based its plan on highly dubious monitoring data. The carbon monoxide strategy for the entire city was based on a single unusually high reading at an extremely congested intersection. The ozone calculations were based on a solitary reading from a monitor that had probably malfunctioned.[59] New monitoring data requested by the court showed that these readings were far too high. According to the new figures, reducing new-car emissions by 90 percent would solve the carbon monoxide problem almost everywhere in Boston. The new information also showed that the EPA had exaggerated the amount of emission reduction needed to achieve the ozone primary standard.[60]

The First Circuit upheld the EPA's legal authority to issue TCPs but remanded the plan to the EPA for better technical justification. Most officials in the regional offices breathed a sigh of relief. The litigation had impressed upon them the folly of relying on air quality arguments to justify highly unpopular federal transportation control measures. Even those who had previously pushed for rigorous enforcement urged Washington to pull back from its TCP policy. Region I, formerly the most aggressive of the regional offices, now tried to convince Washington to abandon the pretense that all TCPs must achieve national standards

59. *South Terminal Corp.* v. *EPA* at 663–67.

60. Memorandum, Alexander Kovel (Region I) to files, "Outline of Analysis of TCP Methodology," September 11, 1974.

by 1977.[61] In arguing their case the revisionists in Region I were aided by the EPA's loss in *Texas* v. *EPA*. In that case the Fifth Circuit also upheld the EPA's legal authority to promulgate TCPs, but remanded much of its control strategy for lack of adequate technical support.[62]

Region I's efforts encountered stiff resistance in Washington. Region I argued that long distance transport of ozone makes city-by-city control strategies unworkable. The transportation office replied that while such transport might occur, giving public credence to this yet unproven possibility would undermine the EPA's transportation planning effort. The OGC contended that the courts would not allow the EPA to issue "nonattainment" plans. The struggle between these two offices and Region I became increasingly bitter. Finally, Administrator Train, apparently impressed by Region I's technical arguments and concerned about the continuing public and congressional opposition to TCPs, approved the regional office plan. The new Boston TCP dropped all mandatory traffic and parking regulations, relied on additional stationary source controls and voluntary mobile source cutbacks, admitted that much of the city's mobile source pollution comes from outside the metropolitan area, and failed to guarantee attainment of the ozone standards by 1977.[63] The coordinator of TCP development in the Office of Transportation and Land Use Planning, correctly interpreting the significance of Train's approval of the new Boston plan, resigned in protest.

The EPA spent the next year developing a new TCP strategy based on the Boston model. The policy it announced in 1976 bore a striking resemblance to that proposed by the OAQPS in early 1974. There were, in fact, only two differences: the EPA stopped short of saying it would *never* require the states to implement transportation control measures, and it reiterated its support for mandatory inspection and maintenance.[64] The EPA had abandoned its attempts to force major cities to restructure their transportation systems.

61. Action memorandum, John McGlennon (administrator, Region I) to the administrator, "Critical Issues on Transportation Control Plans," January 30, 1975; letter, Roger Strelow (assistant administrator) to regional administrators, "Boston Transportation Control Plan Meeting," May 28, 1975.

62. *Texas* v. *EPA* at 321.

63. 40 Fed. Reg. 25152 (1975).

64. Letter, Roger Strelow to regional administrators, "Guidance for Determining Acceptability of SIP Regulations in Non-attainment Areas," December 9, 1976.

The *South Terminal* and *Texas* decisions played a key role in the shift of power within the EPA from those advocating TCPs to those who viewed them with skepticism. The courts educated the lawyers and political executives in the EPA about the dangers of which the technocrats had warned. But of course other courts had made this slow and painful education necessary by helping to remove the engineers from decision-making in the first place. Interestingly, the NRDC and other environmental groups did not challenge the EPA's new policy. They too had been chastened. Moreover, they had moved on to other projects, including efforts to impose inspection and maintenance on the states and to enforce New York's unique TCP. Subsequent court decisions blunted attempts to implement these control measures as well.

The Collapse of Enforcement

Behind the legal argument comparing highways to stationary sources of pollution lay the OGC's assumption that the federal courts would, when called upon, issue detailed injunctions to state officials and monitor their compliance with TCP requirements. EPA lawyers made an analogy between TCPs and desegregation plans. In fact, when one regional official asked a headquarters attorney how the EPA could force cities to buy buses, the attorney replied that federal courts had ordered cities to buy buses to transport school children to integrated schools and would do so again to provide mass transit for commuters. But the courts did not view meeting ozone standards as quite so compelling a cause as achieving racial integration. Their refusal to help the EPA dictate to the states undermined the EPA's remaining efforts to enforce its TCPs.

THE CIRCUIT COURTS BALK. The first court to consider the issue of whether the EPA could issue section 113 orders to states to institute such measures as inspection and maintenance, mandatory bus lanes, and parking restrictions was the only court to side with the EPA. The Third Circuit found that since "the states have, by their transportation policies, contributed to the problem of air pollution from automobile emissions," state officials "can be required to take affirmative actions to correct it." But the court warned that "there may remain a legitimate concern for possible intrusion upon the proper functioning of our federalist system as a result of future developments in the implementation of the Clean

Air Act." It promised to "remain ready to protect that concern in any appropriate case."[65]

A year later the Ninth Circuit, seldom sympathetic to EPA causes, ruled that while the agency could instruct the states to stop polluting, it could not order them to prevent private citizens from polluting. The court saw a crucial difference between the state's ownership of commercial property and its regulation of private parties:

> To make *governance* indistinguishable from *commerce* for the purposes of the Commerce Power cannot be equated to the "unintrusive" regulation of economic activities of the states upheld by the Supreme Court. . . . A Commerce Power so expanded would reduce the states to puppets of a ventriloquist Congress. We will not attribute to Congress any such intent unless it is expressed unequivocally. As we have already pointed out, that was not done in the Clean Air Act.

The circuit court took particular offense at the EPA's claim that the states' failure to comply with its regulations would justify the imposition of such sanctions as

> injunctive relief, imposing a receivership on certain state functions, holding a state official in civil contempt with a substantial daily fine until compliance is secured, and requiring a state to allocate funds from one portion of its budget to another in order to finance the undertakings required by the Agency.[66]

While the circuit court rested its initial decision on statutory interpretation, it later indicated that Congress did not have constitutional authority to specify how a state must regulate its citizens.[67]

Even the D.C. Circuit, the EPA's strongest ally in the federal judiciary, failed to provide it with the enforcement authority it most needed. The court ruled that the EPA could order the states to install bus lanes or to expand their bus fleets and could even prohibit certain motor vehicles from using public roadways. But it said that the act does not authorize the EPA to control "pollution caused by the general public by requiring the states to enact statutes and to administer and enforce the programs contained in the EPA plan." In particular, the court said, the EPA cannot force states to adopt legislation setting up mandatory inspection and maintenance. Such authority would, in effect, convert "state legislatures

65. *Commonwealth of Pennsylvania* v. *Environmental Protection Agency*, 500 F.2d 246 at 261, 263 (3d Cir. 1974).

66. *Brown* v. *EPA* at 839, 831.

67. *Brown* v. *Environmental Protection Agency*, 566 F.2d 665 (9th Cir. 1977).

into arms of the EPA." Nor can it issue orders to state motor vehicle bureaucracies in an attempt to "commandeer the regulatory powers of the states, along with their personnel and resources, for use in administering and enforcing a regulatory program against the owners of motor vehicles."[68]

This was an especially serious loss for the EPA, since it had recently abandoned its efforts to enforce traffic controls and had decided to focus instead on inspection and maintenance. Acknowledging that the court rulings would "virtually paralyze" its efforts to implement inspection and maintenance, the EPA asked the Department of Justice to appeal the decisions to the Supreme Court.[69] The Justice Department expressed serious doubts about the constitutionality of the EPA's claims and forced it to drop its demand that state legislatures adopt specified legislation. This concession, coupled with the EPA's withdrawal of many of its TCP strategies, allowed the Supreme Court to avoid the difficult constitutional issues raised by the case. Noting that the case had "undergone a great deal of shrinkage," the Court ruled the case moot.[70] Thus, by 1977, four years after promulgation of its TCPs, the EPA's enforcement authority remained in limbo.

SOUND AND FURY IN NEW YORK. The EPA lawyers who had first proposed the "highway as source" enforcement strategy blamed their loss on the Department of Justice and claimed that their enforcement strategy would have succeeded if only the EPA had been able to convince the appellate courts.[71] The strange history of the New York City TCP calls the latter assumption into question. The long and tortuous litigation over that plan shows that even when constitutional and statutory bars to enforcement do not appear, federal district courts will avoid entangling themselves in the administration of transportation controls.

In the early 1970s New York City was the only major city in the country with a fully approved state-authored TCP. Shortly before they left office, Governor Nelson A. Rockefeller and Mayor John V. Lindsay approved an ambitious TCP for the city that included mandatory inspection and maintenance, reductions in parking spaces in Manhattan,

68. *District of Columbia* v. *Train,* 521 F.2d 971 at 983, 984, and 992 (D.C. Cir. 1975).

69. 6 *Environment Reporter—Current Developments* 1226.

70. *Environmental Protection Agency* v. *Brown,* 431 U.S. 99 at 103 (1977). Meanwhile the EPA had lost another case in the Fourth Circuit, *Maryland* v. *Environmental Protection Agency,* 530 F.2d 215 (4th Cir. 1975).

71. 8 *Environment Reporter—Current Developments* 45.

expanded use of bus lanes, staggered work hours, selective bans on taxi cruising, and even a contingency plan to bar all traffic from Manhattan's business districts. State and local air pollution officials had written this plan without consulting local transportation authorities. After the EPA approved the plan, the Second Circuit upheld it against a challenge by the Friends of the Earth, who claimed it was too weak.[72]

For over two years the city did nothing to implement its plan. Mayor Abraham Beame and Governor Malcolm Wilson both opposed the plan and refused to carry it out. In 1976 the NRDC asked the federal district court in New York to force the state and the city to put their plan into effect.

New York's legal defense was amazingly weak. According to the district court, the state's attorney

> stated in open court that he had a great deal of difficulty with his clients' arguments. He found that "this plan is a legally enforceable plan, is a legally adequate plan, and that the State is committed to fulfilling its responsibilities thereunder." He went on to say, however, that the State apparently has no intention of implementing certain strategies of the plan and observed, "If there is a valid legal ground for such a refusal, we have not been able to find it, your honor."

Yet Judge Kevin Duffy declined to issue an injunction. Noting that the EPA was negotiating with the state and city on this matter, he concluded:

> In this case discretion dictates that the preliminary injunction not issue because there is, on the one hand, a total lack of expertise in the court and, on the other, the existence of a federal agency of such expertise charged with the enforcement of the highly technical and difficult problems involved.

The judge indicated that the principles of equity condoned this "policy favoring judicial restraint."[73]

The Second Circuit disagreed. It said Congress intended citizen suits "to stir slumbering agencies and to circumvent bureaucratic inaction that interferes with the scheduled satisfaction of the federal air quality goals."[74] The circuit court ordered Judge Duffy to give prompt attention to the case and to enter partial summary judgment for the plaintiff.

Judge Duffy established a compliance schedule for the city. Soon thereafter, however, he granted the city's request for a hearing to argue the constitutional issues raised in the circuit court cases described above.

---

72. *Friends of the Earth* v. *Environmental Protection Agency,* 499 F.2d 1118 (2d Cir. 1974).

73. *Friends of the Earth* v. *Wilson,* 389 F. Supp. 1394 at 1395 (S.D.N.Y. 1974).

74. *Friends of the Earth* v. *Carey,* 535 F.2d 165 at 173 (2d Cir. 1976).

Upon hearing these arguments Duffy revoked his order and ruled that the federal government cannot force the states to implement a TCP.[75] This spurred the Second Circuit again to overrule the district court judge. It found that the state had waived its rights to raise these constitutional claims when it submitted its TCP to the EPA in 1973.[76] It was now 1977, and no part of the TCP was yet in effect.

The third time Judge Duffy heard the suit brought by the NRDC and the Friends of the Earth with the cooperation of the EPA, he ordered the city and the state to install toll booths on thirteen bridges leading into Manhattan, limit downtown cruising by taxicabs, and reduce parking spaces in Manhattan. While the taxi companies agreed to abide by their part of the order, the toll and parking provisions proved harder nuts to crack. After several hearings, the judge gave the state until August 1978 to start collecting tolls. But with the New York congressional delegation sponsoring legislation to eliminate this requirement, Governor Hugh Carey stalled. The issue eventually became moot when the 1977 amendments allowed New York to remove the toll booth requirement.[77]

Rather than issue a specific order on parking reductions, Judge Duffy gave the EPA and the city time to reach agreement on the number and location of spaces to eliminate. The eventual parking compromise, ratified by the court, removed only 134 parking spaces—far fewer than required by the 1973 TCP. Both the EPA and NRDC hoped that this would at least get the city moving in the right direction. Thus after four years of litigation the EPA and environmental groups won what the NRDC presented as a major court victory—the removal of a few parking spaces and reduced taxi cruising. Both these measures required continued policing by the city.

Judge Duffy's reluctance to intervene in this case is typical of the reaction of district court judges faced with complex and controversial questions of relief in environmental cases. Only the commitment of the Second Circuit—one of the most pro-environmental circuits in the country—kept the case in court at all. And the district court had not really gotten to the hard part yet. What could the court have done if the state had refused to build toll booths? What can it do in the future if the city refuses to issue parking tickets for violation of court-ordered

---

75. *Friends of the Earth* v. *Carey*, 422 F. Supp. 638 (S.D.N.Y. 1976).

76. *Friends of the Earth* v. *Carey*, 552 F.2d 25 (2d Cir. 1977).

77. Sec. 110(c)(5)(A). Five years later this amendment itself became the center of legal dispute. See *Council of Commuter Organizations* v. *Gorsuch*, 17 *Environment Reporter Cases* 1897 (2d Cir. 1982).

parking restrictions? Antipathy toward the federal government ran so strong at times in New York that local officials declared they would welcome contempt citations—nothing would aid their reelection bids more. The willingness of state legislators to ignore federal court orders was illustrated again in 1982 when the Pennsylvania legislature refused to provide funds for an inspection and maintenance program that was part of a court order.[78] In short, the more deeply involved courts become in enforcing TCPs, the more they too become dependent on state cooperation.

In retrospect, the attempt of the EPA to rely on the courts to enforce TCPs was doomed from the beginning. SIP regulations written by the states for private stationary sources are relatively simple and noncontroversial compared to TCPs. But, as chapter 7 indicated, even for these sources court-based enforcement is slow and extremely resource-intensive. It took nine years for the EPA to force West Penn Power to begin installing a scrubber at one facility. How long would it take the agency to force New York or Los Angeles to restructure their entire transportation network by threatening them with court action? The attorneys who pushed TCPs and who designed the EPA's enforcement strategy, while perhaps in tune with the sentiments of the D.C. Circuit, showed remarkable lack of understanding of other circuits and district courts or of the process by which the states and lower levels of the federal bureaucracy bring polluters into compliance with the act. The EPA's legalistic orientation on the TCP issue did not serve it well when it reached the final, crucial stages of the legal process.

The Second Time Around

By early 1977 the TCPs promulgated in 1973, including their inspection and maintenance provisions, were dead letters. The *New York Times* quoted Deputy Administrator John Quarles as saying that the courts

78. The Pennsylvania case is similar to New York in that the state (in the form of the governor and the Department of Transportation) agreed to institute control programs (in this case, inspection and maintenance). The legislature refused to go along, and the state kept asking for more time. In 1982, after more than seven years of litigation, the district court judge found that the state had violated its consent decree with the EPA. Rather than order the state to establish an inspection and maintenance program, the judge ordered the federal Department of Transportation to withhold highway funds from the state until it complies with the consent decree. This was a clever move that allowed the court to avoid complex remedies. Whether it will work remains to be seen. These events are summarized in the Third Circuit's opinion upholding the lower court. *Delaware Valley Citizens' Council v. Pennsylvania*, 17 *Environment Reporter Cases* 1151 (3d Cir. 1982).

had dealt a "crippling blow" to the program and that "even a court-ordered plan has little chance of success" in light of the "understandable hostility" of local officials to the plans.[79] The EPA prepared to start all over again under the 1977 amendments. This time it hoped to convince the states to write and enforce their own plans. While the amendments gave the EPA more time and a few more incentives, in many ways the situation was the same as during the early months of 1973.

Both the House and Senate committees conceded that the costs TCPs impose on urban citizens often do not justify their benefits. The 1977 House report declared that the plans were "impractical within the time frame permitted under the current [1970] Act. Some of the measures may never be practicable." The Senate committee admitted that the plans "imposed vast economic and social costs, for relatively small improvement in the quality of the environment."[80]

Instead of specifying which control measures it considered worthwhile, Congress simply extended the act's deadlines. This saved the technology-forcing strategy of the act while appeasing those who objected to the EPA's proposed TCPs. It also ensured that once again the EPA would be faced with the problem of deciding how hard to push the states and that in a few years Congress itself would again have to extend the deadline of the statute.

The 1977 amendments allowed the states to receive extensions of the deadline for attaining mobile source pollutant standards until 1982, provided they submitted by 1979 a plan that (a) established a permit system for stationary sources of carbon monoxide and hydrocarbons, (b) provided for the implementation of all "reasonably available control measures" as expeditiously as possible, and (c) achieved "reasonable further progress" in the interim. Areas unable to meet the national standards by 1982 were eligible for a second five-year extension. But to receive this second extension states had to adopt a specific schedule for adopting and administering an inspection and maintenance program to begin operation in 1982. Surprisingly, the amendments state that almost all the measures included in previous TCPs (with the exception of rationing, retrofitting, and limits on offstreet parking) constitute "reasonably available" controls. States are still obligated to meet the 1987 deadline using whatever controls are necessary.[81]

79. *New York Times*, January 14, 1977, p. 1.

80. *Clean Air Act Amendments of 1977*, H. Rept. 95-294, pp. 228–29; *Clean Air Amendments of 1977*, S. Rept. 95-127 (GPO, 1977), p. 14.

81. Secs. 110(c) and 171–77.

At the same time, the 1977 amendments increased the carrots and sticks at the EPA's disposal. States that did not submit an adequate plan by July 1, 1979, or did not implement the programs in their plans face the loss of federal funds for air pollution control, sewage treatment facilities, and highway construction. More important, the amendments bar the construction of new stationary sources in areas for which there is no approved mobile source control plan. Even federal promulgation of substitute plans will not lift these sanctions; only state cooperation with the EPA can do that. Congress also appropriated funds for local and regional planning agencies in nonattainment areas, required the EPA and the states to coordinate their efforts with local planning officials, and instructed the Department of Transportation to approve funds for only those transportation projects consistent with meeting the national standards.

Even with these new regulatory tools and with the appointment of former NRDC lawyer David Hawkins as assistant administrator, the EPA gave transportation control measures low priority. The agency mounted a major offensive to convince the states to institute inspection and maintenance programs and succeeded in most major urban areas. It also took steps to reduce hydrocarbon emissions from stationary sources. But the EPA has made it clear that it will not repeat the mistake of promulgating its own TCPs. It has not required the states to employ such measures as bus lanes, parking restrictions, and auto-free zones. Although the amendments require the states to implement "reasonably available" controls by 1982, the EPA's regulations insist only that the states establish by 1982 a scheme for *choosing* which controls to implement. The amendments require states requesting extensions to include in their 1979 submittals schedules for the improvement of mass transit, but the EPA asked only that the submittal include a schedule for the *analysis* of such improvements. Rather than requiring state legislatures to approve fully enforceable inspection and maintenance programs, the EPA has allowed states to avoid sanctions by passing vague legislation setting up pilot programs.[82] The 1979 submittal became, in the words of EPA transportation office officials, "a plan for a plan."

In its efforts to avoid antagonizing the states the EPA has imposed sanctions on only those states that have repeatedly refused to cooperate. Although almost every state in the nation missed the 1979 deadline for submitting SIPs, the EPA disciplined only two, California and Kentucky,

82. 44 Fed. Reg. 20372 (1979); and EPA, Office of Transportation and Land Use Planning, "Transportation and Air Quality" (EPA, July 1981), app. B.

which had adamantly refused to endorse inspection and maintenance.[83] It granted conditional approvals to all states making good-faith efforts to complete their plans. Assistant Administrator Hawkins explained that large-scale application of sanctions could have "disastrous effects" and that the EPA prefers the sanctions to become a "historical footnote." One reason for the EPA's restraint was the recognition that Congress would respond to application of the sanctions with further amendments to the act. By mid-1979 120 House members had cosponsored a bill to extend the deadline for plan submittal. By 1982 the question before Congress was not whether to extend the deadlines, but whether to eliminate them altogether. Interestingly, while environmental groups opposed efforts to eliminate the deadlines, most promised not to challenge the conditional approval policy in court.[84]

Thus the court decisions on TCPs produced neither cleaner air nor a statute that makes realistic demands on the EPA and the states. While the experiences of the 1970s taught the EPA and even environmental groups important lessons about the limits of the EPA's power and the futility of trying to justify draconian transportation restrictions on the basis of air quality, the Clean Air Act does not yet reflect this learning process. Only further legislation can bring the EPA's policy in line with the law.

Legislative Histories and Political Coalitions

The EPA's efforts to impose restrictions on the use of private automobiles and on the construction of indirect sources were a complete and costly failure. Die-hard advocates of transportation controls still argue that although these programs produced few concrete results, they at least put the issue on the political agenda. While it is true that TCPs and ISR attracted considerable attention in the early and mid-1970s, the events of that period did far more to discredit the programs than to legitimate them.

---

83. 10 *Environment Reporter—Current Developments* 923; and National Commission on Air Quality, *To Breathe Clean Air* (GPO, 1981), pp. 3.4-9 to 3.4-16.

84. 9 *Environment Reporter—Current Developments* 1351; 10 *Environment Reporter—Current Developments* 923. Environmental groups may have changed their position since the arrival of the Reagan administration. See testimony of Robert Yuhnke (Environmental Defense Fund), *Clean Air Act,* Hearings before the Subcommittee on Health and the Environment of the House Committee on Energy and Commerce, 97 Cong. 1 sess. (GPO, 1981), pp. 92–125.

Some commentators view the failure of the EPA's efforts as evidence of the American political system's inability to control social forces and to act forcefully to reduce threats to the environment and the public health.[85] Yet the air quality gains associated with transportation controls are so small that it makes far more sense to use the history of the EPA's programs as an example of the ability of a pluralistic political system to resist the imposition of unreasonable bureaucratic rules. If some of the control strategies the EPA proposed are worth the burden they impose on the American people, it is not because they reduce air pollution. Their justification lies in the many other benefits of reduced reliance on private automobiles.

Those in Congress who created and defended the "land-use and transportation controls" section of the act tried to use this language to win indirectly battles they had previously lost in direct political confrontations. TCP advocates on Capitol Hill concentrated their efforts on putting into the law little-noted clauses with drastic implications, supplementing these phrases with statements designed to produce a legislative history, and blocking attempts to amend the law. They did not try to explain the possible consequences of their proposals or to build congressional support for them. Agency officials and environmental groups defended their programs against strong political opposition not by explaining their merits but by claiming "that's the law." But "the law" did not supply the political support, the technical competence, or the administrative apparatus necessary to put such massive programs into operation.

The courts' action-forcing decisions played a key role in the history of transportation controls by transmitting the commands of the congressional advocates of TCPs to an agency that originally was astute enough to move cautiously in this area. Knowing that the courts will play this role encourages congressional insiders to address their actions to the courts, not to the rest of Congress or to the public. Such court action also increases the power within the EPA of lawyers who lack an understanding of the administrative, technical, and political constraints on agency action. The courts thus form the critical link between congressional committee members and their eager staffs, on the one hand, and, on the other, those within the agency willing to take risks for which they can evade responsibility.

85. See, for example, Richard Walsh and Michael Storper, "Erosion of the Clean Air Act of 1970: A Study in the Failure of Government Regulation and Planning," 7 *Environmental Affairs* 189 (1978).

One frequently hears the claim that action-forcing court decisions impel Congress to include in legislation only those projects it will stand behind. But the example of transportation controls suggests that nondiscretionary duty suits did not force Congress to become more disciplined in setting goals commensurate with the means it condones. With so many safety valves in the political process, Congress can still avoid making hard choices. These safety valves include the agency's use of enforcement discretion; slippage in the administrative process at the state level; court action such as that in the *South Terminal, Texas,* and states' rights cases; and statutory extensions of deadlines. No one now takes the deadlines and the demands of the 1977 amendments seriously. The law itself will become relevant once again only if environmental groups choose to use it as a weapon.

The courts have the option of refusing to play the middleman between congressional and agency advocates of programs without political support. They can simply refuse to hear cases in which plaintiffs without traditional standing ask the courts to initiate new programs disliked by agency officials. This would permit agencies to allocate their scarce resources—especially political capital—to those programs they view as most productive. If Congress is dissatisfied, it can communicate this directly to the agency in oversight and confirmation hearings, in the authorization and appropriations process, and in its rewriting of the law. Agencies are hardly immune from such political pressure. The greater the support for the program within Congress, the more costly resistance becomes for the agency. Thus the withdrawal of the courts would not leave agencies uncontrolled, but would encourage congressional advocates of administrative programs to build legislative coalitions instead of legislative histories.

CHAPTER TEN

Judicial Capacity and the Regulatory Process

No ONE who studies the evolution of air pollution regulation in this country can deny that the courts have played an important role in shaping environmental policy. In cases on enforcement and standard setting, significant deterioration and transportation controls, variances and dispersion enhancement, the federal courts have neither timidly deferred to administrators nor served as obedient intermediaries for Congress. These cases vividly illustrate the efforts of proponents of the "new administrative law" to reform the regulatory process. The courts' apparent success in improving the performance of the Environmental Protection Agency—proclaimed by a variety of jurists, scholars, and congressmen—has added luster to the reputation of the new administrative law.

This book has called into question the conventional wisdom on the effect of these court decisions on pollution control policy. Looking beyond formal court records and the avowed purposes of judicial action, one discovers a multitude of unintended and undesirable consequences of court action. Just as studies of policy implementation by bureaucracies have revealed the difficulties administrators have in turning statutory mandates into concerted action, analysis of the implementation of court decisions shows that judges frequently issue commands ignored or modified by others, pursue inconsistent policies, and generally "muddle through." Ironically, while the new administrative law was in part a response to academic critiques of bureaucratic policymaking, the courts' attempt to alleviate the shortcomings of administrative agencies has attracted a spotlight revealing similar defects in judicial decisionmaking.

Identifying the long-term consequences of court decisions does not complete the task of evaluating the institutional capacity of the courts, but only exposes its complexity. The courts have not in any simple way corrected administrative policy. But in only one case (variances) was court action counterproductive. Partisans continue to debate the merits of the EPA's program for prevention of significant deterioration (PSD), its guidelines on stack height, its ozone and lead standards, its enforcement record, and its mobile source pollution control strategies. To use a distinction introduced in chapter 1, these are all questions of *policymaking*, which cannot be reduced to *problem solving*. The difficulty one has in labeling individual court decisions right or wrong shows that when the courts enter what Justice Frankfurter called "the political thicket," evaluation of their rulings becomes a political undertaking.

This chapter approaches the task of evaluating the performance and capacity of the courts by looking not at each individual "case and controversy" but at how court decisions taken as a whole have influenced environmental regulation. This broader perspective allows one to examine the coherence of the policies advocated by the courts and to ask whether the courts have helped administrators to design programs that achieve at the lowest possible cost the objectives established by elected officials after enlightened discussion. This perspective is compatible with that of the new administrative law, which seeks to counteract the parochialism of specialists, encourage public debates over regulatory issues, and increase the accountability of unelected bureaucrats to elected representatives.

Taken as a whole, the consequences of court action under the Clean Air Act are neither random nor beneficial. The courts have pushed the EPA in two directions at once, extending the scope of its programs while diminishing its already inadequate resources for achieving publicly proclaimed objectives. Court action has encouraged legislators and administrators to establish goals without considering how they can be achieved, exacerbating the tendency of these institutions to promise far more than they can deliver. The policymaking system of which the federal courts are now an integral part has produced serious inefficiency and inequities, has made rational debate and conscious political choice difficult, and has added to frustration and cynicism among participants of all stripes.

The institutional structure of the federal judiciary contributed directly to this result. Enforcement cases and challenges to rules of general applicability go to different courts. Business firms subject to pollution regulation have devoted their efforts to enforcement cases and have succeeded in convincing judges to restrain the EPA from imposing "unreasonable" costs on industry. Environmentalists have put their resources into expanding regulatory programs and strengthening air quality standards. They have brought their cases to the D.C. Circuit and other courts sympathetic to the argument that the EPA must be prevented from bowing to industry influence. The narrow focus of the adjudicatory process has allowed courts hearing enforcement cases to ignore their effect on air quality and courts hearing cases on general policy to ignore questions of cost and feasibility. Decentralization has prevented the courts from taking a more unified view of the regulatory process and the public interest.

Policy Consequences and Institutional Characteristics

Chapter 1 identified four traits that distinguish courts from the agencies whose actions they review in administrative law cases:

1. Courts provide a ready alternative route of *access* to those who are excluded from agency decisionmaking or unhappy with agency policies.

2. Courts rely on the highly structured *adjudicatory process* rather than their own staff to produce evidence and analysis.

3. The federal court system is more *decentralized* than most bureaucracies.

4. As generalists with lifetime tenure, judges remain *independent* of the administrative responsibilities and political pressures that bear down on those in other branches of government.

The following review of this book's six case studies examines the link between these institutional characteristics and the policy consequences of court decisions discovered in preceding chapters. It will then be possible to show how these characteristics contributed to the dualism that permeates air pollution policy—the divorce between goal setting and enforcement.

Prevention of Significant Deterioration

Judge Pratt's 1972 *Sierra Club* v. *Ruckelshaus* decision was the most important decision issued under the Clean Air Act. Without it there would be no PSD program today. In 1970 Congress provided the EPA with two methods for distinguishing "significant" from "insignificant" deterioration of air quality: national ambient air quality standards and new source performance standards. The EPA had more than enough to do in administering these sections of the act and preferred to concentrate on programs that protected "people, not prairie dogs" (in the words of William Ruckelshaus). The Sierra Club, in contrast, worried that the imposition of uniform national air quality and emission standards would push polluters into presently undeveloped regions, especially the pristine areas surrounding the Rocky Mountains. The club made up for the thinness of its legal argument by persuading almost twenty state attorneys general to lend their support to the cause.

Neither Judge Pratt nor the two appellate courts that upheld his decision explained to the EPA what "significant deterioration" means. In effect, the court instructed the EPA to respond to the Sierra Club's concerns without insisting upon any particular pollution control strategy. Yet the decision was more than a blank check written to the EPA. It influenced policymaking in two subtle but crucial ways. First, the wording of the opinion led the EPA to choose an "ambient increment" control strategy, even though the major alternative, one based directly on emission, is far simpler and deals more directly with the problem of atmospheric loading. The EPA embraced this incredibly complex and poorly understood scheme because its lawyers decided it was more likely to survive subsequent judicial review.

Second, by initiating a program that would go into effect unless vetoed by Congress, the courts gave a decisive strategic advantage to congressional advocates of PSD. Western senators proved capable of blocking amendments to the act, but not of passing legislation to overturn the court action. Moreover, key committee leaders—especially Senator Edmund S. Muskie and Representative Paul G. Rogers—would not allow any set of amendments lacking a strong PSD program to go to the floor. With westerners demanding revisions to the EPA's plan and with a variety of industries clamoring for changes in other sections of the act, Muskie and Rogers adeptly traded concessions on the section of the program most obnoxious to western states for additional provisions extending the scope of federal regulation. The convoluted nature of the ambient increment scheme hid important implications of these additions not just from PSD opponents, but from the EPA and committee staff as well.

The PSD program that finally emerged from the lengthy *Alabama Power* litigation in 1979 has limited pollution increases in the Rockies, protected visibility in national parks, and stimulated the development of sulfur dioxide control technology. But PSD has also added significantly to pollution control costs, retarded the substitution of low-sulfur western coal for high-sulfur eastern coal, and slowed the replacement of relatively dirty existing plants with cleaner new facilities. Moreover, the continuing controversy over PSD and the complexity of the program have forced the EPA to devote a large proportion of its scarce administrative and political resources to this program. With opposition to PSD mounting in the White House and among businessmen, it is not surprising that even some devoted environmentalists are willing to jettison large parts of the program.

To say that the *Sierra Club* decision provided that organization with access to policymaking is an understatement. The club argued its case before the agency and lost; it argued before the court and won. In this case "providing access" really meant "deciding who won and who lost." Of course, it is important to note that the winners here were not environmentalists per se, but only those environmentalists whose primary concern is wilderness preservation.

Not all the parties who prevailed in the original case were pleased with its result. The support of those states that claimed that PSD would end "economic blackmail" proved to be little more than a mirage. Few of the attorneys general who wrote *amicus* briefs had consulted with state air agencies (who shared the EPA's original skepticism) or elected state officials (who resented federal restrictions on their ability to attract taxpaying industry). In recent years PSD has drawn support not from clean air states eager to protect their environment, but from heavily polluted states trying to hang on to existing industry. This indicates that judges cannot always rely on the parties before them to explain fully and accurately the interests of the groups they claim to represent. Recognizing who represents whom requires substantial familiarity with the policy issues under consideration.

The adjudicatory process clearly failed to provide the court with an adequate understanding of PSD. The policy arguments of the litigants and the courts were as rudimentary as their arguments on legislative intent were misleading. The tendency to base highly significant policy decisions on tenuous analysis of legislative intent appeared not just in the hastily argued *Sierra Club* case, but even in the massive *Alabama*

Power case. Moreover, to the extent that adjudication addressed policy issues at all, it focused entirely on identifying problems rather than reviewing possible solutions. The court apparently determined that atmospheric loading and degradation of air quality in pristine western areas were serious problems and ordered the EPA to find a solution. It never reviewed the alternative control strategies or recognized that each solution defined the problem somewhat differently. Nor did it realize that a solution to the problem identified by the Sierra Club could exacerbate the problem of urban pollution.

Supporters of the PSD decisions have argued that only the courts' independence from administrative routine and political pressure allowed them to appreciate the importance of wilderness preservation. They claimed that the EPA was too engrossed in other duties to consider the importance of this goal, and that Congress is too susceptible to interest group pressures to endorse a program imposing large costs on one section of the country. Only the courts could make this tough decision that future generations would applaud. It is important to note, however, that the courts' independence from bureaucratic responsibilities brought with it a lack of concern for administrative feasibility: PSD is one of the federal government's most convoluted regulatory programs. Similarly, independence from political pressure led the courts to underestimate— or perhaps to dismiss cavalierly—the substantial costs, environmental as well as economic, imposed by this immense program.

Dispersion Enhancement

In the winter of 1973–74, as the energy crisis worsened, the EPA found itself caught between two warring forces: on one side were the White House, the Federal Energy Administration (FEA), and the utilities, who demanded that the EPA find ways to permit the burning of coal and high-sulfur oil; on the other side were environmentalists and their congressional allies, who insisted that the EPA force facilities emitting large amounts of sulfur dioxide to install scrubbers despite the economic or energy costs. This controversy focused on the use of two dispersion enhancement techniques, commonly known as intermittent control systems (ICS) and tall stacks. Its resolution came from an unexpected source: the Court of Appeals for the Fifth Circuit. The court ruled that the 1970 act does not allow polluters to substitute dispersion enhancement for available emission reduction control technology.

The EPA soon decided it agreed with the ruling and declined to appeal this section of the Fifth Circuit decision to the Supreme Court. With other courts following the lead of the Fifth Circuit and with the Muskie and Rogers subcommittees refusing to consider amendments to the act, the FEA and the utilities had no choice but to compromise. This compromise, eventually included in the 1977 amendments, prohibited almost all use of ICS. On this front the EPA had used the court decision to get almost everything it wanted.

Yet this was not the end of the dispersion story. It took the EPA almost eight years to formulate stack height rules that satisfied the courts and Congress. In effect the court told the EPA to prohibit the use of tall stacks, but failed to explain how a tall stack differs from a normal one. A literal reading of the decision would have required the EPA to classify *all* stacks as tall. To avoid this extreme, the EPA reinstated the "good engineering practice" rule previously rejected by the courts. When the Natural Resources Defense Council (NRDC) threatened the EPA with contempt, agency lawyers and political executives placed more specific limits on stack height. The guidelines finally approved by the court contained a confusing array of rules and exceptions aimed more at hiding the EPA's misrepresentations to the courts than at formulating an effective, equitable solution to the dispersion issue. The 1977 amendments required the EPA to make substantial revisions in these regulations. It took the agency five years to do so. And now, once again, they are being challenged in court.

The efforts of the courts, Congress, and the EPA to resolve the stack height controversy have continued to flounder because each has tried to use simple engineering formulas to resolve a major deficiency in the structure of the Clean Air Act. By focusing on local ambient air quality, the act ignores the problem of long distance transport of pollution. Limits on dispersion constitute backdoor methods for coping with the latter. But all definitions of the proper stack height are either too vague or too arbitrary to justify the highly significant pollution control policies they produce. It is not surprising that this roundabout method of restructuring the act has itself invited circumvention and has failed to satisfy most of the parties involved.

As was the case in the *Sierra Club* litigation, the court decision on dispersion provided environmental groups—in this case the NRDC—with access to decisionmaking and simultaneously diminished the influence of the White House and the FEA. The fact that the EPA openly broke with the administration on both ICS and PSD led some to suspect that the EPA had deliberately lost these cases to insulate itself from interagency review. While this was the effect of these decisions, there is no evidence that the EPA engaged in collusion or even foresaw this result. Indeed the NRDC firmly believed that the EPA was illegally ignoring the order of the Fifth Circuit. The NRDC's lawyers adeptly used the opinion of that court to force the EPA to recast its stack height guidelines. The aftermath of the NRDC decision illustrates how a victory in court can enhance the bargaining power of an organization that previously had little influence.

The NRDC's bargaining power was based on the extreme nature of the Fifth Circuit's ruling, and this ruling was itself the result of the extreme nature of the Georgia state implementation plan (SIP). The NRDC chose to challenge this atypical SIP precisely because it permitted the complete substitution of dispersion enhancement for emission reduction. By chance this case, rather than one in which industry claimed the right to combine dispersion with emission reduction, came to court first. By focusing on this peculiar example, the adjudicatory process never forced judges to recognize that dispersion enhancement involved not a yes-or-no choice, but rather one of more or less. Having failed to explain this to the court on the first round (probably because at that time they did not fully understand it themselves), the EPA's attorneys refused to make the facts clear in subsequent litigation. Each litigant had an incentive to distort the issue, and the court, apparently tiring of the whole complex matter by 1976, proved unable to sort out the distortions.

Despite this, the courts' independence allowed them to focus the EPA's attention on a serious environmental problem (atmospheric loading) that threatened to become forgotten amid the chorus of demands for an immediate response to the energy crisis. Mounting evidence of the damage caused by acid rain makes the courts look farsighted indeed. Moreover, by taking the matter out of the hands of EPA engineers, the courts helped political executives in the agency see the policy significance of decisions that had previously been justified on narrow technical grounds. Generalists on the bench helped generalists in the agency get control over specialists nominally under the latter's control.

Paradoxically, the courts' political independence and concern for broad policy issues also led to a subtle form of timidity and myopia. While noting the atmospheric loading problem, the Fifth Circuit rested its decision on "legislative intent." It believed or hoped that its interpretation of one small part of the act would solve a problem of major significance—one which Congress itself had never addressed. For a court to construct a more systematic response to the shortcomings of the act would require both a fuller understanding of environmental issues and a willingness to state openly that Congress had erred. Lacking the confidence and extraordinary audaciousness this would require, the courts settled for a stopgap measure. Unfortunately, the appearance of this awkward temporary solution took the steam out of efforts to effect more adequate reforms, such as use of a sulfur dioxide emission tax or imposition of national emission standards. Only now, as the inadequacies of the existing regulatory scheme (as modified by the dispersion decisions) become obvious, have these approaches come out of political hibernation.

Variances

The variance decisions provide the only examples of counterproductive decisions studied in this book. Fearing that administrative leniency would undermine the Clean Air Act's rigid deadlines, several circuit courts prohibited the EPA from allowing states to grant polluters variances after 1975. The EPA first ignored these decisions and then announced ambiguous guidelines designed to appease the courts. These guidelines angered state enforcement officials, many of whom either cut back on their activities or stopped talking with the federal agency. The EPA responded by issuing new guidelines that reassured the states but flew in the face of the court orders. While the Supreme Court eventually reversed the decisions that had caused the EPA so much trouble, it could not repair the damage already done to state-federal relations.

To understand this sequence of events it is necessary to see why variances were an important part of state and federal enforcement efforts. Most state pollution control plans were thrown together hastily to meet the deadline of the act. Many states made their SIPs effective immediately and used variances to give polluters time to come into compliance. Others wrote stringent uniform control requirements, expecting to use variances to avoid closing down sources that did not contribute to air quality standard violations. Just as important, both the EPA and the states found it necessary to use enforcement orders—which differed from variances in name only—to negotiate deals with polluters. Given the arbitrariness of many state regulations, the number of sources out of compliance, the inexperience of the EPA's small enforcement staff, and the reluctance of judges to impose heavy penalties on violators, most polluters knew they could put off compliance for years. State and federal enforcement officials, realizing this as well, offered to extend compliance deadlines, to relax their interpretation of some rules, and even to revise some sections of state plans if sources would take specific steps to install available control technology. Stripped of authority to issue compliance orders giving effect to these agreements, the EPA and state agencies would have been forced either to resort to expensive, time-consuming litigation or to halt enforcement action against the worst polluters.

Why was it that no court—not even the Supreme Court, which sided with the EPA—recognized that variances formed the linchpin of state and federal enforcement efforts? The adjudicatory process failed to probe the inadequacies of the original SIPs, the weakness of state and federal enforcement programs, or the different ways in which the EPA and the states used variances. The original cases were argued and decided well before the EPA had had any experience enforcing the act. Neither the EPA's lawyers nor the NRDC anticipated what was to come. More disturbing still was the failure of the government's attorneys to explain the problem candidly to the Supreme Court in 1975. The EPA's Office of General Counsel and the Department of Justice, themselves far removed from the centers of enforcement, insisted upon arguing "the law" and declined to complicate their argument with a discussion of the fact of widespread noncompliance. Public admission that SIPs were vague, confused, and unreasonable or that the EPA lacked credible enforcement sanctions might further weaken enforcement. Neither the NRDC nor the business groups that intervened in the case saw any advantage in explaining these bleak facts to the Court.

Once again court decisions gave environmental groups greater access to EPA decisionmaking. The EPA's 1974 variance guidelines were the direct result of negotiations with the NRDC. But in the long run these guidelines served only to diminish the influence of environmentalists. Rather than granting fewer concessions to polluters, state officials merely made their concessions in a less formal manner. Consequently, their actions were less subject to scrutiny by environmentalists—and by the EPA. It is interesting to note that the NRDC at first approved of the EPA's rules on variances and only later chose to bring suit. They chose wrong.

Finally, the variance decisions call attention to the decentralized structure of the court system. Disagreements among the circuits kept the EPA's regulations on variances and revisions in limbo for well over two years and led to different treatment of polluters in different parts of the country. At the heart of the variance controversy lay an even more serious split between federal courts. The First Circuit justified its variance decision by claiming that unless it banned post-1975 variances, polluters seeking variances would tie up enforcement in the courts. To do this, of course, polluters would need sympathetic ears in the lower courts. In effect, the First Circuit and its followers intended to prevent district courts from causing such delay. The circuit courts' concern over district courts' commitment to meeting the deadlines of the act proved well founded. But their remedy was clearly inadequate. District courts refused to take the position that "sources of pollutants either should meet the standard of the law or be closed down." Recognizing this, the EPA and the states tried to write compliance schedules that trial courts and polluters would consider reasonable. Even then they had trouble with the lower courts. The variance decisions hampered the EPA without limiting the discretion of federal district courts.

Enforcement

Enforcement cases contrast sharply with the cases discussed above. Here the EPA faces industry lawyers, not environmentalists. District courts, not appellate courts, constitute the principal forum. Policy emerges from the accumulation of rulings on many small cases rather than from landmark decisions. And most important, the pattern of judicial action has been to weaken, not strengthen, environmental regulations.

The most dramatic evidence of this pattern is the Supreme Court decisions preventing regulators from enforcing work rules for hazardous pollutants and SIP requirements for federal facilities. Similarly, circuit court decisions on the feasibility issue prevented the EPA from enforcing emission limitations in the Midwest between 1973 and 1976. By far the most damaging blow to the EPA's enforcement effort, though, has come from the "balancing of equities" by district courts in individual enforcement proceedings. Attempting to discover reasonable solutions to local pollution problems, judges have scrutinized such factors as the financial health of the firm, the health consequences of pollution, the effectiveness of control technology, and even the neighborhood's reaction to sludge removal trucks before setting compliance schedules and imposing sanctions for past violations. The result has been lengthy litigation, lenient schedules, and few fines.

This use of equity power robs enforcement officials of what one such official has called the "shock value" of shutdown. It also gives recalcitrant polluters more time to comply with regulation, often resulting in inconsistent application of pollution control requirements. A close look at the administrative underpinnings of enforcement reveals even more serious consequences. When the EPA must present and defend alternatives to shutdown, litigation becomes extremely time consuming and expensive. Losing a case sets a bad precedent and encourages other polluters to ignore the EPA. To minimize its chance of loss, the agency must concentrate its litigational resources on a small number of cases. It thus has strong incentives to settle other cases before they reach trial. The resulting preference for settlement enhances the ability of polluters to extract from the agency lengthy compliance schedules, permission to use marginally effective control equipment, and formal SIP revisions. Of course, this advantage accrues primarily to polluters sophisticated enough to recognize the EPA's weak bargaining position and absorb the cost of litigation should it occur. Thus the courts' insistence on applying equitable remedies leads to less aggressive and less equitable applications of the law.

These judicial enforcement doctrines clearly increase individual firms' access to agency decisionmaking. The examples recounted in chapter 7 leave little doubt about the enhanced bargaining power of firms owning nonferrous smelters, coal-burning power plants, steel mills, and other problem sources. Conversely, by expanding the number of issues that can be debated, the courts have made it difficult for environmental groups to participate in enforcement cases. They have few experts on control technology, bond markets, or dispersion modeling. This helps explain why so few citizen suits have been brought against polluters.

The adjudicatory process brings to the attention of trial courts many of the issues—especially those relating to cost and feasibility—ignored by appellate courts in the NRDC and Sierra Club cases. District courts, in fact, have demonstrated a nearly limitless capacity to review the peculiar circumstances of individual facilities. The fact that courts have chosen to investigate cost and feasibility in this context, though, has important policy consequences. Here industry litigants far outnumber environmentalists. The interest of the citizens who breathe polluted air seems speculative and ephemeral when compared with the interest of local breadwinners who could lose their jobs, especially if the injured breathers live hundreds of miles downwind. Moreover, consideration of cost on a case-by-case basis rules out the possibility that a cleanup burden found unreasonable by a judge will be redistributed to other polluters. And finally, judges have not used the adjudicatory process to examine how this system affects the EPA's treatment of those thousands of cases that never come to court. Adjudication in this setting magnifies the benefits of leniency and ignores its costs.

It is the courts' decentralized structure that accommodates both their detailed review of the circumstances of each polluter and their inconsistent evaluation of the costs and benefits of regulation. It is only a slight exaggeration to say that trial judges and appellate judges see the entire regulatory world differently. The former not only directly observe the effect of imposing strict regulations, but share responsibility for imposing these burdens on local citizens. The latter, more removed from local concerns, better able to place responsibility for enforcement on others, and more likely to be inspired by statements about broad public goals, value uniformity more than flexibility. To the trial judge justice requires being responsive to the peculiar needs of individual citizens and localities. To the appellate judge it means consistent, unbending application of the laws and the intent of Congress. In their consideration of cases brought under the Clean Air Act the courts have combined responsiveness with accountability by invoking these two views sequentially.

Standard Setting

Federal courts have announced a wide variety of decisions affecting the setting of national air quality standards. They have ruled that the EPA must regulate all pollutants it finds hazardous; that in reviewing scientific evidence the agency must follow "paper hearing" procedures designed by the courts; that the courts themselves will take a "hard look" at this evidence; and that the act prohibits the EPA from considering cost in setting its standards. Environmentalists have won some cases, industry others. Observers have claimed that these decisions have made the EPA's standard setting more thorough and accurate.

Chapter 8 found that these rulings have had a significant substantive effect on the standards subsequently established by the EPA. The courts—primarily the D.C. Circuit, which hears most standard-setting cases—have strengthened the EPA's "lean" toward stringent standards in three ways. First, by focusing their review on the quality of the scientific evidence supporting the EPA's standards, the courts have enhanced the bureaucratic position of public health professionals, the most vocal of whom insist upon using conservative, worst-case assumptions in their analysis of health effects. Second, by prohibiting the EPA from openly considering the costs of its standards, the courts have both weakened the bureaucratic position of the agency's economists and insulated it from pressure to relax proposed standards. Third, by indicating that it is far more likely that a standard will be invalidated as too lenient than as too stringent, the courts have strengthened the incentives of political executives to "err on the side of overprotection" in setting standards and to make any concessions to those hurt by restrictive standards in later stages of the regulatory process.

These conclusions may come as a surprise to those who feared that industry experts would dominate the new rulemaking process established by the courts. To be sure, industry has devoted a great deal of money and time trying to turn its access into influence. But so far it does not have much to show for its effort. Environmentalists have been far more successful in using litigation to force the EPA to regulate new pollutants, listen to public health advocates, and resist pressure from the White House. The reason for this is that the courts have structured debate so as to help those who favor restrictive standards: the relevant question is not whether a standard produces more benefits than costs, but whether the EPA has set the standard at the lowest point at which adverse health effects can be discerned.

Many jurists and scholars have warned that the adjudicatory process is not capable of explaining complex scientific issues to generalist judges. However, the number of occasions on which judges have misread scientific evidence is extremely small. By overturning only those decisions based on glaring error, the courts have managed to avoid becoming enmeshed in disputes between experts. Judges appear to recognize their own limitations when reviewing clinical, epidemiological, and toxicological studies.

What the adjudicatory process has not seemed to convey to key federal judges, though, is the fact that health effects thresholds do not exist for most pollutants. While most scientists agree on this and congressional committees have conceded that the health effects threshold is little more than a myth, the courts continue to insist upon a "health only" approach that rests on the threshold assumption. In part this results from the reluctance of the EPA, environmental groups, and industry to attack the threshold assumption. Environmentalists prefer the search for the elusive threshold to the use of cost-benefit analysis. Industry hesitates to admit that no standard can protect all sensitive individuals. The EPA sees the present arrangement as one that protects its autonomy and sense of mission. In court, no one mentions what everyone knows.

It is highly unlikely, however, that the courts are completely unaware of this fact. What has inspired key judges to cling to their "health only" reading of the Clean Air Act is their belief that the courts, the only branch of government independent of narrow political pressures, have a special interest in protecting the health and safety of private citizens. By pushing for stronger standards the courts seek to counteract political pressures to weaken them; by protecting unorganized victims of pollution they moderate the influence of well-organized polluters. Thus the courts have used the threshold assumption to create something approaching a statutory right to a safe environment. This right rests not on the Constitution or even a careful reading of the Clean Air Act, though, but on these judges' analysis of the politics of regulation.

Transportation Controls

Court decisions on transportation controls came in three waves. The action-forcing decisions of the D.C. Circuit and federal district court in California pushed the EPA into a controversy it had tried to avoid. Subsequent judicial review of the agency's hastily prepared plans led to delay and retrenchment. Still later, court rulings on states' rights dashed the EPA's hopes of enforcing what remained of its transportation control regulations. The courts thus played a pivotal role in a drama that proved to be an unmitigated disaster for the EPA.

The most interesting aspect of the litigation over transportation controls is how court decisions transformed an agency skeptical of efforts to regulate driving patterns into one that led the crusade to reduce Americans' reliance on the automobile. The action-forcing decisions of 1972–73 brought to power within the EPA a small coterie of young lawyers and transportation planners who were long on enthusiasm but short on technical expertise or experience in dealing with local government. Working closely with the NRDC, these transportation control advocates invented the ambitious indirect source review (ISR) program, which eventually succumbed to technical flaws and intense congressional opposition. Sitting in Washington, they used consultants' reports to formulate extreme transportation control plans (TCPs), which attempted to redesign traffic patterns and build mass transit systems for the nation's largest cities. These enthusiasts dismissed challenges to the technical underpinning of their plans by saying that the courts had left the EPA with no choice but to proceed; they answered questions about implementation by assuring skeptics that the courts would order the states to put the plans into effect. Only when the courts invalidated the plans for Boston and Texas and refused to become entangled in the administration of plans for other cities did the transportation control advocates fall from power within the EPA.

The courts first told the EPA to institute transportation controls not because they considered this good public policy (Judge George E. MacKinnon, who voted with the majority in the D.C. Circuit's *NRDC* decision, warned that the order "ignores reality"), but because Congress had clearly ordered the EPA to do so. Not only was the language of the act unambiguous, but the legislative history stressed Congress's commitment to reshaping transportation patterns. Presumably the action-forcing decisions would force Congress to either stand behind this policy or revise it. But history shows that neither happened. Individual congressmen complained bitterly about the plans. The House and Senate authorizing committees labeled them "unreasonable." Yet the 1977 amendments extended the deadline for implementing transportation control measures without addressing the fundamental flaws in the program. So long as the pain of imposing transportation controls could be put off—by either court action or congressional extension of deadlines—Congress as a whole would "ignore reality" and repeat its support for such controls.

The early decisions obviously provided the NRDC and other TCP enthusiasts with access to EPA policymaking. The NRDC's attorney in this case, David Hawkins, worked closely with the EPA officials who wrote the agency's ISR and TCP regulations. He eventually became assistant administrator for air programs. While the Office of General Counsel and the Office of Transportation and Land Use Planning rose to prominence, the offices within the EPA most dubious about these efforts (the Office of Air Quality Planning and Standards and most of the regional offices) were effectively excluded from decisionmaking. The situation was reversed many months later when court decisions began to go against the EPA. Rather than ensuring balanced representation, court action skewed participation first in one direction, then in another.

Did the adjudicatory process fail to reveal to the courts the enormous problems associated with transportation controls? Clearly the courts were not aware of many of these in 1972–73—but then again, neither was anyone else. The EPA explained its doubts to the D.C. Circuit, but the court found these practical concerns irrelevant in light of the clear commands of the statute. When the courts used the adjudicatory process to probe the basis for individual plans, as they did in the *South Terminal* and *Texas* cases, they succeeded in educating not only themselves, but the EPA as well. In the states' rights cases the courts learned of the tremendous burden the EPA's enforcement strategy would place on the states and on the courts. Thus the adjudicatory process provided the courts with all the information they needed to answer the questions they asked. The problem was that they did not take responsibility for addressing all these questions at the same time.

The decentralization of the court system exacerbated the fragmentation of policymaking that characterized the EPA's entire transportation control program. The lawyers who wrote the EPA's plan oriented themselves to the appellate courts (especially the D.C. and Second Circuits) that had insisted upon strict adherence to the mandates of the act. The regional officials responsible for implementing these plans were more attuned to the perspectives of local district court judges, whose help they would need to compel the states to cooperate. Just as the enthusiasm of one group and the caution of the other created conflict within the EPA, the insistence of some circuits that the law be enforced regardless of consequences and the reluctance of district courts to become entangled in the administration of transportation plans created disagreement within the judiciary. The battle between the Second Circuit and District Court Judge Kevin Duffy presents a graphic illustration of this.

Finally, independence proved to be a mixed blessing for the courts in this series of cases. Freedom from political pressure allowed the courts to insist that the law be carried out regardless of cost. But here, as in many other areas, administrators needed more than a push from the judiciary to overcome the many objections to transportation controls. They needed cooperation from those outside the agency. When the EPA called on the courts for this aid, the courts held back. Not only did the costs of compliance seem great, but the courts' lack of an administrative apparatus (the prerequisite of their independence from bureaucratic parochialism) made it difficult for them to provide assistance. Ironically, the courts' retreat from aggressive enforcement forestalled a congressional retreat. Congress could still endorse ambitious plans to control pollution and avoid imposing burdens on constituents. Lack of judicial follow-through thus undermined the logic of action forcing.

The Courts and the Regulatory Process

The history of transportation control measures presents an extreme example of the pattern that characterizes air pollution regulation as a whole. Congress announced ambitious, costly goals. The EPA embarked on an aggressive crusade to meet these objectives, occasionally expanding them and seldom questioning whether it had the resources to prevail. Running into the inevitable opposition, the agency turned to jawboning with those whose cooperation it needed. Deadlines passed; goals remained unmet. Rather than revising these objectives or increasing the EPA's resources, Congress extended the deadlines and told the agency to keep trying. While the EPA has been more successful in controlling stationary source pollutants than those from mobile sources, even its accomplishments in the former area fall far short of the goals set more than a decade ago.

Court action has contributed significantly to this pattern by both thrusting new tasks upon the EPA and reducing its ability to carry out its old and new responsibilities. The clearest case of judicial expansion of agency goals is PSD. But there are many more: the dispersion decisions added the task of limiting total emissions to that of meeting air quality standards; the "nondiscretionary duty" cases led the EPA to announce regulations for asbestos, beryllium, mercury, benzene, vinyl chloride, and, most important, airborne lead; the judicially endorsed "lean" toward stringent standards has kept ambient air quality standards so high as to be virtually—and purposefully—out of reach; and, of course, action-forcing decisions brought forth ISR and scores of TCPs. Court rulings limiting the EPA's enforcement authority not only defanged its transportation control effort, but slowed down stationary source enforcement and even brought it to a halt in some particularly troublesome areas. Adding to the agency's enforcement woes were court decisions that impeded federal-state cooperation (variances) and diverted time, money, and political capital from the administration of existing programs to the formulation and defense of complicated new ones (PSD, ISR, TCPs and lead SIPs).

The federal courts, of course, do not bear sole responsibility for the enormous gap between mandate and resources. The 1970 act, passed by Congress and signed by the president, created it. The EPA made little effort to explain or close it. Congress later widened it. What is most interesting about the courts' activities is how they exacerbated rather than ameliorated the tendency of other institutions to make promises that far outstripped their ability to perform. To paraphrase a slogan of the 1960s, the courts were not part of the solution because they were part of the problem. This was because they dealt with two sets of complaints about regulation—either that it was too strict or that it was not strict enough—in isolation from one another and because they made so little effort to investigate the consequences of their action. Interest groups and their allies in Congress used these characteristics of the judiciary to their advantage. The EPA learned to live with the world the courts had helped to produce. While all sides seem to have gained some benefit from this system, its costs are becoming increasingly apparent and severe.

The Causes of Dualism: Structure and Participation

No single interest group or coalition of groups has dominated Clean Air Act litigation. Consider the diversity of the parties that have won major cases against the EPA: the Sierra Club, Natural Resources Defense Council, Environmental Defense Fund, Friends of the Earth, Kennecott Copper, Alabama Power, International Harvester, Portland Cement Association, Cincinnati Gas and Electric, Duquesne Power and Light, and the states of Texas, Maryland, and California. While the court system has provided access to a broad range of groups, it has not directed them all to the same forum. What is surprising about Clean Air Act litigation is how seldom the two sides that most disagree—industry and environmentalists—come before the same court at the same time. Each side has won its biggest victories by concentrating on issues assigned a low priority by its adversary. When both sides throw themselves into the same case, the result is usually stalemate or a victory for the EPA.

For this reason it is important to examine how interest groups have chosen to deploy their resources. Litigational strategies are partly dependent on court jurisdiction: parties select their cases so as to present their claims to friendly courts. The structure of the judicial system and the statutory allocation of jurisdictions channel the activities of interest groups and help shape their overall political strategies. In discussing access, therefore, one must also ask, "access to what?"

The combination of ambitious policy goals, limited resources, and the jurisdiction of the federal courts has led environmental groups to devote their litigational efforts to challenging regulations of national applicability rather than forcing individual polluters to comply with the law. Only a few local environmental groups (such as the Group Against Smog and Pollution in the Pittsburgh area) have participated actively in enforcement cases. The environmental groups with enough money and staff to mount extensive litigation appeal to a national audience. They are less interested in reducing pollution from a particular facility or city than in shaping national—even global—environmental policy. Not surprisingly, environmental groups, even those founded elsewhere, have gravitated toward Washington. Finding the agency officials, key congressmen, reporters, and federal judges in that city generally sympathetic to their cause, environmental groups have focused their lobbying effort on inducing their allies to use their considerable resources more aggressively, rather than on attacking polluters directly.

Environmentalists are fortunate that the Clean Air Act allows them to bring the cases of greatest interest to them in a forum that is both friendly and located right around the corner from their Washington offices. Section 307 requires challenges to rules of "national applicability" to go directly to the D.C. Circuit Court. Section 304 allows citizens to bring "nondiscretionary duty" cases to any federal district court, including the one in the District of Columbia. Judges in these courts see many more administrative law cases than do other judges. They are neither cowed by federal administrators nor fearful of a powerful federal government. Moreover, influential judges on the D.C. Circuit, especially Chief Judges David Bazelon and Skelly Wright, have read and accepted the literature on agency "capture." They have made a bold and determined effort to balance the scales of justice by increasing the influence of public interest groups and curbing the power of regulated firms. Fear of harming local industry has not diminished their concern for protecting the environment: Washington is a city with a serious pollution problem but no polluting industry.

This does not mean environmental groups have sued or won only in Washington. In its initial challenge to nearly all state implementation plans, the NRDC learned which courts to avoid (especially those in the West) and which ones to focus on (those in the East, especially the First and Second Circuits). The NRDC's litigation on the dispersion issue graphically illustrates how environmental groups have benefited from their careful selection of extreme cases. Georgia's wholesale reliance on dispersion enhancement led the Fifth Circuit to announce equally sweeping restrictions on dispersion credit. Environmentalists have also found sympathetic district courts in the more friendly circuits. The airborne lead case, for example, originated in the federal district court in New York City—where lead poisoning is a serious problem among ghetto children—and was upheld by the Second Circuit. In short, environmental groups have chosen their forums astutely.

The opportunities for successful litigation have reinforced environmental groups' general political strategy of expanding regulatory goals and leaving to others the job of finding the resources to meet them. In the early days of environmental activism, environmentalists, who had then had little experience with the administrative process and tended to equate legislators' and regulators' caution with undue industry influence and lack of vision, paid little attention to questions of administrative and political feasibility. The history of transportation control plans illustrates this. Subsequent experience has shown environmentalists that external constraints and a crowded agenda can reduce the effectiveness and dissipate the energy of a well-intentioned agency. Yet they have not modified their attack. Court rulings on enforcement cases have made it extremely difficult for environmentalists to gain leverage at this stage of the process. At the same time environmental advocates have developed close working relations with congressional staff members and EPA personnel and have become skillful in using litigation and negotiation to push for stringent formal regulations.

Leaders of environmental groups have replaced their naive optimism of the early 1970s with a conscious political strategy: bend on deadlines, but never on goals; keep goals out of reach to put constant pressure on regulators and polluters. Relaxing goals would not only weaken the technology-forcing thrust of the Clean Air Act, but would signal a general retreat from environmental protection. The gap between goals and performance, they argue, increases the opportunity for action-forcing litigation, reminds the public of what remains to be done, and allows environmental groups to shame legislators into providing more resources.[1] Whether this strategy will produce the desired result—or merely reflects the public interest groups' organizational maintenance needs and their attachment to symbolism—remains to be seen. But the elective affinity between their strategy and the structure of court jurisdiction is clear.

The political and litigational strategy of business groups, in contrast, has been primarily defensive, has focused on source-specific emission requirements, and has taken them into different courtrooms. Despite its reputation for effective lobbying, the business community suffered a major defeat when the Clean Air Act was passed in 1970. A few groups, such as automakers and the National Coal Association, fought a losing battle over the act. Most firms and trade associations, though, did not lobby at all, and learned of the act's strict emission limitations only after the states completed their SIPs. Regulated firms always seemed to be one step behind, spending their time and money trying to convince the government to reverse commitments it had already made.

Few firms knew or cared about the EPA's broad goals—attaining air quality standards, protecting PSD increments, reducing atmospheric loading—but only about how pollution control requirements imposed costs directly on them. Despite the weakness of the scientific support for the EPA's original air quality standards, industry challenged only one— the secondary sulfur dioxide standard. Industry failed to intervene in the 1972 *Sierra Club* case or even in the 1974 litigation on dispersion. In their counterattack on the strict regulations produced by these standards and programs, regulated firms argued that they should be subjected only to "feasible" requirements, regardless of statutory objectives. While losing the original feasibility battle, industry gained valuable delay and eventually won the feasibility war. The judicial review provisions of the Clean Air Act allowed industry to pursue its claims first in circuit courts outside the District of Columbia and then in federal district courts. Ironically, the harsh nature of the EPA's regulations helped industry convince these courts that the agency was a cabal of "pointy-headed ecofreaks."

The diversity of the business community reinforced its tendency to focus on source-specific regulations rather than on general regulatory goals. Challenging rules of general applicability creates a "free rider"

1. For a clear statement of this position, see "Dissenting Statement of Commissioners Richard E. Ayres, Annemarie Crocetti, and John J. Sheehan," in National Commission on Air Quality, *To Breathe Clean Air* (Government Printing Office, 1981), pp. 5-31 to 5-39.

problem: each firm has an incentive to let others bear the cost of the challenge. Moreover, the diversity of firms affected by most rules of general applicability makes it hard to agree on a common strategy. Indeed, the fact that firms are economic competitors as well as potential political allies gives them incentives to seek delay and leniency for themselves but to keep the regulatory burden high for their competitors. If the effect of stringent goals and selective enforcement is to redistribute the cleanup burden to a competitor, so much the better.[2]

Industry litigants have broadened their attack only when regulation has had a particularly visible effect on a highly concentrated industry (such as autos, smelters, and utilities burning high-sulfur coal) or a trade association has identified a program that has a drastic effect on almost all members of an industry (such as ISR for shopping centers). These cases, though, go to the D.C. Circuit, which has not been nearly as hospitable as district courts and many other circuits. Industry, to be sure, has won a few cases in the D.C. Circuit. But even these have brought only temporary relief, not permanent changes in regulatory goals. In some instances environmental groups have intervened in cases brought before the D.C. Circuit by industry and convinced the court that the EPA has been too lenient, not too strict.[3] Industry plaintiffs have learned to avoid the D.C. Circuit whenever possible. The chief method of doing this is to challenge regulations as applied to a few sources or in a few states.

Thus, just as the division of labor within the federal judiciary has

2. Raymond A. Bauer, Ithiel de Sola Pool, and Lewis Anthony Dexter noted many years ago the difficulties business firms have joining together in lobbying efforts. *American Business and Public Policy*, 2d ed. (Aldine, 1972). More recently, economists have noticed the differential impact of environmental regulations on firms within a single industry. See C. James Koch and Robert E. Leone, "The Clean Water Act: Unexpected Impacts on Industry," 3 *Harvard Environmental Law Review* 84 (1979).

3. For example, in *ASARCO, Inc.* v. *Environmental Protection Agency*, 578 F.2d 319 (D.C. Cir. 1978) the Sierra Club intervened in a case brought by a polluter and won. In *Lead Industries Assoc.* v. *Environmental Protection Agency*, 647 F.2d 1130 (D.C. Cir. 1980) the NRDC intervened, encouraging the court to announce a strong "health-only" interpretation of sec. 109.

Industry victories in the *International Harvester, Portland Cement*, and *Essex Chemical* cases (discussed in chap. 8) led to delay in the imposition of performance standards for new cars, portland cement plants, and fossil-fired power plants. However, their effect lasted only a year or two. It is too early to tell if the invalidation of a new source performance standard in *National Lime Assoc.* v. *Environmental Protection Agency*, 627 F.2d 416 (D.C. Cir. 1980) will lead to less stringent NSPS regulation. It is very likely that PSD and nonattainment review will bring back stringency on a case-by-case basis.

reinforced environmental groups' tendency to focus on general goals and rules of national applicability, it has strengthened industry's incentive to concentrate on source-specific rules and compliance schedules. While the interests of these two sides seem in direct conflict, both have used litigation to their advantage. Environmentalists can claim that in the long run the decisions of the federal courts will bring cleaner air. Industries can take pride in their ability to delay requirements they consider unreasonable and can recall the words of a famous student of economics: "In the long run we're all dead."

The proclivity of each set of groups to focus on different ends of the regulatory process calls into question the interest group representation analysis that underlies the new administrative law. This analysis assumes that when all major groups participate in policymaking, they confront each other directly, compromise, and thus achieve balanced representation. More specifically, participation by public interest groups supposedly counterbalances the undue influence of regulated industries. But by concentrating their activity on different parts of the regulatory process, these energetic participants have created two instances of imbalance—much as if two children sat facing each other, but on different seesaws.

These two ends of the regulatory process are not completely independent, of course. For example, the combination of stringent air quality standards and lenient enforcement against existing facilities puts a very heavy regulatory burden on new facilities. These connections—and thus the consequences of the pursuit of conflicting policies—are hard to trace. While economists have complained about the disproportionate control costs imposed on new facilities, few policymakers have taken notice.

The institutional structure of the courts helps explain not only why litigants have chosen different forums, but also why judges have not tried to make the various parts of regulatory policy fit together. Judges are asked to decide "cases and controversies," not design coherent regulatory policies. They compartmentalize issues to make them more manageable: this is an enforcement issue; that is an issue of general policy. One finds even the Second Circuit and the D.C. District Court supporting the "balancing of equities" on enforcement cases without connecting this to general policy issues.

To make matters worse, only the Supreme Court reviews the decisions of courts inside and outside the District of Columbia. To the Supreme Court air pollution is a relatively insignificant issue. It sees a Clean Air Act case only once a year or every other year. It resolves conflicts between courts only if these conflicts are clear and serious. When several circuits came to different conclusions on the variance issue, the Supreme Court settled the debate. But the next year it resolved the feasibility dispute by leaving a loophole that undercut the logic of its decision on variances. Recognizing the interconnection of issues presented in different terms takes more familiarity with the overall policymaking process than overworked courts can muster—indeed more than the EPA or Congress has achieved. In theory Supreme Court review brings unity to a decentralized judicial system that promotes participation by a variety of groups. In practice it does not.

The Causes of Dualism: Adjudication and Judicial Perceptions

To a large extent the debate over judicial activism has focused on the ability of the adjudicatory process to supply generalist judges with information sufficient for solving complex social problems. The case studies in this book have provided evidence on both sides of the controversy. In several instances judges failed to understand issues of central importance to the case before them. In others the courts' disciplined analysis of evidence helped educate the EPA as well as the bench. Examples of such illumination through litigation include *South Terminal* v. *EPA, Texas* v. *EPA*, and *Kennecott Copper* v. *EPA*. In recent years several courts, led by the D.C. Circuit, have experimented with new methods for organizing attorneys' arguments and have produced detailed opinions that demonstrate their familiarity with the complex issues before them. Like other institutions, courts both make mistakes and learn from their mistakes.

Surprisingly, the issues that judges either overlooked or misunderstood were not particularly technical ones. Three different courts (the D.C. District Court, D.C. Circuit, and Supreme Court) all reviewed the original *Sierra Club* case, but not one judge noted that "significant deterioration" has no intrinsic meaning. Nor did these courts give any indication what the term might mean. In issuing its rule about "no dispersion unless absolutely necessary," the Fifth Circuit ignored the fact that all industrial facilities use smokestacks to disperse pollutants. In the variance cases several circuit courts established rules on variances without knowing how the EPA and the states used them and without defining what a variance is. A variety of courts ruled that technologically infeasible emission control requirements were invalid, without noting that what is "feasible" depends on what one is willing to spend. The D.C. Circuit continues to insist that the EPA not consider cost in setting national air quality standards. Yet this reading of the act is based on the health effects threshold assumption, which the scientific community and even Congress have rejected.

In each case the court assumed—wrongly—that experts would fill in the blanks left by the court. Air pollution control professionals, the courts implied in *Sierra Club*, could identify significant deterioration of air quality if they put their minds to it. Engineers could distinguish tall from normal stacks and feasible from infeasible control technology. Physicians could say what pollution levels are safe. There are other examples of this excessive judicial faith in the experts: dispersion modelers, the D.C. Circuit has asserted, can learn how to calibrate PSD models using preconstruction monitoring data and can discover how to correlate ozone and carbon monoxide levels with automobile use. In each instance the EPA struggled for years to design workable programs based on faulty premises. The courts never understood the problems they were creating for the agency or the policies they were helping to produce because they never looked behind the abstract terms of their opinions.

The courts fell into this trap by concentrating their analysis on identifying legal rights and wrongs and dealing with remedies almost as an afterthought. If the courts had tried to be more specific in their instructions to the EPA, they would have recognized the inadequacy of their own understanding of the issues before them. Suppose the D.C. District Court had attempted to spell out what PSD regulations the EPA must promulgate. It would have discovered that to do so one must not just specify administrative details, but must choose among conflicting policy goals. Suppose the Fifth Circuit had followed through on its promise to issue "further guidance in accordance with this opinion." It would have struggled with the task of distinguishing tall from normal stacks. Or suppose the First Circuit had tried to define a "variance." It would have faced the questions of whether enforcement orders are variances, whether agencies can use their enforcement discretion to extend deadlines, and whether courts can use their equity powers to do the same. Being more specific about remedies would have led the courts to recognize the complexities lurking behind the abstract legal terms they used.

Other writers have noted that the courts' initial focus on rights often inhibits them from comparing alternative remedies.[4] A right is a right; it should not be denied or attenuated merely because exercising it will put a burden on others. For example, the NRDC's members had a statutory right to breathe air free from excessively high ozone and carbon monoxide levels and thus a right to have the EPA use all its statutory powers to reduce mobile source pollution. That transportation controls would impose substantial costs on millions of citizens and make the EPA the target of anger and ridicule was irrelevant. Identifying individual rights is antithetical to basing policy on cost-benefit analysis.

It goes too far, though, to say that the courts simply identified rights and ignored their cost. For one thing, most of the court decisions hardly involved individual rights at all. What rights did the courts identify in the PSD, dispersion, or variance cases? Only the general right to have the act carried out in accordance with the courts' reading of legislative intent. The courts, in effect, found the EPA's remedies for the pollution problem defective. They mandated new remedies, albeit in a vague and offhanded manner. Secondly, courts hearing enforcement cases devote most of their time to consideration of alternatives to shutdown. They clearly think about the costs of compliance as they design equitable remedies. In fact, district courts have so immersed themselves in the costs of compliance in individual cases that they have tended to lose sight of the clear dictates of the law—such as that air quality standards be achieved by the deadlines.

The contrast between the attention given remedies in enforcement cases and that given in challenges to rules of general applicability is startling. The district court that heard the *West Penn Power* case spent far more time comparing alternative remedies and their consequences than did any of the courts ruling on the PSD, dispersion, variances, or transportation control cases. The adjudicatory process *is* capable of assessing costs and comparing options. But courts have tended to make use of this capacity in small cases, not large ones.

One possible explanation for this contrast is that trial courts hear enforcement cases, while appellate courts hear most challenges to general rules. Trial courts can listen to witnesses, review depositions, conduct inspections, and meet frequently with the parties before them. Appellate

4. For example, Donald L. Horowitz, *The Courts and Social Policy* (Brookings Institution, 1977), p. 34; and Jeremy Rabkin, "Office of Civil Rights," in James Q. Wilson, ed., *The Politics of Regulation* (Basic Books, 1980), pp. 328–38.

courts can seldom do more than listen to the arguments of the parties' attorneys and examine the formal record established by the agency or the court below. (District court judges hearing nondiscretionary duty cases usually treat these suits as motions for summary judgment, conducting no trials and collecting no evidence.) Thus, in enforcement cases there is a rough proportion between the court's ability to review evidence and the complexity of the issue involved. In other cases the issues are far more complex and the capacity of the courts to investigate them more restricted.

Challenges to agency regulations under section 307 go directly to appellate courts not just because there is a need for prompt, consistent resolution of these issues, but because the issues are supposedly disputes of law, not fact. The assumption behind this commonly used distinction is that courts can decide issues of general policy by looking only at the statute and its legislative history, not at facts about the policy environment. Thus, in the standard-setting cases the D.C. Circuit looked at the legislative history of section 109, not at the fact that no thresholds exist for most pollutants. In the *Sierra Club* case the court examined the preface of the act and various fragments of legislative history without examining the facts about various pollution control strategies. In the dispersion and variance cases the circuit courts debated the intrinsic meaning of "emission limitations" and "revision" without looking at the facts that all factories use smokestacks and that all pollution control agencies use enforcement orders.

This does not mean that these courts did not take into account any facts at all. Indeed there is reason to believe that Judge Pratt was influenced by the states' concern about "economic blackmail" and environmentalists' warnings about atmospheric loading and a Grand Canyon filled with smoke. The Fifth Circuit made explicit the finding that dispersion enhancement can lead to dangerous increases in sulfate levels. The First Circuit pointed out that the EPA's predecessor had failed to reduce pollution levels. The D.C. Circuit was obviously impressed with what it saw as the fact that humans "must eliminate or control life threatening chemicals . . . if the miracle of life is to continue and if earth is to remain a living planet."[5] These judges took de facto "judicial notice" of many different factors, picking and choosing among the various pieces

5. *Environmental Defense Fund* v. *Environmental Protection Agency*, 636 F.2d 1267 at 1286 (D.C. Cir. 1980).

of evidence presented to them and failing to subject either the evidence or their inferences from it to careful scrutiny.

In almost all of the cases studied above, the courts interpreted ambiguous sections of the act and its legislative history so as to correct what they saw as flaws in EPA policy. Yet, remarkably, they came to their policy-based decisions without using the adjudicatory process to investigate policy issues. How, then, did they come to their policy conclusions? In part they relied on discussions of policy issues sprinkled through the briefs submitted by the litigants. (The fact that government lawyers for a while insisted on arguing only "the law" while challengers threw in policy arguments helps explain why the EPA lost so many cases in the first few years.) More important were judges' preconceptions of environmental issues and the regulatory process. The most vivid example of this came in the variance cases. The First Circuit sided with the NRDC because it believed regulators are inclined to be timid and lax in the face of industry pressure. The Supreme Court, reviewing the same record and equally ignorant of the way the EPA and the states used variances, assumed that regulators can be trusted to be sufficiently aggressive and interpreted the law so as to restrain excessive regulatory zeal. These contrasting evaluations of the EPA were based not on careful investigation, but on highly schematic views of how regulatory agencies operate.

Most federal courts have adopted one of two images of the EPA. Some circuits, notably the D.C. Circuit and the Second Circuit, have pictured the EPA as a generally competent but occasionally careless agency that from time to time needs to be reminded of the importance of its statutory goals and warned against bowing to demands from the White House and industry. According to this view, the EPA, like all regulatory agencies, is inclined to seek accommodation with those it regulates and to indulge in what the Second Circuit called "administrative foot-dragging." Congress has asked the courts "to stir slumbering agencies."[6] These courts' evaluation of the EPA comes in part from their conclusions on the general importance of environmental protection. The judiciary, the D.C. Circuit frequently repeats, has a "special interest" in protecting "fundamental personal interests in life, health, and liberty," as opposed to mere "economic interests."[7] From this perspective almost all administrative restraint becomes suspect. Environmental groups have

6. *Natural Resources Defense Council* v. *Train*, 545 F.2d 320 at 328 (2d Cir. 1976), and *Friends of the Earth* v. *Carey*, 535 F.2d 165 at 173 (2d Cir. 1976).

7. *Environmental Defense Fund* v. *Ruckelshaus*, 439 F.2d 584 at 598 (D.C. Cir. 1971).

built on these suspicions by pointing out what the EPA has yet to do and by providing examples of ex parte communications between the EPA and industry groups as well as White House intervention on behalf of industry.

Other courts have developed far different views of the EPA and environmental protection. They see an agency wielding great power over private citizens and the entire economy, bent on extending its authority, single-mindedly devoted to protecting the environment, and applying uniform rules in diverse situations. One district court went so far as to call the agency's actions "totalitarian."[8] To these courts the problem is excessive government control over the private sector, not excessive business influence within government. Their response has been to construe statutory authority narrowly, to interpret the requirements of due process broadly, and to use the discretion at their disposal to balance the EPA's regulatory zeal.[9]

These obviously are stereotypes. Most judges do not subscribe to either view in its entirety. Yet, since most see environmental cases relatively infrequently, they fall back on simplified conceptions to guide their review. Unfortunately, the judicial process tends to reinforce rather than correct these images. Jurisdictional arrangements limit the array of cases viewed by each court. Opportunities for forum shopping lead both environmental groups and industry to seek out those courts that share their views. The adjudicatory process, especially as used by appellate courts, produces information only on those subjects deemed relevant by the court. Those more concerned about protecting the beneficiaries of regulatory statutes can focus their attention on these benefits, dismissing the costs as legally irrelevant. Those more concerned with protecting traditional property rights can likewise ignore the environmental and administrative costs of elaborate due process requirements.

The celebrated independence of the courts is essentially a negative quality. It is clear what judges are free *from*: political accountability, administrative responsibilities, the norms of specialized professions. One expects that freedom from these constraints will lead judges to take a broad view of the public interest. Adopting this broad view, though, takes more than independence; it takes broad familiarity with both

8. *Anaconda* v. *Ruckelshaus*, 352 F. Supp. 697 at 704 (D. Colo. 1972).

9. For a sophisticated argument in support of this general perspective, see Eugene Bardach and Robert A. Kagan, *Going by the Book: The Problem of Regulatory Unreasonableness* (Temple University Press, 1982), especially chaps. 3 and 4.

policy debates and the political process. Seeing different parts of the whole, most judges have adopted partial views of what the public interest requires. One view stresses commitment to the regulatory goals stated or suggested in the statute and the Constitution. The other stresses the need for balance, responsiveness to local circumstances, and respect for existing property rights. The judiciary as a whole has not reconciled the divergent points of view adopted by its component parts. Nor have the courts forced Congress to reconcile the competing demands it makes of the EPA.

The Courts and Congress

In every case studied in this book the courts have claimed to act on behalf of Congress. They have interpreted the statutes it has passed, searched to discover its intent, even tried to divine the "spirit" behind its enactments. That the courts have alternated between two contradictory views of regulation as practiced by the EPA is partially a reflection of Congress's internal divisions on the nature of the "bureaucracy problem."

It is hard to find a congressman who does not claim that federal bureaucracies are running out of control. In recent years Congress has employed a number of new mechanisms for reviewing agency activities, including annual authorizations, zero-based budgeting, sunset laws, legislative vetoes, and a unified congressional budget. Congress has also called upon the courts to exercise similar oversight in its name. In fact the Senate has twice passed a bill instructing courts not to show *any* deference to the agencies whose decisions they review.[10]

Congressional unanimity on the need for control of the bureaucracy disguises dissension on the purposes of this control. To many congressmen, controlling the bureaucracy means preventing administrators from taking actions that injure or anger their constituents. The EPA becomes "out of control" when it threatens to close down local industries, tells city dwellers where they cannot park or drive, and prevents states from attracting new industry. Controlled bureaucracies do not take actions congressmen and their vocal constituents consider unreasonable.

To those congressmen who sit on authorizing subcommittees, con-

---

10. *Congressional Record*, daily edition (September 7, 1979), p. S12145. On congressional control of administrative activity, see James Sundquist, *The Decline and Resurgence of Congress* (Brookings Institution, 1981), chaps. 8, 11, 12, and 13; and Arthur Maass, *Congress and the Common Good* (Basic Books, forthcoming).

trolling the EPA has a far different meaning. They expect the agency to obey not just the instructions contained in the statute, but also suggestions made in committee reports and even in committee hearings. These subcommittees usually attract congressmen who strongly support federal regulation of environmental hazards. They object to the watering down of *their* statutes and expect administrators to look to congressional committees, not the White House, for policy guidance.[11]

Congress, in short, is a diverse body whose members have different expectations of the EPA. The majorities that support major pieces of legislation such as the Clean Air Act are uneasy coalitions, not unified armies. Ambiguities in statutory language often indicate the coalitions' failure to reach agreement. Especially when legislation is controversial— as the Clean Air Act always has been—the bill's sponsors must decide what to make clear and what to leave in the shadows, how much to demand and when to pull back. The legislative history of most important statutes reflects this coalition building and shadowboxing. It contains conflicting pieces of evidence that can be interpreted in many different ways by agencies and courts.

The cases studied here provide a number of examples of courts imposing an "intent" on a Congress that at best could be described as undecided. If there were any congressional intent to add PSD to the provisions for attaining the national air quality standards established by the act, then that intent existed only in the minds of the staff members who inserted a few pregnant phrases into the Senate report and the committee leaders who subsequently berated the EPA for refusing to address the Sierra Club's concerns. Although the Fifth Circuit claimed Congress had intended "emission limitations" to mean "standards requiring constant emission reduction," Congress never considered the dispersion issue before 1973. In fact, in late 1973 the House voted in favor of allowing polluters to use dispersion enhancement, and the Senate remained silent. In the feasibility cases several courts (later overturned by the Supreme Court) distorted the wording and history of the act beyond recognition, as did the Supreme Court in the federal facilities case. In reading the "legislative intent" behind the standard-setting section of the act, the D.C. Circuit held tight to the wording of

11. Herbert Kaufman provides a perceptive analysis of congressional criticism of bureaucracy in *The Administrative Behavior of Federal Bureau Chiefs* (Brookings Institution, 1981), pp. 169–72. Also see James Q. Wilson, "The Bureaucracy Problem," *The Public Interest*, no. 6 (Winter 1967), p. 3.

the 1970 Senate report and the 1977 House report, neglecting the implication of the entire PSD title of the statute and various statements by the bill's sponsors acknowledging the collapse of the threshold myth. Either these courts were looking for justification for their policy choices or their extreme carelessness allowed them to be misled by the litigants before them.

Such manipulation of legislative history has a significant effect on Congress as well as the courts. Recognizing that the courts may pick up on suggestions inserted in committee reports, floor debate, and hearings, committee members and their staff lace these parts of the record with their interpretations of ambiguous sections of the statute. Ackerman and Hassler's study of the 1977 amendments shows how House and Senate staff members tried to use the conference report to resolve the extremely important debate about scrubbers without attracting attention from the rest of Congress.[12] Writing these lengthy reports—the 1977 House report alone was over 500 pages long and the legislative history of the 1977 amendments compiled by the Congressional Research Service exceeds 7,500 pages—confers enormous power on the authors, who are usually staff members supervised by only one or two members of Congress.[13] The more attention courts pay to legislative histories, the more powerful these congressional insiders become. Moreover, the more likely courts are to rely on nonstatutory language, the less likely these insiders are to risk indicating their intentions clearly in the statute. Thus, by employing easily manipulated legislative histories to increase Congress's control over the bureaucracy, courts increase the control of subcommittee leaders and their staff over policymaking, but diminish the control exercised by Congress as a whole over its component parts.

While the major beneficiaries of court decisions have been committee leaders and staff, the biggest governmental losers have been White House officials. Especially when statutes are ambiguous, the White House frequently competes with congressional committees for control over agency policy. This competition was particularly keen under the Clean

12. Bruce A. Ackerman and William T. Hassler, *Clean Coal/Dirty Air* (Yale University Press, 1981), pp. 48–54.

13. In *Unelected Representatives: Congressional Staff and the Future of Representative Government* (Basic Books, 1980), Michael J. Malbin provides some fascinating examples of the influence of congressional staff members. One well-known committee staffer created a transcript for twelve days of hearings that never took place (p. 30). In another instance, staff members representing members of a conference committee produced a conference report despite the fact that the committee never met (chap. 5).

Air Act, because during the 1970s the preoccupation of presidents—both Republican and Democratic—with energy and economic policy put them at odds with committees whose main concern was environmental protection. The White House and other agencies opposed PSD, limitations on dispersion, and rapid implementation of transportation controls while these matters were under consideration by the EPA, and later introduced legislation to overturn the courts' decisions. The President's Council of Economic Advisers and its adjunct, the Council on Wage and Price Stability, sought to convince the EPA to consider costs explicitly in standard setting and to raise the ozone standard above 0.12 part per million. They were rebuffed by EPA officials who claimed (probably rightly) that the courts would not allow this. The courts have thus weakened the role of the president and his staff not just by strengthening congressional committees, but also by painting important policy choices as matters for experts, not political balancers, to decide.

On almost all these issues, the House and Senate, which were solidly Democratic during the 1970s, followed the lead of their committees, not the president. Most congressmen examine committee recommendations carefully only if they have received complaints from their constituents. In the absence of widely dispersed complaints, committees generally prevail unless intensely interested minorities can extract concessions by threatening to block congressional action altogether. By affirming committee policies and putting the burden on their opponents to pass contrary legislation, court decisions virtually ensure that these committees will emerge victorious.

The Clean Air Act provides many examples of court-committee symbiosis. Substantial minorities in the House and Senate, composed mainly of members whose states were most directly affected, opposed PSD. Without committee positions, however, they could not construct majorities to overturn the *Sierra Club* decision. If the courts had not acted first, it is unlikely that the committees could have built coalitions large enough to push PSD past each veto point in the legislative process. The same is true of court-ordered limits on dispersion. In this case the House committee lost a key vote when congressmen who were worried about the oil shortage responded to complaints from utilities and the FEA. The Senate committee blocked action in that chamber, and the court decision stood. Only on indirect source review, which was linked in the public's mind with the much-resented restrictions on parking contained in TCPs, did the committees reluctantly bow to pressure from noncommittee members. On the TCPs themselves the committees saved their program by putting off the deadline.

This calls attention to the basic pattern of congressional action on air pollution policy. Committees and subcommittees can generally push the programs of special interest to them unless these programs seem to single out a few states or districts for unfair treatment (as was the case on PSD) or impose visible costs on large numbers of citizens (as did transportation controls). Another major cost imposed on citizens by pollution control is unemployment. This occurs—at least in a visible way—only when enforcement begins in earnest. Recognizing this, committee leaders have supported measures that halt enforcement action threatening to cause unemployment. Allowing courts to "balance equities" is the keystone of this strategy. Despite their complaints about enforcement delay, committee members have encouraged the courts to use their discretion to avoid regulation-caused unemployment. Moreover, they have generally ratified the enforcement policies developed by the EPA, the courts, and the states for such problem sources as smelters, steel mills, and coal-burning power plants. The "local coal" provision of the 1977 amendments represents an extreme example of a policy made to avoid unemployment attributable to environmental regulation. The provision, designed to reduce unemployment among midwestern coal miners, received the support of the House committee, though not of Senator Muskie and his subcommittee.[14]

In short, congressmen are usually content to have committee leaders set the goals of environmental protection programs so long as they do not anticipate immediate or widespread pain to result. The courts have not only helped committee leaders expand agency programs over the

14. In his explanation of the 1977 Senate committee recommendation, Senator Muskie expressed the expectation that the courts would seek to balance environmental protection and economic well-being. "When the courts determine the public health and welfare costs of plant closure are greater than the public health benefits to be achieved from strict adherence to compliance with emission limitations by the deadlines in the statute, the court may rely on a combination of delayed compliance penalty and civil penalties to equalize economic differences while maintaining momentum for compliance with the law." *Congressional Record* (June 8, 1977), p. 18025. Congress has also enacted several special exemptions for problem sources (see chaps. 6 and 7). On the "local coal" amendment, which requires utilities to scrub high-sulfur local coal if switching to low-sulfur coal creates "significant local or regional economic disruption or unemployment," see Ackerman and Hassler, *Clean Coal/Dirty Air*, pp. 44–48.

opposition of the White House and angry congressional minorities, but have provided these committees with a dependable enforcement safety valve as well. Thus, without following the instructions of Congress, the courts have pursued a course that satisfies both its committees and its rank and file—without forcing the latter to keep track of what the former are doing.

So far this analysis has focused on how the courts' reading of legislative history and their use of discretion in enforcement cases have influenced congressional politics. But the willingness of courts to instruct agencies to perform the unambiguous nondiscretionary duties specified in the statute itself has also affected congressional behavior. As mentioned above, most observers see action-forcing litigation both as a way to prevent timid agencies from ignoring congressional commands and as a way to force Congress to stand behind its words. The examples of nondiscretionary duty cases examined in this work, however, suggest that agencies often have better reasons than mere timidity for avoiding these tasks. Especially with transportation controls—but with regulation of airborne lead as well—the agency knew it lacked the technical, administrative, and political resources to carry out programs that would produce only small air quality benefits. Subsequent events showed that most members of Congress agreed with the agency's initial assessment. Instead of thanking the courts for helping them control a "slumbering" agency, most members condemned the EPA for its stupidity and arrogance. Once again, though, their outrage resulted in relaxation of enforcement, not alteration of statutory goals.

As statutes grow longer and more complex they, like legislative histories, receive only fleeting attention from most members of Congress. It is relatively easy for committee leaders to add ambitious provisions to regulatory statutes without attracting much attention. When courts were hesitant to handle nondiscretionary duty cases, the advocates of such programs had to convince balky agencies that Congress really meant what it said, that the wrath of Congress would not fall on them for carrying out statutory instructions, but rather for failure to do so. With courts willing to force action, though, this second step is no longer necessary. Committee leaders and staff can insert provisions, encourage public interest groups to litigate, and hope for the best. If the program succeeds, they take credit; if it fails, blame usually falls on administrators. Unfortunately, this type of statute-writing adventurism has become more frequent without causing Congress as a whole to take a closer look at the statutes it passes.[15]

Thus in several ways the courts have helped committee leaders and staff to push their favorite regulatory programs and to hide the implications of these programs from the rest of Congress. As a result, the coalitions supporting air pollution controls are more fragile than they might at first appear. This helps explain the EPA's fears of congressional backlash, which may seem irrational if one looks only at how Congress strengthened the act in 1970 and 1977. Recognition of this fact also explains the willingness of committee leaders to extend deadlines time after time and to grant special exemptions to the worst polluters. Without following any real congressional intent, the courts have developed a symbiotic relationship with committee leaders who have advocated ambitious goals but feared strict enforcement.

The Courts and the EPA

One might expect that an agency that has lost as many major court cases as the EPA would take a jaundiced view of judicial intervention. Such is not the case. While complaining about some decisions, EPA officials generally credit the courts with improving the agency's competence and programs. One possible explanation for this complacency is that court action helped to free the agency from interagency and White House review. But reducing the influence of other components of the executive branch simultaneously increased the influence of Congress. Court rulings did not significantly increase the EPA's autonomy.

EPA officials speak highly of the courts precisely because court decisions have played such a major role in shaping the agency's structure, strategy, and sense of mission. By forcing the EPA to carry out new programs, the courts created new program offices within the agency. The most vivid example of this was the formation of the Office of Transportation and Land Use Planning, which became a focal point of TCP activity. The *Sierra Club* decision similarly led scores of EPA officials, some new, others diverted from other tasks, to devote themselves

15. John Quarles makes a similar point in "The Transportation Control Plans—Federal Regulation's Collision with Reality," 2 *Harvard Environmental Law Review* 241 (1977). On the general problem of Congress's control over its committees, see Maass, *Congress and the Common Good*, chaps. 5 and 6.

to writing PSD regulations. Those who opposed PSD avoided the program and concentrated on tasks they considered more important. This left the true believers in charge. Court decisions stressing the need for more evidence on the health effects of regulated pollutants and requiring the EPA to set standards for additional pollutants led to expansion of the agency's research staff, the creation of special task forces (such as one for airborne lead), and the establishment of a new office to write criteria documents. In short, a variety of court decisions have produced new bureaucratic units whose task it is to respond to court demands. Since they derive their jobs, their influence, and sense of purpose from court action, it is not surprising that officials in these offices tend to praise judicial review.

The frequency of court challenges has also contributed to the growth in size and influence of the EPA's Office of General Counsel. The OGC was a major actor in every controversy examined in this book. It helped to write PSD regulations. It composed the 1975 variance rules and the 1976 stack height guidelines virtually single-handedly. It used court decisions to win its battle with agency economists over the consideration of costs in standard setting. A small coterie of OGC attorneys dominated agency policymaking on TCPs and ISR. Throughout the 1970s OGC attorneys tended to be young, aggressive lawyers who welcomed the experience of arguing before appellate courts, the influence legal controversy brought to them, and the expansion of regulatory programs produced by court decisions.

Enforcement offices present a different situation. Regional officials often express their frustration with individual district court judges. But they and their supervisors in Washington generally accept the courts' practice of reviewing a large number of factors before deciding upon relief. Preparing for litigation and bargaining with sources over schedules, revisions, and fines has become an integral part of their job. Enforcement officials tend to accept the perspective of the district court judges: while priding themselves on being tough enforcers, they do not want to be so unreasonable as to shut down local employers. Enforcement attorneys object not to the complexity of litigation, but to the reluctance of EPA headquarters and the Department of Justice to file suit. Trial work is the most exciting part of their job and the experience that most enhances their professional reputation. Typically regional enforcement lawyers are young, stay in the EPA only a few years, and view their positions in the agency as stepping-stones to jobs in private law firms. While they hate to lose cases, they welcome the opportunity to become immersed in the legal complexities created by the courts' balancing of equities.[16]

The EPA's political executives and their advisers would seem to have the most to lose from the court decisions examined here. They received the blame both for the EPA's failure to meet its air quality goals and for its controversial entry into transportation planning and land use management. Court decisions have reduced the ability of the EPA's administrators to set agency priorities. This was clearest under the first administrator, William Ruckelshaus. He tried to concentrate the EPA's efforts on meeting primary air quality standards and saw PSD and transportation controls as sideshows that would squander the agency's public support and divert its attention from more important matters.

Later administrators, either because they saw more merit in these programs or because they did not want to rock the boat, came to support these judicially mandated programs. Gradually, these administrators adopted the same general strategy as environmental groups and committee leaders, welcoming expanded programs and promising their opponents enforcement delays. Douglas Costle's actions on the lead standard provide the best example of this. Administrators Russell Train and Costle tended to take the course of least resistance: accept court decisions; when possible, use them to justify expansion of the EPA's budget and to satisfy authorizing committees; avoid antagonizing program advocates within the agency; limit legislative proposals to extending deadlines rather than pruning programs. As the EPA matured, its administrators found it difficult to challenge a pattern established by Congress and the courts and supported by their subordinates.[17]

There is one group within the EPA that has remained skeptical about

16. This view of the incentives of lawyers squares with the analysis of Robert A. Katzmann in *Regulatory Bureaucracy: The Federal Trade Commission and Antitrust Policy* (MIT Press, 1980), pp. 76–85, and Paul J. Quirk, *Industry Influence in Federal Regulatory Agencies* (Princeton University Press, 1981), pp. 148–74.

17. Herbert Kaufman explains why it is hard for bureau chiefs to make major changes in bureaucratic routines and strategies in *The Administrative Behavior of Federal Bureau Chiefs*, chap. 3.

Anne Gorsuch Burford of course viewed many of the programs expanded or created by the courts with skepticism. But her low standing in Congress made it impossible to repeal those sections of the 1977 amendments that incorporated these court-initiated requirements. Consequently, she exhibited leniency in the enforcement process to an even greater extent than her predecessors. Moreover, her unceremonious departure was in part the result of her inability to work with the permanent bureaucracy. The history of her brief reign illustrates the difficulty political executives have in reversing well-established bureaucratic strategies.

the contribution of the courts: the air control professionals, mainly engineers and meteorologists, within the Office of Air Quality Planning and Standards (OAQPS). This office had initially proposed most of the policies overturned by the courts. Court rulings on PSD, dispersion, variances, and transportation controls not only increased the power of other EPA offices at the expense of the OAQPS, but also put additional administrative burdens on it. The OAQPS was handed the thankless task of filling in the blanks left by the courts. It was told to transform the PSD ambient increment scheme into a workable program, to devise dispersion models for TCPs and ISR, to find a specific, technical solution to the stack height problem, and to guide development of SIPs for airborne lead. Although these tasks kept the OAQPS busy and increased its size, it already had plenty to do. Told to perform duties clearly beyond its capacity, the OAQPS received criticism for its incomplete or poorly justified products.

To many environmentalists, congressional staff members, and political executives, the OAQPS was precisely the type of foot-dragging, unimaginative, industry-dominated, parochial bureaucracy that the new administrative law tries to reform. To them, the office represented restraint; it was always telling them what the EPA could not do. The OAQPS never accepted "technology forcing," preferring instead to work with industry to discover the best available control technology. This emphasis on cooperation and engineering solutions led environmental advocates to believe that the OAQPS was "in bed" with industry, the same charge launched at the National Air Pollution Control Agency, from which many OAQPS officials came. Moreover, the OAQPS's air pollution control professionals were primarily interested in reducing air pollution, while their critics wanted to revolutionize transportation patterns, promote land use planning, and discourage industrial growth in rural areas.

Not surprisingly, the leaders of the OAQPS have also dissented from the agency's strategy of setting ambitious goals and then compromising in enforcement. As authors of regulations of general applicability, OAQPS staff members have objected to viewing these rules as guidelines for enforcement officers, not binding rules. As career civil servants who expect to be in the EPA for years, the leaders of the OAQPS are wary of crash programs and interested in preserving the agency's reputation for competence and reasonableness. The OAQPS's geographic location reflects its political position: Durham, North Carolina, is in neither

Washington's sphere of influence nor that of local employers. The principal political point of reference for the OAQPS is neither congressional committees nor district court judges, but rather the increasingly cohesive air pollution control profession, whose major interest, not surprisingly, is finding pragmatic ways of reducing air pollution.

To a greater extent than most EPA personnel realize, the agency is the creation of court action. Court decisions have increased the number and variety of program advocates within the EPA; led enforcement officials to accept slow, piecemeal negotiation and litigation; made it easy for political executives to follow the two-pronged strategy described above; and reduced the influence of the single office within the EPA that focused on pollution reduction, not symbolic victories. In a perverse way the courts helped form offices within the agency that corresponded to their stereotypes of inefficient compromise (enforcement) and overzealous regulation (program advocates) and weakened the office (OAQPS) that corresponded to neither.

The Costs of Dualism

Behind this analysis of the courts and the policymaking system is the assumption that it is poor regulatory policy to set goals that greatly exceed the resources the political community is willing to expend. One could imagine, though, a different evaluation of this pattern of behavior. According to this view, regulation under the Clean Air Act shows how a pluralist system balances competing policy demands, providing something for everyone. Environmentalists get ambitious programs and significant amounts of pollution reduction. Most business firms must only apply available controls and even then get lengthy delays. Committee members receive credit for sponsoring pathbreaking legislation. Other congressmen get credit for standing up to the bureaucracy. The EPA keeps busy writing regulations and preparing enforcement cases. The amount of pollution reduction achieved and the cost sustained represent a balance between the political community's desire for economic growth and its wish for environmental protection. This view maintains that such "muddling through" produces reasonable policy.

What is wrong with this method of setting environmental policy? Many things. First, it increases cynicism and distrust of government. Environmental advocates, seeing the gap between the goals they consider essential to human well-being and the accomplishments of the EPA, conclude that the American government and the free enterprise system have let the people down again. The EPA, many now say, has lost its sense of purpose and been captured by industry. Businessmen, in contrast, see the harsh regulations the EPA publishes, brand the agency as the tool of unthinking "ecofreaks," and attribute reduced enforcement to their own skillfulness and the helpfulness of their allies. The general public hears of excessive red tape, receives draconian commands (82 percent gas rationing in Los Angeles), and worries about unemployment, but knows the air is still dirty. While it is true that nearly everyone gets something, it is also true that everyone concentrates on the promises not kept and the threats not enforced.[18]

Second, the resulting policy is hard to review and to revise. Indeed it is almost impossible to describe what American "environmental policy" is. Policy is not contained in statutes or even in the Federal Register, but in the multitude of orders and rulings of state and federal officials throughout the country. Efforts to coordinate overlapping policies on energy, the economy, and the environment consume enormous amounts of time but produce laughably inadequate results. Every president and every Congress since 1973 has worked to decrease American dependence on oil by increasing the use of coal by utilities. The massive acts passed— the Energy Supply and Environmental Coordination Act of 1974 and its progeny—produced virtually no coal conversion. So far the byzantine nature of environmental and energy policies has allowed the EPA and environmentalists to block many energy programs that would increase pollution. But the sword is two-edged. In 1980 Administrator Costle warned that the complexity of the Clean Air Act would allow business lobbyists to gut the act without the public knowing what had happened.[19] The gap between stated policy and actual policy is so large that intelligent public debate and reasonable adjustment to new circumstances are nearly impossible.

Third, this two-tiered administrative structure creates serious inequities. It discriminates against those who unquestioningly obey the law

18. In his *Discourses on the First Ten Books of Titus Livius,* Machiavelli quotes Tacitus as saying, "Men are more ready to repay an injury than a benefit, because gratitude is a burden and revenge a pleasure" (bk. 1, chap. 29). Consider in this context the advice Machiavelli offers in bk. 1, chap. 32.

19. Costle claimed the act's "very complexities can disguise a legislative retreat," that "not one in 100,000 citizens would willingly read" the act, and that its complexity leads members of Congress to lose interest in and patience with debate. 11 *Environment Reporter—Current Developments* 299.

and favors those who choose to ignore and fight it. Those who hold out the longest sometimes may even be rewarded with windfall "emission rights." Frequently, the extent of a polluter's compliance depends on neither the seriousness of the harm caused nor the cost of control, but rather on the attitude of state officials, district court judges, and EPA regional office personnel; on the importance of the firm as a local employer; and on the skill of its negotiators and lawyers.

Finally, and perhaps most important, this system creates an underlying inequity that increases control costs while reducing environmental benefits. As enforcement leniency and statutory exemption have lightened the load on *existing* facilities, the regulatory burden on *new* facilities has grown heavier and heavier. The 1970 act recognized that installing pollution controls in new plants is generally cheaper than retrofitting old ones: new source performance standards require all new facilities, not just those in nonattainment areas, to install the best available controls. Since 1970 the gap between requirements for new and old facilities has grown so wide that it no longer bears any relation to the relative costs of control. In the words of Lester B. Lave and Gilbert S. Omenn, the result of the existing scheme "is to make siting of a new plant difficult anywhere, with powerful incentives to continue using existing, highly polluting facilities."[20]

Many observers—particularly economists—have noted and denounced this favoritism toward existing sources.[21] They have blamed Congress for pursuing a policy of economic protectionism disguised as a policy for environmental protection. The history of PSD, the local coal amendment, and the 1977 amendments' scrubbing requirement lend support to their argument. What has generally gone unnoticed is how the courts' actions have contributed to this pattern of regulation.

There can be little doubt that court action has reduced emission reduction requirements for existing facilities, especially the dirtiest—smelters, steel mills, and midwestern coal-burning power plants. At the

20. *Clearing the Air: Reforming the Clean Air Act* (Brookings Institution, 1981), p. 41.

21. Lave and Omenn, *Clearing the Air*; Ackerman and Hassler, *Clean Coal/Dirty Air*; David Harrison, Jr., and Paul R. Portney, "Making Ready for the Clean Air Act," *Regulation* (March–April 1981), p. 24; Peter Navarro, "The Politics of Air Pollution," *The Public Interest*, no. 59 (Spring 1980), p. 36; and Robert W. Crandall, "The Use of Environmental Policy to Reduce Economic Growth in the Sun Belt: The Role of Electric-Utility Rates," in Michael A. Crew, ed., *Regulatory Reform and Public Utilities* (Lexington Books, 1982).

same time, the court-initiated PSD program slapped additional restrictions on new facilities. PSD applies not just to areas surrounding national parks, but to all attainment areas. (Even New York City and Chicago are attainment areas for some pollutants.) Forcing firms to comply with restrictions on new facilities is relatively easy: the EPA can simply refuse to approve their permits. Firms seldom devote large amounts of capital to building facilities before they know they can receive necessary approval. Even if a firm begins construction without a permit, the EPA can get an injunction from a federal court. At early stages of construction, the equities, according to legal doctrine, are all in the EPA's favor. Not only have the courts increased restrictions on new sources, but they have been happy to enforce them.

As heavily polluted areas missed the deadline for meeting national air quality standards, the EPA and Congress looked for ways to encourage further cleanup. Once again the burden of these efforts fell on new sources. In 1976 the EPA announced that new facilities could not locate in nonattainment areas unless they offset their emissions by buying emission rights from other polluters. While presenting this plan as a way to allow economic growth in nonattainment areas, the EPA included (and Congress later added) so many restrictions in the offset policy that very few firms have qualified for permits.[22] Similarly, seeing that the courts would not force the states to implement TCPs, transportation control advocates looked for other incentives. The 1977 amendments impose a construction ban in states that fail to submit adequate carbon monoxide and ozone control plans. The EPA invoked this authority when California and Kentucky refused to approve inspection and maintenance plans, and has threatened to ban construction in many other states as well.[23]

In short, new sources have borne the brunt both of the new programs resulting from court decisions and of the courts' failure to take aggressive enforcement action against existing sources. The courts have not been motivated by crass economic protectionism. Although the explanation

22. Lave and Omenn, *Clearing the Air*, pp. 23–25. The EPA's "bubble" policy is also aimed at encouraging firms to replace old plants with new ones. But the courts have limited the EPA's use of the bubble, first in *ASARCO* v. *Environmental Protection Agency*, 578 F.2d 319 (D.C. Cir. 1978), and again in *Natural Resources Defense Council* v. *Gorsuch*, 17 *Environment Reporter Cases* 1825 (D.C. Cir. 1982).

23. 13 *Environment Reporter—Current Developments* 155.

for their behavior is far more complicated, the effect is the same. The courts have formed an integral part of a policymaking system that has bred cynicism, muddled debate, created serious inequities and inefficiencies, and kept pollution levels high in the most heavily populated areas of the country.

Roads to Reform

"Philosophers until now have only interpreted the world," Karl Marx proclaimed in his "Thesis on Feuerbach." "The point is to change it." This could be the motto of current schools of policy analysis. So far this book has concentrated on understanding the world of politics and policymaking. Does this interpretation point to a program of reform? To a limited extent, yes. By showing that court action under the Clean Air Act has not improved regulatory policy or the performance of regulatory agencies, it suggests that judges should show more deference to administrators and less confidence in their own ability to reform complex regulatory programs. A new understanding of administrative decisionmaking and judicial capacity stands behind the new administrative law. To the extent judges recognize the shortcomings of this understanding, their behavior will change. The following proposals are designed above all to impress upon the courts the limits of their knowledge and control.

Information and Expertise

No one would deny that judges are frequently uninformed about the policy issues that come before them. Traditional administrative law responded to this problem by urging judicial deference toward expert agencies. More recently judges have responded by designing mechanisms such as paper hearings to increase the information available to them and by devoting more time to administrative law issues. Judges on the D.C. Circuit have become specialists in administrative law and have spearheaded the effort to improve the courts' oversight capacity.

Most proposals to improve this capacity focus on the need to explain *technical* issues to judges. Judge Harold Leventhal, for example, suggested that judges hire science clerks in addition to regular law clerks. Others have proposed the creation of courts that specialize in scientific and environmental matters.[24]

These reforms are misguided. Despite the technical complexity of most clean air issues, the case studies in this book show that what the courts need most is a better understanding of *administrative* issues, not technical ones. The courts have gotten into trouble when they have relied on general impressions and sketchy evidence to conclude that an environmental or administrative problem exists and then issued haphazard instructions on how the EPA should deal with it.

To perform competently the tasks they have taken on, judges must learn more about the nature of the problem they seek to cure, the policy options open to administrators, and the constraints on those who must carry out their orders. Judges can take a major step in this direction by starting to think about specific remedies as soon as they consider possible interpretations of the law. Linking abstract legal terms to concrete administrative action will help them recognize the difficulties they create for administrators when they issue vague directives such as "prevent significant deterioration," "prohibit dispersion," or "implement transportation controls." Designing specific remedies will acquaint judges with the dilemmas confronting policymakers and the steps necessary for turning general goals into operational programs.[25]

Greater specificity in court orders will, of course, reduce administrative flexibility. But presumably courts overrule agency decisions only when agencies have exceeded the outer bounds of their discretion. If the agency has done something wrong, the court should be able to specify what that wrong is and how the agency should correct it. Otherwise courts will be tempted to overturn agency actions merely on the vague suspicion that something is wrong or the vague hope that the agency could do better.

By paying more attention to remedies, judges will also put themselves

24. Harold Leventhal, "Appellate Procedures: Design, Patchwork, and Managed Flexibility," 23 *UCLA Law Review* 432 (1976); Leventhal, "Environmental Decision-making and the Role of the Courts," 122 *University of Pennsylvania Law Review* 509 (1974); Scott C. Whitney, "The Case for Creating a Special Environmental Court System," 14 *William and Mary Law Review* 473 (1973); Note, "The Environmental Court Proposal: Requiem, Analysis, and Counterproposal," 123 *University of Pennsylvania Law Review* 676 (1975); and Joel Yellin, "High Technology and the Courts: Nuclear Power and the Need for Institutional Reform," 94 *Harvard Law Review* 489 (1981).

25. Robert Katzmann makes a similar argument about institutional reform litigation in "Judicial Intervention and Organizational Theory: Changing Bureaucratic Behavior and Policy," 89 *Yale Law Journal* 513 (1980).

in closer touch with nonlawyers in the agency and reduce the power of agency attorneys. As it is, agency lawyers first filter out the "facts" they view as irrelevant to the "law" and then play a major role in designing agency responses that they think will satisfy the court. If at early stages of litigation judges ask parties for information on possible remedies, agency attorneys must consult with line personnel and report the difficulties they discover *before* the decision is carved in stone. This diminishes the likelihood that courts and agency attorneys will set goals that other agency officials know cannot be achieved.

Thinking about remedies and soliciting the opinions of those with administrative responsibilities will, no doubt, increase judges' deference to administrators. Recognition of the complexity of policy choices and of the obstacles to implementing them will make judges hesitate to label agency caution as "foot-dragging" or to view its power as "totalitarian." Already there are indications that as judges learn more about agency policies and decisionmaking processes they become less inclined to second-guess. In recent years industry, environmental groups, the states, and the EPA have become more sophisticated in their presentation of arguments to the courts. Courts have overturned fewer agency actions and have made smaller adjustments when they have ruled against the EPA.

Jurisdiction

By addressing questions of program design and enforcement in isolation from one another, the courts have increased the gap between administrative promise and performance. One way to bridge this gap might be to adjust jurisdiction so that the same judges hear both enforcement cases and challenges to rules of general applicability. This presumably would reduce the disagreements among courts that have so confused federal air pollution policy.

One possible jurisdictional remedy is to increase the authority of the D.C. Circuit—the court that hears most challenges to EPA regulation—in enforcement cases. Doing so, however, would be difficult. The D.C. Circuit cannot hold trials to determine whether polluters throughout the country have violated the law. Nor could the circuit review the lengthy records these cases produce. Centralization of jurisdiction has proceeded about as far as possible under the Clean Air Act.

Another alternative is to reduce the role of the D.C. Circuit by giving other circuits jurisdiction over challenges to rules of national applicability. Industry groups have supported this change and have defeated efforts to centralize jurisdiction under other statutes. This cure, however, is worse than the disease. The resulting forum shopping would increase the number of disagreements among courts. The Supreme Court would not be able to resolve these differences within a reasonable amount of time. While the D.C. Circuit has in the past been particularly hospitable to environmental groups, it has tended to uphold the EPA more frequently as it has learned more about pollution control. In the long run no one's interest would be served by further fragmentation of policymaking.

In the past few years the Supreme Court has taken halting steps toward unifying the judicial system by ordering the D.C. Circuit to show more deference toward administrative agencies. In the landmark *Vermont Yankee* case the Court described a series of D.C. Circuit opinions on environmental regulation as "judicial intervention run riot" and "border[ing] on the Kafkaesque."[26] This restraint is no doubt beneficial. But given the large number of complex administrative law cases the D.C. Circuit hears and the small number the Supreme Court can review in depth, the Supreme Court cannot by itself exercise much control over regulatory issues. In the words of one scholar, "As a practical matter, the D.C. Circuit is something of a resident manager, and the Supreme Court an absentee landlord" in administrative law.[27]

While maintaining pressure on the D.C. Circuit to avoid unwarranted intervention, the Supreme Court should also put an end to its own practice of reducing the enforcement authority of the EPA. The Supreme Court's decisions on federal facilities, hazardous pollutants, and equitable remedies have had a more serious and inequitable effect on the EPA's enforcement program than the Court has realized. Increasing the discretion of district court judges in enforcement cases is a poor method for curbing the regulation-extending decisions of the D.C. Circuit.

Standing

One sure way to reduce the role of the courts in regulatory policymaking is to raise the barriers that keep plaintiffs out of court. The case

---

26. *Vermont Yankee Nuclear Power Corp.* v. *Natural Resources Defense Council*, 435 U.S. 519 at 557 (1978).

27. Antonin Scalia, "Vermont Yankee: The APA, the D.C. Circuit, and the Supreme Court," 1978 *Supreme Court Review* 345 at 371. Scalia subsequently became a judge in the D.C. Circuit.

studies in this book show some of the difficulties produced by relaxed standing requirements. "Public interest" law firms frequently speak only for a small segment of the population they claim to represent. In the PSD case, for example, the Sierra Club spoke not for all those concerned about reducing pollution, but only for those whose primary concern was controlling pollution in rural areas. Giving environmental groups standing has not made policymaking more balanced, since environmentalists and industry tend to devote their litigational resources to different parts of the process.

This does not mean that groups without a concrete economic interest represent no one or that they have nothing to add to policymaking. Rather than going to the extreme of denying them standing, judges should endeavor to investigate the nature of their interest and to avoid precipitous action that may exclude important parties from participation. The first palliative requires judges to learn enough about policy issues to identify the costs as well as the benefits of the relief sought by public interest plaintiffs. By thinking about specific remedies courts can learn more about these costs and who must bear them. The second consideration should make judges reluctant to grant temporary restraining orders or motions for summary judgment, especially when those who must ultimately bear the cost imposed by these actions are not present to explain their point of view.

Relying on procedural hurdles such as standing to avoid the merits of a case is particularly attractive when a statute unambiguously requires an agency to perform a duty that is beyond its capacity or one that will divert resources from more important tasks. By choosing their cases carefully and by negotiating with agency attorneys, private plaintiffs use nondiscretionary duty suits to determine agency priorities. Judges can usually avoid putting the agency in an untenable position by interpreting "nondiscretionary duties" narrowly. When this is not possible, the courts should take every step possible to force Congress to recognize the consequences of its inclusion of this provision in the statute. They can ask the agency to explain in detail why it previously refused to act, what resources will be required to carry out the letter of the law, and how it intends to implement the entire program. Judges should also avoid letting the agency and the plaintiff reach a consent agreement solely between themselves. If Congress wants to force action, it should be told the full implications of its command and should not have its directives made more palatable by an agreement between the agency and an environmental group.

Reading Legislative History

In several of the cases examined above the courts overturned agency actions not because the agency had ignored the clear meaning of the statute, but because the court found that the Clean Air Act's legislative history required a policy other than that pursued by the agency. The courts' extensive perusal of legislative history has not taught them much about either policy issues or congressional politics. Judges have frequently taken statements out of context to support peculiar readings of the statute. They have also ignored those parts of the legislative history that show that Congress in fact had no unified intent. The courts have used legislative history to increase their own discretion rather than to make sure the agency has obeyed the instructions of Congress.

One result of this use of legislative history is increased judicial intervention. Another equally important consequence is an expansion of the influence of congressional subcommittees and their staff. This in turn has produced a corresponding decline in the influence of the White House and has made it more difficult for Congress as a whole to supervise its committees.

Courts can put an end to manipulation of legislative history by legislators, litigants, and judges by viewing committee reports, hearings, and floor statements as informal directives to agencies, not as guidelines to be interpreted and enforced by the courts. If an agency's action is consistent with the statute, there is no need to go further. If the committee members who helped to write the legislative history are displeased, they can use their already considerable influence to convince the agency to change its mind. This will induce the authors of legislation to say precisely what they mean in the statute rather than leaving hints in various sections of the record.

Judicial Perceptions of Bureaucracy

In the end the courts' success in improving regulatory policies depends on the adequacy of their understanding of the regulatory process itself. If judges cling to untenable images of bureaucracy and regulation, added knowledge of the details of individual controversies will be of little help. Particularly dangerous are the two stereotypes of bureaucracies frequently applied by federal courts to the EPA.

According to the first, the EPA is in constant danger of becoming captured by the business firms it regulates. The courts, according to this view, must counterbalance industry's influence by augmenting the bargaining power of public interest groups and by insulating the EPA from political pressure. According to the second stereotype, the EPA is filled with overzealous regulators unmoved by the economic and social disruption they cause. This view, often held by district courts and western circuit courts, requires the judiciary to rein in these official environmental extremists.

The analysis of the regulatory process presented in this study suggests that the shortcomings of federal air pollution regulation stem from neither "capture" nor overzealousness, but from policymakers' inability or unwillingness to set goals that appear reasonable to those whose cooperation they need to implement environmental protection programs. These groups include industry, state and local officials, Department of Justice attorneys, state and federal district court judges, congressmen who are not on environmental subcommittees, reporters, and common citizens. The major failing of the federal courts has been their inability to recognize the overriding need to bring the agency's goals and authority into better balance.

Given the importance of judges' general perceptions of the regulatory process in resolving administrative law controversies, it is likely that the problems discovered here are not limited to the realm of environmental protection. The "new administrative law" is based on the premise that administrators cannot be trusted to carry out the mission assigned to them by law. Behind this is a suspicion that within a pluralist, capitalist system business groups wield far too much power, especially in the regulatory process. The courts, the only major political institution not controlled by popularly elected officials, should therefore seek to correct this supposed "political failure." This view of politics and regulation has been superimposed on the more traditional view, which emphasized the courts' duty to protect private property against public encroachment. The coexistence of these two outlooks helps explain the dualism in the courts' treatment of Clean Air Act cases. And this is why one can expect the same dualism to afflict other regulatory programs as well. To avoid repeating the mistakes of the past, the courts need, above all, better education on the politics of regulation and American politics in general. For this they must look outside the law.

Index of Cases Cited

General Index

Ackerman, Bruce A., 31n, 229n, 375, 377n, 385n
ACP. *See* Area classification plan
Adams, W. C., 285–86
Administrative Procedures Act, 10, 11, 66, 239, 263
Advisory Panel on the Health Effects of Photochemical Oxidants, 286–87
Air pollution regulation: administrative history, 49–52; administrative organization, 38–43; Congress and, 26, 28–29, 31–35, 57, 58, 373–79; courts and, 1–5, 18–19, 22, 53–55, 367–73; interest groups, 35–38, 360–67; legislative history, 24–26, 28–31; policymaking problems, 383–87; statutory problems, 43–49. *See also* Air quality standards; Dispersion enhancement program; Enforcement; Prevention of significant deterioration; Transportation control programs; Variances
Air Quality Act of 1967, 26, 28, 78. *See also* Clean Air Act Amendments of 1977; Clean Air Amendments of 1970; Energy Supply and Environmental Coordination Act
Air quality standards: congressional actions, 242, 244, 252–55, 263, 283, 284, 293; court decision effects, 241–44, 280–81, 293–98, 355–57; court decisions, 239–41, 261–69, 279; enforcement problems, 47–49, 116, 207–09; lead, 266–81; measurement problems, 46–47; ozone, 281–94; research problems, 244–51, 266–68; standard-setting process, 255–61; statu-

tory problems, 29–30, 43–49; threshold problems, 44–46, 243, 256–57, 272–74, 290, 356–57. *See also* Lead; Ozone
American Industrial Health Council, 36
American Lung Association, 37
American Petroleum Institute (API), 36, 281, 283, 284, 287, 291, 293
Anderson, Frederick R., 4n, 150n
Anderson, Paul, 228n
Animal studies, 246–47
API. *See* American Petroleum Institute
Area classification plan (ACP), 88–91
Armstrong, D. P., 324n
Asbell, Bernard, 32n
Atmospheric loading, 46–47, 83, 120, 153
Ayres, Richard E., 128n, 131n, 140n, 180n

Bach, Stanley, 35n
BACT. *See* Best available control technology
Baker, Howard, 32, 318
Barber, Walter, 283n
Bardach, Eugene, 372n
Barden, Charles, 299
Barth, Delbert, 254n, 283n
Bauer, Raymond A., 36n, 365n
Baum, Lawrence, 14n
Baum, Robert, 79n, 123n, 130n, 241n, 314n, 317n
Bazelon, David L., 1, 3, 12, 60, 69, 296, 362
Beame, Abraham, 335
Becker, Theodore, 14n
Bennett, Kathleen, 77n
Bernstein, Joan, 277n, 278n

397